THE NEW BOSNIAN MOSAIC

The New Bosnian Mosaic
Identities, Memories and Moral Claims
in a Post-War Society

Edited by

XAVIER BOUGAREL
Centre National de la Recherche Scientifique, Paris, France

ELISSA HELMS
Central European University, Budapest, Hungary

GER DUIJZINGS
*School of Slavonic and East European Studies,
University College London, UK*

ASHGATE

Published by
Ashgate Publishing Limited
Gower House
Croft Road
Aldershot
Hampshire GU11 3HR
England

Ashgate Publishing Company
Suite 420
01 Cherry Street
Burlington, VT 05401-4405
USA

Ashgate website: http://www.ashgate.com

British Library Cataloguing in Publication Data
The new Bosnian mosaic : identities, memories and moral
  claims in a post-war society
  1.Bosnia and Hercegovina - Social conditions 2.Bosnia and
  Hercegovina - Politics and government - 1992- 3.Bosnia and
  Hercegovina - Ethnic relations
  I.Bougarel, Xavier II.Helms, Elissa III.Duijzings,
  Gerlachlus, 1961-
  949.7'4203

Library of Congress Cataloging-in-Publication Data
The new Bosnian mosaic : identities, memories, and moral claims in a
  post-war society / edited by Xavier Bougarel, Elissa Helms and Ger
  Duijzings.
      p. cm.
  Includes bibliographical references and index.
  ISBN:13: 978-0-7546-4563-4
  ISBN:10: 0-7546-4563-0
  1. Bosnia and Hercegovina--Social conditions. 2. Pluralism (Social
sciences)--Bosnia and Hercegovina. 3. Bosnia and Hercegovina
--Ethnic relations. 4. Bosnia and Hercegovina--Politics and govern-
ment--1992- . 5. Violence--Bosnia and Hercegovina. 6. Bosnia
and Hercegovina--Economic conditions. I. Bougarel, Xavier.
II. Helms, Elissa. III. Duijzings, Gerlachlus, 1961- .

HN639.A8N48 2006
306.0949742--dc22

2006020606

ISBN-13: 978-0-7546-4563-4

Printed and bound in Great Britain by Antony Rowe Ltd, Chippenham, Wiltshire.

Contents

List of Maps

List of Figures

List of Acronyms

ARBiH
: *Armija Republike Bosne i Hercegovine* (Army of the Republic of Bosnia-Herzegovina)

CRPC
: Commission for Real Property Claims

DGS
: *Državna granična služba* (State Border Service)

DM
: Deutschmark

HDZ
: *Hrvatska demokratska zajednica* (Croat Democratic Union)

HKDP
: *Hrvatski kršćanski domovinski preporod* (Croat Christian Patriotic Rebirth)

HKDU
: *Hrvatska kršćanska demokratska unija* (Croat Christian Democratic Union)

HOS
: *Hrvatske obrambene snage* (Croat Defence Forces)

HSP
: *Hrvatska stranka prava* (Croat Party of Rights)

HSS
: *Hrvatska seljačka stranka* (Croat Peasant Party)

HV
: *Hrvatska vojska* (Croatian Army)

HVIDR-a
: *Hrvatski vojni invalidi Domovinskog rata* (Croat War Invalids of the Homeland War)

HVO
: *Hrvatsko vijeće obrane* (Croat Defence Council)

ICMP
: International Commission on Missing Persons

ICTY
: International Criminal Tribunal for the former Yugoslavia

IEBL
: Inter-Entity Boundary Line

IFOR   Implementation Force

IPTF   International Police Task Force

JNA   *Jugoslovenska narodna armija* (Yugoslav People's Army)

JOB   *Jedinstvena organizacija boraca* (United Soldier's Organization)

KM   *Konvertibilna Marka* (Convertible Mark)

NATO   North Atlantic Treaty Organization

NDH   *Nezavisna Država Hrvatska* (Independent State of Croatia)

NHI   *Nova hrvatska inicijativa* (New Croat Initiative)

NIOD   *Nederlands Instituut voor Oorlogsdocumentatie* (Netherlands Institute for War Documentation)

OHR   Office of the High Representative

OSCE   Organisation for Security and Cooperation in Europe

RS   *Republika Srpska*

SAO   *Srpske autonomne oblasti* (Serb Autonomous Regions)

SBiH   *Stranka za Bosnu i Hercegovinu* (Party for Bosnia-Herzegovina)

SDA   *Stranka demokratske akcije* (Party of Democratic Action)

SDP   *Socijaldemokratska partija* (Social Democratic Party)

SDS   *Srpska demokratska stranka* (Serb Democratic Party)

SFOR   Stabilization Force

UNHCR   United Nations High Commissioner for Refugees

UNPROFOR   United Nations Protection Force

VRS   *Vojska Republike Srpske* (Army of the *Republika Srpska*)

List of Contributors

Ioannis Armakolas Ph.D. candidate in Social and Political Sciences, University of Cambridge, UK. *Main publications*: 'A Field Trip to Bosnia: the Dilemmas of the First Time Researcher', in M. Smyth and G. Robinson (eds), *Researching Violently Divided Societies: Ethical and Methodological Issues*, Tokyo: United Nations University Press (2001); 'Identity and Conflict in Globalizing Times: Experiencing the Global in Areas Ravaged by Conflict and the Case of Bosnian Serbs', in P. Kennedy and C.J. Danks (eds), *Globalization and National Identities: Crisis or Opportunity?*, London / Basingstoke: Macmillan (2001).

Xavier Bougarel (co-editor) Ph.D. in Political Sciences, Institute for Political Sciences, Paris. *Present position*: Research Fellow, National Centre for Scientific Research (CNRS), research unit: Ottoman and Turkish Studies, Paris. *Main publications*: *Local Level Institutions and Social Capital in Bosnia-Herzegovina*, Washington D.C.: The World Bank (2002); *Le nouvel Islam balkanique : les musulmans comme acteurs du post-communisme, 1990-2000* [The New Balkan Islam: Muslims as Actors of Post-Communism, 1990-2000], co-edited with N. Clayer, Paris: Maisonneuve & Larose, 2001; *Bosnie: anatomie d'un conflit* [Bosnia: Anatomy of a Conflict], Paris: La Découverte (1996) (Serbian edition: *Bosna: anatomija rata*, Beograd: Fabrika knjiga, 2004).

Kimberley Coles Ph.D. in Cultural Anthropology, University of California, Irvine, USA. *Present position*: Lecturer, Department of Social Anthropology, University of Edinburgh, UK. *Main publications*: *The Object of Elections: International Workers, Electoral Practices, and the Government of Democracy in Post-War Bosnia-Herzegovina*, Ph.D. Dissertation, Department of Anthropology, University of California, Irvine (2003); 'Election Day: The Construction of Democracy through Technique', *Cultural Anthropology*, 19/4 (2004); 'Ambivalent Builders: Europeanization, the Production of Difference, and Internationals in Bosnia-Herzegovina', *Political and Legal Anthropology Review*, 25/1 (2002).

Isabelle Delpla École normale supérieure, Paris-Ulm; Ph.D. in Philosophy, University of Clermont-Ferrand, France. *Present Position*: Assistant Professor, University of Montpellier, France. *Main publications on Bosnia*: 'Is There a Right to Return?', *Filozofski godišnjak*, 14 (2004); 'La justice internationale dans l'après-guerre: la difficile évaluation des critères de justices' [International Justice in the

Aftermath of War: The Difficulty of Evaluating the Criteria of Justice], *Balkanologie*, 8/1 (2004); 'Une chute dans l'échelle de l'humanité: les topiques de l'humanitaire pour ses récipendiaires' [A Fall in the Scale of Humanity: Humanitarian Aid Topics from the Perspective of Recipients], *Mots*, 73 (2003).

Ger Duijzings (co-editor) Ph.D. in Anthropology, University of Amsterdam, Netherlands. *Present position*: Reader in the Anthropology of Eastern Europe, Head of the Department of East European Languages and Culture, School of Slavonic and East European Studies, London. *Main publications*: *Geschiedenis en herinnering. De achtergronden van de val van Srebrenica.* [History and Memory. A Background Account to the Fall of Srebrenica – Annex to the Srebrenica Report of the Netherlands Institute for War Documentation (NIOD)], Amsterdam: Boom (2002); *Religion and the Politics of Identity in Kosovo*. London: Hurst (2000); *Kosovo – Kosova: Confrontation or Coexistence*, co-edited with D. Janjić and S. Maliqi, Nijmegen: Peace Research Centre (1997).

Hannes Grandits Ph.D. in Southeast European History, University of Graz, Austria. *Present position*: Lecturer, Department for Southeast European History, Graz University; Research Fellow, Centre for the Studies of Balkan Societies and Cultures, Graz. *Main publications*: *'Distinct Inheritances'. Property, Family and Community in a Changing Europe*, co-edited with Patrick Heady, Münster: LIT Verlag (2004); *'Birnbaum der Tränen'. Lebensgeschichtliche Erzählungen aus dem alten Jugoslawien* ['The Pear Tree of Tears'. Live Stories from the Former Yugoslavia], co-edited with K. Kaser, Wien: Böhlau (2003); *Familie und sozialer Wandel im ländlichen Kroatien. 18.-20. Jahrhundert* [Family and Social Change in Rural Croatia, 18th-20th Century], Wien: Böhlau (2002).

Elissa Helms (co-editor) Ph.D. in Cultural Anthropology, University of Pittsburgh, USA. *Present position*: Assistant Professor, Department of Gender studies, Central European University, Budapest. *Main publications*: *Gendered Visions of the Bosnian Future: Women's Activism and Representation in Post-war Bosnia-Herzegovina*, Ph.D. Dissertation, Department of Anthropology, University of Pittsburgh (2003); 'Women as Agents of Ethnic Reconciliation? Women's NGOs and International Intervention in Post-War Bosnia-Herzegovina', *Women's Studies International Forum*, 26/1 (2003); 'Women's Activism and Post-War Reconstruction in Bosnia-Herzegovina: The Use of Gender Essentialisms', in W. Giles, M. de Alwis et al. (eds), *Feminists Under Fire: Exchanges Across War Zones*, Toronto: Between the Lines Press (2003); 'The "Nation-ing" of Gender? Donor Policies and Women's NGOs in Post-war Bosnia-Herzegovina', *The Anthropology of East Europe Review*, 21/2 (2003).

Stef Jansen Ph.D. in Anthropology and Sociology, University of Hull, UK. *Present position*: Lecturer in Social Anthropology, University of Manchester, UK. *Main publications*: *Antinacionalizam: etnografija otpora u Beogradu i Zagrebu* *polovinom devedesetih* [Antinationalism: Ethnography of the Resistance in Belgrade and Zagreb in the Mid-1990s], Belgrade: XX vek (2005); 'National Numbers in Context: Stats and Maps in Representations of the Post-Yugoslav Wars', *Identities: Global Studies in Culture and Power*, 12/1 (2005); '"Why Do They Hate Us?"* the Bosnian Way: Everyday Serbian Nationalist Knowledge of Muslim Hatred', *Journal of Mediterranean Studies*, 13/21 (2004); 'The Violence of Memories. Local Narratives of the Past after Ethnic Cleansing in Croatia', *Rethinking History*, 6/1 (2002).

Larisa Jašarević Ph.D. candidate in Cultural Anthropology, University of Chicago, USA.

Torsten Kolind Ph.D. in Anthropology, University of Aarhus, Denmark. *Present position*: Assistant Professor, Centre for Alcohol and Drug Research, University of Aarhus. *Main publications*: *Post-War Identifications. Counterdiscursive Practices in a Bosnian Town*, Ph.D. dissertation, Institute for Anthropology, Archaeology and Linguistics, University of Aarhus (2004); 'Non-Ethnic Condemnation in Post-War Stolac. An Ethnographic Case-Study from Bosnia Herzegovina', in S. Resic and B. Törnquist (eds), *Cultural Boundaries in Europe: The Balkans in Focus*, Lund: Nordic University Press (2002).

Ivana Maček Ph.D. in Cultural Anthropology, University of Uppsala, Sweden, 2000. *Present position*: Assistant Professor, The Uppsala Programme for Holocaust and Genocide Studies, University of Uppsala. *Main publications*: *War Within. Everyday Life in Sarajevo Under Siege*, Uppsala: Acta Universitatis Upsaliensis (2002); 'Sarajevan Soldier Story', in P. Richards and B. Helander (eds), *No Peace, No War: An Anthropology of Contemporary Armed Conflicts*, Athens, OH: Ohio University Press (2005); 'Predicament of War: Sarajevo Experiences and Ethics of War', in B. Schmidt and I. Schröder (eds), *Anthropology of Violence and Conflict*, London / New York: Routledge (2001).

Anders Stefansson Ph.D. in Anthropology, University of Copenhagen, Denmark. *Present position*: Research Assistant, Institute of Anthropology, University of Copenhagen. *Main publications*: *Under My Own Sky? The Cultural Dynamics of Refugee Return and (Re)integration in Post-War Sarajevo*, Ph.D. dissertation, Institute for Anthropology, University of Copenhagen (2003); *Homecomings: Unsettling Paths of Return*, co-edited with F. Markowitz, Lanham, MD: Lexington Books (2004); 'Refugee Returns to Sarajevo and their Challenge to Contemporary Narratives of Mobility', in L.D. Long and E. Oxfeld (eds), *Coming Home? Refugees, Immigrants and Those Who Stayed Behind*, Philadelphia, PA: University of Pennsylvania Press (2003).

Acknowledgements

This book has been a long time in preparation, undergoing several titles, the addition of a third editor, changes in contributing chapters, and endless negotiations about the structure of the introduction. First and foremost, we therefore thank the contributors for their incredible patience and understanding during this process. We also thank Caroline Wintersgill and Mary Savigar, our editors at Ashgate, for their flexibility and patience. Ger and Xavier are especially thankful to Elissa for agreeing to become the third editor and thereby helping to see this project to completion.

Several scholars doing fieldwork in Bosnia were at one time or another part of this project, even though, for various reasons, their work was not included in the book in the end. These include Andrew Gilbert, Paul Stubbs, Paula Pickering, and Natalija Bašić. We are especially grateful to Cornelia Sorabji, whose input strongly influenced the ultimate form of the introduction and whose chapter is sorely missed in this volume. Thanks also to Isabelle Delpla for her careful comments on parts of the introduction.

The editors enjoyed the hospitality of Ivan Čolović, Marko and Gordana Živković, Orli Fridman and Jessica Greenberg in Belgrade, Edin Hajdarpašić, Armin and Marina Alagić, and Ugo Vlaisavljević in Sarajevo, Ger Duijzings in Nijmegen, and Xavier Bougarel in Paris during several working meetings.

We are also grateful to the Association française pour le développement de l'expression cartographique (AFDEC) for producing the maps included in this volume, and the research unit 'Etudes turques et ottomanes' of the French Centre national de la recherche scientifique (CNRS) for sponsoring them. Ivana Maček's chapter first appeared in *Narodna Umjetnost*, 34/1 (1997); we thank the Institute for Ethnology and Folklore Research in Zagreb for permission to reprint a revised version, and the Art Group *Trio* in Sarajevo for the illustration included in that chapter. Likewise, University of California Press and the American Anthropological Association granted us permission to reprint a revised version of Kimberly Coles' chapter, which first appeared in the *Political and Legal Anthropology Review*, 25/1 (2002). We are also grateful to the Organization for Security and Cooperation in Europe (OSCE)'s mission in Bosnia-Herzegovina for allowing us to reproduce two posters as illustrations in Coles' chapter. Edin Hajdarpašić generously offered his photo of the UNUTIC towers in Sarajevo for the book's cover and gamely accompanied us in search of other, more obscure pictures than the one ultimately chosen.

Pronunciation Guide

The following is a simple guide to pronunciation for names and terms in Bosnian, Croatian or Serbian included in this book. These are different variants of the same South-Slavic language, formerly known as Serbo-Croatian, with differences in vocabulary and grammar akin to those among American, British and Australian English. While all three are official languages of Bosnia-Herzegovina, everyday usage typically references only one or avoids a designation altogether, calling it 'naš jezik' ('our language'), or 'materni jezik' ('mother tongue'). The chapters therefore use the terms applied by the communities under study.

Spelling is phonetic; each sound has its own corresponding letter in both the Cyrillic and Latin alphabets. Both alphabets are used in Bosnia-Herzegovina, though generally only Serbs or people in Serb areas use Cyrillic. We list only the Latin versions, as they are found in this book, and only those letters that differ significantly from English.

a	a as in *father*
c	ts as in *cats*
č	ch as in *cherry*
ć	ch as in *chile* but softer
dž	j as in *jump*
đ	a softer j; d as in the British *duke*
e	e as in *get*
g	hard g as in *go*
h	h as in *hot*, but sometimes more from the throat
i	long e as in *he*
j	y as in *yellow*
lj	lli as in *million*
nj	ny as in *Sonya*
o	o as in *not*
r	r rolled with one flip of the tongue
š	sh as in *she*
u	u as in *rule*
z	z as in *zebra*
ž	zh; s in *measure*

Introduction

An Old Bridge for a New Bosnia?

Along with the siege of Sarajevo, the concentration camps of Prijedor and the Srebrenica massacre of July 1995, the destruction of the *stari most* (old bridge) of Mostar on 9 November 1993 has become one of the main symbols of the war in Bosnia-Herzegovina.[1] Its reconstruction eleven years later, on 23 July 2004, was hailed as a triumph for the 'international community' and a step towards reconciliation among the three constituent *narodi* (peoples[2]) of Bosnia: the Muslims/Bosniacs,[3] the Serbs and the Croats.[4] The dual symbolism of the destruction and rebirth of the *stari most* made it an apt image to grace the covers of several books about wartime and post-war Bosnia. As always, however, such symbolism conceals as much as it reveals about the realities of the war and its aftermath: what appears on book covers is in large part a representation produced by and for the international community, along with the local elites who are linked to it. In other words, the *stari most* is most often perceived 'from above' (from the top down).

---

[1]   The term 'Bosnia' hereafter refers to the state of Bosnia-Herzegovina as a whole.

[2]   In socialist Yugoslavia, a clear distinction was established between the six South-Slavic constituent *narodi* (peoples) of the Yugoslav federation (Serbs, Croats, Slovenes, Muslims, Macedonians and Montenegrins) and the national minorities – also called *narodnosti* ('nationalities') – living in the country. Although the English term 'people' is the official translation of the term '*narod*' in post-war Bosnia, contributors to this book were given their own choice of terminology (nation, nationality, ethno-national group, etc.).

[3]   The name 'Muslim' (*Musliman*, with a capital 'M') has been used to designate the Slavic-speaking Muslims of Bosnia since the end of the 19th century, but became their official national name only in 1968. In September 1993, the *Bošnjački sabor* (Bosniac Assembly) declared 'Bosniac' (*Bošnjak*) to be the new national name. The latter should not be confused with the term 'Bosnian' (*Bosanac*), which applies to all inhabitants of Bosnia-Herzegovina. Whereas 'Bosniac' was introduced in 1995 into the new Bosnian Constitution, the name 'Muslim' is still frequently used in everyday conversations. Therefore, contributors to this book had the choice of using either of these terms.

[4]   According to the population census carried out in 1991, on the eve of the war, Bosnia-Herzegovina had 4,364,574 inhabitants, of whom 1,905,829 (43.7 percent) declared themselves as Muslims, 1,369,258 (31.4 percent) as Serbs, 755,895 (17.3 percent) as Croats and 239,845 (5.5 percent) as Yugoslavs.

In the first place, the *stari most* retains its symbolic power as a bridge between Croat and Muslim erstwhile enemies only if one ignores some realities on the ground, starting with the fact that the bridge does not actually connect Croat and Bosniac parts of Mostar but two banks of the Bosniac sector – the line of division in most of the town runs more to the west, along the main boulevard. A detailed inquiry would further reveal a variety of meanings attached to the bridge by local residents, only some of whom treat it as a symbol of multi-ethnic Bosnia. When the keystone was placed in the top of the arch of the 'new old bridge', it was covered with lilies, the flower that has become a symbol of the Bosniac people. A few hundred meters away, in the Mostar Franciscan monastery, a fresco depicts Ottoman soldiers throwing Catholic monks from the bridge. Further investigation would also show discord between French and German architects competing for control of the reconstruction, and the dismissal of local stonemasons, trained especially for the project, when a Turkish firm was given the final contract for the work. The 'new old bridge', meant as a symbol of reconciliation, can thus also be perceived as an object of intense material and symbolic rivalries involving both local and global actors (see e.g. Grodach 2002).

In this book, we aim to offer a similar reversal of perspectives by considering post-war Bosnia 'from below'. In the existing literature, Bosnia is often presented as an 'ethnic mosaic' that has been undone by ethnic cleansing (Jansen 2005). What this volume demonstrates, however, is that the Bosnian 'mosaic' has always been and continues to be multilayered: while there are still some forms of interethnic coexistence in Bosnia, the war has not only affected ethno-national identifications, but also a large array of other categories such as urbanity and rurality, gender, generation, class and occupation. The chapters of this book thus shed new light on the multiple social groups and conflicts, individual and collective memories, moral categories and claims that shape Bosnian society, the various interactions unfolding between local and global actors, and the ruptures and continuities of the post-war period. This introduction contextualizes these studies by reviewing the dramatic events experienced in Bosnia since 1990 and the ways in which they have been represented by scholars and other analysts. We then discuss the approach 'from below' underlying this collection and present the chapters themselves along with the main themes they address.

The War in Bosnia and its Aftermath

The beginning of the war in Bosnia in April 1992 cannot be explained outside the larger context of the break-up of socialist Yugoslavia. To be sure, the existence of Bosnia pre-dates the creation of the Yugoslav state in 1918, but its inclusion into a multinational state at least partially explains its preservation as both an autonomous territorial entity and a multiethnic society. In 1939, the growing rivalry between Serbs and Croats within the Kingdom of Yugoslavia led to the first territorial partition of Bosnia. Two years later, Bosnia was annexed by the

WESTERN BALKANS

Map 1   The Western Balkans

Independent State of Croatia (*Nezavisna Država Hrvatska*, NDH), and the war opposing the Croat fascist *ustaše* allied with Axis forces, Serb royalist *četnici*, and communist Partisans took more than 300,000 lives. In 1945, the new socialist and federal Yugoslavia re-established Bosnia-Herzegovina as a republic within its former territorial boundaries. This contributed to the restoration of the interethnic balance that had been profoundly disturbed by World War II, and to the silencing of Serb and Croat territorial claims on Bosnia. Twenty-three years later, in 1968, the League of Communists recognized the Muslims as the third constituent people of the republic, thus elevating them to the same status as the Serbs and Croats.

In the 1980s, the crisis of socialist Yugoslavia and the rise of nationalist ideologies (see e.g. Gagnon 2004; Hayden 1999; Woodward 1995a) thus represented a threat to the very existence of Bosnia-Herzegovina, which did not escape the rise to power of nationalist parties (see Andjelic 2003). On 18 November 1990, the first free elections were won by three parties organized along ethno-national lines: the (Muslim) Party of Democratic Action (*Stranka demokratske akcije*, SDA), the Serb Democratic Party (*Srpska demokratska stranka*, SDS) and the Croat Democratic Union (*Hrvatska demokratska zajednica*, HDZ). During the following year, Slovenia, Croatia and Macedonia proclaimed their independence, while the Yugoslav People's Army (*Jugoslovenska narodna armija*, JNA), together with various Serb paramilitary formations, seized about one third of Croatia's territory. Already by this time, the Serbian and Croatian presidents, Slobodan Milošević and Franjo Tuđman respectively, were contemplating the partition of Bosnia as a possible solution to their territorial ambitions. On the ground, the nationalist parties in power began to confront each other more and more violently over the political fate of the republic. In the autumn of 1991, the SDS and HDZ began to create Serb and Croat 'autonomous regions'. In March 1992, the organization of a referendum on independence, its boycott by the SDS and the creation of a self-proclaimed 'Serb Republic of Bosnia-Herzegovina' (*'Republika Srpska'*, RS) announced the collapse of the consociational mechanisms that had been meant to ensure the institutional cohesiveness of Bosnia.

On 6 April 1992, war extended into Bosnia (see e.g. Bougarel 1996; Burg and Shoup 1999; Magaš and Žanić 2001) and Serb forces began their siege of Sarajevo. At first, the Army of *Republika Srpska* (*Vojska Republike Srpske*, VRS) with the support of the former Yugoslav army and of neighbouring Serbia, confronted the Army of the Republic of Bosnia-Herzegovina (*Armija Republike Bosne i Herzegovine*, ARBiH) and the Croat Defence Council (*Hrvatsko vijeće obrane*, HVO). In May 1993, however, the HDZ's creation of the self-proclaimed 'Croat Republic of Herceg-Bosna' (*Hrvatska Republika Herceg-Bosna*) led to fierce fighting between Muslims and Croats in Herzegovina and central Bosnia. This conflict was ended in March 1994, under strong diplomatic pressure from the United States, by the Washington Agreement, which established the Federation of Bosnia-Herzegovina (*Federacija Bosne i Herzegovine*) based on strictly consociational institutions and divided into ethnically defined cantons. The readjustment of the military balance after the discrete US circumvention of the UN weapons embargo and the dramatic reconfiguration of frontline positions between July and October 1995 then led to the opening of peace negotiations at a US military base in Dayton (Ohio), and to the signing of the General Peace Agreement on 14 December 1995.

From April 1992 to December 1995, the war was increasingly internationalized (see e.g. Burg and Shoup 1999; Gow 1997). At the diplomatic level, various peace plans were put forward by the EU, the UN and the great power 'Contact Group', before the United States imposed its own solution. On the ground, humanitarian aid was provided by the United Nations High Commissioner for Refugees (UNHCR) and numerous non-governmental organizations (NGOs), while the mandate of the United Nations Protection Force (UNPROFOR) was repeatedly extended (for the reopening of the Sarajevo airport, then for escorts of humanitarian convoys, and finally, to protect the 'safe areas' created by the UN Security Council in May 1993). At the same time, the North Atlantic Treaty Organization (NATO) became more and more involved in the progression of the war, as illustrated by the February 1994 ultimatum directed at Serb forces besieging Sarajevo and the bombing campaign against Serb positions in Autumn 1995. This internationalization of the war hastened the redefinition of the role of various regional and international organizations in Europe and prompted some major changes in international law, such as the recognition of the right to use force for humanitarian purposes, and the creation of the International Criminal Tribunal for the former Yugoslavia (ICTY) in February 1993.

The increasing internationalization of the Bosnian war is due as much to the larger post-Cold War climate as to its sheer brutality. The war was the most deadly conflict in Europe since World War II with an estimated 100,000 – 150,000 people killed. 'Ethnic cleansing' (*etničko čišćenje*), the violent expulsion of certain populations in order to create ethnically homogenous territories, was used systematically by Serb and Croat forces and resulted in the displacement of more than 2,100,000 people, or about half of the pre-war Bosnian population (see e.g. Bassiouni 1994; Gow 2003). Only the cities of Sarajevo and Tuzla, which were controlled by the Bosnian Army, maintained relative ethnic diversity, while Banja Luka was emptied of most of its non-Serb population and Mostar was divided into Bosniac and Croat sectors. Ethnic cleansing meant serious war crimes committed against the civilian population, including murders, torture and rape, which have been documented by the UN and various human rights organizations. In July 1995, Serb forces overran the erstwhile UN 'safe area' of Srebrenica, killing about 8,000 Bosniac men and expelling the rest of the population. The Srebrenica massacre led the ICTY to charge Radovan Karadžić and Ratko Mladić, respectively the highest-ranking political and military leaders of the RS, with genocide. In August 2001, General Radislav Krstić, former commander of the Serb forces in eastern Bosnia, was convicted of genocide by the ICTY for his participation in the Srebrenica massacre, and the sentence was upheld by the ICTY Court of Appeals in April 2004.[5]

In December 1995, the Dayton Peace Agreement made official the existence of two distinct entities (the Federation and the *Republika Srpska*) within a minimal common institutional framework, and drew a demilitarized Inter-Entity Boundary Line (IEBL) beyond which the three warring parties had to withdraw (see e.g. Bieber 2005; Bose 2002). In this way, the peace agreement endorsed the territorialization of the constituent peoples of Bosnia and therefore also the main result of war and ethnic cleansing. At the same time, however, it confirmed the existence of Bosnia-Herzegovina as an independent state and prioritized the implementation of human rights, beginning with the right to return for all displaced persons (DPs) and refugees. These founding paradoxes of Dayton, with the diverging implications of its military and civilian aspects, the gap between its institutional mechanisms (based on ethnically defined territorial units) and its demographic aims (return of DPs and refugees), have made it the object of never-ending polemics at both the local and international levels. At the same time, Bosnian institutions themselves have become more and more elaborate: in 1999, the municipality of Brčko was turned into a neutral District; in 2002, important constitutional amendments extended the constituent status (*konstituivnost*) of the Bosniac, Serb and Croat peoples to the whole territory of Bosnia and introduced new complex consociational mechanisms at all institutional levels (Bieber 2005; ICG 2002c).

At the military level, the Dayton Peace Agreement created the Implementation Force (IFOR), renamed the Stabilization Force (SFOR) one year later, to replace the wartime UNPROFOR. This new international force numbered 60,000 troops and fell under NATO command; its mandate was to supervise the implementation of the military part of the peace agreement (separation of the warring parties, control of the IEBL) and, further, to contribute to lasting internal security. The civilian aspects of the peace agreement were entrusted to a foreign High Representative,[6] whose main role was originally to ensure that the signatories to the agreement implemented it and to coordinate the activities of the various international organizations and agencies present on the ground, beginning with the Organization for Security and Cooperation in Europe (OSCE) (elections, democratization), the International Police Task Force (IPTF) (monitoring of police forces), the UNHCR (return of displaced persons and refugees), the Commission on Real Property Claims (CRPC) (restoration of confiscated real estate), the EU and the World Bank (humanitarian aid, reconstruction) (see e.g. Bose 2002; ESI 2000).

It is possible to divide the post-war period into several distinct periods according to the internal social and political evolution and to the transformation of

---

[5]   For all ICTY indictments and rulings, see <http://www.un.org/icty>.

[6]   The High Representative is appointed by an international Peace Implementation Council, to which he presents regular progress reports (see <http://www.ohr.int>).

Map 2   Bosnia and Herzegovina (with the sites discussed in this volume)

the international presence. The first period, from January 1996 to July 1997, was dominated by the consolidation of the peace, with the deployment of SFOR, the transfer to the Federation of most of the Serb-held neighbourhoods and suburbs around Sarajevo, the establishment of the IEBL and provisory common institutions, and the reconstruction of basic infrastructure (roads and bridges, electricity and telecommunication networks, etc.). But the political elites tied to the war maintained their hegemonic position. In September 1996, the first post-war general elections were won by the SDA, the SDS and the HDZ, despite a split in the SDA that had led to the creation of the Party for Bosnia-Herzegovina (*Stranka za Bosnu i Herzegovinu*, SBiH) by wartime Prime Minister Haris Silajdžić.[7] Laws on 'abandoned' real estate and the privatization of public enterprises were passed by ruling parties in both entities in the attempt to consolidate the results of ethnic cleansing. At that time, international actors largely accepted this situation: the High Representative restricted his role to mediation between the ruling nationalist parties; OSCE endorsed the results of the elections despite massive fraud and political pressures; SFOR refused to consider the arrest of war criminals as part of its mission; and the World Bank turned to the dominant political elites to implement its reconstruction programs. The RS, however, was subject to financial sanctions, following its refusal to participate to the common institutions established by Dayton.

During the second period, from July 1997 to July 1999, the hegemony of the nationalist parties began to weaken and the international community became more directly involved in political and social processes. In July 1997, a serious crisis broke out between the leadership of the SDS, closely linked to Radovan Karadžić and hostile to the peace agreement, and Biljana Plavšić, President of the RS, who took a more conciliatory stance. Finally, SFOR prevented a coup attempt against Plavšić and, following special elections in the RS in December 1997, pressure from the High Representative facilitated the appointment of Milorad Dodik, leader of the Party of Independent Social Democrats (*Stranka nezavisnih socijaldemokrata*, SNSD), as the new RS Prime Minister. This successful move then led the Peace Implementation Council to grant new powers to the High Representative (the 'Bonn powers'), which allowed him to dismiss elected politicians and civil servants deemed to be obstructing the implementation of Dayton, and to impose legislative measures when Bosnian political actors could not reach a compromise.

In the months that followed, High Representative Carlos Westendorp pushed through various laws on new state symbols and personal identification documents, a common currency (the *Konvertibilna Marka*, KM) and uniform car number plates, while thoroughly amending the entity laws on 'abandoned' real estate. These moves, along with the expansion of the activities of other international organizations, strongly contributed to the restoration of relative freedom of movement throughout Bosnia and to the beginnings of an effective return and

---

[7]   For all electoral results, see the website of the Election Commission of Bosnia-Herzegovina, <http://www.izbori.ba >.

restitution process (41,191 'minority returns' in 1998, out of which 6,586 in the RS). Nevertheless, the political changes brought by the general elections of September 1998 were limited: in the Federation, the SDA and HDZ still dominated political life in spite of some electoral losses; in the RS, the *Sloga* ('Harmony') coalition led by Milorad Dodik retained its majority in the National Assembly thanks to the support of Bosniac and Croat representatives, but the ultra-nationalist Nikola Poplašen defeated Biljana Plavšić in the presidential election. Thereafter, international pressures became even stronger, as evidenced by Poplašen's dismissal in March 1999 following his refusal to reappoint Dodik as Prime Minister.

The 'Bonn powers' thus enabled the High Representative to remove some major obstacles to the implementation of Dayton, but in the long run this threatened to distort Bosnian political life and deprive local institutions of any real power and legitimacy. From July 1999 onward, the priority of the new High Representative Wolfgang Petritsch was thus to unify the political forces opposed to the nationalist parties and to hand over responsibility for implementing the peace agreement to local actors. At first, this 'ownership' strategy enjoyed some significant successes. In the Federation, the general elections held in November 2000 resulted in a severe defeat for the SDA and the rise to power of the Alliance for Change (*Alijansa za promjene*), led by the Social Democratic Party (*Socijaldemokratska partija*, SDP) and the Party for Bosnia-Herzegovina (SBiH) (ESI 2001b; ICG 2002a). This success, however, was tarnished in the RS by the collapse of the *Sloga* coalition and the return to power of the SDS in alliance with the Party of Democratic Progress (*Partija demokratskog progresa*, PDP). Ultimately, attempts by the HDZ to establish a third Croat entity in the Spring of 2001, the political conflicts and personal rivalries that undermined the Alliance and the enduring paralysis of state-level institutions compelled Petritsch to resort to the 'Bonn powers': he dismissed several high-ranking Croat politicians in March 2001 and imposed a new election law in August 2001, as well as significant constitutional amendments in April 2002.

The period stretching from July 1999 to November 2002, which most of the chapters of this book address, is therefore especially crucial. For the first time, political forces supported by the international community were in power. On the ground, 'minority returns' (261,617 between 2000 and 2002, with 109,156 in the RS) and property restitutions (67.8 percent of reclaimed properties having been restored by the end of 2002) were gaining momentum without leading to outbreaks of violence as some had anticipated. Against this background, Bosnia's future became closely linked with the potential success of the Alliance for Change and the 'ownership' policy promoted by Petritsch. From this perspective, however, the political and social changes of this period remain quite limited. The 2002 constitutional reforms extending the constituent status of the Bosniac, Serb and Croat peoples to the whole territory of Bosnia significantly modified the institutional framework established by Dayton (Bieber 2005; ICG 2002c). Other important reforms were launched in the fields of civil service, taxation, the armed forces, secret services, justice, and education, with the aim of strengthening common institutions and turning Bosnia into a viable state. Yet all of these reforms were implemented only partially and with utmost difficulty, and the return and restitution process itself turned out to be extremely complex (see e.g. Cox 1998; ICG 2002b; Ito 2001; O'Thuatail and Dahlman 2005; Philpott 2005). The economic situation in the country remained appalling, with the unemployment rate close to 40 percent of the working-age population and strong social tensions resulting from the dismantling of the social welfare system inherited from the socialist and wartime periods.

Furthermore, while all these changes reflect a gradual normalization of the political and social climate in Bosnia, they are probably due less to the actions of the Alliance for Change than to the repeated interventions by the international community and to changes in the regional context, especially the death of Tuđman in December 1999, the electoral defeat of the HDZ in Croatia in January 2000, and the fall of Milošević in Serbia in October 2000. This fact underscores some of the limits and paradoxes of Petritsch's 'ownership' policy. When he left Bosnia in June 2002, the role of the Office of the High Representative (OHR) in local institutional and political contests was probably more important than ever. Four months later, after the general elections in November 2002, the three nationalist parties were back in power. Thus, two years after the election of the Alliance had aroused such great hopes, Bosnia seemed to be back to the situation of November 1990 (ICG 2003).

It would be misleading, however, to label this a 'return to the beginning'. On the contrary, as the nationalist parties regained power, international actors abandoned their last hopes that the consequences of war and ethnic cleansing could be completely undone. Whereas the restitution process was close to completion (92.5 percent of the reclaimed property having been restored at the end of 2003), the number of 'minority returns' had started to decrease sharply (44,868 in 2003, with 18,051 in the RS; 17,948 in 2004, with 7,718 in the RS), and the on-going crisis of the Bosnian economy and public finances presented additional obstacles to the implementation of the 2002 constitutional amendments. On the other hand, the return of the nationalist parties did not lead to a renewal of ethnic violence. Economic recovery and integration into Europe became the international community's new priorities, as evidenced by Bosnia's admission to the Council of Europe in October 2002 and the handover to the EU of missions previously administered through other international organizations (IPTF was replaced in January 2003 by the European Union Police Mission, EUPM, and SFOR in December 2004 by the European Military Force, EUFOR).

At the same time, the new High Representative, Paddy Ashdown, became more hesitant: after trying to garner support from the nationalist parties for the implementation of reforms initiated by his predecessor, Ashdown also resorted extensively to the 'Bonn powers'. In June and December 2004, after NATO rejected Bosnia's candidature to its 'Partnership for Peace' program due to the RS's refusal to arrest war criminals, the High Representative dismissed several high-ranking members of the SDS. The resulting institutional paralysis, together with the approach of the tenth anniversary of Dayton, reactivated simmering debates about the need to revise the Constitution attached to the peace agreement (see e.g. Bieber 2005; Chandler 2005; Solioz 2005). The last months of 2005, however, were marked by some institutional breakthroughs: the RS National Assembly accepted the principle of unified military and police forces, and, on 25 November 2005, negotiations between Bosnia and the European Commission on a Stabilization and Association Agreement began.

Dayton: A Distorting Lens for Post-War Bosnian Realities?

Since 1992, editorialists and social scientists have often used the case of Bosnia to point to a return of 'ethnic nationalisms', the rise of a specific kind of 'new war', or the failure of 'traditional peacekeeping'. Similarly, since the mid-1990s, Bosnia has occupied a prominent place in peace studies and international relations theory. It is difficult to establish an exhaustive assessment of the literature on post-war Bosnia, as it involves authors with a wide range of perspectives and academic backgrounds. Moreover, this literature has evolved over the years, reflecting changes in the Bosnian situation itself. The first observation that must be made is that the ways in which post-war realities have been analyzed largely reflect perceptions of the war itself. Between 1992 and 1996, most of the literature on Bosnia consisted of testimonies, journalistic enquiries and official reports on the ongoing war and ethnic cleansing campaigns (e.g. Bassiouni 1994; Gutman 1993; Rohde 1997). Academic publications were much less common; those that appeared were mostly based on research done before the war (e.g. Bax 1995; Bringa 1995; Donia and Fine 1994; Malcolm 1994b). Most of these strove to refute the thesis put forth by bestselling authors that Bosnia was a country torn apart by 'ancient hatreds' (Kaplan 1993) or a 'clash of civilizations' (Huntington 1997). This wartime literature played a key role in revealing war crimes to a large international audience and in preparing the ground for a better understanding of the country. However, because it was influenced by the central issue of the definition of the war – civil war or foreign military aggression – this literature often neglected the role of economic motivations in the dynamics of war and ethnic cleansing (see e.g. Andreas 2004; Bojičić and Kaldor 1999), or the full complexity of political and military configurations on the ground (see e.g. Bax 2000; Bjelaković and Strazzari 1999; Duijzings 2002a, 2002b, 2002c). Moreover, the will to 'deconstruct nationalism' (Campbell 1998) and to valorise 'betrayed traditions' (Donia and Fine 1994) led some authors to oversimplify the history of interethnic relations in Bosnia and to reify other aspects of Bosnian social realities, such as the cleavage between town and countryside (see e.g. Allcock 2002; Bougarel 1999b).

Early analyses of the post-war period were similarly driven by various critical stances toward the war, including toward the role played by international actors. This was especially true in the first years following the signing of the Dayton Peace Agreement. At that time, the literature on Bosnia remained structured around binary oppositions: the two dominant scenarios for Bosnia – 'gradual reintegration' vs. 'definitive partition' – tended to reflect the two definitions of the war as 'aggression' or 'civil war'. In the first scenario, obstruction by nationalist parties was perceived as the main obstacle to the 'undoing' of ethnic cleansing and the 'restoration' of a multiethnic Bosnia, and the international community was once again criticized for its lack of determination (e.g. Cousens and Cater 2001). In the second scenario, all attempts at preserving the existence of Bosnia were dismissed as illusory, as the war was said to have revealed the futility of imposing a common institutional framework onto irremediably hostile populations (e.g. Chandler 1999). These two scenarios, however, share an important feature: both draw on the political projects and interpretative schemes that dominated the war period, thereby obscuring a more nuanced understanding of what are complex, changing and often paradoxical realities.

At the end of the 1990s, academics and other experts began to more closely scrutinize important phenomena such as the role of clientelistic networks and practices in the maintenance of nationalist party hegemony (ESI 1999), the impact of neo-liberal policies on the (non)restoration of the state (e.g. Donais 2005; Pugh 2002, Stojanov 2001), and various attempts to promote 'civil society' through new-style NGOs (e.g. Belloni 2001; Chandler 1998; Smillie 1996). Case studies on topics like 'minority returns' or local institutions also began to supplement more general work that was not based on field research. At the same time, the political and social transformations experienced in Bosnia led to a gradual reformulation of the debates that dominated the immediate post-war period. On one hand, the strengthening of the powers of the High Representative and of the international organizations present on the ground prompted growing questions about the possible unintended effects of the transformation of Bosnia into a 'quasi-protectorate' (e.g. Bose 2002; ICG 2003; Zaum 2003) and the need to develop an 'ownership' policy that would return the responsibility for the peace process to local actors (e.g. ESI 2001a; ICG 2003; Solioz 2005). On the other hand, the precarious consolidation of state-level institutions, the increasing pluralization of Bosnian politics and the incomplete return of DPs rendered obsolete those analyses based on the 'reintegration vs. partition' binary. These were replaced with more balanced discussions on the adaptation of institutional frameworks and territorial divides inherited from Dayton (Caspersen 2004; ESI 2004; Solioz 2005), and on the reform of key state sectors such as the armed forces, justice and education. Within a decade, Bosnia thus became the object of a very rich and diverse literature, through which an impressive amount of data has been collected. This literature has also contributed to the crystallization of larger debates about contemporary peacekeeping and state-building operations and the place they occupy in the 'new world (dis)order' (see e.g. Bellamy and Williams 2004; Paris 2005).

In spite of their contribution, however, many analyses of post-war Bosnia share some common flaws, starting with the perception of post-war Bosnia through the lens of Dayton. Much of the existing literature takes the Dayton Peace Agreement as a starting point in order to assess its (non)implementation and ultimately to consider conceivable long-term political solutions. From such a perspective, the various realities of post-war Bosnian society are either framed in terms of the legal categories set forth in the peace agreement or simply dismissed as trivial because they do not fit into this framework. To be sure, political and social processes on the ground are indeed influenced by Dayton and its implementation, but they can in no way be reduced to it. Over the years, assessments of Dayton have become more nuanced and better informed. Nevertheless, the literature on post-war Bosnia remains dominated by legal scholars and political scientists, producing an overemphasis on institutional and electoral issues, excessive influence by the main international organizations on academic research, and an over-reliance on these organizations' official reports and websites or interviews with their representatives. The main consequence of this approach 'from above' is that the way Bosnian citizens relate to the experience of war and the uncertainties of the post-war period have been either ignored or reduced to data from opinion polls and interviews with local 'experts' and NGO leaders.[8]

A related flaw that appears in many analyses is the reduction of Bosnian realities to their ethnic dimensions. This 'ethnic bias' is obvious in the work of authors who favour partition scenarios and therefore tend to emphasize ethnic conflicts. In a more indirect and unexpected way, though, this has also been present among the advocates of a unified Bosnia. Not only do some of them give in to interpretations of the war in terms of collective guilt, but they also tend to reduce its impact to the spatial separation of ethno-national groups, a process they argue that the marginalization of nationalist elites and the revision of Dayton would be sufficient to 'undo'. Paradoxically, such analysts therefore tend to focus on the very constitutional issues that nationalist parties want to keep at the top of the political agenda. Moreover, the increased use of ethnic quotas following the 2002 constitutional reform, along with the continued proliferation of ethnic statistics and maps by the organizations in charge of the return process, show how the very notion of 'undoing ethnic cleansing' risks trapping the Bosnian population within the ethno-national categories these very organizations purport to reject (Jansen 2005). At the same time, other changes and continuities have gone largely unnoticed or are still subordinated to a normative reading of the war and its aftermath. It was only after the defeats of the *Sloga* coalition and the Alliance for Change, for example, that the majority of commentators discovered that authoritarianism and corruption were not limited to nationalist parties (see, however, Chandler 2002), and that such political practices were partly inherited from the socialist period (see, however, ESI 1999).

The difficulties international organizations have met in their endeavours to 'rebuild the state' and 'promote civil society' in post-war Bosnia and other post-war contexts have led specialists of peace studies to place increasing emphasis on

---

[8]   Paradoxically enough, such a tendency appears even in work that strives to develop a critical approach to international intervention.

the (lack of) interaction between local and international actors (see e.g. Pouligny 2004) and the (non)regeneration of social and political bonds (see e.g. Pugh 2000; Stover and Weinstein 2004). A comparison with the existing anthropological literature on peacekeeping operations (see e.g. Cockburn and Žarkov 2002; Duijzings 2002a, 2002c), return and reconciliation processes (see e.g. Grandits and Kosztonyi 2003; Leutloff-Grandits 2005) or non-governmental organizations (see e.g. Sampson 2002b; Stubbs and Deacon 1998) in former Yugoslavia reveals both points of convergence and divergence. Against this background, we now turn to a discussion of the ethnographic perspectives used in this book, in hopes of demonstrating their advantages in contributing to a better understanding of post-war Bosnia, and of encouraging a fruitful dialogue between anthropologists and other social scientists working on post-war societies.

From Socialist Ethnology to Socio-Cultural Anthropology

The impetus for this book came out of the editors' own experiences: as we conducted research in post-war Bosnia (Duijzings 2002b; Helms 2003a; World Bank 2002), we were struck by the disconnects between 'top-down' political analyses and what we and other researchers were seeing 'on the ground'. Inevitably, because of the focus on local-level fieldwork, most contributors to this volume are anthropologists, but we also included authors from other disciplines who use ethnographic methods. The goal is to describe and theorize the dynamics of social and political life from the perspective of those who do not appear in dominant, 'top-down' historical and political analyses (see e.g. Eriksen 1995). As Chris Hann has pointed out in the context of post-socialist Europe, ethnographic studies focus attention on ordinary people and marginalized segments of the society, giving voice to their preoccupations and worldviews rather than denying them agency (Hann 1994).

Following the assertions of anthropologists working on other post-socialist (e.g. Burawoy and Verdery 1998; Hann 2002) and war-torn societies (e.g. Das and Kleinman 2000, 2001; Nordstrom 1995), we argue that a local-level approach to post-war Bosnia has much to offer, since it provides for a more nuanced and holistic understanding of local contexts and is better able to represent the complexities of everyday life. Careful attention to local dynamics reveals historical continuities and discontinuities as well as systems of meaning that are not always immediately obvious to the outside observer. Further, by describing local conditions along with the experiences and strategies of the actors involved, this approach allows for a disengagement of scholarly analysis from various agendas (whether 'local' or 'Western') and a deconstruction of the essentialist bias through which Bosnia has often been represented and understood. Approaching social and political realities 'from below' can thus offer explanations from an 'insiders' perspective', illuminating such questions as, for instance, why nationalism is still a dominant force in Bosnia, but also why local actors do not always behave according to nationalist logic.

In order to further contextualize the studies presented in this volume, we find it useful to briefly outline the history of local-level research done in Bosnia since 1945. In socialist Yugoslavia, as in all of Central and Eastern Europe, this primarily took the form of ethnology, a largely descriptive and atheoretical discipline that was mostly concerned with documenting rural material culture, folklore and customs as a way of 'discovering' the national 'Self'.[9] During the socialist period, the political climate in Bosnia was one of the most repressive in all of Yugoslavia, which meant that ethnographic research on ethnicity, religion, or interethnic relations was especially controlled. Ethnology was allotted few resources, had little visibility, and ethnologists were forced to restrict themselves to 'harmless' topics such as material culture (Beljkašić-Hadžidedić 1988; Buturović and Kajmaković 1988). As a consequence, while ethnologists in Zagreb, Ljubljana and Belgrade would eventually adopt some of the more theoretically-driven approaches of Western social and cultural anthropology, such a development did not occur in Bosnia.

Too much scrutiny of interethnic relations would have risked exposing what Mahmut Mujačić observed in 1972, that 'in everyday life, in the relations among ... [ethno-]national groups, the [ethno-]national question is in some way present; "that spark is smouldering" and it's enough for people to start talking about it ... for the spark to ignite' (Mujačić 1972: 1092). It was thus impossible for Bosnian ethnologists to develop a research agenda that would tackle such problems as the rising interethnic tensions in the 1980s (Beljkašić-Hadžidedić 1988: 72). During the socialist period, the rare Bosnian scholars who did venture to write about local-level interethnic relations were historians, sociologists or political scientists, rather than ethnologists.[10] These researchers emphasized the ambivalence of *komšiluk* (good neighbourliness) or the importance of rural/urban migrations, clientelistic networks, religious institutions and collective memories. However, some of them fell afoul of the Bosnian League of Communists, or published their work only as confidential reports. Against this background, foreign (Western) anthropologists played an important role in addressing these issues in unconcealed terms, despite

---

[9]   Whereas classical ethnology sought to 'discover' the national 'Self', socio-cultural anthropology has developed in the West around the 'discovery' of the colonial 'Other' (see for example Asad 1995 [1973]). On the history of ethnology in Central and Eastern Europe, see among others Hann, Sarkany and Skalnik 2005. On Yugoslavia, see among others Hammel and Halpern 1969; Naumović 1999; Rihtman-Auguštin and Čapo Žmegač 2004.

[10]   See among others Ćimić 1966; Hurem 1972; Mujačić 1972; Tomić 1988. As rare examples of Bosnian ethnographic work dealing with local-level interethnic relations, see Stojaković 1982, 1986-1987.

their own difficulties in getting access to and carrying out research in Bosnia.[11] The work of anthropologists William Lockwood, Cornelia Sorabji and Tone Bringa showed, among other things, that ethno-national identifications in Bosnia were fluid and contextual, that interethnic relations were based on stable rules of reciprocity that were nonetheless negotiated on a day-to-day basis, and that peaceful coexistence did not amount to a blurring of ethnic boundaries (Bringa 1995; Lockwood 1975; Sorabji 1989).

Cornelia Sorabji, for example, has used her insights from fieldwork in Sarajevo in the mid 1980s to challenge some misleading interpretations of official Yugoslav nationality policy and terminology, outlining the complex ways in which ethno-national categories and interethnic relations were perceived by Bosnians themselves before the war. While socialist Yugoslavia recognized six separate South-Slavic peoples or nations, Sorabji showed that, in everyday life, 'the notion of *narod* is more multifaceted than that of nation and that Bosnian citizens understood it in different ways in different contexts' (Sorabji 1995: 89). She also emphasized the importance of the concept of *komšije* (neighbours), which mirrors that of *narod*: 'the *narod*s were separate, but even their separate existence was predicated upon their interconnectedness; neighbours were warm, trusting and united, but at another level this unity was predicated upon difference' (Sorabji 1995: 90). Sorabji pointed out that Bosnians already had a sense of ethno-national belonging before the war, but 'for the most part tolerance, good will and a conscious desire for cooperative and civil relationships filled the joints between the three populations. At the same time, non-ethnic differences, differences of class and status, of rural and urban origin, and of access to resources, were far more salient than much current analysis suggests' (Sorabji 1993: 33-4).

These differences between Western anthropologists and local ethnologists should not be overstated, however. East European ethnological traditions historically modelled themselves on strands of ethnology in 'the West', particularly the German tradition of *Volkskunde* with its strong emphasis on the 'discovery' of the national 'Self'. In more recent years, since the late socialist period, social and cultural anthropology has become more and more influential in Slovenia, Croatia and, to a lesser extent, in Serbia (see e.g. Baskar 1998; Naumović 1999; Rihtman-Auguštin and Čapo Žmegač 2004). In the 1990s, local ethnologists came under pressure to produce work that supported new nationalist ideologies. However, in both Serbia and in Croatia, some ethnologists – such as Ivan Čolović and Milena Dragićević-Šešić in Serbia or Ivo Žanić and Reana Senjković in Croatia – have worked to deconstruct nationalist categories and myths by scrutinizing, among other things, local newspapers, popular literature and neo-folk songs (Čolović 2002; Dragićević-Šešić 1994; Senjković 2002; Žanić 1998). After the war broke out in 1991, Croatian anthropologists developed a theoretically informed, though

---

[11]   This situation confirms Chris Hann's general observation for Eastern Europe that Western anthropologists have often been in a more privileged position to discuss sensitive issues than local ethnologists (see Hann 1987).

nationally centred, 'anthropology of tears and fears' focusing on everyday experiences of war and exile, local-level transformations of (inter)ethnic relations, new war heroes and rituals associated with civilian victims and fallen soldiers (e.g. Čale-Feldman, Prica and Senjković 1993; Jambrešić Kirin and Povrzanović 1996). Anthropologists from Western countries, such as Robert Hayden, Bette Denich and Mart Bax were among the first to investigate the political uses of memories of World War II (Bax 1997; Denich 1992; Hayden 1992), while Cornelia Sorabji, Mirjana Laušević and Lynn Maners explored cultural transformations taking place in Bosnia (Laušević 1996; Maners 2000; Sorabji 1994).

One could even say that the Yugoslav wars have revealed the value of the ethnographic data collected during the socialist period. For example, during the war in Bosnia, when outside observers were asking how erstwhile neighbours could suddenly turn on each other, Sorabji offered a crucial explanation of the character of the violence. Coming back to the notion of *narod*, she wrote that 'brutality is aimed at humiliating, terrorizing and killing the "enemy" population in order to remove it from the territory, but also at transforming the assumptions held by both victims and perpetrators about the very nature of identity groups and boundaries in order to prevent any future return of the exiled population. ... The creation and, more importantly, the maintenance of ethnically pure territories ... requires that the first [divisive] view of *narod* be retained and reinforced while all others are jettisoned. In this project personalized violence involving the killing of neighbour by neighbour, colleague by colleague and friend by friend acquires a particular importance' (Sorabji 1995: 81, 90). The relevance of such analyses appear fully in Tone Bringa's documentary film *We Are All Neighbours*: returning in 1993 to the village where she had conducted fieldwork in the late 1980s, she witnesses the deterioration of relationships between local Muslims and Croats and the expulsion of the Muslim population by the Bosnian Croat army, the HVO (Bringa 1993).[12]

Both foreign and local anthropologists, to varying degrees, have countered nationalist and essentialist interpretations of the Yugoslav wars, which of course does not mean that they were immune to bias and disputes among themselves (see Povrzanović 2000; Povrzanović-Frykman 1997, 2003). The most striking example of such a conflict is probably the tensions between the editors of a special issue of *The Anthropology of East Europe Review* and some of the contributors from Croatia, who decided to withdraw from the project when it was turned into an edited book (see Halpern and Kideckel 1993, 2000; Rihtman-Auguštin 2004). While Bosnia often occupied a central place in the arguments of anthropologists taking part in these discussions (including those who had done fieldwork in other parts of the world – see e.g. Borneman 1998, 2002; Bowman 1994; Hann 2003), field research in Bosnia effectively came to a halt, and the work of Bosnian academic institutions was hampered by the difficult war conditions (see e.g.

---

[12] A sequel chronicles the return of some of the displaced Muslims to their pre-war homes (Bringa and Loizos 2001).

Buturović 2000; Sijarić 1996). Despite a growing 'fieldwork-under-fire' literature (Nordstrom 1995), few social scientists carried out fieldwork in Bosnia during the war, and those who did made only short research trips, for obvious practical reasons (Bougarel 2002; Bringa 1995: XV-XXI; Maček 2000: 11-44).

Against this background, this volume reflects a new generation of researchers who conducted fieldwork after the war or, like Elissa Helms and Stef Jansen, first came into contact with the region through local NGO work during the war. A few, however, had previous research experience in Bosnia (Xavier Bougarel) or in other parts of former Yugoslavia (Ger Duijzings) before the war, and Ivana Maček did her fieldwork during the war itself. Inevitably, for various reasons, we were not able to include all members of this new generation.[13] Nevertheless, despite some significant omissions, we feel this volume offers a relatively good sample of recent local-level research on post-war Bosnia.

Another feature of this volume, which could be considered a drawback, is that nearly all contributors come from Western Europe or North America. The only authors from the region are Ivana Maček and Larisa Jašarević, both of whom have been educated in Western countries. However, we argue that this should not come as a surprise, nor should it necessarily be viewed negatively. The first reason for the preponderance of foreign researchers is the lack of a tradition of anthropological research in Bosnia. Moreover, university structures dominated by scholars still influenced by Titoist or nationalist ideologies, along with the emigration of many young Bosnian scholars and the recruitment of others by international organizations and NGOs, have forestalled a badly needed change of generation. However, some of the most promising new scholars of Bosnia are Bosnians now being trained in contemporary theories and methods, and some modest attempts are being made to introduce socio-cultural anthropology in Bosnian universities.

There are admittedly other limitations of this volume, one of them being the uneven geographical spread of the contributions and the disproportionate attention to Bosniac-held territories. Far from a result of editorial design, this imbalance is more a reflection of the state of current ethnographic research on Bosnia. Most contributors to this book conducted fieldwork in the Federation (Sarajevo, Tuzla, Zenica, Mostar and Stolac) where research conditions for Western scholars have generally been more favourable than in the RS. This is also a continuation of a similar tendency among pre-war anthropological studies, such as those by Lockwood, Sorabji and Bringa, which focused on Bosnian Muslims and, to a lesser extent, Croats. Indeed, Croat communities have largely been studied where they

---

[13]   These include social policy scholar Paul Stubbs (e.g. Stubbs 1999, 2000b; Stubbs and Deacon 1998), anthropologists Kristof Gosztonyi (e.g. Gosztonyi 1999, 2003; Grandits and Gostonyi 2003), Mare Faber (Faber 2001) and Andrew Gilbert (e. g. Gilbert 2003, 2005), political scientist Paula Pickering (e.g. Pickering 2003, 2006), psychosociologist Natalija Bašić (e.g. Bašić 2004), and several graduate students working on doctoral dissertations.

co-exist with Muslims (Lockwood 1975; Bringa 1995) or because of the specific context of the Catholic pilgrimage site of Međugorje (Bax 1995; Claverie 2003), while the Bosnian Serbs have been largely ignored (see, however, Maners 2000). This is partly because most anthropologists studying particular ethno-national groups in pre-war Yugoslavia tended to carry out fieldwork in the group's 'home' republic or province: Bosnia was considered the home republic of the Muslim people, which presented an interesting case of 'nation-building' in contemporary Europe. Following a similar logic, interest in the Muslim, or Bosniac, population has been replicated by anthropologists during and after the war, with Bosniacs being perceived as the most 'Bosnian' of the three major groups. At the same time, this imbalance is also likely a reflection of wartime political preferences and a tendency among anthropologists to identify with underprivileged, voiceless or victimized groups. This volume does not overcome such biases: Armakolas, Delpla and Duijzings are the only contributors who conducted substantial fieldwork in the RS, and only Armakolas deals primarily and only with Bosnian Serbs living in the Serb entity.

Finally, this collection presents analyses based upon fieldwork conducted mostly between 1999 and 2003, after the end of the war rendered Bosnia much more accessible. The only exception is Ivana Maček's opening chapter, which deals with everyday life in besieged Sarajevo and provides a vivid account of the war conditions that have so profoundly affected Bosnian society ever since. The rest of the chapters deal primarily with the time period when the Alliance for Change came to power in the Federation. As noted above, the Alliance was only a partial and short-lived success: it proved impossible to 'undo' the outcomes of the war and in November 2002 the nationalist parties regained political control. This period is thus particularly apt, given that this volume aims not only to illuminate the complexity of the situation on the ground and the worldviews and practical choices of Bosnians themselves, but also to provide a critical perspective on international (Western) intervention in Bosnia.

Bosnia from Below

The book is divided into three sections, deliberately reflecting themes through which post-war Bosnia has often been analyzed: ethnic identities and conflicts, collective memories and 'ancient hatreds', 'protectorate' and 'transition' to democracy and a market economy. Our intention, however, is to show that local-level realities defy reduction to such simple categories. It is not enough to presume that ethnic nationalism informs every aspect of Bosnian political and social life. Nor can memories and narratives of the war be reduced to Serb, Croat, and Bosniac 'versions', as if these were uniform and uncontested. Likewise, in post-war Bosnia, the impact of international presence is not limited to one-way 'monitoring' and 'implementation' policies, and 'transition' is in no case an unproblematic given. In the following overview of the sections and chapters of this book, we also discuss the themes by which they are grouped. Because they are prominent aspects of post-war Bosnian life in general, these themes are not (only) confined to the specific sections but reappear throughout the chapters.

Beyond 'Ethnicity'

Section One deals primarily with the social and cultural categories through which participants in post-war processes act, react, and make sense of their lives. Some of these categories have been carried over from the socialist era, albeit transformed by the war; others are direct products of wartime experiences (see also Vlaisavljević 1997). Not surprisingly, the chapters show that, after war and ethnic cleansing, ethno-national categories have become more pervasive and rigid (see also Halpern and Kideckel 2000; Sorabji 1995), as well as more closely linked with religious markers and institutions (esp. Bougarel, Maček, Grandits; see also Bougarel 2001b; Bringa 2002). At the same time, however, they demonstrate that ethno-national identifications are still relative, changing and contested (see also Jansen 1998; Kolind 2004), and that some forms of interethnic cooperation have survived the war (see also Maček 2000; Pickering 2003).

Taking the reader 'beyond ethnicity', all of the book's chapters reveal the diversity of social groups and conflicts that have been transformed or produced by the war: the rural/urban divide and senses of local belonging have been reshuffled by massive population movements (see also Rolland 2004; Stefansson 2004a, 2004b); socio-professional groups and social classes linked with pre-war economy have disintegrated (esp. Jašarević, Maček, Jansen); new social groups and constituencies such as displaced persons (esp. Stefansson, Armakolas, Grandits; see also Stubbs 1999; Wesselingh and Vaulerin 2005), war veterans (esp. Bougarel, Grandits; see also Bašić 2004; Maček 2001, 2005), or families of missing persons (esp. Delpla, Duijzings) have appeared; gendered roles and representations have been redefined by wartime experiences (esp. Helms, Delpla, Bougarel; see also Cockburn 1998; Helms 2003a; Lilly and Irvine 2002). All these social groups and categories rely on specific war experiences and memories (see Section Two), and are often expressed through strong moral categories. Terms referring to victimhood (*žrtve*) and war crimes (*zločinci, dželati*); heroism (*heroji, gazije, šehidi*), cowardice (*podrumaši, pobjeglici*) and treason (*izdajnici*); poverty (*sirotinja*), illegitimate enrichment (*lopovi, bogataši*) and organized crime (*mafijaši, ratni profiteri*) inform public discourses as well as everyday conversations, and add a dramatic dimension to social conflicts.

Against this background, clashing interests and demands are quickly transformed into unyielding moral claims and intense struggles for legitimacy. In cities overwhelmed by displaced persons, the competition for scarce resources such as housing, jobs and collapsing public services is expressed through strong moral categories opposing 'cultured' urbanites to 'uncultured' newcomers, an opposition carried over from the socialist period (Bringa 1995: 58-65) but intensified by the war (esp. Stefansson, Jašarević, Kolind). More specifically, the acceleration of the restitution and return process in the early 2000s pitted displaced persons and (minority) returnees against each other: the former emphasized their material needs and their right to settle in their new place of residence, while the latter demanded their pre-war property rights and redress for wartime injustices (esp. Maček, Stefansson, Armakolas, Kolind; see also Philpott 2005; von Carlowitz 2005).[14] At the same time, veterans lamented the loss of their wartime status and the ingratitude of society (esp. Bougarel, Jansen) while civilian victims longed for recognition of their own suffering (esp. Delpla, Helms; see also Delpla 2004b; Stover and Shigekane 2002).

This exploration of the inner complexity of Bosnian society would remain incomplete without taking into account two major issues. The first concerns the resilience of war-related groups and conflicts after the war. As all the chapters demonstrate, the social divides and conflicts running through Bosnian society are still largely informed by wartime roles and experiences. This is explained to a great extent by the sheer brutality of the war and ethnic cleansing, while material insecurity and lack of economic perspectives also play a role (esp. Maček, Jašarević, Jansen). More concretely, however, many war-related categories are deliberately nurtured by various actors, beginning with the main nationalist parties. In a dire economic situation, the distribution of housing, jobs and social benefits according to wartime roles and status not only contributes to nationalists' control over their respective ethno-national groups, but also perpetuates various kinds of war-related conflicts, inscribing them into the core of society (esp. Grandits, Bougarel; see also Cox 1998, 2001; Stubbs, 1999, 2001; World Bank 2002: 9-55). Within this context, the fact that the international community has sometimes contributed to the perpetuation of these conflicts becomes even more noteworthy (see Section Three).

The second issue is how ethno-national categories relate to others that have been produced or transformed by the war. Depending on the circumstances, war-related categories can undermine, override, reinforce, or complicate ethno-national identifications, at times even rendering them all but irrelevant (esp. Maček, Stefansson, Jansen, Jašarević). In the early 2000s, the restoration of freedom of movement and the increasing number of 'minority returns' favoured the (re)invention of new spaces and forms of cooperation (esp. Kolind, Armakolas, Jašarević; see also Bringa 2005; Grandits and Gosztonyi 2003; Helms 2003b; Pickering 2006). At the same time, however, competition over scarce resources, the ongoing restitution process and the granting of specific material support to (minority) returnees have aggravated interethnic tensions, at least in the short term and at the local level (esp. Stefansson, Armakolas, Kolind; see also Cox 1998; Ito 2001; Stubbs 1999, 2000b; World Bank 2002: 9-55). It is against this background that nationalist parties proved to be very skilful in (re)mobilizing ethno-national categories by adapting pre-war clientelistic practices to new war-related groups and conflicts and stirring up widespread feelings of insecurity and injustice (esp.

---

[14]   On the restitution process in Croatia, see Leutloff-Grandits 2005.

Grandits, Bougarel). In a similar way, moral categories and claims sometimes strengthen ethno-national identifications and conflicts, as is often the case with notions of heroism and victimhood (esp. Duijzings, Bougarel, Delpla). However, they can also exacerbate social and political divides *within* each ethno-national group (esp. Stefansson, Delpla, Helms), and lead ordinary Bosnians to reject nationalist ideologies by denouncing *en bloc* 'armchair politicians' (*foteljaši*) and 'profiteers' (*profiteri*) (esp. Grandits, Kolind, Helms) as opposed to the individual qualities of 'decent/honest people' (*pošteni/fini ljudi*) (esp. Kolind, Stefansson, Jašarević).

This first section, 'Beyond Ethnicity', begins with a look back at the realities of the war period, a time in which so many of the social and moral categories at work in the post-war period were solidified or given new meanings. Ivana Maček's chapter (Chapter One) addresses the four-year siege of Sarajevo, analyzing its impact on the everyday life of the city's inhabitants. She movingly reflects on their reactions to the pervasiveness of physical danger, irregular supplies of food and other staple commodities, sudden and drastic impoverishment, dependency on black markets and international humanitarian aid, the illegal occupation or looting of abandoned properties, and brutal ruptures in the bonds of family, friendships and relations between colleagues and neighbours. The break with pre-war normality and its associated values gave rise to feelings of deep insecurity and humiliation, a loss of meaning that in many cases led to serious states of depression. Material and psychological dependency also rendered the population more receptive to shifts in ethno-national identification encouraged by the nationalists in power, beginning with the increased presence of Islam in the public sphere. However, as Maček argues, Sarajevans did not just passively endure the chaos of war: their everyday strategies for survival were accompanied by a will to maintain some semblance of routine and normality, to regain a hold on their own war experience and lives and thereby recover a positive meaning for that part of their lives.

In Chapter Two, Anders Stefansson carries the focus on Sarajevo into the post-war period, exploring the social and cultural transformations experienced in the city after the departure of a large portion of the pre-war population and a massive influx of people displaced by the war. As a result of these shifts, many Sarajevans consider themselves 'in exile' in a city they do not recognize any more. At the same time, they deny the 'invaders' the right to settle in their new place of residence. For similar reasons, some of those who left during the war have hesitated to return. The demographic changes in Sarajevo have not only led to the ethnic homogenization of the city but also to the aggravation of the long-standing conflict between the urban, marked by 'culture' and 'European-ness', and the rural, associated with 'non-culture' and 'backwardness'. Other divides compound this central one, as illustrated by the tensions between Sarajevans who stayed to endure the siege and those who fled abroad, or among displaced persons from various regions. All of these divisions relate to each other in complex and changing ways depending on the circumstances in which they are invoked. In general, Stefansson observes, Sarajevans seldom acknowledge that, far from revealing essential cultural or moral qualities of classified groups, differences in ways of living in the city are fundamentally a reflection of different war experiences and access to scarce resources such as housing and financial income.

While Stefansson discusses the primarily rural 'invaders' of Sarajevan urban space, Armakolas (Chapter Three) draws our attention to some of those who left: Serbs displaced from Sarajevo to the small, semi-rural setting of nearby Pale, the wartime capital of *Republika Srpska*. During and after the war, as the Serb entity was inscribed into the political landscape, the modes of identification of these urban Serbs were also transformed away from any association with the now Bosniac-dominated city of Sarajevo and the Bosnian state it symbolizes. In the post-war period, due to the trauma of war and exile and to their resentment towards the international community, displaced Sarajevan Serbs have nurtured an intense longing for security. It is on this basis that they initially justified their rejection of any Bosnian state and their unwillingness to return to Sarajevo. However, their attachment to their city of origin has not disappeared altogether. Over the course of several field visits, Armakolas observes how factors such as the symbolic stigmatization of the RS and the increasing pressure put on its leaders by the international community, the restoration of freedom of movement between the entities, the restitution of illegally confiscated property, and the concentration of job opportunities in the Bosnian capital have gradually induced these same people to visit Sarajevo, to settle there, and to resume relations with the rest of the population. Through these spatial practices, Armakolas argues, they indirectly call into question the nationalist rhetoric still dominant in the RS.

The final two chapters in the first section deal with the part of Herzegovina which has been controlled by Croat nationalists since 1993. Hannes Grandits (Chapter Four) scrutinizes local political practices and discourses among Croats of the region in an attempt to explain the absolute hegemony exerted by the Croat Democratic Union (HDZ) there throughout the 1990s. He locates the main factors supporting this hegemony in strong Croat national feelings tied to a vigorous Catholic faith, the memory of post-World War II communist repression, and enduring economic underdevelopment. This hegemony also reflects the capacity of the HDZ leadership in accommodating various factions with diverging ideological origins and material interests, channelling financial resources from Croatia and the Croat diaspora through parallel institutions, and redistributing them on a clientelistic basis. Against this backdrop, the allocation of material perks such as housing, jobs or social benefits to new social groups created by the war (displaced persons, veterans, etc.) plays a key role. As Grandits chronicles, during the 2000 electoral campaign, the HDZ relied heavily on these groups and their symbolic prestige in its confrontation with the international community and its related efforts to re-mobilize Croat voters – people who had become more and more critical towards their own leaders, whom they increasingly perceive as opportunistic and corrupt politicians.

Grandits' discussion of Croat politics and HDZ tactics in Herzegovina provides relevant background for Torsten Kolind's study (Chapter Five) on Stolac, a small

Herzegovinian town whose Bosniac inhabitants were expelled by Croat forces in 1993. Faced with the pervasiveness of ethnic divisions in everyday life, the Bosniacs who have returned to the town since the late 1990s have developed a counter-discourse based on non-ethnic cultural and moral categories. First of all, these Bosniacs recognize several categories of Croats (locals vs. refugees, urbanites vs. peasants, 'fascists' vs. 'good Croats', and the like). More generally, they contrast 'decent people' with corrupt and cynical politicians, denounce politicians and 'politics' in general as fundamentally immoral and removed from 'the people', and hold them responsible for the war. Through these stances, Kolind argues, Stolac Bosniacs strive to give meaning to the chaos and violence of war, to overcome their own feelings of insecurity and suspicion, and to restore the cognitive and normative frameworks that regulated everyday interethnic relations before the war. Kolind concludes that this counter-discourse, without being openly political, calls into question the ethnicization of everyday life; it renders ethnic categories more complex and flexible, and facilitates the creation of new spaces and new forms of peaceful coexistence.

Beyond 'Ancient Hatred'

Section Two focuses on war memories. Due to the very aims of the recent war, these memories have a clear ethno-national dimension, which nationalist parties strive to perpetuate (see also Torsti 2003, 2004; Wesselingh and Vaulerin 2005). War memories, however, are less related to ethnicity as such than to place – such as, for example, the side of the frontline on which people were trapped during the war (esp. Maček, Armakolas, Jansen; see also Maček 2000; Povrzanović-Frykman 1997) –, social status that predates the war or emerged along with it (esp. Jašarević, Helms, Bougarel; see also Jambrešić Kirin and Povrzanović 1996), and personal experiences of interethnic violence or cooperation (esp. Maček, Kolind, Delpla; see also Sorabji 2006). Thus, conflicts of memory not only pit ethno-national groups against each other, but also reflect other divides such as those between war participants and returning refugees (esp. Stefansson, Jansen), believers and secularists (esp. Bougarel, Jansen), and supporters of nationalist parties and their opponents (esp. Jansen, Helms, Kolind).

All these memories are expressed through various means: from commemorative events and public monuments (esp. Duijzings, Bougarel, Grandits; see also Robinson, Engelstoft and Pobric 2001; Torsti 2004) to private rituals and conversations (esp. Jansen; see also Jansen 2002; Sorabji 2006), from official reports and schoolbooks (see Perry 2003; Torsti 2003) to personal diaries and photo albums (see Willekens 2003). This diversity is at times reduced to an opposition between 'official' and 'hidden' memories, collective and individual ones. In reality, however, official narratives and personal stories, political strategies and psychological needs constantly meet, confront and influence each other (esp. Duijzings, Delpla, Jansen). Thus political actors do play a key role in the shaping of war memories, but are also often met with resistance from the population (esp. Duijzings, Bougarel, Kolind, Armakolas; see also Sorabji 2006). By and large, however, the pervasiveness of war memories contributes to the perpetuation of war-related social categories and to their expression through unyielding moral claims (see Section One). As shown by most of this book's chapters, what is at stake in the conflicts over memories in post-war Bosnia is not only the (re)interpretation of the past, or the (de)legitimization of the results of the war and ethnic cleansing. These conflicts also reflect divergent material and symbolic interests (esp. Bougarel), and represent attempts to promote new moral hierarchies and definitions of justice (esp. Delpla, Kolind, Helms). As is the case with war-related social categories, taking an approach 'from below' to war memories therefore raises several new and important questions.

Many analysts have faulted the Titoist 'politics of memory' for celebrating fallen and living Partisans, remaining silent on the fate of civilians, demonizing political adversaries and, last but not least, striving to 'de-ethnicize' the bloody events of World War II. As has been shown by historians and anthropologists alike, the collapse of this official narrative coincided with that of the Yugoslav federation itself (see e.g. Denich 1994; Hayden 1994; Höpken 1994, 1999). Policy makers and NGO activists therefore insist that reconciliation must be based on truth instead of state censorship or nationalist propaganda, and on justice and individual responsibility instead of impunity, revenge or collective guilt (see e.g. Bass 2000; Neuffer 2001; Stover and Weinstein 2004). It is beyond the scope of this book to re-examine how socialist Yugoslavia legitimized itself through ideological representations of the past and the future (see e.g. Höpken 1994, Lilly 2001). A closer comparison with post-war Bosnia, however, reveals important continuities. In many cases, individual memories of the recent war are influenced by those of World War II and the socialist period (esp. Armakolas, Kolind, Jansen, Jašarević). At the political level, nationalist parties reject the Titoist narrative of World War II, but they also draw on commemorative practices inherited from that period (esp. Duijzings, Bougarel, Grandits), while 'civic' forces cultivate the image of a pre-war Bosnia suffused with the spirit of 'Brotherhood and Unity' (esp. Helms).

International organizations also play an active role in the shaping of war memories (see Section Three), and their presence in Bosnia contributes to one of the main aspects distinguishing the present period from that following World War II, that is the existence of a pluralistic political and media landscape. But this major difference raises further questions. In such a diverse and fragmented public sphere, the question of whether reconciliation can best be achieved through the establishment of a shared narrative of the war or through the recognition of divergent war memories (esp. Duijzings, Jansen; see also Borneman 2002; Bougarel 2001a; Halpern and Weinstein 2004) becomes a very practical and puzzling one. In the early 2000s, for example, the trial of General Krstić at The Hague resulted in the classification of the Srebrenica massacre as genocide (ICTY 2001). Subsequent international pressures compelled the *Republika Srpska* authorities to finally acknowledge, in October 2004, the reality of the massacre (RS

Commission 2004). At the same time, however, war-related monuments and commemorations continued to reshape space and time along ethno-national lines (esp. Duijzings, Bougarel, Grandits; see also Robinson, Engelstoft and Pobric 2001; Torsti 2004). In everyday life, too, the coexistence between local hegemonic ethno-national groups and 'minority returnees' is most often accompanied by the silencing of sensitive issues such as wartime events and responsibilities (esp. Kolind, Armakolas, Jašarević; see also Grandits and Gosztonyi 2003; Wesselingh and Vaulerin 2005).[15]

The first two chapters of this section centre on publicly expressed narratives of the war. Ger Duijzings (Chapter Six) addresses divided war memories and separate commemorations in eastern Bosnia, which seem to undermine any attempt to reach consensus about what happened during the war or to bring about reconciliation. The text looks particularly at the afterlife of the Srebrenica massacre (July 1995), that is the way in which it has been remembered and commemorated by the Muslim community, resulting in the inauguration of the Potočari Memorial Centre in 2003, and the parallel counter-commemorations organized by local Serbs. Duijzings places these competing commemorative practices in historical perspective, especially focusing on how World War II memories were locally managed under socialism. Because of their varying historical experiences and allegiances, local Serbs and Muslims developed 'different ways of being in history': the former were able to commemorate their victims, while the latter had to keep silent. The 1990s saw the rise of a new official narrative of Muslim or Bosniac victimization, in which the Srebrenica massacre has become a key symbol. Duijzings also shows that the commemorative practices related to the Srebrenica events cannot be properly understood without taking into account the interventions into the local 'commemorative arena' by international bodies, most importantly the OHR, which played an active part in the opening of the Potočari Memorial Centre.

In Chapter Seven, Xavier Bougarel describes the rise of a new cult of *šehidi* (martyrs to the faith) in Bosniac-dominated parts of Bosnia, as part of the re-islamicization efforts ushered in by the SDA. In principle, only fallen soldiers are considered to be *šehidi* but, during and after the war, the very definition of this concept, and the rituals attached to it, have remained much more ambiguous and fluid. The population itself has both resisted the cult of *šehidi* and co-opted it to fit its own needs and perspectives. The resulting tensions relate not only to the process of defining a new Muslim/Bosniac national identity, but also to divergent interpretations of the war and to the crystallization of new social groups and moral hierarchies within the Bosniac population. In particular, the heroic figure of the *šehid* has played a central role in the construction of the veteran population (veterans, war disabled, and the families of fallen soldiers) as a social group with a specific material and moral status. Bougarel shows how this process was made evident in 2001, when the attempt to reform the system of war pension benefits led

---

[15] On similar processes in Croatia, see Jansen 2002; Jansen, forthcoming.

to an open confrontation between veteran associations and the newly-elected Alliance for Change.

The final chapter in this section (Chapter Eight) examines the issue of war memories and narratives from the perspective of individual and everyday interactions. Stef Jansen relates the encounter among three former work colleagues in October 2000 in Tuzla. Samir and Hasan are both Bosniacs, but the first fought in the Bosnian Army, whereas the second was in Germany when the war broke out. Robi, a Serb, has come back to Tuzla after having spent several years in Serbia. It rapidly becomes clear that humour will not be enough to ease the strained atmosphere, and Hasan takes Robi to task for having left Tuzla in the first days of the war. Robi tries to justify himself, but then an even more violent argument breaks out between Hasan and Samir: Hasan implicitly accuses Samir of abandoning his people and the latter takes full responsibility for his choice not to participate in 'a dirty war between Balkan nations'. This discussion, Jansen argues, shows that the various war memories in conflict with each other in Bosnian everyday life are not only related to ethnic divisions but are also influenced by divergent assessments of the socialist past, personal experiences of the war and people's relationships to the state and politics. It also illustrates the way in which Bosnian citizens incorporate the normative categories of an omnipresent international community into their own modes of justification and everyday conversations.

Beyond 'Protectorate'

In many analyses, the international organizations present in post-war Bosnia appear as a force acting on local society and politics 'from above': the very terminology reduces this relationship to a 'quasi-protectorate' in which a benevolent 'international community' exerts a one-way influence (through 'implementation strategies', 'monitoring mechanisms', etc.) on problematic local practices (such as 'obstructionist tactics', 'democracy deficits', etc.). In contrast, the third and final section of this book reveals some of the ways in which 'international actors', in their many guises, roles, and initiatives, have both a formal and informal impact on local level dynamics, just as 'local actors' affect the choices and possibilities of the international community.[16]

An approach 'from below' thus sheds new light on the trials and tribulations of the international presence in post-war Bosnia. The very fact that this presence involves a large variety of actors with their own agendas means that international

---

[16] For the sake of brevity, both inter-governmental organizations and international NGOs are referred to here as 'international actors', in spite of their differences in modes of functioning and fields of intervention. By contrast, 'local actors' are social and political actors who come from and primarily operate in Bosnia. Part of our argument, however, is that 'local actors' are quite often 'transnationalized local actors' (Ferguson and Gupta 2002: 995) that act within transnational networks and systems of meanings.

policies can contradict each other and even backfire. From a 'top-down' perspective, constitutional reforms, removal of obstructive politicians, support to non-nationalist parties and NGOs, and 'minority returns' appear as convergent moves towards a common aim: the progressive reintegration of Bosnia. On the ground, however, 'minority returns' are most strongly resisted in places where they are perceived as a threat to the political *status quo* (esp. Grandits, Duijzings; see also Cox 1998; Ito 2001), institutional changes can lead to renewed support for the nationalist parties (see Grandits on the 'Croat crisis'), and compliance with the decisions of international organizations can weaken non-nationalist forces (see Bougarel on the 'veteran crisis').

Beyond the issues dealt with in the mainstream literature, international actors also contribute to the reshaping of the social categories, war memories and moral claims described in Sections One and Two. Helms and Delpla, for example, explore the impact of the ICTY, the OSCE and foreign NGOs on gendered roles and representations (see also Bougarel on the World Bank's impact on veterans' status). Local level studies also reveal how the allocation of international aid according to war-related categories – including that of 'minority returnee' – can contribute to their reinforcement, and thus, indirectly, to the perpetuation of interethnic tensions (see e.g. Gilbert 2003, 2005; Stubbs 1999; World Bank 2002: 9-55). From this point of view, the case of the restitution and return process, which reached its peak in the early 2000s, is especially telling: at the local level, it has not only led to awkward situations and difficult compromises, but has also produced much more limited and ambivalent results than those expected by its advocates (esp. Armakolas, Kolind; see also Dahlman and O'Thuatail 2004; O'Thuatail and Dahlman 2005; Philpott 2005).[17]

The strong and pervasive international presence in post-war Bosnia does not mean the absence of local agency. Several chapters show how 'locals' in turn perceive, react to and influence the activities and discourses of international actors, be it at the political level (esp. Grandits, Duijzings, Delpla, Helms) or in everyday life (esp. Jašarević, Armakolas, Jansen). Local actors, beginning with nationalist parties, sometimes openly resist international interventions (esp. Grandits, Duijzings). Even in the case of nationalist parties, however, the relations between international and local actors are most often located somewhere between 'collision and collusion' (Wedel 1998): the international community places strong political pressure on nationalists, but at the same time indirectly contributes to the financing of their clientelistic networks (see e.g. Bliesemann de Guevara 2005; Cox 2001; Donais 2005; Pugh and Cooper 2004; Stubbs and Deacon 1998). In the longer term, this sort of relationship has led to the 'domestication' (Creed 1998) of the international presence, with local actors adopting new cultural patterns, legal frameworks and political practices and fitting them into their own interests and representations. At the same time, international actors themselves experience

---

[17] On similar processes in Croatia, see Babić 1999, 2000; Leutlofff-Grandits 2005; Povrzanović 1998.

processes of 'hibridizations and creolizations' (Gupta 1995: 393) adopting some of the practices and representational forms of the local society, as shown by several studies on the behaviour of UNPROFOR soldiers during the war (see e.g. Cockburn and Žarkov 2002; Frankfort 2002a, 2002b; Thiéblemont 2001).

The diversity of interactions taking place between the international community and the local society means that, on the ground, the distinction between international and local actors becomes blurred. New-style NGO activists, together with the 'local staff' of major international organizations and foreign NGOs, belong to a new transnational elite (esp. Coles, Helms, Jansen; see also Sampson 2002a, 2002b; Stubbs 1997).[18] More generally, boundaries between 'locals' and 'internationals' are continually renegotiated and redrawn in everyday life: the international community is a major source of income for many Bosnians and 'locals' and 'internationals' directly interact on a regular basis, though this does not mean they escape the reassertion of various legal and symbolic hierarchies (esp. Coles, Delpla, Jansen; see also Coles 2003). Despite this continual interaction on the ground, international and local actors do not always share the same values, expectations and symbolic frameworks (esp. Delpla, Jašarević, Duijzings; see also Helms 2003b; Sampson 2002b).

Against this background, international actors are often unaware of their full impact on local society, leading at times to unexpected results, including the cultivation of new nationalist mobilizations. International organizations and foreign NGOs, for example, want to encourage reconciliation and, therefore, to influence the way local war memories are shaped (esp. Duijzings, Delpla, Helms). But their own aid policies tend to reproduce the very war-related social groups and categories on which nationalist memories and discourses are based. The reverse case exists as well, in the sense that international decisions not related to the war can indirectly call into question war-related social and moral hierarchies (esp. Bougarel, Jašarević). One could argue, for example, that some of the actions of the international community contributed to the November 2002 defeat of the Alliance for Change, the very coalition it had painstakingly helped over several years to build. Finally, everyday interaction between local and international actors can also undermine international policies: Kimberley Coles, in particular, demonstrates that the way 'internationals' live beyond the scope of Bosnian authorities and perceive Bosnian society in essentialist terms works against the restoration of a viable state in Bosnia and its integration into the European Union (see also Coles 2003).

Isabelle Delpla's chapter (Chapter Nine) examines the impact of the ICTY in Bosnia. She argues that the Hague Tribunal is one of the rare institutions which embodies moral values, though it remains distant for most Bosnian citizens, addressing only a small fraction of post-war injustices. Focusing on some victim associations primarily made up of Bosniacs, Delpla shows that their primary concern is to achieve official recognition of their status as victims. Furthermore, their concepts of justice do not overlap entirely with those put forth by ICTY

---

[18] On similar developments in Kosovo, see Lafontaine 2002.

promoters. Advocates of international criminal justice hope to contribute to the restoration of basic universal values and a common humanity. Though victims endorse some categories of international criminal law, they still understand justice in a narrower, more personal or local sense, focusing on the individuals whom they knew before the war and who committed atrocities in their municipalities of origin. Hence, the ICTY matters for them mainly through arrests and punishments of those specific war criminals. Moreover, Delpla argues, trials going on at The Hague have very little social effects beyond municipal boundaries. This localism in victims' approach to (international) justice is linked to a strong sense of local belonging from before the war, and to the key role played by municipal authorities in ethnic cleansing campaigns. But paradoxically it might also be reinforced by The Hague tribunal itself, through its policy of selective indictments focusing on a few symbolic municipalities.

In Chapter Ten, Elissa Helms examines the activities and self-representation strategies of Bosnian women involved in local NGOs and political parties. During the war, women were above all depicted as passive victims of ethnic cleansing and mass rape, and therefore as symbols of the victimization of their respective ethno-national groups. Beginning especially in 1996, however, and in response to direct and indirect international intervention, a variety of local women's NGOs were created and gender quotas were later made part of the new electoral law. Since politics is perceived as a typically male activity, while its corrupting nature is symbolized by a morally negative female figure ('politics is a whore'), women who are active in the public sphere must constantly justify their social commitment and simultaneously avoid any question of their own moral and sexual reputations. Against this backdrop, the discursive strategies they adopt are based on a denial of the political nature of their activities and/or insistence on their status as civilian victims of the war. This is expressed through reference to moral qualities deemed to be typically female and especially associated with motherhood, such as unselfishness, concern for future generations, and a willingness to compromise. Such strategies reveal changes experienced during and after the war in gendered roles and representations, as well as in the boundaries of public and private spheres.

Kimberly Coles (Chapter Eleven) examines the ways in which the 'internationals', or Westerners working in Bosnia, create new physical and symbolic boundaries between themselves and the local society. As members of a new transnational elite, they are beyond the reach of the Bosnian state, living as they do in their own distinct legal space with its own identification cards and social welfare system. At the same time, their involvement in the efforts to restore the authority of the Bosnian state and their everyday relations with Bosnian colleagues prompt 'internationals' to reproduce prejudices about the 'lack of competence' or the 'cultural deficits' of the local population. In so doing, they perpetuate an essentialist vision of post-communist Balkan societies, which they contrast with the ideal and apolitical picture neo-liberal Europe imagines for itself. It appears, therefore, that the efforts to turn Bosnia into a viable nation-state are undermined by the very forms of privatized and supranational governance in which the 'internationals' participate. What's more, as Coles shows, the wish to integrate Bosnia into the European Union is accompanied by the symbolic exclusion of Bosnian society from the normative frameworks of the new European project.

The volume concludes with a study by Larisa Jašarević (Chapter Twelve) that brings together elements of international intervention with local moral hierarchies in the context of post-war struggles for economic survival. Jašarević compares the open-air market 'Arizona', located in the neutral Brčko District, with the traditional peasant market *(čaršija)* as described by William Lockwood in the late 1960s. Arizona has little in common with the traditional *čaršija*, the collapse of the production economy having forced both independent peasants and wage-earners to move into trade activities that were previously considered marginal and degrading. But Arizona's traders still refer to the key symbolic figures of the *čaršija* – the 'peasant-producer' and the '*švercer*' (smuggler) – in their attempt to endow their new activities with a positive meaning. At the same time, traders object to the neo-liberal market models promoted by the OHR and the District authorities. Instead, they invoke a morality of exchange based on non-economic criteria which aims at ensuring the possibility of survival to the greatest portion of the population. Arizona is therefore neither a 'traditional' nor a 'transitional' market. Moreover, despite the wishful pronouncements of many foreign observers, it is not primarily a site of interethnic reconciliation, but a place where conflicts common to all of Bosnia, between an impoverished population and new economic elites and between an ethics of shared survival and the logic of unbounded accumulation, come to the fore.

Bosnia and Beyond: Toward an Anthropology of 'State-Building'

On the basis of the material presented here, it is possible to outline some directions for an anthropology of 'state-building' which could draw on other topics such as the anthropology of 'transition', the anthropology of state, or the anthropology of violence and recovery.

All of the chapters in this volume show that the social and political ruptures of the war and post-war periods should not be allowed to overshadow important continuities. For example, the frequent assumption that 'civil society' is something new in Bosnia must be re-examined, since charities, cultural societies and trade-unions appeared there at the end of the 19th century (see e.g. Hadžibegović and Kamberović 1997), and various voluntary associations were also active in socialist Yugoslavia (see e.g. Hann 1996; Stubbs 2000a; World Bank 2002: 68-118).[19]

---

[19] Taking a broader definition of civil society, anthropologists have also explored the roots of interethnic conflict or tolerance through social practices continued from the socialist period and before (for contrasting views see Hayden 2002; Sorabji forthcoming; and for a discussion see Hann 2003).

Similarly, and despite the burden of the war legacy, the political difficulties faced by post-war Bosnia share much in common with those experienced by other post-socialist countries. The clientelistic manipulation of the gap between legal entitlements and available financial means or the ethnic legitimization of informal power networks are practices that were already present in socialist Yugoslavia and, indeed, contributed to its final demise (see e.g. Sekelj 1993; Woodward 1995a, 1995b). Ambivalent perceptions of the state as both illegitimate predator and provider of physical and material security, the surrender of the public sphere to 'corrupt' political elites, the withdrawal into the private sphere and reliance on kinship solidarities and personal connections (*veze*) were all existing patterns that the circumstances of the war and the post-war periods only encouraged and reshaped (see e.g. Gosztonyi and Rossig 1998; Sorabji forthcoming). Finally, a comparative study of the Austro-Hungarian, early socialist and the present periods would demonstrate that even the imposition of imported modernization projects and their 'domestication' by the local society is nothing new in Bosnia.

Against this background, an anthropology of 'state-building' in Bosnia will inevitably have much in common with anthropologies of post-socialism.[20] As with 'transitology' in general, the literature on post-war Bosnia is often based on the notion of a linear 'transition' to democracy and market economy.[21] In the minds of Dayton's main architects, such a 'transition' was meant to allow for the removal of its initial ambiguities: together with the return process, the establishment of democracy and market economy was to have led to the replacement of the nationalist elites and the rebirth of a shared economic space and political community. Anthropologists working on post-socialist countries, however, have shown how the notion of 'transition', with all its normative presuppositions, is unable to reflect the complex processes taking place in post-socialism, as well as their effects in everyday life (see e.g. Burawoy and Verdery 1999; Hann 2002). This is all the more true for Bosnia, which is both a post-socialist *and* a post-war country.

Beyond issues specifically linked with post-socialism, it could therefore be useful to consider recent insights offered by anthropologies of the state. Akhil Gupta, for example, argues that an ethnographic study of the state should encompass 'both the analysis of the *everyday practices* of local bureaucracies and the *discursive construction* of the state in public culture' (Gupta 1995: 375; emphasis in the original), since at the local level, what one is most likely to

---

[20] As some anthropologists have pointed out, parallels can also be drawn between post-socialist 'transition' and post-colonial 'development' (see e.g. Barsegian 2000). For anthropological approaches to 'development' policies, see e.g. Escobar 1995; Ferguson 1994; Grillo and Stirrat 1997.

[21] In 2002, Wolfgang Petritsch himself talked about Bosnia going through a 'transition from war to peace, and from a Communist system to a market democracy' (speech to the Council of Europe Parliamentary Assembly, 22 January 2002, available at <http://www.ohr.int>).

encounter on the ground are 'blurred boundaries' between 'state' and 'civil society' (Gupta 1995: 384; see also Ferguson and Gupta 2002; Mitchell 1999). In a similar way, Michel-Rolph Trouillot emphasizes the fact that the state 'is not necessarily bound by any institution, nor can any institution fully encapsulate it' (Trouillot 2001: 126), and that, in the context of globalization, 'state practices, functions, and effects increasingly obtain in sites other than the national but never entirely bypass the national order. The challenge for anthropologists is to study these practices, functions, and effects without prejudice about sites or forms of encounters' (Trouillot 2001: 130-1; see also Ferguson and Gupta 2002; Kalb 2002).

Post-war Bosnia is indeed being shaped by a variety of state and state-like effects. As shown by Grandits in this volume, the state itself is struggling, fragmented, and contested, due to the institutional framework in place since Dayton and to an enduring crisis of legitimacy in the eyes of the population. Many of its functions have been taken over by intergovernmental or non-governmental organizations, in a unique exercise in international intervention (esp. Coles, Duijzings, Grandits, Jašarević; see also Gosztonyi 1999, 2003; Stubbs 2000a, 2000b, 2005). The efforts of foreign donors to 'promote civil society' and the role of both international and local new-style NGOs in the delivery of public services and social benefits have introduced new distinctions between 'national' and 'international', 'governmental' and 'non-governmental', 'political' and 'humanitarian' (esp. Helms; see also Sampson 2002a, 2002b; Stubbs 2000a, 2001; Stubbs and Deacon 1998). International intervention has clearly produced state-like effects at the local level, and both practices by and expectations of 'the state' have undergone deep transformations. These new forms of 'governmentality' (Foucault 1991) are characterized by multiple layers of government and by 'blurred boundaries' between 'the local' and 'the global' (see e.g. Ferguson and Gupta 2002; Gupta 1995; Trouillot 2001).[22] Against this background, the ways in which ordinary people experience international policies and the level of trust they place in various local, foreign, and international institutions make a difference, as several of the chapters in this book demonstrate (esp. Grandits, Delpla, Bougarel, Jašarević). In other words, the final outcome of international policies depends also on local practices and worldviews, and it is only by 'going local' that one can hope to fully understand the state or state-like effects of international intervention and, more broadly, of globalization (see e.g. Burawoy 2000; Gupta 1995; Trouillot 2001).[23]

In support of such anthropological approaches to 'state-building', we would like to come back to one the main findings of this volume: the pervasiveness of moral categories and claims in post-war Bosnia. In all the chapters, it is especially

---

[22] On new forms of transnational governmentality in Eastern Europe, see e.g. Kalb 2002; Pandolfi 2002, 2003; Stubbs 2000a, 2005; Wedel 1998, 2001, 2004.

[23] At the same time of course, political violence and processes of globalization represent new challenges for ethnographic fieldwork (see e.g. Burawoy 2000; Greenhouse 2002; Marcus 1995; Nordstrom 1995).

striking to see how war-related social and cultural categories bolster and are bolstered by competing moral claims, and that this competition is pervasive throughout all of Bosnian political and social life. Notions of culture and morality, justice and common good reappear throughout the chapters. This central (but often neglected) feature of post-war Bosnian society reflects not only a lingering confrontation over the causes and outcomes of the war, or the exacerbation of social conflicts over scarce material resources, but, more fundamentally, the need *and* the difficulty of restoring common normative frameworks after the collapse of the pre-war legal order and the gross violation of commonly accepted norms of comportment.

In the aftermath of violence, issues of rule of law, definitions of justice and everyday moralities are closely related and much more intricate than many 'top-down' analyses suggest (see e.g. Das and Kleinman 2000, 2001). On the one hand, the moral categories and claims so prominent in post-war Bosnian society apply to various issues and temporalities – from the recognition of historical misdeeds (esp. Duijzings, Grandits) to the allocation of scarce material resources (esp. Stefansson, Bougarel, Jašarević), through the prosecution of war crimes (esp. Delpla) and the hierarchization of wartime sufferings and merits (esp. Duijzings, Helms, Armakolas, Jansen). Even the distinction frequently made between retributive, reparative and distributive justice is not sufficient to understand how these different registers reinforce or contradict each other (esp. Grandits, Bougarel, Delpla), and are mobilized, renegotiated and reshaped at the local level (esp. Kolind, Stefansson, Helms, Jašarević,). On the other hand, what is common to all these moral categories and claims is their utmost rigidity. The articulation of social and political conflicts in moral terms is by no means peculiar to Bosnia, or to post-war societies. In the Bosnian case, however, the ubiquity of a narrow selection of moral categories and claims ensues from the need to ascribe meaning to wartime experiences and to the uncertainties of the post-war period. It can also be perceived as a legacy of totalitarian ideologies and imposed historical narratives. In this light, the main question is whether such categories and claims contribute to the restoration of common normative frameworks or, by turning social conflicts into unyielding moral hierarchies, prevent Bosnian society from successfully managing its inner contradictions.

As illustrated by the issues of war crimes and the return of the displaced, local level studies call for nuanced answers to this fundamental question. The activities of the ICTY contribute to the restoration of a minimal consensus on the necessity to punish war criminals and, together with the pressures exerted by the OHR on the authorities of the RS, to the establishment of truth and the recognition of victims (Delpla, Duijzings). At the same time, the management of war memories remains a highly contested process, both in and among ethno-national groups (esp. Duijzings, Bougarel, Kolind), and the restoration of interpersonal cooperation often implies the avoidance of sensitive topics or the recognition of diverging war experiences (esp. Armakolas, Jašarević, Jansen). In a similar way, the amendment of the entity laws on 'abandoned' real estate in the late 1990s may have only had a limited impact on the return process, but these amended laws did allow for the nearly complete restitution of reclaimed property and, after a period of heightened tension between legal owners and *de facto* occupants, for the restoration of a minimal consensus on the legitimacy of pre-war property and occupancy rights (esp. Stefansson, Armakolas; see also Delpla 2004a; Philpott 2005; von Carlowitz 2005).

In their own work on violence and recovery, anthropologists Veena Das and Arthur Kleinman point out that, after violence has led to 'the distortion of local moral worlds' (Das and Kleinman 2000: 1), coming back to everyday life implies, 'on the one hand, creating a public space in which experience of victims and survivors can not only be represented but also molded, and, on the other, engaging in repair of relationships in the deep recesses of family, neighbourhood and community' (Das and Kleinman 2001: 3). In such a context, 'community healing ... means repair but it also means transformation – transformation to a different moral state' (Das and Kleinman 2001: 23), and 'the fresh attempt to build communities or neighbourhoods is never purely a local affair', since 'it is simultaneously an attempt to redefine and re-create the political society' (Das and Kleinman 2001: 4). In Bosnia, the painstaking elaboration of common normative frameworks is indeed accompanied by the crystallization of new forms of governmentality: the activities of the ICTY have also indirectly contributed to the reform of the Bosnian judicial system, and the restoration of pre-war occupancy rights has been followed by the privatization of socially owned apartments. The production of new normative frameworks, new forms of governmentality and new allocations of power and wealth appear as complementary aspects of what is labelled 'state-building' by mainstream literature. It is against this backdrop that the difficulties met by the international community in its endeavour to establish a viable state and a shared political community must be reconsidered.

International organizations have played a key role in the removal of certain physical and social divides inherited from the war (esp. Duijzings, Armakolas, Kolind). But international policies and the forms of governmentality they produce can also complicate the reformulation of common normative frameworks and represent new challenges for a shattered political community. This is evident in the way the collapse of the production economy and the socialist welfare state has forestalled consensus on the definition of legitimate income and social justice (esp. Jašarević, Bougarel, Jansen). Once again, it becomes clear that the difficulties encountered by the international community are attributable not only to deliberate obstruction by the nationalist parties, but also to a widespread, longstanding perception of 'politics', as shown by the fact that 'internationals' and NGO-activists are themselves perceived as 'corrupt' by many Bosnians (esp. Coles, Helms). Paradoxically enough, some international practices and discourses feed this perception, and can thus work against the emergence of a shared political community in post-war Bosnia.

PART 1
Beyond 'Ethnicity'

Chapter 1

'Imitation of Life':
Negotiating Normality in Sarajevo under Siege

Ivana Maček

Introduction[1]

During my fieldwork in Sarajevo in 1994 and 1995 I found that people often used the concept of 'normality' in order to describe some situation, person, or their way of living. The concept was charged with a sense of morality, of what was good, right or desirable. A 'normal life' was a description of how people wanted to live, and a 'normal person' was a person who thought and did things people found acceptable. Thus, 'normality', in its locally understood meaning, communicated social norms according to the person using it, and as such also often indicated her ideological position.

When used as an analytical concept, as I use it here, it is important to bear in mind that social norms are always in a process of change. Each member of a society continuously defines and redefines her/his norms of conduct and perception of reality in accordance with her/his daily experiences. This process, which I refer to as 'negotiation' for lack of a better term, can exist unnoticed, and it is not seldom that the people involved perceive 'normality' as a stable entity. Indeed, an essential feeling that 'this is how things *really* are', seems to be tremendously important in creating a feeling of security. The human need for security can, in turn, be used by actors in a political arena to promote their own versions of reality, and consequently those with more power have more to say about what normality is.

By highlighting the process of negotiating normality in violent circumstances I want to give an outline of, and suggest a way of interpreting, life in Sarajevo during the war. The interpretation is grounded in research conducted in the last

1 This chapter is based on fieldwork conducted during 1994 and 1995 in parts of Sarajevo controlled by the Bosnian Government. An earlier version was published in *Narodna umjetnost*, 34/1 (1997): 25-58 (© 1997 by the Institute of Ethnology and Folklore Research; used with permission). I would like to thank this book's editors for helpful suggestions on the text of this version.

decade by social scientists working in similar circumstances of systematic violence against civilians, as well as in my own experiences from Sarajevo.

Between Chaos and Resistance

When members of a society are exposed to systematic physical destruction, or a fear of it, the normality of their daily lives as they lived them in peaceful times is seriously jeopardized. In wars where civilians and civilian lives are the main targets of destruction, the destruction of normality stretches itself through all levels of social life. As Carolyn Nordstrom has shown for the cases of Sri Lanka and Mozambique,

> Maimed *bodies* and ruined *villages* are obvious casualties of dirty wars. Maimed *culture* – including crucial frameworks of knowledge – and ruined *social institutions* are not as visible, but they are equally powerful realities and their destruction might have a much more enduring and serious impact than the more obvious gruesome casualties of war. (Nordstrom 1992: 261; emphasis added)

The destruction, however, rarely happens suddenly and totally. Rather, the lives people are used to living are disrupted gradually and continuously. This leaves space for people to come to terms with the disruptions: to feel them, to think about them, to explain them, and to find their own ways of acting – in other words, to negotiate their normality.

Michael Taussig's *Nervous System* (Taussig 1992) is a distressing account of such social processes in a 'true state of emergency', to use his words. The expression stands not only for the effects of Colombian state terrorism on civilian life, but also characterizes a global phenomenon. Central to Taussig's account are notions of 'terror as usual' and 'normality of the abnormal' which 'requires knowing how to stand in an atmosphere of whipping back and forth between clarity and opacity, seeing both ways at once' (Taussig 1992: 17). He continues:

> I am referring to a state of *doubleness of social being* in which one moves in bursts between somehow accepting the situation as normal, only to be thrown into a panic or shocked into disorientation by an event, a rumour, a sight, something said, or not said – something that even while it requires the normal in order to make its impact, destroys it. (Taussig 1992: 18; emphasis added)

Characteristic of the type of wars described in this chapter is the initial notion of chaos and abnormality. In such circumstances of permanent insecurity, each small incident that disrupts normality produces an ontological and epistemological vacuum (Nordstrom 1992: 261, 267-8). This condition stays for a shorter or longer period of time until the disruption is dealt with, interpreted, understood, and normality is re-established.

Taking examples from World War II, Elaine Scarry posits that this enables implantation of new 'truths', explanations of events and reality, by those who hold power over the destruction (Scarry 1985). As the cases from Latin American 'dirty wars' show (Green 1999; Suárez-Orozco 1992; Taussig 1992), an individual's struggle to make sense of her situation and the world around is indeed subjected to the 'truths' defined by politico-military elite. But people do not just automatically accept new explanations, ideas and norms. It is better to say that the negotiation of normality takes place in a political space where the power over defining 'truth' is highly contested.

In his *Grammar of Terror*, Marcelo Suárez-Orozco (1992) describes the stages of reaction to systematic terror to which civilians were subjected during the Argentinean 'dirty war'. The first reaction was a denial that people were disappearing. Then came rationalizations for why somebody had disappeared, which implied that this could not happen to oneself. Coping with the loss of a loved one without knowing her destiny also caused reactions of anger against the authorities held responsible or anger turned inward in the form of depression, 'mummification' of the disappeared person's belongings, and eventually acceptance of the situation. This is the state where people are full of doubts about what is true and real, which produces still more fear and a withdrawal into one's own shell of privacy. 'Every possibility is a fact' (Taussig 1992: 34) and paranoia becomes social theory and social practice.

Still in the domain of the private, when terror becomes the order of the day ('terror as usual' in Taussig's words), the shared experience of survival often turns into 'despair and macabre humour' (Taussig 1992: 18). This, like the sharing of trauma among women in Guatemala through talk about their sicknesses (Green 1999), is the first sign of resistance to the imposed order of terror. When experiences, traumas, desires and ideas get expressed – voiced – they become shared. The forms of expression can be various: humour, jokes, poetry, rock-music, paintings, theatre or talking about sicknesses. The naming of the trauma is not only a form of resistance but can also be a way of healing.

Material Uncertainty, Humiliation and Shame

> If I have three children, I shall call them Electricity, Water, and Gas!
> – a ten-year old boy in Sarajevo

It is not hard to understand the basic needs for food, water and some source of energy for the sustenance of bare physical life. Because of their basic and obvious nature, I perceived the problems of providing them as fairly banal, and yet, I found myself from the very beginning very attentive to whether water or electricity would come at some point of the day. On the days when this happened, my fieldnotes inevitably begun with something like: 'Today around twelve o'clock I heard the water coming on...' The explanation for this preoccupation lies in the fact that these things were necessary for physical survival. More importantly, however, it points us to a phenomenon necessary for understanding the war in Sarajevo: everyday uncertainty.

Characteristic of the war situation in Sarajevo was the scarcity and irregular availability of life-sustaining basics rather than a total lack of them. This was one of the central strategies used against ordinary life and the civilian population in this war. Whether aware of its effects on the population or not, authorities from both warring sides alternated between cutting off and letting through supplies to the population as a way to reach their goals (which most often appeared to be military or political). This caused confusion among the people of Sarajevo. I was told that all the cables and pipelines went through Serb-held territories, which meant that the Serb side could easily cut Sarajevo off completely. Thus, people wondered why the Serb side sometimes let them have electricity, water and gas. As the war went on, many Sarajevans lost their illusions about how much their own government cared about them. In September 1994 people were convinced that it was not only 'the Serbs' but also their own government that was causing the cuts. The general opinion was that this was done in order to victimize the population of Sarajevo and thus gain points in the international political arena.

The effect of these 'strategies' was that any daily routine became impossible. During the periods when there was no water at all, whole days went to queuing up at the cisterns and then transporting the water home. Often in freezing temperatures, under random shell fire, accompanied by the physical hardships of transporting water and the emotional exposure to the nervous, depressed or angry outbursts of fellow citizens, the experience of accessing water in Sarajevo became engraved in people's bodies and memories as something to avoid at all costs. Everyone therefore waited eagerly for the occasional sound of water starting to drip from the taps in order to catch every precious drop. This usually did not last for more than half an hour, nor did it happen every day, but still the waiting was worth it. Anything to avoid water queues.

The same happened with random electricity supplies once the electricity started coming. These were people who were forced to spend long winter evenings by the light of one precious candle or the weak light of a small bulb powered by a car battery; people whose homes were filled with modern electrical appliances that sat useless for more than two years; people who were tired of washing clothes by hand in tiny quantities of precious water; people who were ashamed of their homes which had once been vacuumed weekly: these people welcomed every second of electricity in order to re-establish the standard of living they considered decent.

The occasional arrival of water and electricity made people feel that they were able to live more normally, that is normally according to pre-war standards. Its randomness, on the other hand, had a disastrous effect on their coping with the situation. For example, a young woman told me that her mother used to leave the bathroom light on so that if the electricity were to come on during the night (as it often did during the initial period), she would wake up and be able to vacuum. When the electricity came on one night at three o'clock in the morning, the daughter, too, woke up. She saw that her mother was too tired to do any work so she begged her to go to bed. The woman returned to her bed, but she could not give up the idea and could not fall asleep for a long time.

In the family where I lived I witnessed similar situations. One day the water and electricity came on at the same time. For anyone in charge of a household this felt like winning the lottery and my hostess' reaction was no different. Although she knew that both the water and electricity could disappear any second, this was her happy moment and she hurried to start the washing machine. As predicted, it was less than half an hour before the power for the machine disappeared again and she ended up rinsing everything by hand.

Interestingly, these conditions persisted even after the final ceasefire was declared; it was thus no longer directly connected to the military situation. In October 1995 I noticed a calendar in the kitchen of one of my friends in Sarajevo. It was filled with small notes. My friend explained that her father had marked the days when the authorities had said there would be water, electricity or gas. The scheme was very complicated but it was possible to work out on which days one would have, for instance, both water and electricity so that laundry could be planned for that day. A month later, water, electricity and gas were once again cut off, coming on just occasionally and randomly.

Being forced in this manner into a state of waiting and complete subordination to the whims of destiny, or the authorities, the unpredictability became incorporated into every person, and the alertness to the coming of water, electricity and gas became a survival instinct. The message that slowly but surely engraved itself into people was that they had no power over their lives. Consequently, they started feeling that their lives were worthless and that they could not understand the logic governing them.

Important to note in this process are feelings of shame. When talking about their situation Sarajevans would not only use the notion of 'normal life' but also express the shame they felt: because they could not invite me for a decent (normal) meal, because their homes were not as tidy as they wanted them to be, because they had lost their dignity by losing control over their lives and destinies, or because they no longer cared if somebody had been killed that day (as long as it was not somebody they knew).

Scarcity and irregular availability not only affected water, electricity and gas, but also food and wood – although the question of how these were supplied was different in character because humanitarian aid and the 'black-market' were involved (Maček 2000: 86). Before the war, the population of Sarajevo had been used to a standard of living which generally coincided with that of any Western city of the same size (about half a million). During the first year of the war almost all Sarajevans went from being fully employed professionals providing a decent standard of living for themselves and their families to being charity recipients dependent upon the good will of a range of organisations (from the United Nations, Western NGOs, religious relief organisations such as *Caritas* and *Merhamet*, to Islamic humanitarian NGOs coming mostly from Saudi Arabia and Kuwait).

Examples I am about to give show how shame can gradually turn into the (normal) state of things, which indicates that a change in what is considered to be normal has taken place.

The couple I was staying with were university educated people in their late fifties. Throughout their lives they had been able to provide for themselves a decent living that included much more than basic food provision. Even during the first months of the war they had been able to buy their own food and fuel (that is wood or coal, needed when the electricity and gas were cut off). They simply could not face the humiliation of receiving 'mercy from foreigners', as they expressed their view on humanitarian aid. Queuing for hours in the cold and under the threat of shelling in order to be given a few kilograms of food that would only last a few days was unthinkable. But after some months their reserves of Deutschmarks (DM) were gone, and they were compelled to apply for help from foreigners as if they were charity cases. It was a public statement of their social degradation caused by the war. By September 1994 when I stayed with them in Sarajevo for the first time, queuing for humanitarian aid was a part of their everyday life. They explained the original humiliation they felt but it no longer bothered them.

On the other hand, they still refused to take charity from '*šejhovi*' ('sheikhs'), private donors from Muslim countries in whose name bread was occasionally distributed free of charge. They preferred to use their own precious flour and yeast, spending almost a whole day walking to the house of a relative who had a wood-burning oven in order to bake their own bread. They also had to use up valuable coal and were obliged to somehow return the service to the relative later on. They could still afford it, however, so they refused charity from the '*šejhovi*'. Receiving help in the name of Allah was perceived as much more degrading than losing social status. If there was a social logic behind it, then it must be that one could become poor and still live in the same society with the same norms, whilst accepting charity in Allah's name would, for my secularized hosts, mean accepting another kind of society with a whole range of different norms.

The question I asked myself at that time was how long it would take before my hosts would have to accept this sort of charity. The answer can perhaps be given through another example of a friend of mine who was a medical doctor and from a Catholic Sarajevan family. From our first meeting in September 1994, she commented from time to time on the proliferation of Islam in civil and official everyday life, most often brought by 'Arabs', which she found disturbing. When I visited in October 1995, Saudi Arabia had established a new donation to medical doctors in Sarajevo who had been working throughout the war for free or for a minimal monthly salary of 10 DM (5 €) in Bosnian coupons.[2] The Saudis had now decided to donate 50 DM (25 €) per medical doctor per month, which my friend was happy to receive. She made no remarks about it, either, although it meant going every month with her ID card to two Saudi representatives (one man and one

---

2 Bosnian Coupons were the only currency in which salaries were paid at the time. Since very few goods could be bought for Coupons, most households had plenty of them.

woman, the woman veiled in a very strict way, a style perceived as a sign of an extreme form of Islam, alien to Sarajevo). The money was not as much as she would have needed, but it was a welcome increase in the family budget, and at that point she was glad for it, no matter from whom and how it came.

Another friend of mine, also a medical doctor, from a secularized Muslim Sarajevan family jokingly commented on the same situation: 'Since the *hadžije* came, I feel that I can make small gifts to myself and my family. Last week I bought a chocolate bar for my seven-year-old nephew.' A *hadžija* is a Muslim who has completed the *hadž*, the religious pilgrimage to Mecca that every Muslim should, if possible, make once in his/her lifetime. To call the Saudi donors '*hadžije*' (pl.) implied that their involvement in Bosnia was merely allowing them to gain some spiritual credits. As we shall see later on, this sort of joking played an important role in Sarajevans' resistance to the abnormality of the circumstances.

Ideological Shifts and Everyday Life

To be clear, the discomfort a lot of people in Sarajevo felt about Islam had very little to do with the religion as such. People were used to Islam's presence in their surroundings and had always respected religious Muslims, their beliefs and customs, as any other religious people. What caused the uncertainty was the growing importance (and power) of Islam in public space, which had been completely secularized before the war. This was readily visible in politics, the army, education and the media (Maček 2000, 2001; Bougarel, this volume).

The Bosnian Government fought hard to present itself as democratic, respecting the rights of all its citizens, regardless of nationality. This was, of course, very hard in a war which was designed as a war between Bosnia's major nationalities (*narodi*) and which took place in the middle of the process of a new ideological and political constitution of these nationalities, displacing the Yugoslav ideology of 'Brotherhood and Unity'.

Many people I knew in Sarajevo believed in their government's good intentions. In this way they were able to think of their new country as a continuation of the previous one. It was others who had become different and broken all the norms of morality – 'the Serbs' on the other side, especially their political leaders. Specific instances of injustice against non-Muslim and non-religious citizens were explained by the war situation. This was a way of dealing with the destruction of the previous experience of political life: a tolerant dismissal of disruptions, a sort of denial and rationalisation in order to protect normality (Suárez-Orozco 1992). Some citizens critical of the Bosnian Government's policies, however, interpreted all this as a mask, and every occurrence that promoted Muslims or Islam was taken as proof of the government's real intentions.

The part of the population that wanted to live in a secular Western-style democracy was usually very sceptical towards the government's policies and often pointed out the growing tendencies towards Muslim domination and islamicization of the society. They lived and fought for the ideals they were living by before the war. Often they were called '*jugonostalgičari*' ('Yugonostalgics'), although this was misleading. For example, in several official places people refused to remove Tito's picture from the office walls, not because they were nostalgic about the old regime – often they were very critical of it – but rather as a protest against the new regime. The picture simply said: 'I do not accept *this!*'

In an article entitled '*Merhaba, gospodine!*' ('Merhaba, Sir!'), a Sarajevan linguist argued that it was a sign of 'political pathology' that during the war 'foreign, Oriental' words were increasingly being used in everyday language ('*Merhaba*' is a Turkish greeting, itself Arabic in origin), pushing out the well-established 'European' pre-war greetings like '*Dobar dan*' ('Good day' in former Serbo-Croatian). At the end of the article she encourages Sarajevans to use the pre-war greeting with other 'old Sarajevo folk' in order to at least preserve a memory of the Sarajevo that once was (Stančić 1994). The argument was very characteristic of feelings shared by many people I met. The bitterness these critical people felt was first of all directed towards the so-called 'neo-Muslims', or 'April Muslims' – those who had become vocal and dedicated Muslims only after the beginning of the war in April 1992. On the other hand, people who were known to have been religious Muslims all their lives, and who used Turkish words in private, were respected.

People who supported the government's policies and accepted these new tendencies in society could basically be divided into three categories: those who felt that they could accept the new situation and that, after all, this was their government, and every government had its good and bad sides; those who completely re-interpreted their pre-war experiences and perceptions of religion as well as the relations between nationalities; and those who had always considered that more of the (mostly Ottoman) traditions of Bosnian society should be part of daily socio-political life. Regardless of the category to which they belonged, however, they all justified the changes that had been introduced, arguing that there was a tradition of both Islam and Turkish loan words in Bosnia. Greetings like '*Merhaba*', for example, were explained by the presence of a large number of Turkish loan words in the Bosnian variant of the former Serbo-Croatian language, words that had been in use all along but had been abolished from official language by the previous regime. The same goes for other language changes like the (re)introduction of the letter 'h' into some words, sometimes in the most curious places, (re)interpretations of literature and history, and the general revaluation of Islam's importance for the society (Maček 1997; Maček 2000: 153-207).

Yet very few people supported the incorporation of Arabic loan words into the local language, nor did they approve of the disturbing presence of 'Arab missionaries' who seemed to hold quite a bit of power over socio-religious issues. The idea that (Islamic) 'fundamentalism' was gaining ground in Bosnia was also strongly opposed. These reactions were closely connected to the fear of a new islamicization of Arab provenance, which was seen as something non-Bosnian, an attempt to change the society and customs from outside. The Arab language had always been a part of religious practice and education, the argument went, but traditionally there had been very few Arabic loan words in the Bosnian language, and that's the way it should stay.

The following anecdote illustrates this tension. One day I went for a walk with my hosts in the old part of town. We came to a small mosque and my host wanted to show it to me from the inside. As it happened, there was a prayer session going on so we decided to wait until it was over. When people came out of the mosque, we asked a man who was responsible for the building if we could take a look and he agreed, but then suddenly a young man who was sitting near the entrance said that non-Muslims were not allowed to enter a mosque. He was dressed very formally in a dark suit and tie, he was dark-haired and had a carefully cut beard and moustache – obviously a foreigner, one of the 'missionaries'. My host and another elderly local man started arguing with him that this was not true. The young man told them that this was what the Qur'an said. I could see how anger escalated in the faces of my host and the elderly local man, both of whom had a quite good knowledge of the Qur'an and Islam. It did not help. The 'missionary' was determined on this point, so we left the place without being allowed into the mosque. I could see a sort of apology on the local elderly man's face.

Afterwards the people to whom I told the story referred to the young 'missionary' as an 'Arab'. A young *bula* (female teacher of Islam), for example, was upset that the 'Arabs' had come to Sarajevo with the thought that they could teach Islam to Sarajevans. The notion that she shared with other religious Muslims in Sarajevo was that they had been Muslims as long as the 'Arabs' had and that in Bosnia they had their own way of practicing Islam. According to this stance it had always been possible to enter a mosque or a church, no matter your own religion, as long as you did not disturb the religious sermon. The *bula* and her husband, along with their whole families, had always been Muslim believers and they were obviously disturbed by these new tendencies. He, an officer in the Bosnian Army and an activist in the ruling Party of Democratic Action (SDA), was also upset by the image of Bosnia he felt was spreading abroad based on the presence of foreign Muslims. '*We* are the "fundamentalists" they are talking about [in the West]?!' he complained. Since he was not prepared to consider the 'Arab missionaries', the foreign *mudžahedini* (mujaheddins), or any other sign of a more dogmatic islamist presence as parts of Bosnian society, he perceived himself as being unfairly labelled 'fundamentalist' just because of his Muslim faith and practice of praying five times a day, as well as because he fought for his government, his country and his people.

In this reaction he was not alone. People in Sarajevo were all upset about the 'fundamentalist' label. No matter to which of the above mentioned categories of (Muslim) government supporters they belonged, or of which nationality or faith they were, this was a unifying point for the Sarajevo population.

On the other hand, it could be said that during the war an almost complete division of the population along nationality lines was accomplished. In the case of those people who adopted new national ideologies this was very obvious. But, although such people were numerous, this was not the most typical attitude I met in Sarajevo. In fact, most of the people expressed tolerance towards all nationalities and religions, but when it came to the way they told their stories (anecdotes, or jokes), the 'side' with which they sympathised and identified could easily be seen.

Broken Bonds: Relatives and Neighbours

> You should take just one family, any family in Sarajevo, and describe its destiny. That will give you the best picture of what this war did to each one of us.
> – my host in Sarajevo

More than two-thirds of the families I knew in Sarajevo lost a close family member (a child, wife, brother or sister, parent) during the war, either because the relative left town or because s/he was killed. If we consider all the family members that were part of daily life, as well as those who were wounded, the amount of the population affected by such losses is likely to approach the total. This is exactly how it felt to Sarajevans themselves.

In the beginning of the war people considered only the physical dangers when they decided to separate for some time. Nobody thought about the effect that a separation of several years, along with the anxiety of not knowing how ones' loved ones were, would have on their relations. People in Sarajevo, as well as refugees abroad who had somebody left in the town, assured me time after time that they had initially thought that the war would be short. Had they known that it was going to last for years, they would never have separated from each other.

The opportunity to leave the town by plane, provided to Sarajevans – mostly old people, women and children – in the beginning of the war by the former Yugoslav People's Army (JNA) was re-evaluated after the realization of what this separation did to people. Many Sarajevans I met in Zagreb or Sweden told me that they had left town on 'the last plane' or 'the last bus'. 'Sarajevo looked like Saigon in those weeks' a middle-aged woman told me in Zagreb in Autumn 1993. A man in Sarajevo interpreted the former JNA air-bridge as an indirect way of ethnically cleansing Sarajevo (as opposed to some other towns and villages that were cleansed in a more obvious way). He maintained that 'the Serbs knew'[3] that the men who stayed behind would not last long before leaving the town to join their wives and children. This was exactly what happened in many cases after the initial phase of local patriotism, anger and defiance ('We felt we wanted to defend the town against the *papci* [hillbillies] up there in the mountains') faded away and turned into disappointment and emotional exhaustion. The Sarajevan art group *Trio*, designed a sharp comment in relation to these feelings (see Figure 1.1).

---

[3]   On the widespread opinion that 'the Serbs knew' what would happen, see also Jansen, Armakolas, this volume.

Sgt Pepper logo redesigned by "Trio" - Sarajevo

Figure 1.1 **'Sarajevo's Lonely Hearts'**

(© Art Group *Trio*)

However, not all of those who left left at the beginning. As the situation failed to get better with the passage of time, many decided to leave during the course of the war and even after the war. These people knew the conditions – they had to make the decision never to come back. Mostly, of course, they were the ones whose families were already abroad, people who could organize a flight for the whole family or young people in search of a better start to their adult lives.

The circumstances of separation were devastating for inter-personal relationships, especially marriages in which the bond between the spouses was not strong. Some of the men, left alone in the town, found other women after some time. Other families split apart when one of the spouses decided to flee the town. Most frequently, however, the way Sarajevans dealt with separation and the associated emotional pain had much in common with the 'mummification' that Suárez-Orozco found characteristic in Argentina. In both cases, the remaining members of the family were forced to deal with the fact that a close person was no longer around, although her definitive disappearance from their lives was not certain. In the case of Argentinean *desaparecidos*, a family would keep the rooms and belongings of the victims intact, exactly as if they were still living there. In Sarajevo this was not often the case – mostly because it was impossible from a practical point of view – but the need to keep absent loved ones in one's life was similar. This integration into daily life was often accomplished by making the missing person into the purpose of one's life. I knew people in Sarajevo who fought for their lives only because they did not want to worry their family members who had left the town. Perhaps the lack for many Sarajevans of any kind of strong ideological commitment accentuated even more the importance of, and commitment to, one's family.

Leaving the town was one of the most obvious ways of avoiding the disrupted normality. As I have already mentioned, in the beginning of the war the rationale behind the decision to leave was to preserve physical lives as well as the standard of living. But it was also an ideological escape for many people who felt that they could not live in a state where a division of people into nationalities was to be the new socio-political order (see also Stefansson, Jansen, this volume). Life in exile showed, however, that such an escape was possible only to a certain degree. One's own life was certainly protected. The material conditions of living were sometimes worse, sometimes better. On the other hand, the social position, self-esteem and social networks were lost, and only some of the refugees managed to re-establish conditions comparable to those they had regarded as normal before the war. The concern for one's own life was substituted by the concern for the lives of loved ones who had stayed in Sarajevo, and the need to deal with ideological and political changes in Bosnia was at least as strong for those who left as it was for those who stayed.

Especially sensitive were instances of Serbs leaving for Serb-held territories since the chances of being accused of collaboration, or at least of sympathy for the (Serb) enemy, were very high. This could be devastating for the family members who remained on the Bosnian Government side. Family members, friends, acquaintances and neighbours who fled to the Serb side were generally condemned for their choice. In mainstream public discourses they were seen as traitors to a multiethnic Bosnia and the ones responsible, together with the enemy, for the tragedy of the war (see also Armakolas, Jansen, this volume). Even the people who were critical towards their government, and for whom nationality and religion had never played an important role, condemned those who fled to the Serb side, but mostly in cases where personal contact was lost. For example, one young woman told me about her friend who was a medical doctor, so she knew that he was not carrying a gun or part of an armed force. She was sure that he was helping people. Yet he had chosen to help only one nationality – the Serbs, whilst she who had stayed on the Bosnian Government side was helping everybody, regardless of nationality. He had made his choice for only one nationality.

Mistrust and ostracism were general phenomena, used not only against Serbs or those of different nationalities, but also against those who had left and fallen out of touch. This sort of sentiment was also apparent in popular songs during the war, most of which talked about love for Sarajevo and contempt, rather than hatred, for the people who had left. One of the rationales behind staying whilst a part of the family left the town was therefore to increase the whole family's chances of returning. By staying in the town during the whole war, one could prove one's ideological and moral righteousness. To have some sort of job would certainly count as an advantage after the war, and what was perhaps most important, one could take care of one's apartment and possessions.

A lot of Sarajevans experienced the plunder of the apartments left by those who fled as one of the shameful episodes of this war. Many of these apartments and houses were occupied by refugees from other parts of Bosnia, mostly eastern Bosnia, and from Sandžak in Serbia. Generally, Sarajevans felt contempt for these people, but at the same time they understood their need for shelter. Sarajevans could empathise with refugees who had lost everything material, and often even family members, because they themselves were experiencing similar losses. Many of their own belongings had been sold in order to buy food, books and furniture were burned for warmth, and some homes had been destroyed more or less completely by shells. But what they could neither understand nor accept were the people, Sarajevans like themselves, plundering everything down to the last fixture in the apartments of their neighbours who had fled. This behaviour was so disturbing that everybody I knew felt ashamed. At the same time, this was the reason why many were afraid to leave their apartments unguarded. The idea of one's neighbours, people one knew and had largely depended upon during the war, rummaging among one's personal possessions was so revolting that it made the thought of leaving impossible. The same was true of the ones who had left; one of the reasons for not wanting to return was the thought of living in a town where one's neighbours did this sort of thing.

The idea of neighbours as people one could trust, a sort of social security, had been widespread and established in Bosnia before the war (Bringa 1993; Bringa 1995: 55, 65). The story of a man selling his house for two hundred gold coins illustrates this very well. The house was objectively worth only one hundred and when the surprised buyer asked why the price was two hundred when the house was worth only one, the answer was: 'The neighbours are worth as much as the house.' Neighbourly trust also remained a norm during the war (Maček 2000: 128-38), which may be one of the reasons why the flight of the population was so decisive and why the return of refugees to their original homes is so difficult. If old neighbours were to live as neighbours again as before, they would have to re-establish the neighbourly trust that is still considered a social norm. Such a process is a painstaking emotional and social endeavour, something that can hardly be regulated 'from above' by political agreements or well-meaning but often poorly informed outsiders.

Countless times during the war I heard people say that Sarajevo would never exist again. The town may survive and be rebuilt but the absence of the people who left meant that life in it would never be the same. This is because these people and the way of life in the town *were* Sarajevo. To complete the social picture of Sarajevo, it is important to note that in a town that had had 525,000 people before the war, UN statistics for 1994 estimated the population at 440,000, of which 140,000 were refugees from outside Sarajevo (UNHCR 1994: 7). This means that by 1994 only slightly more than half of the pre-war population still lived in Sarajevo. My host told me that he did not have any friends to visit and talk with anymore. A young working woman told me during my stay in October 1995 that she had rarely encountered anyone she knew in the town even before that, but that after summer 1995, when she walked down the main street she no longer met anybody familiar. When I asked people to tell me about their friends and what had happened to them, the answer I usually got was that all of their friends had left. Some people knew where their friends were because they kept in contact, and those were the friends that were missed the most. Others had just disappeared and, as mentioned above, those were the ones people condemned.

Danger, Vacuum and the Worth(lessness) of Life

When I asked one of my friends how she had felt after a shell exploded in her garden only a few seconds after she had gone into the house (she felt the explosion even though she was in the house), she answered, 'miserable'. What she usually did after such an experience was to call a friend and just talk, make something special to eat or drink, or do some other nice thing in order to forget about it. Her 'technique' was actually to reaffirm life in a way that brought back a feeling of comfort and security.

The day after I myself was shot at from Grbavica (the part of town near the centre then held by Serb forces) in front of UN soldiers in their tanks who did not do the slightest thing to protect me, also I felt utterly miserable. The feeling was strong and paralyzing in the sense that I lost the will to do anything. When I thought about it afterwards I understood that what was happening inside me was a realization that my life – everything I had ever done, all my qualities and qualifications, and the righteous purpose, as I saw it, of my being in Sarajevo – was no longer worth anything. After a day, when I managed to convince myself of the purpose of my stay and when I had worked out a way to expose myself as little as possible to potential gunfire, the misery disappeared. My world was re-established through the reaffirmation of my own values: my work and my life.

As I outlined above, another way of dealing with danger was to deny it. In Sarajevo, there was nothing one could do about the physical threat of shells and sniper bullets, and the only way of dealing with them was to find ways to ignore them. From my own experience I discovered that being with somebody else and talking was a good way of forgetting that you were constantly within the sight and reach of shells and bullets. When walking alone, the best thing was to actively think about something else: about things you had to do, people you had met, or things that were said.

Rationalising away the danger was still another way of dealing with it. The probability of being killed in Sarajevo was not larger than in any big city in the world – the number of people killed by crime or traffic accidents in New York was larger than the number of injuries by shells and snipers in Sarajevo I had been told. There were also stories going around about people hiding during the whole war in cellars because they were afraid of getting wounded. When, after two or three years, they came out for the first time, a random shell fell and they were killed on the spot. The moral of the story was, as in the previous one, that there is no use hiding or thinking about the dangers. A young soldier told me that a way of keeping your senses at the front was to realize that the soldiers on the other side were just as scared as you were. 'Everybody is scared. The important thing is not to panic, because then you're dead', he concluded. Of course, it was impossible to keep these rationalizations continuously intact. Everyone went though periods of not caring followed by periods of fear and feeling exposed, in this way swinging constantly between strength and anxiety.

As I discussed in the beginning of this chapter, between disruption and the re-establishment of normality there is an epistemologically empty space, a vacuum. This was something that each Sarajevan was constantly exposed to and forced to deal with.

As far as the people I knew were concerned, periods of strength (whether a re-established purposefulness of life – normality – or just a successful dismissal of the situation and its dangers) were followed by periods of depression, or broken normality, and then again by strength in a seemingly never-ending cycle. People with whom I one day had the most rewarding discussions on politics and their private situation could some other day express feelings of chaos. Nothing made sense, there were no explanations, no logic, they were tired and feeling weak. This made me realize that notion of chaos functioned as a pause, a break from the exhausting enterprise of creating normal life. Sometimes it could also be accompanied by a sort of plea: people asked me to provide them with an answer, an explanation, which I rarely could. When their own energy was insufficient, people often turned to others for explanations. Explanations were sought not only from me, the anthropologist, but also from neighbours, relatives, politicians, journalists, priests, in rumours, as well as in the media. In such cases the new normality was no longer based on one's own experiences, but rather the other way round: everyday experiences were interpreted in accordance with this new normality coming in 'from the outside'.[4]

'*Prolupati*' was an expression used during the war that is hard to translate: it is a verb literally meaning 'to break through'. The expression appeared as early as the period of the 1991 war in Croatia and was afterwards also used in Bosnia. What it described was a state of mind of people who acted normally in their daily routines (supplying food, water, fuel), but who at the same time did not care much about anything any longer. These people had lost their hope for the future; they had no more strength with which to re-establish some sort of norms in their lives and they did not care if they were killed or not. When I first noticed them it was because they could calmly stand in an exposed place whilst the shelling was going on. Or, for example, there was the elderly man I met in March 1995, who was not at all interested in the opportunity he suddenly got to move from Sarajevo to a house he had in a peaceful coastal part of Croatia where his wife, daughter and grandson already were. He had no energy, no will to act and improve the conditions of his life. Whether this was a permanent state of mind or just a temporary condition which could be changed was impossible for me to judge. What was characteristic of such people was that they could appear to be more stable than the people who negotiated their normality. For the people who had 'broken through', there was no longer anything they could be disturbed by, there was nothing they longed for. They had escaped from the exhausting process of the negotiation of normality.

'Imitation of Life' and Existential Creativity

> But I made new friends during the war. These friendships can never be like the ones we had in peacetime – they are short, and they are informed by this horrible situation. But perhaps just because of the sharing of the most difficult moments they are as strong as the old ones.
>
> – a young woman in Sarajevo

So far I have discussed the disruptions that war caused in Sarajevans' normality. I have also noted the processes of integrating the new conditions into the everyday life and attitudes, a process which caused a change in what was perceived as normal. In several places, though, I have noted the ways in which people resisted

---

4   This is why it is important to have in mind that the negotiation of normality always takes place in a political space where several possible truths exist and the power over defining normality is highly contested.

the conditions that forced them to give up parts of their pre-war standards, as for instance with the norms for hygiene, forms of greeting, or neighbourly trust. Now I would like to take a more systematic look at the forms of resistance that existed in Sarajevo during the siege.

To accept one's living conditions and adapt to them (a change in normality) is a way of surviving, and certainly a way of negotiating normality, but it cannot be seen as resistance. People themselves were very well aware of their survival techniques. That was why they often referred to their lives as an 'imitation of life': a preservation of normal forms of life through activities that were highly abnormal and humiliating. On the other hand, I suggest that a creative acceptance of one's conditions is a form of resistance.[5]

The tremendous creativity that Sarajevans demonstrated during the war was one of the most important characteristics for the everyday process of fighting for norms. Creativity is a word often associated with artistic work, but the war conditions forced literally everybody in Sarajevo (including the artists, of course) into an amazing mental and emotional display of creative power. It could be seen in all aspects of war life: in tasty meals made from insufficient and monotonous food supplies, fantastic machines constructed out of scrap as alternative energy sources, new types of war friendships, or in the emotional and spiritual fight to hold onto the will to achieve a meaningful life.

For example, all the very imaginative methods Sarajevans used in order to make their monotonous, tasteless food of miserable quality into tasty and varied meals was a way of resisting the humiliating conditions that also threatened their health and lives. Another example was the hard work put into finding employment, because having a job to go to not only meant economic benefits and social contacts, but most importantly it provided structure for a daily routine. It could be said that people accepted the situation, but this was only as resistance to the destructive effect of irregularity and broken norms that accompanied the war.

The need to resist the war also resulted in an amazing explosion of cultural life. Art was popular with Sarajevans not only because it was 'imitating normality' but also because it was a means by which everyday common problems and traumas could be expressed and shared.[6] Similarly, the public life of the town – street cafés, restaurants and fashionably dressed youth – flourished as much as it could. All of these things, as well as some industries that continued their production, even at very low levels, throughout the whole war, including the well known daily *Oslobođenje*, was the pride of Sarajevans. These were the symbols of resistance proudly pointed out to every visitor in the town.

Naming or expressing the disruptions in one's normality was another way of resisting outside conditions and creating, or preserving, one's own norms. This form of resistance flourished in Sarajevo during the war. My host told me that he found it difficult to be a man in this war because men were supposed to be brave. 'Of course, everybody is scared, but as a man you're not supposed to show it', he

---

5   On everyday forms of resistance after the war, see Kolind, this volume.
6   On art as a means of expressing the inexpressible, see Aretxaga 1997.

told me. However, he himself, as well as most of the men I talked to, expressed their fear quite clearly. Somehow during the war it became commonly accepted that everybody felt fear, and this shared knowledge helped enormously in coping with it.

Another typical way of commenting on the situation, its destructiveness and humiliation was through jokes. For example, the joke, 'How does a smart Bosnian call a stupid one? With a phone call from abroad!' basically expressed one of the most acute dilemmas during the war – to leave or not to leave. In sharing the joke, people were letting each other know that they shared the same problem.

Of course, jokes and art were often not just expressing problems, but also offering sarcastic comments or critique (for example, the work of the art group *Trio*, discussed above). I referred earlier to Taussig's notion of 'despair and macabre humour' (Taussig 1992: 18) because I found it highly true of the situation in Sarajevo. Many of the jokes were impossible to tell outside of the town because people who did not have the same macabre experiences had no references with which they could appreciate this kind of humour. Instead, they tended to find such jokes disturbing and morbid.

In their daily lives, Sarajevans often took verbal revenge against those they saw as the cause of a certain disruption. For instance, the seemingly 20-year-old high-protein biscuits that were sent as humanitarian aid from the USA were called 'Vietnam cookies', implying that the U.S. was getting rid of food reserves left over from the Vietnam War. In jokes snipers were made fools of and Muslim donors were called '*hadžije*', implying that they were using Sarajevans' tragedy to win points with Allah. That this sort of phenomenon is to be expected in any similar situation can be inferred, since even the UN soldiers stationed in Sarajevo adopted the same sense of humour. They called their air bridge to Sarajevo *Maybe Airlines*, insinuating that anything could happen, and that in Sarajevo no 'normal' rules could be counted on.

Lastly, I would like to come back to a reflection on new friendships by a young woman I quoted earlier. I have witnessed, and even experienced myself, many such newly built friendships that were characteristic of the wartime. During the relatively short time I spent in Sarajevo I made at least some friends for whom I felt as strongly as for any of my out-of-Sarajevo peacetime friends. This would not have been possible without the war conditions we shared. In the same manner I acquired a war family. The feeling I often had of being the 'wrong person' when meeting parents, siblings or friends of refugees I knew from Zagreb and Sweden, was induced by the warmth and happiness they showed towards me, as if I was the person they missed. In the beginning I felt bad about this. I felt guilty for having the privileged status of freedom of movement that these people lacked. I also felt bad about receiving all this emotional capital that I had not earned in any way except by knowing the persons that were so much missed. After some time, however, I started to build new social and emotional bonds myself, and in talking with people I realized that these new bonds were something very common during the war. Filling old needs with new people was normal in Sarajevo. It was not a substitution for the ones who were missed but a substitution for the social and emotional needs they had once fulfilled.

Conclusion

In this chapter, I have tried to present the complex experiences of war and political violence in Sarajevo in terms of a process of negotiation of normality. We have seen how the everyday presence of physical violence forced Sarajevans into a constant struggle to understand their life situation, interpreting their experiences of war and thus establishing their normality anew, only in the next second to witness its destruction. We have seen Sarajevans' reactions and shared cultural methods of dealing with experiences of everyday violence. While some of this resembles what other authors have described in similar conditions in other parts of the world, the local Sarajevan concepts such as 'imitation of life' and their concern with 'normality' bring some new elements into our understandings of life and culture in circumstances of war. They point us toward an important human need for the feeling that life is normal, that it is recognizable, predictable and thus also safe. This is a subjective feeling which is existentially crucial for every individual to maintain, no matter what the 'objective' circumstances are. The Sarajevan example teaches us that through an understanding of the meanings of normality in a certain context, we can better grasp the social, cultural and ideological processes taking place. This is especially true of circumstances of political violence where these processes easily remain obscured by terror and the chaotic nature of the everyday experience of violence.

In the post-war context, experiences of violence are no longer shared on a large scale as they were during the war (although for some people, violence and fear of violence are certainly still present in their everyday lives). Instead, the experience of violence becomes increasingly part of individual memory and public constructions of truth and history. At the same time, people often feel for the first time that they have a chance to look with hope into the future. They hope that their lives will become normal in the sense that it was understood before the war, while at the same time they are well aware that it is not possible to re-establish it. In this situation it is crucial that the visions of the future, of the new post-war normality, leave space for individual memories of violence to be formed and communicated, as well as to satisfy the need for a recognisable, predictable and safe everyday life. As was the case during the war, even after the war the process of individual negotiation of normality will take place in a politically contested space. For this reason I suggest that the method of understanding and describing the meanings of normality would be a fruitful one in any post-war context.

Chapter 2

Urban Exile:
Locals, Newcomers and the Cultural Transformation of Sarajevo

Anders Stefansson

Introduction[1]

For the locals, there is no doubt: Sarajevo is not, and will never become, the city it once was before the recent war. The sense of radical transformation is not only caused by the manifest destruction of the material and economic urban landscape. After all, houses, apartment blocks and public facilities can be rebuilt, the economy reinvigorated. But war-related population displacements and migrations have also brought about cultural changes that are not easy to measure, and even more difficult to reverse. In demographic terms, the locals' sense of a fundamental upheaval is hardly an illusion. Indeed, the arrival of at least 90,000 internally displaced persons (DPs) from other parts of Bosnia-Herzegovina and the exodus of an estimated 240,000 pre-war inhabitants in the course of the recent war have had an obvious impact on the population structure of Sarajevo. These displacements simultaneously decreased the overall number of inhabitants from 510,000 in 1991 to 360,000 in 1999 and changed the ethno-religious structure of Sarajevo, as the Bosniac part of the local population increased from about 50 percent prior to the war to 87 percent in 1997, while the majority of Bosnian Serbs and 'Yugoslavs' left town (ICG 1998; UNHCR 1999).

In my conversations with *Sarajlije*, the pre-war Sarajevo inhabitants,[2] comments on the eroding cultural standards of life in the city were extremely common:

---

[1]   The findings of this chapter are based on nine months of fieldwork carried out in Sarajevo during 1999 and 2001, in connection with a Ph.D. project on the process and experience of refugee return (Stefansson 2003). The main informants were repatriated refugees from different host countries, people who stayed behind in Sarajevo during the conflict, DPs, visiting refugees and representatives of international and local organizations.

[2]   Throughout the chapter, the terms '*Sarajlije*' and 'locals' will be used to refer to members of the pre-war population in Sarajevo.

Sarajevo is not a city anymore.
Sarajevo has become one big village.
We have been invaded by peasants.
We have become minorities in our own city.
There's no culture in this place anymore.

Thus, *Sarajlije* portray themselves as 'cultural strangers' within their 'own' city. According to some informants, there are things, phenomena and groups of people that do not belong in a city like Sarajevo and as a result, they ought to be expelled in order to restore the proper cultural standards of life. From the *Sarajlije*'s point of view, the prime source of cultural disturbance is both the influx (or 'invasion', as it is often termed) of DPs and other groups of *došljaci* (newcomers) who came during the war and are all seen as having come from rural and backward areas, and the simultaneous departure of a large portion of the urban population.

This chapter explores the dual meaning of 'urban exile'. On the one hand, a significant number of people from other parts of Bosnia-Herzegovina sought refuge in Sarajevo during the war. On the other hand, according to *Sarajlije*, the city itself – that is the core values which defined the city and the people who embodied those values – has been 'exiled'. Throughout the analysis, the socio-cultural cleavage between locals and various groups of newcomers is related to the wider Bosnian assumption of a ranking among cultural mentalities, placing urban and rural, as well as 'cultured' and 'non-cultured' behaviour at opposite ends of a normative hierarchy. The discussion primarily rests upon *Sarajlije*'s perspectives, but it also takes into account the voices of the stigmatized newcomers. By highlighting this particular aspect of social relations in post-war Sarajevo, the chapter presents an image contrary to that of the many studies which portray ethno-religious identity (*nacionalnost*) as the paramount source of social division in Bosnia-Herzegovina and in the former Yugoslavia in general.

Classifying (Non-) Culture

In Sarajevo, the distinction between locals and newcomers is not solely a matter of different territorial origins or regional cultural characteristics. It also relates, in rather complex ways, to other important cleavages between urban and rural people, as well as between 'cultured' and 'non-cultured' people. It is not the mere influx of newcomers that *Sarajlije* lament, so much as that these newcomers all allegedly stem from more provincial, backward and less 'cultured' parts of the country. In Bosnia-Herzegovina, the deep-seated assumption of the existence of a cultural hierarchy encompasses a range of other oppositions:

Being 'cultured' [*kulturni*] or 'non-cultured' [*nekulturni*] refers to a whole set of ideas associated with other sociological oppositions, such as town versus village, educated versus uneducated, poor versus rich, modern and Western versus backward and Balkan. (Bringa 1995: 58)

In this respect, Sarajevo is a special location. As the capital, it is by far the largest town in Bosnia-Herzegovina, which, in addition to its long history of economic, cultural and political power in the country is also perceived by its native inhabitants as the most urbanized, developed and 'cultured' place of the country. A term like '*sarajevski duh*' ('Sarajevan spirit') alludes to the cultural superiority of its native population. In the popular imagination, relative wealth, high levels of education, cosmopolitanism, 'Europeanness' and low levels of religiosity characterize the refined urban, 'high' culture of Sarajevo. In contrast, *Sarajlije* depict Bosnia-Herzegovina beyond Sarajevo as more or less rural, poor, primitive, traditional, religiously radical and 'non-cultured'.[3] Thus, in Sarajevo, the three central socio-cultural dichotomies – local/newcomer, urban/rural and 'cultured'/'non-cultured' – are interconnected in such a way that, ideally, the native, 'cultured' locals are opposed to the rural newcomers with inferior cultural habits and knowledge.[4]

Ridiculing and ostracizing culturally inferior newcomers and arguing against their right to settle in new destinations is not a phenomenon unique to Sarajevo, but rather widespread throughout the former Yugoslavia. Nor is stigmatizing newcomers a recent practice caused by the massive displacements of people in many parts of the region (e.g. Duijzings 1996; van de Port 1998: 52-3). According to informants, the same negative attitudes towards rural newcomers were common in pre-war Sarajevo. The reasons for the importance of the urban/rural and 'cultured'/'non-cultured' distinctions in the former Yugoslavia are complex and, while largely lying beyond the scope of this chapter, deserve a few observations.

A proper account of the importance attributed to urban, 'civilized' values in the former Yugoslavia, that is, to be regarded as *fini ljudi* (decent people) (van de Port 1998: 37-66; Kolind, this volume), would have to include the region's long history of political, economic and cultural marginalization within Europe, especially during the centuries of Ottoman rule. Within the Balkans, there exists a profound

---

[3] In fact, the term 'non-cultured' is somewhat of a misnomer. When informants characterize other groups of Bosnians as *nekulturni* they are in fact not claiming that these people have no culture at all but that they have the *wrong* kind of culture. *Nekulturni* people thus do not have the right 'high' culture but possess an abundance of the traditional peasant culture from which Bosnians are generally eager to distance themselves (see Jašarević, Kolind, this volume).

[4] Obviously, in more provincial areas of Bosnia-Herzegovina and the former Yugoslavia, locals are not necessarily urban and newcomers are not always rural. The influx of DPs and returning refugees from rural areas to Sarajevo and other major towns in Bosnia-Herzegovina is paralleled by a less well-researched movement of urban people to the countryside, notably the Sarajevan Serbs leaving for areas in *Republika Srpska*. On a couple of occasions, I visited such Bosnian Serb DPs who all complained (and joked) about the 'ruralization' of their living conditions (see also Armakolas, this volume).

longing for 'Europe', a desire to escape the stigmatization of the Balkan label and to be considered a part of Europe and as 'real' Europeans (e.g. Balić-Hayden and Hayden 1992; Todorova 1997). On the perceived fringe of Europe, the idea of 'Europe' carries much more explosive, symbolic weight than in the heartlands of Europe. Thus, people in Sarajevo and other parts of the former Yugoslavia value, articulate and strive to behave according to the ideals of the educated, refined, cultivated, knowledgeable and highly bourgeois European citizen, perhaps more than is the case in countries closer to the centre of Europe. A case in point is the Bosniacs. Indeed, most stress that they belong in Europe despite their (cultural) Muslim identity, that they are 'European Muslims' with a much more detached relationship towards Islam than among Muslims in the Arab world (see also Maček, this volume).

The influx of 'peasants' to the cities is not a new process, although it accelerated drastically during the war. The Communist party, which came to power in the aftermath of World War II, turned rapid economic progress, that is urbanization and industrialization, into the centrepiece of its political project. From the 1950s onwards, people from the countryside started migrating in large numbers into major cities like Belgrade, Zagreb and Sarajevo, looking for jobs and better living standards.[5] Communist leaders strove to bring Yugoslavia out of its 'backwardness' by imposing education and the right (West European) *kultura* on the masses (Doder 1978: 196). In so doing, however, they indirectly demonized the large peasant part of the population and turned it into a collective scapegoat:

> The rural population were [sic] a symbol of the mentality, life-style and living conditions that the new socialist Yugoslavia was to leave behind. (van de Port 1998: 46)

According to Yugoslav social scientists, this rapid urbanization resulted in what Cvetko Kostić terms the 'peasantization of the cities'.[6] As the concept indicates, due to the rapid pace of urbanization, the cities had to adapt to the rural migrants' way of life (and not the other way around), for example in relation to the significance of kinship ties:

> [E]ven in the largest urban centers, an ideology rooted in kinship solidarity and multistranded reciprocity has survived virtually intact, and has been projected into non-kinship social arenas as well. (Simic 1983b: 209)

This continuous reliance on kinship networks apparently alleviated the social problems that often go along with rapid urbanization, such as impoverishment and crime. At the same time, however, other 'maladaptive aspects of traditional

---

[5]   According to Michael Spangler (1983), Bosnia-Herzegovina had the lowest rate of urbanization of all Yugoslav republics. However, many Bosnians migrated to major cities in the neighbouring republics.

[6]   *Politika*, December 1969, quoted in Spangler 1983: 83. See also Simic 1973, 1983b.

culture' produced an urban environment in which 'rationally' working large-scale institutions and a 'contemporary mentality' were not very well developed (Simic 1983b: 203-4).

The academic notion of the 'peasantization of the cities' is supported by many ordinary Bosnians who claim that before, during and after the recent war, many people who migrated to a city like Sarajevo kept their rural mentality instead of transforming themselves into decent, 'cultured' urbanites. In Bosnia-Herzegovina, people do not believe that such a transformation can happen overnight. In fact, even after living in the city for years, even generations, one can still be labelled by others as a peasant and a newcomer. Thus, these stereotypes refer less to actual social facts than to ascribed cultural mentalities. On the inertness of the rural mentality, Adnan, a refugee in Denmark, remarked:

> People who came to the city after the [communist] revolution quickly got money and education, but here [pointing at his head], they stayed primitive. It was normal in Yugoslavia that a person had a good education, TV and satellite dish but when he talked, you could hear that he was 'a man of yesterday'.

Urbicide: War Against Civilization

As the term 'peasantization' may indicate, in Bosnia-Herzegovina and the former Yugoslavia, social scientists are among the foremost proponents and reproducers of the notion of hierarchically ordered urban/rural cultural mentalities. Bosnian sociologist Alisabri Šabani, in a striking example of this tendency, focuses on the huge number of 'new refugees' who entered Sarajevo during the recent war from a predominantly poor, rural environment and examines the way in which this 'invasion' or 'attack', as he terms it, has transformed the character of Sarajevo. As the newcomers fear and disapprove of the 'urban life style', characterized by 'impersonal relationships', 'indifference, apathy, and cosmopolitanism', they have ruralized the city by bringing with them their 'rural habits'. They have turned Sarajevo into 'a sad urban phenomenon' where 'socio-pathologic events' like crime, prostitution and black markets prevail (Šabani n.d.: 4-5). In this process, 'urban people became strangers and minority groups in their own city' (Šabani n.d.: 5) and Sarajevo found itself in 'its own urban exile' (Šabani n.d.: 88). Although *Sarajlije* did their best to resist this sociocultural deterioration in a sort of 'rural-urban war' (Šabani n.d.: 4), they were up against a superior force. For example, according to Šabani, the incoming rural people's affection for group behaviour, contrasting with the individualistic preferences of the true 'metropolitan person' (Šabani n.d.: 4), has unfortunately infected the post-war revival of the strong urban tradition of taking walks along the main street of Sarajevo.

The value of this article clearly does not lie in its scientific merits but in its unintentional, and all the more revealing reflection of the cultural stereotypes which prevail among the local population, as we shall see in the following. The massive scale of displacement taking place during the war and in the 1990s has intensified and brought a new meaning to the cultural stereotyping of rural newcomers. Besides blaming them for bringing about the cultural deterioration of Sarajevo, *Sarajlije* also accuse the rural population of having caused the war in the first place: 'In Sarajevo the onset of war was widely understood as an urban/rural conflict between civilized citizens and barbaric peasants.' (Sorabji 1994: 125; see also Maček, Kolind, Jašarević, this volume)

According to many informants, due to their backwardness, aggressiveness and cultural ignorance, people in the countryside were much more inclined to support the nationalist parties in the early 1990s and, when the crisis escalated, to take up arms against their neighbours of different ethno-religious backgrounds. This idea is mirrored in the works of several Western scholars who seem to uncritically adopt the Bosnian model of hierarchized cultural mentalities, portraying the urban population, especially the eloquent intellectuals, in highly idealistic ways:

> The difference between a sophisticated and cosmopolitan urban population on the one hand and a backward rural population [on the other hand] is, according to many observers, actually one of the causes of the exceptionally embittered and cruel nature of the present fights. (Østergård 1993: 14-15; translated by A.S.)

> These urban cultured Europeans, representing *the best in Bosnia*, never wanted partitions or ethnic cantons… (Donia and Fine 1994: 9; emphasis added)

Such analyses tend to neglect the fact that the ideology employed for stirring up ethno-religious antagonisms for political purposes largely emanated from (factions of) the urban intellectuals based in the major cities, like Belgrade, Zagreb, Sarajevo and Banja Luka, as is usually the case with nationalist movements.

More surprisingly, many *Sarajlije* describe the war as an attempt by the rural population, masked in ethno-religious disguise, to destroy the cities and the urban way of life:

> At the start of the war, many Sarajevans, for instance, claimed that it was being waged by country folk [*seljačine*] who hated the city because they could not understand it. (Bringa 1995: 240, note 14)

Among these 'sackers of cities' (Bogdanović 1993: 36) are of course the Bosnian Serb leader, Radovan Karadžić, and his supporters. For *Sarajlije*, the shelling of Sarajevo by the Yugoslav/Bosnian Serb Army situated on the hills around the city epitomizes rural attacks on urban values; it is the ultimate emblem of 'primitiveness' attacking 'civilization', 'non-culture' violating 'culture'. Therefore, *Sarajlije* continually emphasize the fact that Karadžić is neither a native of Sarajevo nor even of Bosnia-Herzegovina. He is in fact a 'double newcomer' who grew up in the rural parts of Montenegro before moving to Sarajevo and apparently suffered from an inferiority complex due to his rural upbringing. Therefore,

Karadžić might have used the war to take revenge against Sarajevo and its local intellectual circles from which he allegedly felt excluded. One can almost sense the pleasure it subsequently gave the author of a tourist guide to Sarajevo to label Karadžić 'a Serb peasant from the Montenegrin mountain of Durmitor'! (Dizdar 1998: 36) Karadžić spent his adult life in Sarajevo, where he completed university, practiced as a psychiatrist, and published collections of poetry. It thus does not make much sense, from a Western viewpoint, to characterize him as a 'peasant'. However, seen through the Bosnian cultural lens, in which urban life is closely associated with refinement, tolerance and culture, the actions of Karadžić clearly reveal his 'primitive peasant mentality'.[7]

Foreigners entering Sarajevo are therefore likely to be in for a surprise if they expect the local population to subscribe to the popular notion of a 'civil war' that was fought between antagonistic ethno-religious communities (*narodi*), carrying out brutal ethnic cleansing fuelled by an ancient history of communal hatred in this unruly and conflict-ridden Balkan region. While not dismissing the 'ethnic' explanation altogether, *Sarajlije* tend to portray the siege and the shelling of Sarajevo as a war that village or mountain people waged against the urban population and its refined style. Similarly, the central social cleavages in post-war Sarajevo seem to be those separating *Sarajlije* from newcomers, urban from rural people, returning refugees from those who stayed behind, and the economic elite from the lower classes, all of which, in today's Sarajevo, often amounts to an internal conflict among Bosniacs, and not between the Bosniac, Bosnian-Serb and Bosnian-Croat parts of the population.

At least in Sarajevo, the distinction between 'cultured' *Sarajlije* and rural newcomers has become a pervasive, emotional issue, surrounded by such a small degree of rhetorical restriction that it appears to sideline the cleavages between the various ethno-religious communities. Whereas criticism of other people's (lack of) culture was voiced with great emotion by the vast majority of informants, critical remarks directed against other nationalities were rare and carefully expressed. This probably testifies both to genuine, surviving multiethnic beliefs as well as to a sense of 'political correctness'. In socialist Yugoslavia, publicly expressed negative attitudes towards specific ethno-religious communities could lead to harsh sanctions. Likewise, in post-Dayton Bosnia-Herzegovina, the Sarajevo authorities are still officially committed to the ideals of a multicultural society. In fact, *Sarajlije* consider open criticism against other nationalities to be one of the most obvious signs of a non-Sarajevan, 'non-cultured', rural mentality.[8]

---

[7]   It is important to point out that, within the former Yugoslavia, there also exist more positive attitudes towards the countryside and the peasantry. Particularly in Serbia, various nationalist movements cultivate a 'cult of the primitive' (van de Port 1998: 87), both in the past and in relation to the recent conflict, in which the peasant population is regarded as the incarnation of the unspoiled, 'pure' Serb.

[8]   The impossibility of criticizing other nationalities, and the political system in general, may, at the same time, partly explain the popularity of classifying people in terms

Peasants in the City: *Gorštaci*, Goats, and the Sound of Garbage

The antagonistic attitudes of *Sarajlije* towards the newly arrived groups of people are already suggested by the terminology used to describe newcomers. The most common collective terms for the newcomers are '*došljaci*' (literally 'those who have arrived', but in the former Yugoslavia, the term usually carries negative connotations) and '*došljo*' (a form of the same word, but even more patronizing). More overarching terms are '*seljaci*' (peasants/villagers), '*seljačine*' (literally 'big peasants', country bumpkins), '*papci*' (literally: hooves, meaning bumpkins, hillbillies), '*gorštaci*' (people from the mountains) and '*primitivci*' (primitives). The newcomers are sometimes referred to as '*Indianci*' ('Indians') and '*Afrikanci*' ('Africans'). I also came across the expression '*oni koji su došli sa Romanije*' ('those who have come from Romanija', a mountain range close to Sarajevo), whether or not the people in question actually originated from this particular (and, in the popular imagination, extremely rural) region. Apart from that, specific groups of newcomers are labelled according to their regional origins, as in Herzegovina, eastern Bosnia or Sandžak, with the accompanying ascribed cultural mentalities (which are discussed later on in this chapter).

Asked about their attitudes towards the newcomers and the transformed cultural environment of Sarajevo, informants usually evoked lengthy, emotional and colourful descriptions of the primitive, 'non-cultured' behaviour of the newcomers, which is clearly inappropriate in an urban setting. Jelena, a Sarajevan returned refugee from Norway, pointed to some of the typical complaints against the newcomers:

> Everything they do, they do in a way that has no place in a city. They behave non-cultured, they are uneducated, illiterates, have some customs that are strange to us, wash carpets outside, shake them out of the window, dump garbage out of the window. All this doesn't belong in the city. The way they talk. When they call on the telephone they ask 'Hamo, is that you?', instead of telling their name. All this bothers me. The only thing that can change this is the return of the original Sarajevan population.

Many of the stories referred to the newcomers' unfamiliarity with the 'proper' public behaviour in a densely populated urban environment, and their 'monopolization' (and hence 'ruralization') of the public space. The newcomers' handling of garbage was a prime cause for contempt. When asked his feelings toward the newcomers, Dragan, a Sarajevan returnee from Germany, simply exclaimed: '*Fuj!!*' ('Yuck!!'), before starting to describe the way in which the newcomers in his suburban high-rise block threw garbage out of their windows instead of placing it in the containers by hand. Dragan explained that, while

---

of cultural mentalities, as this might have served, and continue to serve, as a 'valve' for other sorts of social cleavages linked with the economic and political conditions in the country.

watching TV in the evenings, he was constantly disturbed by the sound of garbage hitting the ground below. Obviously, the result was messy and not very hygienic.

Sarajlije despise another characteristic of the newcomers: some of them are allegedly grazing herds of goats and cows on the outskirts of town and sometimes letting hens and other types of animals move into their homes.[9] As Hamid, a young refugee in Denmark said with disgust in relation to his former home town, Banja Luka:

> People from the countryside brought their horses with them up the stairs to the empty apartments [that they occupied], gathered grass for them and let them have their own room! They don't understand the way I've been living in the city.

The newcomers' conspicuous way of dressing, walking and talking make them even more vulnerable to criticisms in Sarajevan public life:

> I was going to the post office close to the *vječna vatra* ['eternal flame'[10]] and a woman in her fifties with curlers in her hair, wearing a coat and slippers walked in and directly past the queue [to the counter]! You can tell who are cityfolk and who are newcomers just by looking at them. Also young people. You wouldn't see a girl from the city wearing heavy make-up and wearing totally tight-fitting clothes in the middle of the day. (Jasmina, Sarajevan returnee from Germany)

> Sometimes you can see how they walk in the city, talking too loud, often yelling out for each other from long distances. (Vlatko, Sarajevan returnee from Germany)

The newcomers are perceived as uneducated because of the improper greetings and obscene vocabulary they use. They also have the reputation of being illiterate. For example, Mirsad, a Sarajevan returnee from Canada, claimed that 42 percent of the post-war population in Sarajevo are illiterates, most of them DPs.[11]

Taking into consideration the subtle Bosnian sense of humour – most Bosnians have a seemingly inexhaustible stock of jokes – it is not surprising that the newcomers have become the primary target for new popular jokes. These jokes typically ridicule them in their inability to grasp the nature and purpose of the technical 'wonders' of urban civilisation, such as toilets, water taps, electric heating, modern cooking facilities and elevators. One such joke deals with a rural DP who, when asked if and when he would return to his pre-war house in the countryside, answers, 'Yes, when "rain drops" have been installed in my house!', rain drops evidently referring to the shower.

---

[9] On the cultural prejudices between locals and DPs in Sarajevo and other urban environments in Bosnia-Herzegovina, see also Cattaruzza 2001; World Bank 2002: 26-7.

[10] A memorial to the dead Partisans of World War II situated in the main street of Sarajevo.

[11] I do not have any statistics on post-war illiteracy rates, but this figure is clearly exaggerated.

In a less benign way, the newcomers are considered to nurture fundamentalist religious, ethnic and political attitudes which threaten the 'fine and complicated', even 'fragile', cultural pluralism of Sarajevo (Karahasan 1994: 16):

> The newcomers create disorder in Sarajevo. They inflict Islam on us. We in Sarajevo have always respected each other [across ethno-religious boundaries]. But now, extremist tendencies are imported from outside, and I don't want to accept that. No matter what nationality people have, I think that everybody must return to their own places. I wish the old [demographic] structure would be restored. (Aida, Sarajevan returnee from Norway)

Newcomers are described as aggressive and, due to their low level of education, as easy prey for manipulation by the nationalist parties. Phenomena like mafia-style criminality, corruption, nepotism and nationalism are blamed on the newcomers.

This miserable state of affairs and the cultural deterioration of Sarajevo are bad enough in themselves, but what makes it even more depressing is that *Sarajlije* do not believe that the situation will change in the immediate future. This is because most *Sarajlije* consider the newcomers to be people who were first forced to flee their home areas but then came to enjoy (peasantized) urban life and the better living conditions Sarajevo offers. They therefore do not wish to return to their backward and war-devastated places of origin. They are here for good, like it or not. In the standard saying, the newcomers have 'caught the asphalt' ('*dočepali se asfalta*'):[12]

> Sarajevo has become a village. People who arrived from the countryside are having a good time in Sarajevo. They've caught the asphalt. They've discovered how it is not to work hard as they did their whole life. They don't want to do it again. (Marina, Sarajevan stayee)

In other words, after spending some time in Sarajevo, the newcomers have come to realize the pleasures of urban life:

> They [the DPs] didn't come here [to Sarajevo] because they wanted to, at that time, and it was difficult for them to leave their hearth and home [*kuća i ognjište*]. But I see that most of them don't want to leave the city and go back to their villages now that they have tasted the city life. There is a proverb: 'He who drinks water in Baščaršija [the old Turkish centre of Sarajevo] will never leave Sarajevo'. That's the way it is with these people. You can't compare life in Srebrenica or Žepa [provincial towns in eastern Bosnia] with life in Sarajevo, or in Ilidža or Hadžići [Sarajevan suburbs] where most of them live. Who would want to get away from here when they have transportation right

---

[12] '*Asfalt*' ('asphalt') and '*beton*' ('concrete') are widely used Bosnian metaphors for city life (see also Jašarević, this volume). Thus, many informants stressed that 'I was born on the asphalt', in order to classify themselves as true urbanites, in opposition to the newcomers who have just recently 'caught the asphalt'.

to their door? This is city life compared to village life. They're just playing when they say, 'I would like to go to my own place'. And everyone prays to God that they won't have to return [to their pre-war places of residence]! (Alma, Sarajevan stayee)

Sarajlije are generally not convinced by the newcomers' assertion that they would like to return to their pre-war homes but just cannot do it because of security risks and ethnic obstructionism. On the contrary, *Sarajlije* believe that the DPs *could*, in fact, return to their place of origin but do not because they refuse to resume their hard, uncomfortable peasant life:

Interestingly enough, very few want to return to their own, not even those who have an 'open road' back home. It's a lie when they claim that they cannot return. Nobody wants to because it's better to live here. But why didn't they realize this before the war? At that time, they probably were doing better where they lived, or perhaps not. But the important thing is that they didn't want to go to Sarajevo even given the chance. In order to live in the city at that time, you had to be cultured and have an education. Since this was out of their reach, they worked as farmers. I respect that, but they also have to respect me [my way of living]. But they don't know how to behave decently. (Hasan, Sarajevan returnee from Norway)

Dropped from the Moon: The Return of the Urban Refugees

Against the backdrop of such unflattering accounts, locals and newcomers appear worlds apart in terms of cultural mentalities. Vlatko, a returnee from Germany, characterized the two groups as being as different as 'heaven and earth'. He said that upon his (involuntary) return from Germany, the shock of the state of affairs in Sarajevo made him feel like 'I had been dropped from the moon'. Some *Sarajlije* did not realize the lack of refinement of their rural compatriots until recently. For others, this fully dawned upon them only in the course of war or during their stay in exile:

I didn't know that such stupid people lived in my country before I met them in the refugee centres in Denmark. (Zlatko, refugee in Denmark)

As noted earlier, urbanization is not a new phenomenon but, according to *Sarajlije*, migration greatly accelerated during the war, so that the city lost its former capacity to transform the 'non-cultured' rural newcomers into 'cultured' urbanites. To the contrary, it is the city people who are pressured to adapt to the village manners:

Sarajevo has changed a lot. They [the newcomers] bring along the primitive. The city radiates primitivism. A lot of new people have come who, I think, should adapt themselves to the city and to the new conditions. But quite the reverse, they expect the city to adapt itself to them. I'm certain that people who have left for the US or other places try to adapt themselves. (Ivanka, Sarajevan returnee from Serbia).

'It will take thirty years for them to learn how to live like urban people, and I don't have the time to wait for that to happen', said Dženana who had returned from Canada with her husband because she missed the cultural atmosphere of Sarajevo and Bosnia-Herzegovina. Like many other returnees, however, she had become so disillusioned with the economic, political and cultural situation of her home country that she was considering settling abroad once again, this time permanently.

Sarajlije portray themselves as a marginalized, colonized minority, confronted with the massive influx and dominating behaviour of newcomers. This sense of powerlessness may explain why they tend to exaggerate the number of newcomers. One informant said, for instance, that locals only make up about 20 percent of the total population, and a second informant claimed that, during the war, 300,000 city people had left Sarajevo and 300,000 had arrived from other parts of the country. Moreover, *Sarajlije* feel marginalized economically and politically by the newcomers who, in their view, stick together and use extended kinship, village or regional networks to quickly gain access to sources of livelihood, notably jobs and housing, at the expense of the local population. Whereas locals consider themselves true to their tolerant and multiethnic beliefs, they describe the newcomers as opportunists who, on the one hand eagerly enlist in the dominant nationalist parties, and on the other, fake religious devotion in order to raise their social status. According to *Sarajlije*, influential municipal institutions are entirely in the hands of newcomers who use their offices for personal enrichment. It is a common assumption that when one person from a certain village or area gets a job in the public administration, 'thirty others' from the same place quickly follow.

Due to this sense of cultural marginalisation, *Sarajlije* nurture nostalgic and often clearly exaggerated images of the cultural standards of life in pre-war Sarajevo. They describe what was once a 'European city', even a 'European centre', and how it has been transformed into 'one big village', 'Africa', 'the Middle East', 'a place without culture', or in a standard expression, how it has 'moved hundred years backward in time'. Pre-war Sarajevo and post-war Sarajevo seem to be two diametrically opposed cities, the former sophisticated cosmopolitanism being replaced by plagues of cultural primitivism.

For *Sarajlije*, the rural population's influx has brought about a cultural deterioration of the city, and the only factor that could challenge and reverse this process is the return of the pre-war urban population from foreign host countries or from their temporary places of residence in other parts of Bosnia-Herzegovina. These Sarajevan refugees are portrayed as 'civilized', 'cultured' and cosmopolitan people, that is true urbanites, *Sarajlije*. In this context, their decision to flee a town experiencing rapid cultural and moral decay is sometimes presented as a reflection of their non-violent, anti-nationalist, tolerant urban values, both by the local stayees and especially by the (returning) refugees themselves. *Sarajlije* carry highly nostalgic images of those who left town. Common observations are that 'everybody who's worth something has gone' and that 'the smart ones left'. The foreign observer sometimes gets the impression that the return of the urban natives would immediately bring Sarajevo back to its former state. That the returnees who return to their pre-war homes in Sarajevo in many cases belong to the non-Bosniac minorities, or to 'mixed' families, is a fact that once again emphasizes the fallacy of arguments reducing the extraordinary sociocultural complexity and 'hybridity' of Bosnia-Herzegovina to 'the banalities of ethnic essentialism' (Campbell 1998: 56).

However, the attitudes of those who stayed behind in Sarajevo towards those who left town are ambivalent and contextually changing. When Sarajevan stayees talk about Sarajevo's cultural decay and the newcomers' 'non-culturedness', the return of urban refugees is a highly appreciated phenomenon indeed. But when they evoke their experience of suffering, (potential) returnees appear in a much less favourable light, as people who 'betrayed' Sarajevo and Bosnia-Herzegovina. They are also referred to as *pobjeglice*, cowards,[13] who not only lacked the courage and moral integrity it took to stay, but who also left for economic considerations (Al-Ali 2002; Maček 2000: 144-6; Jansen, this volume). Those refugees who return from Western host countries, whether voluntarily or involuntarily, are considered to enjoy various economic privileges in contrast with the stayee population. Often, these accusations directed against the returnees, different war experiences, and the development of new cultural identities in exile cause social distance between the two groups and the development of distinct 'moral communities' of stayees and returnees (Stefansson 2004a, 2004b).

The stayee/returnee cleavage cuts into the local/newcomer and urban/rural distinctions, as repatriated refugees encompass both *Sarajlije* and Bosnians who originate from other parts of Bosnia-Herzegovina but, for various reasons, are unable or unwilling to return to their pre-war homes. Only returnees who lived in Sarajevo prior to the war are welcomed back by the local stayees (if they are welcomed at all); these returnees are not targets of, but active participants in the cultural stereotyping of newcomers. In contrast, the non-local returnees are exposed to this sort of cultural discourse. However, as will be shown, this does not exclude them from directing the same type of cultural stigmatisation towards *other* groups of culturally inferior newcomers.

The Cultural Hierarchy among Newcomers

Newcomers are not (always) treated by *Sarajlije* as a homogeneous, equally detestable group, but are placed (and place each other) within a hierarchy of 'culturedness', most often corresponding to regional origins and ascribed cultural

---

[13] Not very easy to translate into English, the term '*pobjeglice*' is a recent linguistic invention which plays on '*izbjeglice*' (refugees), but with negative connotations, suggesting running away, scared for no reason.

mentalities. *Sandžaklije*, people from Sandžak,[14] are at the bottom of this cultural hierarchy, at least when it comes to groups of newcomers from within the former Yugoslavia. In *The Murder of Sarajevo*, the Sarajevan journalist and writer Željko Vuković expresses the widespread feeling of being outnumbered and marginalized by the well-connected people from Sandžak:

> During the war, Sarajevo has become 'Sandžaklian'. *Sandžaklije* control most of the municipal, political and military power. Their lobby is the dominant one. On the eve of the war, about 160,000 people originating from Sandžak lived in Sarajevo, and migration from this region had not yet reached its peak. ... Their new [Sarajevan] neighbours hardly hide their discontent, first of all due to the fact that they are imposing a different way of life, and enjoying specific privileges. *Sandžaklije*, more easily than others, manage to get water and food. They stick together and their own people are in power ... *Sarajlije* realize that they have lost their city. (Vuković 1993: 78-9; translated by A.S.)

Vuković readily admits that, before the war, *Sandžaklije* were 'second-rank citizens' and 'ghettoized strangers' (Vuković 1993: 78). Their stigmatization by *Sarajlije* continued during the war, despite their clear over-representation in the ranks of the Bosnian Army and in the lists of fallen soldiers. In August 1992, for example, the Sarajevan writer Sead Fatahagić declared that 'if Sarajevo is not governed by *Sarajlije* after the war, it will be difficult to stay in it'.[15] The feeling that the war was, for *Sandžaklije*, an opportunity to climb the social ladder with a speed that would have been unthinkable otherwise, a kind of social upheaval, is also present among informants:

> Uh, I get a headache thinking about them! They have a different kind of mentality, a different way of life. We're not used to the system that people from Sandžak import to Sarajevo. And we *Sarajlije*, who are now a minority, fight against this. There's a joke which goes: A man from Sandžak comes [to Sarajevo] and tells the first person he meets, 'show me where the city hall is, when I get to the city hall, I can manage the rest myself since I know everyone there'. And it's a fact that when a *Sandžaklija* comes to Sarajevo, he gets the rest of his [extended] family to this place, and of course they all get jobs and apartments. (Aida, Sarajevan returnee from Norway)

According to *Sarajlije*, *Sandžaklije* enjoy the protection of (and have colonized) the Party of Democratic Action (SDA), which promoted immigration from Sandžak in order to increase the Bosniac population in Sarajevo and other parts of Bosnia-Herzegovina. This situation stirs up the animosity of the locals towards

---

[14] Sandžak is a region situated on both sides of the border between Serbia and Montenegro. It is demarcated to the south-east by Kosovo, and to the north-west by Bosnia-Herzegovina. In 1991, according to the population census, 52.5 percent of the Sandžak population was Bosniac, 25.7 percent was Serb and 19.2 was Montenegrin.

[15] *Oslobođenje*, 31 August 1992, quoted in Vuković 1993: 79.

other groups of newcomers as well – those who, in contrast, highlight the cultural differences between Bosnians and *Sandžaklije*. Newcomers from various parts of Bosnia contrast their own attitude to Islam with the much more traditional and fervent religious behaviour ascribed to the *Sandžaklije*. They further state that *Sandžaklije* stem from a rather homogeneous Bosniac region, and thus do not share the Bosnian experience of living in a pluralistic ethno-religious environment. The fact that many *Sandžaklije* speak Bosnian (Serbo-Croatian) with a Serbian or Montenegrin accent does not improve their situation either.

To a certain extent, the widespread unflattering attitudes towards *Sandžaklije* among both *Sarajlije* and Bosnian newcomers are probably due to the fact that the *Sandžaklije* originate from outside Bosnia-Herzegovina and are therefore not considered 'real' Bosnians. They are a sort of 'double newcomers', cultural strangers in both Sarajevo and in Bosnia-Herzgovina as a whole. In contrast, the large groups of Bosnian DPs from eastern Bosnia and from Herzegovina have an advantage. *Sarajlije* view them as culturally Bosnian and as genuine victims of aggression and ethnic cleansing from areas now dominated by Serbs or Croats. But, less positively, in the popular imagination, eastern Bosnians originate from rural areas or provincial towns in the least developed parts of Bosnia-Herzegovina, and remain the incarnation of the ridiculous, 'non-cultured' villagers who not only live with animals, but also dress in traditional peasant clothes. The attitude of *Sarajlije* towards *Hercegovci* (people from Herzegovina) is more nuanced.[16] *Hercegovci* are not perceived as rural and backward nor as religiously strict as the eastern Bosnians. The difference between *Sarajlije* and *Hercegovci* is therefore generally not interpreted through the lens of the urban/rural, 'cultured'/'non-cultured' dichotomies, but rather in terms of regional cultures. *Sarajlije* insist on the differences between a temperate Bosnia, dominated by hills, dense forests and green pastures, and the barren, stony, dry and warm Herzegovina, projecting these differences into the nature of their inhabitants. Whereas the Bosnians are seen as hearty, sincere, hospitable and generous to the point of naivety, *Hercegovci* have a reputation of being distrustful, closed, stingy and politically radical. While Bosnians enjoy *druženje* (social gatherings), *Hercegovci* are much more reserved. However, *Hercegovci* consider themselves to be hard-working people, smarter than the rather dumb, laid-back average Bosnian.

Other groups of newcomers come from outside the former Yugoslavia. Of all newcomers, the so-called *mudžahedini* (mujaheddins), former soldiers and religious activists from Muslim countries, are looked upon as the most threatening and culturally different group, by both (Sarajevan) Bosniacs and members of minority groups (see also Maček, this volume). Due to their perceived fundamentalist Islamic attitudes, they are described as completely 'non-Bosnian', as aggressive and 'non-cultured' people:

---

[16] As the name indicates, Bosnia-Herzegovina consists of two different parts. Herzegovina makes up the southern part of the country, including the towns of Mostar, Konjic, Jablanica, Stolac and Trebinje. Bosnia is the remaining part of the country.

Do you know what I fear the most in life? *Mudžahedini*. They're the complete opposite of us in Bosnia-Herzegovina. Many [native Sarajevan] Serbs return, reclaim their apartments and then sell them to the *mudžahedini*. They've got money. The Serbs don't care about who settles in our city, but for us who live here it's terrible. Not just for me but for all those Bosnians who are oriented towards Europe. Nothing shocks me anymore, I've survived the war and I could have been dead a thousand times. We've been hungry and without clothes, but this ... Some *mudžahedini* live in the apartment above me and I fear them terribly. (Emina, Sarajevan stayee)

The *mudžahedini* get large amounts of money from the Muslim world. From the *Sarajlije*'s perspective, however, this financial assistance is unfortunately being spent for wrong and political extremist purposes, like building mosques, religious schools and institutions, and promoting Islamic values, instead of using their wealth for more secular purposes, such as (re)construction of houses, public schools and factories.

Much more positive but still ambivalent feelings surround the presence of *stranci* (foreigners), that is SFOR soldiers and the expatriates employed by a plethora of international organizations (see Coles, this volume). In *Sarajlije*'s eyes, 'internationals' play an invaluable role in post-war Bosnia-Herzegovina by securing peace in the country and pouring money into the miserable economy. Besides, they embody the values of Western civilization and urbanity, thus constituting a temporary counterweight to the cultural deterioration and political radicalisation of Sarajevo that other groups of newcomers have brought about. At the same time, however, many *Sarajlije* believe that 'foreigners' have come merely to make money, leaving as soon as their stationing has ended, and considering Sarajevo and Bosnia-Herzegovina as primitive, backward places inhabited by 'savages' or 'monkeys', in the words of several informants.

Conclusion: The Demonization of Newcomers

This chapter has explored the immense discursive power of the local/newcomer distinction in post-war Sarajevo, and the related stereotypes of urban/rural and 'cultured'/'non-cultured'. The ultimate indication of the importance of hierarchically ordered cultural mentalities in Bosnia-Herzegovina is perhaps the fact that, paradoxically enough, it is often reproduced by the newcomers themselves. As the local/newcomer distinction concerns not merely geographical origins, but also ascribed cultural mentalities and behaviours, it becomes possible for everyone, *Sarajlije* as well as newcomers, to employ the repertoire of cultural stereotyping to distinguish and stigmatize groups of people who are perceived as less culturally advanced. Thus, while *Sarajlije* hold negative attitudes towards newcomers in general, specific groups of newcomers ridicule and distance themselves from newcomers coming from other regions or countries. Sometimes, the distancing even takes place in relation to newcomers from one's 'own' category. For example, one informant, Esad, in a rather patronizing tone claimed that '*ljudi sa sela*' ('village people') who came from eastern Bosnia during the war did not want to return because, in Sarajevo, they did not have to work and could live well on humanitarian assistance. But, later on in the conversation, it turned out that he was from Rogatica, a small town in eastern Bosnia; he and his family had been expelled from there at the beginning of the war, and had no plans to return! He did not seem to pay attention to the apparent contradiction inherent in his statement, which of course, is due to the fact that he does not consider himself a 'peasant', but someone working in his new hometown, Sarajevo. Thus, in Bosnia-Herzegovina, nobody categorizes oneself as 'non-cultured', while everybody points to *others* who undoubtedly meet the definition of this label.

Furthermore, the experience of being (or having been) a newcomer oneself seldom turns into sympathy and empathy with other groups of newcomers. For instance, Džemo had twice been a newcomer, first as a refugee in Germany and later, upon repatriation, in Sarajevo, before he and his family finally managed to return to their pre-war residence in a village near Čapljina, in Herzegovina. Nevertheless, he described the displaced Bosnian Croats in his home village as the incarnation of the primitive newcomers:

> There are many *došjlo* [newcomers] here. They're from the mountains around Konjic [a town in the Bosniac-held part of Herzegovina]. It's fucking wild people!

Not only in Sarajevo but all over Bosnia-Herzegovina, local populations consider newcomers, especially the DP population, as culturally different, politically radical and threatening, though to different degrees. Even as a foreigner, it is difficult not to be absorbed by the powerful native cultural discourse and not to start explaining how things work (or do not work) and how people (mis)behave in terms of the local/newcomer, urban/rural, 'cultured'/'non-cultured' distinctions – especially as an anthropologist professionally striving to 'go native'! Dealing with the public bureaucracy, riding on smelly buses and looking at the garbage thrown around in public places in Sarajevo, it is tempting to blame it all on the 'peasant' newcomers who simply do not know how to behave in a city. It is all too easy to forget the fact – and *Sarajlije* seem to constantly ignore it – that, in a society recovering from years of war and economic decline, things cannot be expected to function as smoothly as in Frankfurt. It is easy to forget that what is experienced as the 'peasantization' of Sarajevo is, to a great extent, an almost inevitable consequence of difficult living conditions in general, not of the newcomers' lack of culture. And pre-modern, 'non-cultured' practices, like growing vegetables outside apartment blocks and keeping poultry or goats in the city, may not signify backwardness, but rather constitute an economically rational strategy during hard times. Thus, the 'wildness' ascribed to newcomers is not grounded in any inherent cultural primitiveness but in the fact that these people have in many cases lost their old homes, are economically destitute, and feel insecure about the future. As a result of their vulnerable position, newcomers are forced to compete with the local population for scarce material resources and to seek the protection of their 'own' nationalist parties. Demonizing them is an easy, legitimate and apparently non-political way to explain and give vent to the frustrations of strained living conditions and political stalemate in post-war Sarajevo, as blaming the rural population and backward regions was a common way to voice other types of grievances in pre-war socialist Yugoslavia.

Nevertheless, it would be misleading to describe the cultural categorization of people into 'cultured' city people and (more or less) 'non-cultured' newcomers as all-encompassing, unchanging and uncontested. Depending on the context, the same informants can refer to the repertoire of Bosnian cultural hierarchies in a very collective, indiscriminate way, or use it with much more nuance. Before the war, Norwegian anthropologist Tone Bringa had already noted that:

> Terms such as *nekulturni* and *seljačina* were used as individual value judgments and were neither categories with fixed content, nor, once conferred on a person, constantly used for that individual. Rather, these terms depended on the specific social contexts within which these individuals moved and on those with whom they interacted. (Bringa 1995: 59-60)

In post-war Sarajevo as well, collective cultural stereotypes usually give way to more individual assessments in everyday interactions. Informants acknowledged that, when it comes to actual individuals, *Sarajlije* do not always live up to the ideal of the 'cultured' urbanite, and newcomers do not necessarily comply with the image of the 'non-cultured' peasant. Collective distinctions between locals and newcomers or between urban and rural people do not prevent close social and friendly relationships from developing between *Sarajlije* and DPs from, say, Trebinje in Herzegovina or Srebrenica in eastern Bosnia. Actual social relationships often transcend geographic typographies and are grounded in common interests.

Various informants themselves questioned the value of the local/newcomer and urban/rural distinctions. Newcomers often stressed that they did not grow up on a mountain or in a village, but in one of the other major towns in Bosnia-Herzegovina such as Banja Luka or Mostar. Sometimes, they also claimed that these towns were in fact more ordered, decent, and cultured than Sarajevo, thus turning the argument the other way around. However, these kinds of remarks, and criticism of Sarajevan arrogance towards the rest of Bosnia-Herzegovina, go back long before the recent war, and in the end resort to a similar, though more subtle use of the urban/rural cultural hierarchy. Even those few informants who tried to put this distinction into question made ambiguous statements:

> Every war mixes up the population, the rural and urban population. I was born on the asphalt, but that doesn't mean that my grandfather was too. Therefore, I have no right to say that you're a peasant and I'm a city person, because we're all descendants of peasants. Also in that war [World War II], there were migrations from the countryside to the urban areas, and during the last fifty years those people have melted into the city,

have emancipated and cultivated themselves, and when they have finally become city people, we're once again in a situation where we have to transform the rural population into city people! But we're all citizens of the same state, and nobody is worth less than others. As long as they're humans [*ljudi*]! (Alma, Sarajevan stayee)

It is not entirely clear which kinds of cultural stereotypes Alma was 'deconstructing' and which ones she was 'mobilizing'. For example, what did she mean by 'humans'? My guess is that it has something to do with 'culture'!

Chapter 3

Sarajevo No More?
Identity and the Experience of Place among Bosnian Serb Sarajevans in *Republika Srpska*

Ioannis Armakolas

Introduction[1]

In focusing on the propaganda effects of Serb nationalist discourses, many researchers have failed to examine the details of the style in which the new community has been imagined, thus forgetting one of Benedict Anderson's (1983) most useful lessons. In several ways, this gap becomes obvious the closer one examines the case of the Bosnian Serbs. For example, analyses of Serb nationalism have been dominated by the category of time: the conflation of the past, present and future into one linear and solid span that makes sense only in relation to ethnicity (e.g. Judah 1997). Space as a meaning-creating element has been neglected, although it is always constitutive of the speech acts that make up nationalist discourses (Keith and Pile 1993; Shields 1991).

In a similar way, most analysts have viewed the *Republika Srpska* merely as a tool of territorial expansion and a mask for the nationalist project to build a Greater Serbia, thereby failing to capture the constitutive effects of this statelet in the identities of the population residing there. However, as Anderson emphasizes, 'to see how administrative units could over time come to be conceived as fatherlands ... one has to look at the ways in which administrative organizations create meaning' (1983: 53).

[1] This chapter is based mostly on material collected during fieldwork conducted as a Tip O'Neill Fellow in Peace Studies (1998-99). I wish to thank the Initiative on Conflict Resolution and Ethnicity and the American Ireland Fund for giving me the opportunity to conduct my research as their fellow. A smaller part of the material for this chapter was collected during a visit to Bosnia for my doctoral research, made possible by funding from the Greek State Scholarships Foundation, the Cambridge European Trust, and the Faculty of Social and Political Sciences at Cambridge University. I would also like to thank Daniel Korski and the editors for many useful comments on earlier drafts of this chapter.

Finally, against a backdrop of deterministic views expressed in the form of historical traumas or media manipulation, the identification of agency is of central importance. In *Republika Srpska*, the hegemonic claims of the 'international community' and of Serb nationalists have enabled different kinds of agency to be realized. Their competing articulations of space can only be empowered by agency – by thinking, feeling, doing individuals that confirm or jettison them (Keith and Pile 1993).

This chapter focuses on those Bosnian Serbs who left Sarajevo for the *Republika Srpska* (RS), specifically the municipality of Pale, part of what has been called Srpsko Sarajevo ('Serb Sarajevo') since 1996.[2] It is a chapter about their displacement, their identities, and their intricate experience of place. The example of Sarajevan Serbs in the RS will illustrate that identity is expressed not only through discursive, but also spatial practice, and that space itself is a site of power and symbolism (Massey 1993). Similarly, their narratives and practices will illustrate the complexity and ambivalence of experience in a nationalist environment, along with instances of upholding but also of the subversion of hegemonic meanings.

The chapter is based on fieldwork conducted in 1999 and supplemented by discussions I had with some of my interviewees in 2002. Pale, the fieldwork site, is situated about 15 km east of Sarajevo. Before the war it was one of the rural municipalities belonging to the wider Sarajevo area. When the leadership of the Serb Democratic Party (SDS) set out to create a Serbian state in Bosnia, Pale made a meteoric jump in significance since it was the place where the Serb leadership decided to site its capital.[3] Its non-importance up to that moment was its attraction, according to Radovan Karadžić, the wartime leader of the Bosnian Serbs.[4] Rather than Banja Luka, an important and safe city in western Bosnia, he opted for Pale to stress the transitory character of the capital and to be close to Sarajevo, one of the main war aims of the Bosnian Serb Army. Only much later, in 1998, did pro-reformist forces under the leadership of Prime Minister Milorad Dodik move the RS capital from Pale to Banja Luka.

According to the last pre-war census, conducted in 1991, the population of the municipality of Pale was 16,355, of which 69.1 percent were Serbs. Eight years

---

[2]   A significant part of Sarajevo's suburbs was controlled by the Serb forces during the war. Under the Dayton Peace Agreement, Pale was the only Sarajevan municipality to be assigned to the RS, along with some smaller semi-rural suburbs and villages and a few apartment blocks at the south-eastern end of the urban suburb of Dobrinja (see Sell 2000). These scattered remnants of the wider Sarajevo area were merged into Srpsko Sarajevo in 1996, but the project to turn this new 'city' into a Serb counterpart of Sarajevo itself has remained an empty wish.

[3]   International public opinion has generally regarded Pale as a symbol of extreme Serb nationalism and an incomprehensible war. On doing fieldwork in such a 'location of evil', see Armakolas 2001a.

[4]   Interview with Radovan Karadžić in *Nin*, 10 February 1995, quoted in Vujović 2000: 134-5.

later, as a result of the war, the percentage of Serbs had rocketed to 99.9 percent, and the total population to above 25,500 people (Repatriation Information Centre 2000). The Muslims of Pale decided to leave the town at the start of the war when the local police said it could not guarantee their security. The local authorities provided transportation and the police escorted them to Sarajevo. There were no recorded violent incidents. In the opposite direction, Pale was one of the first destinations of the Bosnian Serb population leaving Sarajevo. Bosnian Serbs that came to Pale left Sarajevo in two waves: the first at the beginning of the war, and the second after the Dayton Peace Agreement assigned most of the Serb-held parts of the wider Sarajevo area to the Federation.[5] Many Sarajevan Serbs found refuge in the houses of friends and relatives. Those who had weekend houses in the hills around Pale were luckier since they moved to their own property. Others arranged informal property exchanges with Pale Muslims. From the beginning of the war, probably somewhere between 15,000 and 20,000 Serb refugees stayed for a short or longer period in Pale. Of these a good number remained there. In 2000, there were still 9,700 registered displaced persons in Pale who were originally from Sarajevo, although adding those that were not registered would likely increase the number another 30 percent.[6]

The Formation of *Republika Srpska*: Geography and the Imagination of Community

As a process which unifies the discursive and the empirical, spatial production is a necessary component of successful nationalist discourses (Liggett and Perry 1995; Shields 1991). In the case of the RS, two stages can be identified in the process of articulating a particular exclusivist meaning. The first was the separation of people, which created the necessary physical space for a distinct territory within Bosnia-Herzegovina. This territory was meant to serve as a necessary transitory entity before the long-term goal of uniting different parts of Croatia and Bosnia with Serbia/Yugoslavia could be realised. This process had started in 1991 with the creation of Serb Autonomous Regions (*Srpske autonomne oblasti*, SAO) and the official proclamation of the RS on 9 January 1992. It continued through violent action after war broke out in April 1992. In Sarajevo, the attempt was to create separate districts for the Serbs; in Karadzić's words: 'Either it is ours or it will be two cities.'[7]

Territoriality is putatively easy to communicate since it requires only one kind of marker: the boundary (Sack 1981). However, communicating such a message was patently difficult in Bosnia since dividing lines ran through villages,

---

[5]   See note 2.

[6]   Estimates from the Pale Office of the Ministry for Refugees and Displaced Persons and of the Pale municipality Red Cross (personal communication).

[7]   Quoted in Vujović 2000: 135.

neighbourhoods and families. Moreover, the geography of the RS grew out of the realities of political and military balances of power. The second stage was therefore the application of the various characteristics of statehood and nationhood that would give specific meaning to an otherwise arbitrary territory. On the one hand, it meant showing the international community that Bosnian Serbs had legitimate claims to self-determination and statehood; cultural and political codes that were meaningful to an international public embedded in nation-states were deliberately used (Frost 1996). On the other hand, it required a 'particular' naming of the new state and the deployment of all the 'natural' characteristics of states. The arbitrary carve-up of the country was subsumed under the huge symbolic significance of the speech act of naming the place (Carter, Donald and Squires 1993).

If people felt they needed their own ethnic state to secure their physical existence, the creation of this state and naming it the 'Serb Republic' confirmed and reinforced those feelings. The 'proof' of their security was there now, and so was the 'proof' of their lack of security in the neighbouring territory. At the same time, a series of other state characteristics were deployed. All the elements of 'banal nationalism' (Billig 1995) that make nation-states seem natural were present in the RS. The newly-formed state had its own government, its own army, its own flag, its own currency,[8] and so on. All were specific to the RS and, being Serb, characteristically distinct from any similar elements to be found in Bosnia-Herzegovina, whether all-Bosnian, Bosniac or Croat.

If separating people had the effect of drastically disrupting the experience of co-existence, the deployment of statehood and nationhood elements were meant to have even more profound and pervasive effects: to prove that the RS, albeit with its transitional character, was the natural order of things for the Serb population in the area. For the years of the war and the early post-war period these people would be informed by the foreign news section of their media about what was happening in the 'neighbouring' state of Bosnia-Herzegovina, they would be taught in schools and universities about the geography of their country, the RS, and they would go about their everyday lives without encountering any signs of the Bosnian state or administration. Thus, for a population that had tried to resist the disintegration of Yugoslavia, the 'disappearance' of Bosnia, and the appearance of 'former Bosnia-Herzegovina', came as a natural development, something that did not need to be disputed because it was evident in their daily lives.

Such processes had the effect of naturalising the new situation, making it appear like common sense (Shields 1991: 64). During my fieldwork in 1999, the appeal of the RS among ordinary Serbs was felt everywhere. In everyday life the RS was talked about as if it was a separate state. People would even hesitate to admit that the RS was part of Bosnia-Herzegovina. All interviewees, including the most moderate and open-minded, would confirm that if it were up to them to

---

[8]   The RS's own currency was in fact short-lived, but, at least in Pale, the Yugoslav Dinar remained the main currency in everyday exchanges well into 1998.

decide they would like to be part of Serbia/Yugoslavia, and would complain that the Bosniacs or the international community were not allowing them to realize this desire. As a reminder of the unfulfilled political goal of unification, they would often mention that in sports they always support Yugoslavia or even that they considered the latter to be 'their' country, contrary as this was to post-Dayton political realities.

At the same time, however, post-war realities and constraints were also crucial elements determining how Bosnian Serbs saw their future. People would still consider 'their' country to be Yugoslavia but would admit that achieving their 'dream' was now beyond them and that the RS would probably remain forever within Bosnia-Herzegovina. Moreover, emotional connections with the Serbs beyond the Drina River remained undiminished, but the mood toward the Belgrade regime seemed to have changed considerably. The Dayton Peace Agreement appeared as a traumatic event that marked a psychological division between Bosnian Serbs and the regime in Serbia. The view was widespread that Slobodan Milošević had agreed to a settlement in Bosnia-Herzegovina and sacrificed the Sarajevan Serbs in return for benefits for Serbia.

> Persida (age 44): Slobo thought that if he gave Bosnia to the Americans, the international community wouldn't touch Kosovo, but now there's war in Kosovo. Slobodan Milošević – he expelled the Serbs from Sarajevo; he thought that they wouldn't touch him, but he was wrong. He wanted to be a man of peace for the whole world. That war in Sarajevo ended; there is now war in Serbia. They are bombarding him now.
> IA: What did you think of him before the war started?
> Persida: I had a very good opinion about him, and I thought because he's Serb... But now I'm very hurt by his behaviour at Dayton. He gave Sarajevo to the Muslims and expelled the Serbs from Sarajevo.

Many people in Pale also complained bitterly about the nepotism and war profiteering of their own politicians, including the fact that the leaders had kept their own sons away from the frontline. I was once even shown around the neighbourhood where local politicians were building luxurious houses, and heard it mockingly referred to as 'Dedinje', the elite neighbourhood of Belgrade where Slobodan Milošević had his residence. At the same time, however, my informants were ready to support and justify the leadership associated with all of the above. They differentiated between the social and political functions of their leaders, between their individual behaviour and their role as head of the 'state'. In fact, this was the best illustration of the success of the 'statehood' of the RS.[9]

---

[9]   On similar tendencies among Bosnian Croats, see Grandits, this volume.

The Paradoxes of the Post-Dayton RS: Marginality and the 'Clash of Hegemonies'[10]

In the post-war period, however, other important developments have impacted the social and spatial identity of the RS. After having forged a geography of necessity, which enjoyed the support of its inhabitants, the RS found itself on the margins.[11] Throughout the Bosnian conflict, the RS was generally viewed in the West as a statelet created through ethnic cleansing or even genocide. Given such a bad reputation, it is a huge paradox that the Dayton Peace Agreement maintained the RS as an entity within the new Bosnian state, thereby to some extent legitimating it. Post-Dayton RS exists as a product of the nationalist project, but at the same time it carries the stigma of that project. Although constitutionally equal with the Federation, it is still perceived as the 'dirty backyard' of Bosnia-Herzegovina, a safe haven for war criminals, and a place where political and economic activity is enmeshed with the criminal underworld.[12]

The RS inhabits a place in the symbolic realm of cultural significations. As this symbolic realm has gone unchallenged, the essential nature of the RS as a culturally inferior place in Bosnia-Herzegovina is also not questioned. This is despite the extent of the political and mental shifts that have taken place in recent years or the fact that separatist and exclusivist attitudes are also evident in the Federation. The complex histories, identities and experiences of the people of the RS lose their importance under the enormity of this wartime image. The former Sarajevans in the RS are a case in point. Their much celebrated urban identity has been completely neglected because they found refuge in the RS (see also Stefansson, this volume). The same can be said for their different experiences, including the traumatic experience of exile and displacement. Instead, they are treated as part of the same homogenous Serb whole, a generalization they strongly resent.

In 1999, this perception of the RS's marginal position was clearly visible in the narratives of my informants. Their identities were in large part constructed around opposition to the international community and what they saw as its one-sided

---

[10] 'Hegemony' here refers to structures of meaning (see Howarth, Norval and Stavrakakis 2000; Laclau and Mouffe 1985).

[11] Being marginal does not necessarily imply a geographical periphery. Marginal places are places in between, both connected to and estranged from the cultural/political centre. They are placed on the periphery of cultural systems of space; they 'carry the image, and stigma, of their marginality which becomes indistinguishable from any basic empirical identity they might once have had' (Shields 1991: 3).

[12] This kind of place image is perfectly illustrated in the titles of reports by the influential International Crisis Group: in *War Criminals in Bosnia's Republika Srpska: Who Are the People in Your Neighbourhood* (ICG 2000), the title communicates marginality and spatial symbolism. Similarly, the title of another report, *The Wages of Sin: Confronting Bosnia's Republika Srpska* (ICG 2001) communicates the wartime stigma of RS. Both reports are available at <http://www.crisisweb.org>.

involvement in Bosnia (Armakolas 2001b). 1999 was still early in the post-war period and a sensitive time due to the war in Kosovo and the NATO bombing of Serbia. Emotions were running high, although a series of shocking political events had changed the mood among Serbs in the RS considerably. These included the indictment for war crimes of the wartime leaders Radovan Karadžić and Ratko Mladić, and a political crisis that pitted the western and eastern parts of the RS against each other. People complained about a series of political decisions, from the indictments issued by the International Criminal Tribunal for the former Yugoslavia (see Delpla, this volume) to the policies encouraging minority return and property restitution, which to them demonstrated the fact that Serbs were discriminated against. A focal point of discontent was the peace agreement itself. This is important with regard to the shift in attitudes in the subsequent three years, as will be shown below.

In terms of political attitudes, the effect of this marginality was resignation, submission and cynicism.[13] This is beautifully illustrated in the words of Ilija, who, when asked whether the ethnic groups (*narodi*) of Bosnia could live together again as they had after World War II, responded:

> Ilija (age 47): Then there was a man who came [to power]: Tito. There was communism after the war. I don't know how he managed it. We were one nation, Muslims, Croats and Serbs.
> IA: There is nothing that can unite the people of Bosnia again?
> Ilija: Maybe another Tito. Perhaps Westendorp is the new Tito! [laughs]

A sense of submission to the policies of the international community was evident at that time, yet so was a certain cynicism about them. Placing Carlos Westendorp, the High Representative at that time, on the same level as a figure of the magnitude of Tito was enough to trivialize the current political situation in the country. At the same time, it showed the enormity of the task: the High Representative was supposed to succeed where even Tito, judging from the recent war, had failed.

Does the marginality of the RS imply that there can be a straightforward articulation of space compatible with the objectives of the international community in Bosnia-Herzegovina? Such an operation is never unproblematic since hegemonic and counter-hegemonic articulations of the spatial and the social can be present within the same geographic area (Keith and Pile 1993: 6). The RS has especially been the battleground for two competing hegemonic claims. The international community has increasingly managed to force the implementation of a core set of its own ethical imperatives and cultural/political objectives. It is clear, however, that the pre-existing exclusivist project is still in operation in the RS. Obstruction to minority returns, official discourses about Serb interests, electoral

---

[13] One should keep in mind that these people have lived under three different state systems (federal Yugoslavia, wartime *Republika Srpska*, and post-Dayton Bosnia-Herzegovina) in less than ten years.

results, as well as the narratives of ordinary people themselves are only a few indicators of the continued significance of the old mindset.

One could, in fact, more controversially perhaps, talk of a 'clash of hegemonies', a state of affairs whereby both the discourse of the international community and the formerly powerful exclusivist Serb discourse have secured important roles. For example, one can identify a space where two types of officially sanctioned nostalgias compete. Both rely to some extent on a degree of silence in their narration. For the increasingly dominant discourse promoted by the international community, there is a silence about cross-border connections and similarities with Serbia and Croatia, and to some extent about the reality of the common state that was former Yugoslavia. For the enduring exclusivist discourse within the RS, there is a silence about previous coexistence among the ethnic groups, about the similarities and common destinies of the peoples of Bosnia-Herzegovina, and of course about the ethnic cleansing that created a virtually ethnically pure RS (see Duijzings, this volume).

All of this is a result of the paradoxical position of the RS as both legitimated by the peace agreement and marginalised by the perception of the war upon which international community policy is based. The international community clearly takes precedence, as it to a large extent exercises control over the Bosnian political scene. However, the official recognition of the RS, the lack of a discursive place for Serbs, and the factual marginality of the entity continue to provide Serb nationalists with arguments supporting their claims. In this context, ordinary Serbs in the RS receive powerful messages, usually contradictory but somehow coexisting, from two different sides. They realize that their future is beyond their control but, as will be shown below, their adoption of the new discourses and practices promoted by the international community has been slow, hesitant and full of confusion (see also Duijzings, Delpla, this volume).

Leaving Sarajevo: Fear, Conviction and Conformism

When asked in 1999 about their reasons for leaving the city, ex-Sarajevan Serbs cited two major types of changes which had driven them away. The first type has to do with problems affecting the social atmosphere as a whole. Although in general interviewees stressed the peaceful character of the period before the early 1990s, some singled out events they thought were evidence of change. The 1990 multi-party elections that resulted in the victory of the nationalist parties was one such event. Others stressed the arrival of people from Kosovo and Sandžak in the 1980s (see also Stefansson, this volume). Another example referred to was the rise in popularity of Islamic religious customs (such as Arabic greetings) in the same period, whereas a few went as far back as the death of Tito in 1980.

The second type of explanation has to do with the factors that directly influenced the decision to leave Sarajevo. This is where the issue of security becomes central. Fear of the Muslim paramilitary, the *'zelene beretke'* ('Green

Berets'), figured prominently in these narratives. Rumours or unconfirmed information about 'plans' devised against Serbs, often spread by local SDS activists, had done much to produce or intensify feelings of insecurity. The well-known incident of the killing of a Serb by a Muslim during a wedding procession in the centre of Sarajevo was remembered by nearly everybody as an example of the heightened emotions and fears in the last days before the outbreak of hostilities.[14] Some mentioned examples of changed attitudes among Muslim acquaintances and, to a lesser extent, friends. Yet a large majority admitted that their neighbours had been friendly to them up to the last minute. Ilija had left with his family during the first wave of the Serb exodus from Sarajevo. In discussing neighbourliness in Sarajevo and the responsibility of ordinary people, he told me he had not changed the way he sees his former Muslim neighbours, nor did he blame them for anything:

> No, I haven't even changed my opinion now [as a result of the war]. I don't want to go to Sarajevo because of this Muslim government, not because of my neighbours. If it were only my neighbours I would go. But it is this government. And my neighbour had to do what his government told him in the war.

Attitudes seem to have changed rapidly after the war started, however. Zlatomirka (age 51), who decided to leave after the outbreak of the war, remembered that by that time there was already mounting hostility against those who wanted to leave Sarajevo. Fearing for her security, she hid the fact that she was planning to leave.[15] One day she did, but in order not to raise suspicions she left without taking any extra clothes; she even, as she stressed, left behind her Turkish coffee grinder.

Another common theme was the fear that the Serbs would be marginalized and reduced to the status of minority in an independent Bosnia-Herzegovina dominated by the Muslims. The triumphalism over independence displayed by the Muslims and Croats also added to the Serbs' discomfort. For Mate (age 51), on the other hand, as a former officer in the Yugoslav Army and a Croat from Croatia married to a Serb, the decision to leave Sarajevo was consistent with his continued belief in a common Yugoslav state. Since he was against the decisions of the Slovenes, Croats, and Muslims to break away from Yugoslavia, he made his way to what he saw as the only territory in Bosnia-Herzegovina that guaranteed some future connection to the remaining Yugoslav federation.

---

[14] On 1 March 1992, during the second day of the referendum on Bosnian independence, a Serb taking part in a wedding procession was killed in front of the old Orthodox Church in Sarajevo. This incident was used by the SDS as an illustration of the threats represented for Serbs by Bosnian independence, and as a pretext to set up barricades around Sarajevo.

[15] On the widespread opinion among Bosniacs that 'the Serbs knew' what would happen, see Jansen, Maček, this volume.

Following the example of relatives and Serb neighbours also seems to have played an important role. The more people decided to leave, the more difficult it became for those who had at first been hesitant.

In an interesting paper based on fieldwork in Croatia, Stef Jansen stresses that authoritative discourses are evoked in narration to justify action or inaction, to deny responsibility, to make sense of social processes, or simply to conform to the regime of the day (Jansen 2002). During my fieldwork, conformism also seemed to be a natural response to authority. When Ilija (in the above quote) said that his neighbour had to do what his government told him to in the war, he was also recognizing that individuals ought to comply with the authorities, be they 'legitimate' or 'war' administrations. And when conviction is not enough, fear can play a role.

Many analysts have viewed the Yugoslav wars as a proliferation of 'anarchical' situations. However, the existence of administrative and governing systems and their success in constraining individual action evidently goes against such analyses (see also Grandits, Duijzings, Bougarel, this volume). A crucial function of any state administration is to control and regulate movement and also to decide who is subject to its authority. In 1999, Anastazija (age 24), who had been a teenager at the beginning of the war remembered the separatist actions of the local Serb militias in this way:

> On Tuesday my father set off for the centre of Sarajevo to go to work, but they stopped him at the barricades in the middle of our neighbourhood; they told him that he was a traitor. He was against the Serbs because he was going to the Muslim side. He told them that there are a lot of Serb people in Sarajevo – why [did they single out] just him because he wanted to go to work? He didn't want to lose his job – on TV they said that whoever doesn't show up [to his post] will lose his job, and he wanted to go, but they didn't allow him. So he chose another way to go and arrived at the office and spent few hours talking to his friends. Everybody was afraid. ... My parents went to work during all of April. After the 1st of May it was forbidden for anybody to leave that left side of the Miljacka River. ... If you went there you had to stay there or maybe some guy with a sniper gun would kill you. Everyday they went to work they risked being killed.

In Bosnia, quasi-state administrations not only existed during the early stages of the conflict, but people also recognized those authorities as speaking 'for them' and abided by their decisions, either out of conviction or out of fear. For the Serbs that left Sarajevo in 1992, a combination of fear, conviction, imitation and compliance with authorities made their decision to move to Serb-dominated areas only natural. A similar combination of concerns can be found for those who left in 1996.[16]

---

[16] For an analysis of the factors that influenced the decision to flee Sarajevo in 1996, see Sell 2000.

Ex-Sarajevan Serbs: Diasporic Experience and Nostalgia for Place

De-territorialization and displacement typically have the effect of intensifying processes of meaning construction (Malkki 1995; Väyrynen 2003). In Bosnia, the traumatic experience of forced migration produced perplexing effects. The ambivalent experience of ex-Sarajevan Serbs in places like Pale is illustrated by their position in their host places: they are both inside, belonging to the 'ethnic self', and outside when they invoke their (former) urban identities. On the one hand, new connections with the local population have been created in a variety of ways. For young people, for example, this sense of a new life is reinforced when they date or marry local young people or find a job in the host place. A conscious decision that 'there is no going back' to what they increasingly see as 'unfamiliar' territory now underlines new connections established in the host areas. On the other hand, the constant invocation by Sarajevan Serbs of their former urban identity can be seen as an attempt to create a boundary between themselves and the local population. Among young people this is usually expressed through complaints about the backwardness of local people, their lack of style, or their funny preferences when it comes to entertainment. Socializing, going out and dating mostly with 'their own' people is one consequence of this. A hesitant acceptance or denial of locality, of local culture and people, maintains a dis-placed sense of place.

The above, however, should not drive us to mistaken conclusions regarding the political consequences of nostalgia for Sarajevo. In 1999, nostalgia for a lost authentic experience of place was omnipresent in the narratives of ex-Sarajevan Serbs. Pre-war Sarajevo took on a romanticised image in those narratives. Asked whether the death of Tito or the political struggles of the 1980s made her insecure or presented problems, Anđelka (age 37) replied:

> No, they didn't. Sarajevo was a united city and a very safe city. You could stay all night in the park and you wouldn't have any problems. There were a lot of nationalities and it was one of the most free cities in Yugoslavia at that time.

Pre-war Sarajevo was depicted in ideal terms, but at the same time, nostalgia was transformed to fit current concerns. If insecurity was believed to have made a difference, then pre-war Sarajevo had to be presented in exactly the opposite terms. The memory of how the city used to be was employed to present contemporary Sarajevo as different. This relates to another common feature in the narratives, that of the changed social fabric of Sarajevo (see also Stefansson, this volume). In fact, almost all the interviewees singled out newcomers as a source of insecurity, differentiating between the old inhabitants of Sarajevo and people who came in 'from the villages'. Newcomers were central to these narratives of a changed Sarajevo. Nikodim, a young man in his early twenties, was still going to Sarajevo to socialize with and date locals. He continued to hang out with old friends 'who have not changed much'. They all agreed that 'Sarajevo is not like it was' since the newcomers had changed the city. His friends would rather not go out in the evenings, preferring to stay at home to drink or do drugs. In fact, narratives of insecurity and unfamiliarity remained central and were invoked even when contrary to the economic logic of that time:

> IA: Would you ever go back?
> Živadinka (age 53): No.
> IA: How about your children?
> Živadinka: No, of course not. I would like to live there if the situation was like it was before the war, but in a situation like it is now, I do not want to live in that town.
> IA: What if some of your children find work there?
> Živadinka: Maybe, if the child has a job it's a different situation ... But, I don't think so, in this situation as it is now, no, no, only if the situation was like in 1990. Now I go to Sarajevo often and walk the streets there.
> IA: Do you find any specific things that have changed?
> Živadinka: Yes. These people are not familiar to me, I don't have contact with them.

In Živadinka's answers, the practical rationale of a job or career prospect seems to prevail at first, but she quickly switches to the security of the original narrative line. At the same time when nostalgia and fascination for the city – demonstrated in her frequent visits and walking through the streets – is revealed, newcomers offer a safe argument about the changed character of the city. For all its romanticism, nostalgia for old Sarajevo is perfectly compatible with the conventional versions of recent history in the RS, be they strongly radical or more flexible: in brief, pre-war peaceful coexistence, happiness and prosperity changed when the other ethnic groups decided they did not want to live united in one state. Unaware of this, one could be shocked by the way in which ex-Sarajevan Serbs nonchalantly switch from nostalgia for a multi-ethnic Sarajevo to 'never again together' talk and other powerful separatist messages and back. Nostalgia for place, then, is fully compatible with and functional within the hegemonic Bosnian Serb discourse.[17]

In this changed context, the urban/rural distinction, though present, inhabits a more perplexing place that what is often assumed in the literature. Ex-Sarajevan Serbs in Pale continued to identify with some sort of urban identity, but its salience was subsumed under the enormous weight of the ethnic factor. Needless to say, the character of the RS during the war did much to instil an ethnic dimension into all aspects of life, including urban identities. By 1999, but I suspect also much earlier,

---

[17]   Another issue with regard to nostalgia for Sarajevo is uneasiness about the terrible fate of the city during the war. In 1999, people tended to rationalize the situation with words like 'it was war' or 'what can you do?' Such comments sound like a justification for the siege of Sarajevo, but it is certain that sensitivity about the issue was there even if not expressed openly. Hesitation to answer was one of the signs of the inconvenience of this question. It was in that context that I was actually advised by my language assistant, also a Sarajevan Serb refugee, that it was better not to ask questions about such sensitive issues.

what could be found was an 'ethnicized' urban/rural distinction: urban identity was always filtered through ethnicity. During my fieldwork I did not meet anyone in Pale who hoped for the reintegration of Bosnia-Herzegovina so that their formerly salient urban identity could be reinstated. In fact, even the most moderate of my informants hoped for unification with Serbia, even though this would mean that their old urban identity would be lost forever. Many people were nostalgic about Sarajevo, but always within the limits of the ethnic reading of events. In the end, far from compromising exclusivist attitudes, the ethnicization of urban identity can have the opposite effect, that is, mostly among young people, an additional hostility toward the ethnic other ('Muslims want all the cities for themselves') and towards the international community ('Dayton gave all the cities to the Federation'), since the Dayton Peace Agreement was seen as having deprived them of the ability to express their urban identity in practice.

Crossing the Line: Spatial Practices and Perceptions of the Boundary

No other place is better suited than Pale for illustrating agency and spatial practices in the RS. Most places in the RS have some predominantly Serb city like Banja Luka or Belgrade nearby and are relatively distant from Sarajevo. Pale, with its large number of ex-Sarajevans and its proximity to Sarajevo and the Inter-Entity Boundary Line (IEBL), is different. In 1999 there was a conscious effort to avoid the 'natural' surroundings that now belonged to the Federation – 'alien' territory. In contrast, interaction with parts of Bosnia that were now in the RS were suddenly highly amplified: under different circumstances, studying in Pale,[18] leaving Pale to study in Foča, going on outings in Sokolac or Lukavica, or paying regular visits to towns like Bijeljina or Banja Luka would probably not have been the natural choice of the people I talked to.[19] This was acknowledged by the people themselves, who stressed at every occasion the provinciality of those places and, in fact, of Bosnia in general. Many ex-Sarajevan Serbs also paid occasional visits to Serbia, where many of their relatives had ended up. Some younger people went to

---

[18]   During the war, a university was created in Pale that was still in operation in 2002. Many younger Serbs, including those who were students in Sarajevo before the war, continued or began their studies in Pale. This is one of the sites where connections to Serbia seem to have increased. The teaching staff of the university is comprised of large number of 'shuttle' lecturers and professors from Serbia.

[19]   Sokolac, Foča (renamed Srbinje by Serb authorities) and Bijeljina are small or mid-sized towns, and Lukavica is a semi-rural suburb of Sarajevo, part of what is now called Srpsko Sarajevo. Like Pale itself, none of these places would attract any particular interest, especially by former urban dwellers, were it not for the war and its effects. The case is different with Banja Luka, the RS capital and one of the biggest Bosnian cities. Still, due to its distance from our area of interest it would, under 'normal' circumstances, present a much smaller attraction for the population living in Sarajevo and its vicinity.

study in Belgrade, and those who could afford a moderate summer holiday at the coast now preferred Montenegro to Croatia.

In that same period, however, people had started visiting Sarajevo again. Crossing the IEBL was made easier by the policies of the High Representative, especially the adoption of a common currency and license plates for all of Bosnia-Herzegovina, as well as the creation of a unified public transport system in the Sarajevo area.[20] People started visiting their properties, especially when it became clear that the property exchange arrangements made during the war would not be legally recognized. Shopping provided a good opportunity for occasional glimpses into the 'forbidden fruit' of Sarajevo urbanity. Young people quickly realised that no one could 'recognize' them in the centre of Sarajevo. Visits for leisure and entertainment became more frequent, although parents often worried or forbade such travelling. Some young people also started looking for jobs with international organizations in Sarajevo rather than in Pale.[21] However, by 1999 only a handful of my interviewees had re-established old friendships or developed new ones in Sarajevo. Especially the young people were only visiting the safely impersonal city centre. Yet even this was not a journey into unfamiliarity. More than six years since they had left the city, people started rediscovering old favourite places and habits. No matter how much they struggled to communicate difference, this was 'familiar territory' in most respects other than in their political imagination.

Crossing the line, however, was not an unproblematic endeavour. Stories about violent incidents involving people found in the 'wrong' territory circulated, and this did much to maintain the symbolic power of the boundary separating the two entities. During my fieldwork, the recent killing of a driver from the RS in Sarajevo was often mentioned as an example of how Serbs were not safe in the Federation. The fact remains, however, that once activated, the spatial practices of regular visits to Sarajevo were not significantly altered as a result of such situations. People increasingly embarked on visits to the other side. In that way they created a space for optimism, since they were in practice discarding the most radical of the separatist messages.

But it was only that. In 1999 people still hesitated to accept that such spatial practices also implied an altered disposition toward the ethnic other. This would

---

[20]   Naturally, even without a direct bus connection, there was always a way to get from Pale to Sarajevo. Buses from all over the RS ended up in the bus station of Srpsko Sarajevo, only a few hundred meters from the beginning of the federal part of Sarajevo. This was a tiresome journey, however, which added an extra hour or so to the time needed for a direct connection to the centre of Sarajevo. In 1999, it was also impossible to go by taxi from Pale to Sarajevo or vice versa. The journey necessarily entailed transferring to the vehicle of a taxi driver colleague 'from the other side' at the IEBL. This inflated the price of the taxi ride, kept drivers from both sides happy, and of course kept the symbolic power of the border intact. By 2002, this taxi arrangement had disappeared.

[21]   On the place of international organizations and NGOs in the local job market, see also Coles, Jansen, this volume.

gradually change only later, as it will be shown below. The practices of visiting Sarajevo demonstrated a fascination for the city and its life and a dependency on the urban complex; Pale, after all, had been tied to Sarajevo even before the war. At the same time, however, people continued to believe that living together was dangerous and for that reason impossible:

> IA: Do you think the peoples of Bosnia can live together again?
> Zlatomirka: The best would be to live close to each other but not together.
> IA: How about Sarajevo and your property there?
> Zlatomirka: I liked Sarajevo like it was before the war, but not Sarajevo now. Now I am not interested in Sarajevo anymore. Now I am only interested in my property there.

Returning to Sarajevo was out of question for my interviewees in 1999. Some of them did not even bother to claim their property. Others tried to sort this out in an attempt to move on smoothly with their lives in their host place. Another informant responded:

> Dobrila (age 55): Maybe we can have our economies together, but our own [separate] states, not one state. We would also like to solve these questions about the property we have in Sarajevo.
> IA: Would you sell your property in Sarajevo?
> Dobrila: I will try to exchange it for this place or sell it, but I won't go there, that's for sure.

The logic of living close by but not together predominated: the economy can be shared, but one's own state is essential since the state, rather than the economy, provides security at the end of the day. People convinced that living in mixed areas was one of the causes of the war should also believe that living separately would spare them from having to experience a new war in the future. In the words of Jelisije (age 27), who disregarded both the 'stories about Brotherhood and Unity' and the 'multi-cultural ideals' of the international community:

> The reality is that every generation in the last 2,000 years has been fighting. One more generation has confirmed that we cannot live together.

There were also a few interviewees who rejected even the most limited forms of communication. Persida, who had left in 1992 with the first wave of refugees and had exchanged away her Sarajevo flat, maintained that she never visited Sarajevo, nor did she find any benefit for people to be able to. On the contrary:

> Persida: Of course it is wrong [that people can cross the line]. Why did we have this war? Because now you can go to Sarajevo and they can come here. Why was there this war, what was the point of this war, then? The only interest of the international community was to kill more people here. We didn't get anything by this war then.
> IA: You wonder why this war happened... Why was it?

Persida: Because we couldn't live together anymore.
IA: Did the war take place to separate the people then?
Persida: Yes, because of that. Serbs wanted their own independent state, but Muslims want to have all of Bosnia only for them.

This in fact illustrates the importance of spatial practices in subverting the mainstream nationalist discourse of separation (see also Kolind, Jašarević, this volume). Persida does not say that it is dangerous to visit the 'other side'; after all, the experience in the vast majority of the cases proves the opposite. She does, however, question this with regard to the war that was fought to separate (read, secure) the people. The existence of the boundary provides the argument for the necessity of the war and separation. If the boundary is removed, especially if it is removed without violent consequences, then one has to answer the painful question 'Why was there this war then?' or again blame the international community.

Three Years Later: Together and Apart

I returned to Bosnia nearly three years after my 1999 fieldwork. Many things had changed in the meantime: Franjo Tuđman was dead, Alija Izetbegović had retired, and Slobodan Milošević was in The Hague. Things had changed and things had also stayed the same. Although the international community kept changing the rules of the game in Bosnia-Herzegovina, nationalists still maintained their hold on power in large parts of the country. However, at least in theory, the political developments in the previous few years should have given a push towards the integration of Bosnian Serbs into the common state. With this in mind, I tracked down some of the people I had interviewed in 1999.

After three years, some of the narratives from 1999 increasingly began to seem as if they had come from the nationalist bubble of that time. The future of the RS and of Serbs in Bosnia, however, was still viewed as a case of marginality. What my findings from 2002 may show becoming clearer is the extent to which standards are set by others. Against this background, maintaining the old separatist mindset is a recipe for disappointment and frustration.

At the same time, ordinary people from Pale had to deal with the difficulties of making a living. They realized that in such hard times it was a luxury not to try to find employment in Sarajevo simply on the grounds of a separatist outlook. If life could be made easier by getting a job in Sarajevo, many reasoned, then so be it. Moreover, as a consequence of the property restitution policies throughout Bosnia-Herzegovina, many people found themselves back in the places they had left with no intention of returning. Some of the Serbs from Sarajevo who had declared in 1999 that they would never go back were left with no choice for the moment but to occupy their former residence in the city.

As a consequence, many Serbs were again in the position in which they might encounter the ethnic other. While, three years earlier, the visits to Sarajevo had for most people meant no exchange with other groups, in 2002 they meant working together, socializing, developing friendships, and dating. Of course, these job opportunities and city life attractions did not mean all was well. Political arguments did sometimes occur, which can also be a positive sign. Even if they were not conscious of it, boundaries were already being redrawn. Not surprisingly, the boundary had to be emphasized at the points where it was less clear: people from the RS not only encountered ethnic 'others' – Bosniacs and Croats – but also other Serbs.

The best illustrations of these changes are the cases of Persida, Vojka and Jelisije. Back in 1999, Persida was probably the most uncompromising of my interviewees. Neither she nor her daughter Vojka accepted that they would ever go back to Sarajevo. In the meantime, however, Vojka found a job with the international community in Sarajevo and told me employment was the single most important issue for her. She wouldn't mind working in Pale, she said, but to be sure there were more prospects in Sarajevo. Vojka's views were shared by her mother. Persida was very happy that Vojka had a job and was contributing considerably to the family income. Persida herself had never been employed again since 1992. Her family had been living on her husband's salary, and later his pension all those years.

Vojka's work schedule was highly irregular. She and her mother quickly realized that she needed to move to Sarajevo. Vojka first moved to a Serb landlord's house, a friend of a friend, in a suburb of Sarajevo that had been held by Serbs during the war. Finding transport from there was difficult and after a few months she decided to move to a more convenient place. This time she found a Bosniac landlord; she wasn't sure 'if he would accept a Serb', but he did. When her parents were told they were very upset and feared for her safety. Coincidentally, the family was soon after evicted from their residence in Pale and repossessed their flat in Sarajevo. They had made their claim for repossession not long before, 'only because everybody did', with no real intention of going back. Thus, in 2002 Vojka was back in the old family flat and her parents moved between their relatives' house in Pale and their pre-war place of residence in Sarajevo.

Vojka was happy to be back in Sarajevo and finally living in a big city again. She would have preferred to be in the Serb sector, though, 'just in case'. She said she thought that Serbs in general were still afraid to live in the Federation. In the pattern of the 1999 interviews, Vojka also stressed that the RS was at a disadvantage since the international community shares the Bosniacs' views about the war. This time, however, she had personal experiences from nearly a year of living in Sarajevo. Coming from the RS presented both advantages and disadvantages. An advantage was that there were quotas for the different ethnic groups and Serbs were therefore in demand, as there were fewer of them; international employers were sensitive about this issue, trying to avoid discrimination for fear of being sued. But Vojka did not mention in her job application that she was living in Pale. Her birthplace and repossessed property in Sarajevo were very convenient in that respect.[22]

Vojka was very surprised at first to find so many Serbs at her job in Sarajevo. She initially socialized mostly with Serbs. However, after a while she started going out with Bosniac friends from work and very quickly discovered that there were no problems in socializing with them. Her acceptance by the locals was quite smooth. She had only one incidence of a conflict with a Bosniac at work. The most serious argument, in fact, was with a local Serb stayee from work who was very hostile toward Serbs from the RS. She considered this an isolated example; in fact her work colleagues supported her when she was attacked. She also said she was sure she 'does not hate the Muslims', although she thought that most Serbs would prefer to be separated by a wall from them. Thus, while she may have thought this way in the past, she had had a significant change of opinion and was now glad there was contact with the other groups.

Persida seemed to be stuck even more between her previous nationalist views, which she most likely still holds, and the reality of a future with the other groups; a reality she seemed to know was beyond her control. Her clumsy and puzzled attempt to adopt some of the multi-cultural ideas promoted by the international community only revealed political resignation and conformism. After all, only three years before she had been the most hard-line of my interviewees, and even in 2002 we talked in a house in Pale decorated with a picture of Radovan Karadžić. In everyday life, Persida was reconnecting with Serb former neighbours – stayees or others who had repossessed their properties. Some had a 'wait and see' attitude, hoping that enough Serbs would decide to stay in the neighbourhood so that they could stay too. Many people, however, said they would stay only for a while until they could sell or exchange their property. Persida declared her intention to do the same. She said she felt quite safe in the Federation, but she confirmed her previous view that Sarajevo is not like it was. Nothing was the same, especially with Bosniac former neighbours. Talking to various Serbs in the neighbourhood, she also confirmed that life was very difficult for those who decided to remain in areas under Sarajevo Government control. In the end, Sarajevo was the city but Pale was different; Pale had people from the same nationality and she felt safer.

Jelisije was also working for an international organisation in Sarajevo in 2002, but he drove from Pale to his job every day. It had been hard at times, especially in the winter, and he did sometimes consider moving to Sarajevo. Jelisije said he would feel safe living in the Federation, but he would prefer Srpsko Sarajevo. He wished that the process of property exchange that started before and during the war would come to an end. He thought it would just start again after the official repossession process ended, since it was only natural to expect that most people would want to live with their own people for security reasons.

---

[22] Her hunch was correct; being from Pale would automatically disqualify her from some positions, the non-discrimination clauses notwithstanding. This was related to me by a person who sorted applications at an international community agency in Sarajevo.

Jelisije is very conscious of his identity. In the office at work, some Bosniacs told him that they had not joined the Bosnian Army. It was a well-intentioned lie aimed at not making Jelisije feel uncomfortable. He did not think this necessary, however. He had never hidden the fact that he had been in the Bosnian Serb Army. As a citizen of that 'state' it was his duty to go, and he did it within the limits of what is acceptable in a war. For him that was but one example of the essentially different experience of the RS Serbs. That experience makes them different, not only from Bosniacs and Croats, but also from Serbs that stayed in government-controlled areas. Back in 1999, he would have said that those Serbs were scared and terrorized. Three years later, he was ready to accept their choice, but he held that there was a clear boundary to be drawn between them and the RS Serbs. He thus resented the role of political bodies like the House of Peoples in the Federation where Serbs are supposed to be represented by that 'loyal' group.

Jelisije also thought that there were many more major and minor examples of how the RS was being forced into secondary status. According to him, the fact that the international decision makers live in Sarajevo was one reason for their support for Bosniacs; another was that the RS was not doing enough for Bosniac minority return. This was a big shift from 1999, when he said that the internationals were against the Serbs *in principle*. He also admitted that the Serbs had committed more war crimes than the other ethnic groups and said he would like to see the perpetrators in The Hague along with the often overlooked war criminals from the other groups. However, he resented the image of the RS as genocidal because it stereotyped all Serbs and was used to further the constitutional dismantling of RS 'from inside' (see Duijzings, Delpla, this volume).

Both Vojka and Jelisije still considered 'their' country to be Yugoslavia. They saw themselves as obliged to live in Bosnia-Herzegovina and did not find any emotional connection to that country. For Jelisije this was a result of the Serb defeat in the war. All of these statements sound familiar from my 1999 interviews. What was new was the realization that even their Dayton 'state', what they had seen back then as a sell-out, was gradually being dismantled. In fact, in 2002, the Dayton Peace Agreement had become popular among some pessimistic Serbs: that 'sell-out' has turned into a 'line of defence' for an increasingly marginalized RS. [23] For Vojka, Serbs are separate only 'on paper' and in the end there will be no RS. Both Vojka and Jelisije felt this trend would be difficult to reverse since it is driven by a biased international community. Further, when asked whether it was at all necessary to have this RS, Vojka fell back into familiar story lines. The RS should exist because there had been a war for it: 'It should be accepted. ... If this entity for Serbs goes away there will be war again after twenty-thirty years.'

---

[23] For a comparison with the Croat case, see Grandits, this volume.

Conclusion

The fascinating mixture of division and dependence, proximity and distance from Sarajevo is what first prompted me to write about the Sarajevan Serbs who had taken refuge in the town of Pale. Their narratives and spatial practices perfectly illustrate the complexity and ambivalence of social and political realities in post-war Bosnia-Herzegovina. From my first stay in Pale in 1999, I thought that this unnatural division of Sarajevo (and Sarajevans) would be particularly difficult to uphold, that Pale's distance from Serb urban centres and its proximity to the Bosnian capital would propel people toward interaction sooner or later. Proximity, after all, allowed for frequent first-hand experience of the urban other, a chance that only few locations in the RS really offered; to most RS Serbs, Belgrade or Banja Luka were closer than Sarajevo. During my fieldwork, it was obvious that many people, despite their exclusivist narratives, were tempted by the neighbouring urbanity. When conditions allowed, they started an interaction which intensified with the passing of time under the influence of material considerations that slowly won out over ethnic/nationalist concerns.

At first, however, it was simply a question of choice, of spatial practice, merely a decision about whether to visit Sarajevo for coffee. That was the period in which many people, by deciding to go to places where they might encounter the ethnic other, started transcending the boundaries erected by previous separatist political projects. Even when individuals did not assign any importance to such encounters, their spatial practices were unwittingly a first defeat for the separatist cause. They demonstrated through their actions that political projects and their spatial manifestations are always unstable.

The scene had been set beforehand by the refugees from Sarajevo whose urban identity and poor adaptation to their host community, and their familiarity with, nostalgia for and imagination of the city were clearly present even when they were claiming they wanted nothing to do with their old city. At the same time, of course, external influences had catalytic effects. This was not a situation in which ordinary people had the power to decide their own futures independently. The policies of the international community seriously constrained their decisions. In 2002, I encountered many Serb refugees who found themselves, even if temporarily and often against their will, in their former homes after having been evicted from their wartime residences and repossessing their Sarajevo property in accordance with international community rules.

This should by no means necessarily be understood as an emotional reconnection of the divided people of Sarajevo, however. The war and its causes have left deep rifts which will hardly be overcome by forcing people together. The issue of security is still there for the Serbs, even those who have happily embarked on a new experience in the city. Security remains important, both as a factor in itself and for communicating difference. This is the point at which optimistic observers must face reality. To be sure, people have started to reintegrate, out of conviction or because of the political realities of the common state. Yet the success of Serb nationalist discourses and the politics of identity in the RS should not be ignored. Like it or not, these are important factors and will remain so for some time. The gradual formation of new identity cleavages led by the same people taking part in the reintegration is a case in point. Different experiences, different identity politics and different physical spaces throughout the 1990s have seriously influenced identities and this must be understood and acknowledged. All of these, however, are illustrations of the ambiguity and complexity of contemporary Bosnia, of the existence of competing political projects and the instability of their meanings and spatial manifestations, of old and new identities, and of the boundaries of community that are being drawn and redrawn.

Chapter 4

The Power of 'Armchair Politicians':
Ethnic Loyalty and Political Factionalism among Herzegovinian Croats

Hannes Grandits

Introduction[1]

Years after the signing of the Dayton Peace Agreement in December 1995, the call
for national groups (*narodi*) to stay '*zajedno*' ('together') has not disappeared from
political rhetoric in Bosnia-Herzegovina. One was made aware of this reality
almost everywhere during the election periods of Spring and Autumn 2000: it was
used as the key word on the election posters of all three leading nationalist parties
in the country. This argument was also continually put forward in sermons given
by religious leaders of the three national groups. At the same time, the expression
'*foteljaši*' ('armchair politicians') also became very popular. '*Foteljaši*' was
applied in the same way to politicians from all ethnic or national groups: it was
often used by ordinary people when complaining angrily about corrupt politicians
who, as they said, sat in powerful and comfortable positions, working only for their
own personal welfare (see also Kolind, Helms, this volume). These politicians
were said to ascend party and governmental hierarchies with the help of influential
patrons and networks, enriching themselves while the population lived in
catastrophic economic conditions.

The two terms, '*zajedno*' and '*foteljaši*', can be used to characterize two
opposite tendencies in post-war Bosnian society: a continuing ethnicization of
political life on the one hand, and its crumbling due to a growing disappointment
with the political elites on the other hand. The results of the November 2000

---

[1]   This chapter is based on fieldwork conducted in various rural municipalities and
Mostar in 2000 and 2001. This research was made possible with the financial support of the
Austrian Science Fund (FWF). I am also grateful to Joel Halpern, Karl Kaser, Carolin
Leutloff, Elisabeth Katschnig-Fasch and the editors of this volume for their comments. My
greatest debt is to my hosts and friends in Herzegovina, for their hospitality and various
kinds of help.

general elections in the Federation, one of the two entities that have made up Bosnia-Herzegovina since 1995, best reflect this conflict. These elections brought to power the Alliance for Change (*Alijansa za promjene*), a coalition led by the ex-communist Social Democratic Party (SDP). This coalition received a majority of seats in the Federation Parliament, where the nationalist Party of Democratic Action (SDA) and Croat Democratic Union (HDZ) had until then predominated. While it lost many votes, however, the HDZ remained clearly dominant among Croat voters, especially in its stronghold of Herzegovina.

This regional centre of power for the HDZ will be the focus of this chapter. Compared with other regions of Bosnia-Herzegovina, the hegemony of the HDZ has always been extraordinarily strong in Herzegovina, as shown by election results (Pugh and Cobble 2001). In the first pluralist elections of November 1990, the HDZ candidates won between 94 and 100 percent of the votes in the four predominantly Croat municipalities located west of the Neretva River (Grude, Ljubuški, Posušje, Široki Brijeg), which have belonged to the Western Herzegovina Canton since 1995. After the war, in the first general elections of September 1996, the HDZ won nearly 90 percent of the votes in these four municipalities. One year later, in the municipal elections, it again managed to garner between 68 and 95 percent of the votes. In all three elections, similar hegemonic levels of support for the HDZ among Croat voters was to be found in the divided city of Mostar and in the five smaller municipalities located in Central Herzegovina – those alongside or immediately south-east of the Neretva river that are part of the Herzegovina-Neretva Canton (Čitluk, Čapljina, Stolac, Neum, Ravno).[2] In the subsequent general elections in September 1998, municipal elections in April 2000, and general elections in November 2000, the HDZ sustained some losses in both numbers and percentages of votes, but the party's domination among Croat voters in Herzegovina largely remained.[3]

Ten years after the breakdown of the communist system, another period of one-party rule thus reigned in this particular region of Bosnia-Herzegovina. How can this be explained? It makes sense to approach this question from a diachronic point of view, and to examine how centripetal dynamics, that is ethnic mobilisation around elites, and centrifugal ones, that is the growing distance between the population and the elite, developed over a period of time. An understanding of the reasons why political dynamics go into one or the other direction requires more knowledge about the relationship between ethnic mobilisation and networks of power (Bentley 1987; Grandits and Leutloff 2003). Generally, mass support for ethnic mobilisation depends on the ability of the elite to be identified with the moral values or the national cause of 'its' population. But such support is most

---

[2]	Whereas the municipalities of Čitluk and Neum were already predominantly Croat before the war, Čapljina and Stolac were ethnically mixed. The predominantly Croat municipality of Ravno was carved out of the municipality of Trebinje.

[3]	For all electoral results, see the website of the Election Commission of Bosnia-Herzegovina, <http://www.izbori.ba>.

often limited in time and bound to specific situations. Over a period of years, material living conditions count considerably. Direct material benefits or protection from losses in property or income help to win over the population in favour of ethnic mobilisation. Both moral and material resources, therefore, play an important role (Gledhill 2000: 127-52; Sundhaussen 1994).

The whole project of ethnic mobilisation is also influenced by control of the institutions of government, and their effective control depends in turn on the internal functioning of the leading nationalist party. The success or failure in keeping a balanced party structure, therefore, often determines the permanency of political power. Factions within a party can work together on the grounds of common interest but, in case of internal conflict they can also block the chain of command. Breakaway factions can threaten the unity of the ethnic group if they are able to attract a serious portion of the party following. The ability of the leading elite to handle factional divisions within the party and the electorate determines much of the future of ethnic mobilisation (Bailey 1970; Köhler and Zürcher 2003: 1-22).

This chapter deals with the question of why the HDZ has succeeded in maintaining overwhelming support among the Croat population in Herzegovina throughout the 1990s. First it will be shown that Herzegovinian Croat logic, according to which it is necessary to stay *zajedno*, has roots in some aspects of the breakdown of the communist system, as well as in new memories, social identities and economic dependencies which have been produced by the recent war. The focus will then shift to the development of the HDZ during the 1990s, and especially during the last years of that decade. The strategies of the party elite for monopolising political and economic life in Herzegovina will be analysed together with the way this elite managed its own heterogeneity. Finally, it will be shown that the success of the HDZ was threatened by the growing distance between the Croat population and its elite, but that this party was able to mobilize the ethnic loyalties of Herzegovinian Croats again for the elections held in November 2000, before going through a harsh confrontation with the international organisations present in Bosnia-Herzegovina.

Croat Identity, Catholic Faith and the Memory of World War II

During my interviews, when informants remembered the communist period, they always emphasized that too open an expression of their Croat national identity had been strictly forbidden. People frequently mentioned wedding celebrations, for example. Although afraid of the authorities and of possible 'spies', it happened from time to time that in the course of such celebrations people began to sing forbidden patriotic Croat songs. This almost always led to interrogations at the police station, and often ended with harsh punishments or even prison terms for those found responsible. With the weakening of the communist system, however, the expression of Croat national consciousness became increasingly public in Herzegovina. The tradition of putting a Croat flag on the top of the houses of a bride and/or bridegroom and carrying it at the head of the bridal procession began in 1990 and became very common in the following years. In 2000, the failure to use the Croat flag on such occasions was often even seen as a sign of opposition to the (HDZ-dominated) political mainstream, at least in rural Herzegovina.

The second topic that people often stressed when reflecting on the period following the end of the communist system was the role of the Catholic Church. Although religious services and folk celebrations on church holidays were permitted under communist rule, the open expression of faith carried negative consequences at the level of employment. In the first years after World War II, even to insist openly on the importance of the church was grounds for punishment, so that many were sent to do extra 'voluntary' community work or even to prison. In the 1980s, however, worship of the *Gospa*, the Virgin Mary, began in the village of Međugorje, which lies in the middle of Herzegovina. In the following years, Međugorje developed as a world-famous site of Catholic religious pilgrimage and tourism (Bax 1995). At the beginning of the 1990s, the importance of this pilgrimage centre increased enormously for the local population, attracting masses for the various church holidays. At the same time, in the traditionally observant Catholic villages of western Herzegovina, the decline of the communist power led to a re-emergence of religious life in the public sphere (Vrcan 2001: 101-51). In most of my interviews, this was interpreted explicitly as an expression of anti-communism and seen as a factor towards the democratisation of society.

As a consequence, the expression of Catholic observance became an increasingly important part of political life in Herzegovina. Catholic liturgy replaced communist symbols and rhetoric. This can easily be seen in the local newspapers published by some western Herzegovina municipalities. Until 1990, their front pages were dominated either by photographs of Tito or by various communist symbols and photos depicting the 'social, economic and industrial progress' in the region. Later on, the practice changed completely and photos of church buildings or Međugorje were placed on the front pages, followed by stories about the history of Catholic faith in the region. Of course, the increased influence of the Catholic Church also affected the attitude of local politicians. It became nearly impossible to advance in the new hierarchy of the HDZ without being, at least officially, bound to the church. As a consequence, a wave of baptisms of former communists and their children took place in the early 1990s.

As early as 1990, and especially after the war started in 1992, another topic became ubiquitous in public discourse: the issue of the Herzegovinian Croats killed at the end of World War II.[4] Western Herzegovina had been a stronghold of the *ustaša* movement in the inter-war Kingdom of Yugoslavia. During World War II, many officials and ordinary soldiers from this region served in the Independent

---

[4]   On the memory of World War II, see also Duijzings, Bougarel, this volume.

State of Croatia (NDH) set up by the Nazis in 1941, and to which Bosnia-Herzegovina belonged until the establishment of socialist Yugoslavia in 1945. At the end of the war, many of these Croats fled towards Austria in an attempt to escape the victorious Partisans but, in May 1945, near the Austrian town of Bleiburg, they were handed over to the Yugoslav communists by the Allies. In the course of the weeks that followed, thousands of them were killed. There were also reprisals and killings of former or alleged *ustaša* members at the end and immediately after the war in Herzegovina itself.

After having been suppressed as a public topic of discussion during the communist period, the killings of these Croats became a focus of interest in the 1990s (Denich 1994; Grandits 1998; Hayden 1994). HDZ leaders and Croat nationalist intellectuals systematically launched discussions about the Bleiburg massacres and the killings in Herzegovina in 1945 and 1946. In the context of the early 1990s, such discussions stirred people's fear that losing a new war could again result in events similar to what happened at Bleiburg. Furthermore, this discourse about Croat 'martyrdom' was used to thoroughly demonize communism, reducing the whole communist period to a 'continuation' of the Bleiburg policy against the Croats of Herzegovina. In Croatia and Croat Bosnia-Herzegovina in general, the idea that nothing short of a historic reconciliation between the antagonistic camps of World War II, the *ustaše* and the Croat communists could bring an end to Serb domination and pave the way for independence was a very popular notion promoted by the HDZ in the years before and during the war. These were the ideological terms through which the HDZ tried to explain its role among the Croat people. Even after the recent war, the issue of Bleiburg remains omnipresent in Herzegovinian public discourse. It has become a synonym for the persecution of Croat soldiers and, by extension, all Croats.

Remembering Fallen Soldiers and Organizing Veterans

The early 1990s were also remembered as the beginning of the threat to Croats in western Herzegovina. In popular accounts, as the war escalated in Croatia in the summer of 1991, the Yugoslav People's Army (JNA) began to station tanks at every strategic point in Herzegovina. At this time the last of the young Croat villagers completing their military service who had not already deserted left the JNA, as the local population had already begun to perceive the JNA as a Serb army. Almost all households with adult males bought weapons, which they still kept at home after the end of the recent war. This helped the HDZ as it began to organize the defence against the JNA and the Serbs. At first the local military units consisted only of volunteers, but after more intense fighting broke out in April 1992, all males up to age 45-50 were systematically drafted into the Croat Defence Council (HVO), the military arm of the HDZ.

In 1993, the military alliance of Croats and Bosniacs opposing Serb forces dissolved. Many soldiers died between May 1993 and March 1994 in the Croat-Bosniac fighting that followed. Mostar and the towns and villages south-east of the Neretva valley became battlefields and were heavily destroyed. The region was ethnically cleansed by the HVO, which expelled the Bosniac population. Although not far from the frontline, the municipalities west of the Neretva did not become a site of direct military confrontation, but the war cost many victims there, too. As the war escalated, the HDZ and HVO gained more and more power and required absolute loyalty. By way of example, local newspapers published lists of names of men who had been drafted but subsequently fled abroad. They were labelled '*izdajnici*' ('traitors') who had abandoned the community in its most difficult moments.

Towards the end of the war, and even more in the first years after it, the most important element contributing to deep ethnic solidarity and unity was the mourning of dead soldiers. Parallel to intimate remembrance among relatives or neighbours, public commemorations were organized at the local level by the church and the local authorities, that is the ruling HDZ. These ceremonies were often accompanied by the dedication of memorials.[5] In most of them, soldiers killed in both the recent war and in World War II were linked in a joint commemorative plaque: this was to express the continued struggle of the Croats against their various enemies. Another important HDZ activity was providing care for the families in which a father, husband or son had been killed in the '*Domovinski rat*' ('Homeland war'): the widows and parents of such fallen soldiers received cash assistance, jobs and new apartments.[6] As long as HDZ rule lasted in Croatia, the availability of financial resources was not at all a problem in Croat Herzegovina, especially given the general situation in Bosnia-Herzegovina. These war-related social benefits were given to thousands of families and were perceived by the population as an act of responsibility on the part of the HDZ. The delivery of these benefits was of course controlled by the local chapters of the party and, most often, close relations with local leaders and activists turned beneficiaries into loyal supporters of HDZ rule.

In addition, many of the beneficiaries were also members of various associations founded during the war such as the Association of Volunteers and Veterans of the Homeland War (*Udruga dragovoljaca i veterana Domovinskog rata*), the Association of Families of Croat Soldiers Killed or Missing in the Homeland War (*Udruga obitelji hrvatskih branitelja poginulih i nestalih u Domovinskom ratu*), and the Croat Disabled Veterans of the Homeland War (*Hrvatski vojni invalidi Domovinskog rata*, HVIDR-a). Of course, all these associations had close links with the HDZ and enjoyed a prominent place in local public life. They were especially active when they felt that Croat 'national rights'

---

[5]   On the Bosniac and Serb cases, see Bougarel, Duizings, this volume.

[6]   On war-related social benefits in the Bosniac part of the Federation, see Bougarel, this volume.

('*nacionalna prava*') were being endangered, issuing public statements and organising protest meetings or street demonstrations. Despite all their ideological and symbolic differences, these associations linked to the ruling party recall the communist period when associations made up of former Partisans likewise played a crucial role in public and political life (Roksandić 1995).

Regional Underdevelopment, Economic Dependency and Patron-Client Relationships

The role of veteran associations and war-related social benefits in the maintenance of HDZ hegemony among Herzegovinian Croats has to be considered against the background of the general economic situation in Herzegovina. In the communist period, western Herzegovina was one of the poorest and most peripheral regions of Yugoslavia. Since it had been the most prominent stronghold of the *ustaša* movement it was first treated very harshly, and real modernisation and regional development efforts started only in the late 1960s.[7] At that time, in many western Herzegovinian villages, more than two thirds of the households had at least one member in Germany or Austria, and *Gastarbeiter* ('guest workers') remained the main source of support for many households throughout the difficult 1980s and 1990s. In the late 1980s, the breakdown of the socialist order was accompanied by hyperinflation and a growing economic crisis. In western Herzegovina, the collapse of several banks with local offices in the region was particularly resented. Many families had held considerable assets earned by *Gastarbeiter* and lost at least part of their savings. At the same time, some people close to the League of Communists were able to take advantage of the situation through financial speculations. In interviews, people described how the growing anarchy of this period affected state institutions as well as everyday life, and hastened the end of the communist system.

During the war, as already mentioned, two different scenarios developed in Herzegovina. The region of western Herzegovina maintained a sound economy until the late 1990s. During and after the war, most of the financial help from Croatia was channelled into this region, due to its strategic importance and the strength of the 'Herzegovinian lobby' in Croatia itself.[8] By the time HDZ rule collapsed in Croatia in January 2000, about 600 million Deutschmarks (DM) (300 million €) had been transferred into Herzegovina every year, mainly from the

---

[7]   In 1966, the Mostar conference of the League of Communists of Bosnia-Herzegovina decided to put an end to the political ostracism of western Herzegovinian Croats and began to promote some of them in the party apparatus.

[8]   Throughout the 1990s, the 'Herzegovinian lobby' in Croatia was led by Gojko Šušak, the Croatian Minister of Defence (see note 14). It consisted of Herzegovina-born people who were exceptionally loyal to Croatian President Franjo Tuđman and belonged to the right wing of the HDZ.

budget of the Ministries of Defence, Reconstruction, and Social Affairs.[9] Through large-scale trading and smuggling, western Herzegovina also developed into a powerful trade centre. In the first years after the war, money from returning *Gastarbeiter* and mass tourism to Međugorje was an additional factor contributing to the economic boom of the region. The standard of living improved rapidly in western Herzegovina and, in contrast with the period before 1990, it became one of the few relatively well-off parts of Bosnia-Herzegovina. This reality also strengthened its role as the political centre of Croat politics in this country.

On the other hand, the city of Mostar and the region south-east of the Neretva were directly affected by war activities and suffered large-scale destruction. Almost all of the Bosniac and Serb population fled or was expelled from those areas controlled by the HVO while Croats were forced out of Serb-held eastern Herzegovina and the Bosniac-held eastern part of Mostar. Beginning during the war and continuing afterwards, these Croats, along with a much more numerous group of Croats from central Bosnia, were systematically resettled in West Mostar, Čapljina, and Stolac, formerly mixed municipalities of central Herzegovina now held by the HVO (see Kolind, this volume). Croat displaced persons were given the right to settle in the houses and apartments that had been inhabited by Bosniacs or Serbs before the war, and new settlements were also built for Croats with financial help from Croatia. In the years following the war, however, expelled Bosniacs and Serbs started returning to reclaim their properties with the support of international organisations like the United Nations High Commissioner for Refugees (UNHCR) and the Commission for Real Property Claims (CRPC). This implementation of the right to return was met with strong resistance; for Croats living south-east of the Neretva and, to a lesser extent, in Mostar, the call to remain *zajedno* was often understood in very emotional terms as defending their very presence against the interests of the returning people.[10] For these Croats, the HDZ, which held almost all the Croat seats in municipal administrative bodies, represented their only support in this 'defence'.

As a result, economic dependency and patron-client relationships tended to be stronger in the war-torn parts of Herzegovina in the 1990s, especially among displaced persons. In the municipalities west of the Neretva, people were less dependent on their respective *foteljaši* and their position in the party hierarchy. Throughout Croat Herzegovina, however, large parts of the labour market were dominated by powerful patrons belonging to or closely linked to the HDZ. Many people were also employed because they enjoyed good relations with such a patron as part of that patron's clientele. Direct pressure was not always exerted on clients, but loyalty was expected, and people working in the public sector or in private enterprises led by HDZ members had to 'take care' (Gosztonyi and Rossig 1998).

---

[9] *Globus*, 12 November 1999.
[10] For a comparison with Croatia, see Leutloff-Grandits 2005.

In the heated atmosphere of the first post-war years, political disagreement could cause people serious problems and even cost them their jobs.

The HDZ in the 1990s: Political Hegemony and Internal Factionalism

This description of the political hegemony of the HDZ among Herzegovinian Croats needs to be augmented by an analysis of the elites of this party. Above all, and this can be stressed in advance, they are anything but a monolithic and homogenous group; political life within the HDZ has been characterized by deep divisions throughout the 1990s. What unites all factions of the HDZ in Bosnia-Herzegovina are varying degrees of commitment to Croat nationalism and a formal deference to the Catholic Church.[11] The various factions, however, stand for diverging political options and material interests that are supposed to be subsumed into one party. Decision making in the HDZ has developed into a process of shifting alliances between various factions, and there is often a real sense of uncertainty about the decisions that will be taken in the party.

The HDZ of Bosnia-Herzegovina has undergone a series of transformations since it was founded in August 1990 as a national mass movement. From its very beginning, this party was an alliance of religious figures and anti-communist émigrés on the one hand, and previously middle-rank functionaries of the Bosnian League of Communists on the other hand.[12] The cleavage produced by these different backgrounds never fully disappeared and as early as September 1990, the founding president of the HDZ, Davor Perinović, a deeply committed anti-communist, was replaced by Stjepan Kljuić, a former communist. Although the HDZ was an offshoot of its 'mother-party' in Croatia, its national leadership was at that time based in Sarajevo and favourable to an integral Bosnia-Herzegovina. This seemed to be reasonable since Croats were living in different parts of the republic, and the HDZ leadership reflected this reality: at the party convention held in March 1991 in Mostar, for example, only 53 out of the 341 delegates present came from Herzegovina.[13]

In February 1992, however, as the war in Croatia began to expand into Bosnia-Herzegovina, a Herzegovinian faction led by the former communist manager Mate Boban, which stood for the territorial partition of Bosnia-Herzegovina, took over the leadership of the party. This coup was made possible by the massive political, financial and military support coming from neighbouring Croatia, and especially from the Croatian Ministry of Defence led by Herzegovinian-born Gojko Šušak.[14]

---

[11]   For a comparison with Croatia, see Zakošek 1998.

[12]   The other leading nationalist parties in Bosnia-Herzegovina and Croatia have similar origins (see Katunarić 1991).

[13]   See the interview with Stjepan Kljuić in *Globus*, 29 October 1999.

[14]   Gojko Šušak migrated to Canada in the 1960s. In the late 1980s, he was one of the organizers of financial support to Franjo Tuđman and the HDZ among the Croat diaspora. After he 'returned' to Croatia, he took part in the organisation and financing of Croatian

From this time on, western Herzegovina became the absolute centre of the HDZ in Bosnia-Herzegovina and, together with Gojko Šušak and Franjo Tuđman, Mate Boban directed the developments of Croat politics in this country.

During the first year of war, the HDZ and its military arm, the HVO, developed a functioning hierarchy of power in the areas under their control. This process included the integration of self-organized fighting units into the HVO. In Herzegovina, for example, a conflict arose between the HVO and the Croat Defence Forces (HOS), a paramilitary organization close to the right-wing Croat Party of Rights (HSP), which ended in July 1992 with the murder of the HOS leader, Blaž Kraljević, and the subsequent enlistment of most of the HOS fighters into the HVO (Bjelaković and Strazzari 1999). At the same time, the HDZ and the HVO became more and more intertwined, so that political activists sometimes held functions in both organisations simultaneously. Heated struggles for power and material resources were also fought throughout the war between civil and military leaders at the local level, or between former officers of the JNA and self-proclaimed commanders of paramilitary units (Vego 1993).

The outbreak of Croat-Bosniac fighting in the first months of 1993 and the proclamation of the 'Croat Republic of Herceg-Bosna' on 24 August of that year led to the further entrenchment of the Croat para-state, which was strongly supported by Croatia, but also to signs of its disintegration (Ribičič 2000; Rotim 1997). In central Bosnia, the defeat at the hands of the Bosnian Army, the isolation of Croat enclaves there, and the increase in smuggling activities led to the progressive disintegration of the HVO (Bougarel 1996: 121-38). In November 1993, the Croatian Army intervened directly in the Croat-Bosniac fighting and installed General Ante Roso as head of the HVO in an attempt to reorganize it. Due to the unfavourable military situation and the massive international pressure that was put on Croatia, the HDZ was compelled to at least formally renounce the para-state of 'Herceg-Bosna' and on 1st March 1994, the Federation of Bosnia-Herzegovina was officially established by the Washington Agreement, merging the Bosniac and Croat-held territories into a single 'entity'. Mate Boban stepped down from the HDZ Presidency, and was replaced by Krešimir Zubak, a politician from Doboj in northern Bosnia.[15]

On 14 December 1995, the Dayton Peace Agreement confirmed the legal existence of the Federation and the ten cantons into which it was divided. In the first years after the end of war, many other leaders of the HDZ left their positions in the party apparatus (Hoppe 1998: 19-26). This did not necessarily mean the loss of their political or especially their economic power, however. Resignation from public functions even developed into a strategy by powerful politicians which

---

forces and became Minister of Defence in September 1991. He occupied this function and remained the second most powerful politician in Croatia until his death in 1998.

[15] After the signing of the Washington Agreement and his withdrawal from the HDZ leadership, Mate Boban was given a high-ranking position in the Croatian state oil company, INA. He died in 1997.

allowed them to escape pressure from international organisations in charge of the implementation of the peace agreement, most prominently the Office of the High Representative (OHR). In this way, the HDZ was able to maintain the functioning of the para-state of 'Herceg-Bosna' despite the fact that it had been officially dissolved, and that the HDZ held key positions in the governments of the Federation and of Bosnia-Herzegovina (Gosztonyi 1999, 2003; Koschnik 1995). In the Federation, the HDZ found a congenial partner in the Bosniac SDA, such that the coalition government led by Prime Minister Edhem Bičakčić (SDA) was in reality a front hiding two parallel systems of power (ESI 1999; ICG 1999). In a similar way, the HVO was officially integrated into a common Federation Army (*Vojska Federacije*) after agreements were reached in January and May 1997, but was able to maintain its independence. In fact, it even managed to become more centralized and professional with the help of the Croatian Army and the US military assistance program *Train and Equip* (Džanić and Norman 1998).

State Capture and the Economic Dimensions of Factionalism

Most analyses of factionalism within the main nationalist parties of Bosnia-Herzegovina focus on the kinds of cleavages that have been described above, that is according to different regional and ideological origins on one hand, and by political aims and strategies on the other hand. However, divergent material interests must also be taken into consideration. During and after the war, many key political leaders have used informal power networks to exploit the state and were therefore able to transform their political influence into personal capital. Others who belonged to nationalist parties or had good connections in them were also able to become 'successful' businessmen through a system of reciprocal aid and patron-client relationships. Of course, some were more successful than others, but the number of *tajkuni*, the local term used for those who rapidly grew rich in the 1990s, is not insignificant among any of the three national groups.

In the Federation, the SDA and the HDZ have eagerly participated in the division of state institutions and public companies into two separate fields of interest. In Croat Herzegovina, exploitation of the state functioned in different ways. For example, the non-payment of taxes at custom posts controlled by the para-state of 'Herceg-Bosna' allowed some businessmen to make immense profits by opening private petrol stations and selling petrol throughout the region. The same happened with other goods like cars, cigarettes and all kinds of food products. Other individuals with the right connections established successful businesses on the basis of very favourable contracts with state institutions and public companies. The HVO itself was used as a tool of illegal enrichment: for example, over the course of several years, huge amounts of wine were allegedly sold at a high price to some army barracks in quantities that were ten times higher than what the employees there could ever consume,[16] and a large number of people were paid by the Federation Ministry of Defence who never appeared at their jobs.[17] International money was also embezzled: in Čitluk, for example, the Stabilization Force (SFOR) for several years paid a yearly rent of one million DM (500 million €) for the use of a tourist resort as a barracks, yet no one can say where the money finally ended up.[18] Many western Herzegovinian private entrepreneurs, however, were able to build up successful enterprises without being involved in dubious affairs, for example by investing the money they had earned as *Gastarbeiter* in Germany.

In the internal cleavages of the HDZ, material interests play an important role. In May 2001, a local journalist tried to differentiate the factions within this party in the following way:

> On the one hand you have the right-wing ideologists, who really believe in their national mission. Most of them are not at all or not too much involved in business affairs. Then you have the army generals. Here you have two groups: the calm ones and the 'involved' ones [in dubious economic activities]. Then you have the *mafijaši* [mafiosi], those who are really deeply involved in illegal or even criminal business. And a major part of the party leaders are pure technocrats or you can call them moderates, who stay in the party because it is better for them and their business interests to be in the party and not out of it.[19]

A look at the development of the banking system offers an even more precise insight into the cleavages and balances of power within the HDZ. In the 1990s, it was possible to distinguish three major factions based on divergent financial interests and on links to one of three banks in the Croat part of Mostar. Their power is concentrated in Herzegovina, but is also influential in central Bosnia. The first was the *Hrvatska Banka Mostar*, founded in 1992, which was the financial institution through which support came in from Croatia. After these financial flows were re-routed to the *Hercegovačka Banka* in 1999, *Hrvatska Banka Mostar* came to represent economic rather than political centres of power in Croat Herzegovina. A second bank linked to a group of influential HDZ politicians was the *Dubrovačka Banka*. This bank was originally based in Dubrovnik, but when it was threatened with collapse in April 1998, it transferred large sums of capital under very unclear circumstances to the newly established *Dubrovačka Banka Mostar*. At that time, this bank represented the second most powerful faction within the HDZ. At the end of the 1990s, however, the most powerful faction was linked to *Hercegovačka Banka*, a bank founded in late 1997.

---

[16] See the interview with Mijo Anić, the Federation Minister of Defence, in *Feral Tribune*, 12 May 2001.

[17] *Feral Tribune*, 24 March 2001.

[18] *Oslobođenje*, 19 April 2001.

[19] Personal conversation with L. M. on 3 May 2001 in Mostar.

Hercegovačka Banka was explicitly founded in order to support Croat 'national interests' and its initial capital was provided by eighteen Herzegovinian public companies and the three cantons of Herzegovina.[20] Several HVO generals, notably Ante Jelavić[21] and Ljubo Ćesić-Rojs (who was in fact a general in the Croatian Army),[22] played a very active part in the founding of this bank. The church, and especially the head office of the Franciscan Province in Mostar, supported the initiative with its authority among the Croat population. Fra Tomislav Pervan, later the head of the Herzegovina Franciscans, and Fra Ivan Ševan, another influential clergyman, were members of the supervisory board of the bank, together with generals Ante Jelavić, Ljubo Ćesić-Rojs, and Ivan Medić. Initially, this military church coalition even formed the majority on the supervisory board. The third group in the founding of *Hercegovačka Banka* was made up of directors of public companies, especially Mijo Brajković, the director of *Aluminij*, a Mostar based company which was to become one of the most significant and profitable industrial complexes in Bosnia-Herzegovina after the war.[23]

The example of *Hercegovačka Banka* shows clearly that factions within the HDZ are strategic alliances between persons of different social backgrounds and representing different interest groups. It also shows how political options and material interests intermingle in the factions of the main Croat party of Bosnia-Herzegovina. In the decision-making process on important issues, however, the divergent positions of all these factions must be brought to terms. The mobilisation of ethnic loyalty is thus often a means of bringing them into a common line. As will be shown below, the November 2000 general elections and the ensuing 'Croat

---

[20]   These three cantons are the Western Herzegovina Canton, the Herzegovina-Neretva Canton and the Livno Canton.

[21]   Before the war, Herzegovina-born Ante Jelavić was an officer in the JNA. He joined the HVO in 1992 and soon held a key position in its main logistics centre located in Grude. Later, he became one of the most influential officers within the HVO. He used this position to accumulate a remarkable financial base, and became one of a group of co-owners of the construction company founded by Ljubo Ćesić-Rojs (see note 22).

[22]   Before the war, Herzegovina-born Ljubo Ćesić-Rojs was a bus driver. When the war began in Croatia, he volunteered and, through good relations with Gojko Šušak, advanced rapidly in the Croatian Army. In Herzegovina he was initially influential in the main HVO logistics centre in Grude. Later, he was made the head of the so-called '66th Pioneer brigade', which was in charge of building strategic roads in Croatia and Herzegovina. After the war, he became a member of the Croatian Parliament, and the (co)-owner of one of the biggest private construction companies in Bosnia-Herzegovina.

[23]   Mijo Brajković was already a leading industrial manager in the 1980s. He made a career in the HDZ during the war and became Mayor of Croat-held West Mostar between 1994 and 1996, and later also Governor of the Herzegovina-Neretva Canton. In 1997 he was appointed director of *Aluminij*, an industrial plant which manufactured aluminium and employed about 800 people at the time. Although he never held a major official position in the HDZ, he was always one of its most influential figures.

crisis' constituted such an attempt by the *Hercegovačka Banka* faction to once again mobilize ethnic loyalty, both within the population and within the party.

The *Hercegovačka Banka* Faction and the Crisis of HDZ Hegemony

In May 1998, during the party convention in Mostar, the *Hercegovačka Banka* faction took over the leadership of the HDZ. This takeover was called the 'generals' putsch', since several high officers entered the top leadership of the party and Ante Jelavić was elected as its new president over Božo Ljubić, the candidate supported by Krešimir Zubak. Krešimir Zubak himself had been elected as the Croat member of the Bosnian Presidency in September 1996, and was linked to politicians involved in the *Dubrovačka Banka* affair. He was believed to want to go beyond what had until then been the prevailing policy of paying lip service to the Federation, and to support Croat interests throughout the country rather than focusing primarily on Herzegovina. It seems that this last issue was one of the decisive factors in his defeat. But it was also of relevance that the party convention took place only two weeks after the death of Gojko Šušak, which lent an atmosphere of patriotic mourning to the whole event, and that Ante Jelavić was supported by the two envoys of Croatian President Franjo Tuđman, Ivica Pašalić and Ljubo Ćesić-Rojs, both originally from Herzegovina. The new power relations which emerged from this party convention triggered the most serious factional fighting within the HDZ since the signing of the Dayton Peace Agreement. It ended in June 1998 when Krešimir Zubak's founded a new political party, the New Croat Initiative (NHI).

In the following general elections in September 1998, the coalition formed by the NHI and the Croat Christian Democratic Union (HKDU) was believed to threaten the unity of the Croat electorate. The NHI in particular expected good electoral results among the Croats of Posavina and central Bosnia, because of their discontent over the dragging return process there. The HKDU intended to present an alternative to the HDZ in Herzegovina, where it had been active for years in some municipalities. But the NHI-HKDU coalition suffered a painful defeat throughout Bosnia-Herzegovina, with the relative exception of the Posavina Canton, where it got 21 percent of the vote. In Herzegovina in particular, but also in central Bosnia, the HDZ had been successful in portraying Krešimir Zubak and his followers as 'traitors' who wanted to divide the Croats of Bosnia-Herzegovina.

Led by Ante Jelavić, the new Croat member of the Bosnian Presidency, the HDZ continued the same policy as before: it participated in the Bosnian and Federation governments, but was keen to protect its fields of interest from any external influence. This especially concerned the Croat component of the Federation Army (HVO), Mostar based pension funds, telecommunication and electricity distribution companies, the *Aluminij* and *Soko* firms, and other important Croat 'national interests' like the low tax and flexible border regime prevailing in areas controlled by the HDZ. Throughout 1998 and 1999, however, HDZ leaders were increasingly hindered in their efforts by the actions of international organisations present in Bosnia-Herzegovina. This included the creation of a unified customs administration by the High Representative in January 1999, the raid by SFOR troops on Croat secret services in Mostar in December 1999, the arrest of some Croats indicted by the Hague Tribunal and, more generally, increased pressure on local HDZ politicians blamed for obstructing the implementation of the Dayton Peace Agreement. At the same time, international organisations were increasingly successful in organising the return of displaced persons and refugees, even in the war-affected regions of Herzegovina (see Kolind, this volume). The return process furthered local discussions about the implementation of property laws, the occupation of private properties and the privatisation of public companies and infrastructure, especially in war-affected areas. The alleged mismanagement of public funds and the barely functioning public institutions also began to tackle the every day interests of the broader population.

Finally, the death of Franjo Tuđman in December 1999 and the parliamentary elections of January 2000 ended the domination of the HDZ in Croatia, and this soon had important consequences in Herzegovina as well. Especially in Zagreb, Croatian public opinion began to develop strong anti-Herzegovina sentiments. For weeks, Croatian magazines and newspapers were full of sensational reports about the 'dirty businesses' of the Herzegovinian HDZ politicians and the 'Herzegovinian Mafia', which were blamed for many problems in 'democratic Croatia'. Since the daily newspapers, magazines and broadcasts from Croatia were the primary sources of media for Herzegovinian Croats themselves, they very soon realized that the tone had changed, which triggered an increasingly critical attitude among them. The nature of the HDZ's domination of political and social life in Herzegovina began to be threatened.

During the first years after the war, the HDZ had been able to transmit the message that it was the only party able to defend common interests and the unity of the Croats in Bosnia-Herzegovina. It claimed that those who had led the Croat people to victory through the hard days of war should also lead them through negotiations with the other national groups and the international community. In a situation that remained tense all over Herzegovina, and particularly in Mostar, all attempts to organize a serious opposition to the HDZ failed. The political parties in real opposition to the HDZ did not succeed in organising any serious network of activists in the region, since the HDZ accused them of having been 'traitors' during the war, or tried to compromise them in other ways. The secret service organisations controlled by the local and regional power holders also scared many out of open political confrontation with the HDZ.

In 2000, however, economic inequality and social insecurity were starting to become the most important topics in public discussions. People talked with increasing disgust about their HDZ leaders who were driving expensive limousines and living in luxurious houses built during or after the war. There was almost no discussion about the political situation in which this problem was not brought up. Many people were also disappointed, as politicians' promises of improved social welfare had fallen far short. Moreover, the new government in Croatia had cut off much of the earlier flow of financial assistance to Herzegovina, and most of those who had until that time received social benefits lost them or received drastically reduced payments.

In the April municipal elections, the argument that it is better to have a united Croat majority in municipal councils to control local affairs was still convincing for Croat voters living in the formerly mixed municipalities of central Herzegovina and central Bosnia. Since many opposition parties also had no viable Croat candidates at the local level, the HDZ maintained its hegemonic position throughout Croat Herzegovina. In the predominantly Croat municipalities of western Herzegovina, however, the elections were characterized by a very low voter turnout and the HDZ lost a large portion of the votes it had won in September 1997.[24] This can be seen as a sign of discontent with the political situation, as was also shown by the relative success of small and poorly organized Christian Democratic parties, which won between 15 and 24 percent of the votes. This outcome furthermore reflected frustration over the results of the elections in Croatia, in which Croats of Bosnia-Herzegovina have been entitled to participate since the early 1990s. Despite these negative trends, the overall domination of the HDZ among Croat voters in Bosnia-Herzegovina was not called into question. This was not the case for its coalition partner in the Federation, the SDA, which lost its longstanding majority among Bosniac voters in the same municipal elections, in some places to the Social Democratic Party (SDP) and elsewhere to the Party for Bosnia-Herzegovina (SBiH).

With the general elections scheduled for November 2000, the HDZ in Bosnia-Herzegovina was threatened with the same fate that had befallen the SDA in the local elections and, earlier, the HDZ in Croatia. Several parties or coalitions had begun to build up stronger local chapters in Croat areas and were also able to win over some well known candidates to join their election lists, including many former HDZ members. In Herzegovina, the SDP presented local Croat candidates for the first time and was expected to benefit at least somewhat from the success of its sister party in Croatia. Several Christian Democratic parties presented candidates, as did the independent list *'Radom za boljitak'* ('Through Work to Well-being'), supported by a group of Croat businessmen. Even parties that had closely collaborated with the HDZ throughout the years expected some electoral gains, as did, for instance, the Croat Party of Rights (HSP) which tried to present itself as a right wing alternative to the HDZ.

---

[24] A comparison of the number (rather than the percentage) of votes for the HDZ shows that, between September 1997 and April 2000, the party lost 2,625 votes (about 42 percent) in Grude, 3,987 votes (57 percent) in Ljubuški, 3,558 votes (59 percent) in Posušje and 6,146 votes (60 percent) in Široki Brijeg.

The 'Croat National Congress': A Last Attempt at Restoring Ethnic Loyalty

As the general elections approached, the HDZ united its ranks and plunged itself vigorously into the election campaign in Herzegovina and all other Croat areas of Bosnia-Herzegovina. In one strategy continued from earlier election campaigns, it began to attack all Croats prominent in opposition parties. With the help of the media under its control, the HDZ tried to discredit non-HDZ Croat candidates by revealing 'true' details of their pasts, such as their failure to observe the Catholic faith or to join the HVO during the war, their readiness to cooperate with non-Croat parties, or their own financial misdeeds. Epithets such as 'communists', 'traitors' and 'Judases' were systematically sprayed on opposition campaign posters. At the same time, the HDZ began what emerged as a key component of its eventual success by launching an aggressive campaign to end the rampant 'discrimination' against Croats in Bosnia-Herzegovina. This campaign became even more convincing for a large portion of the Croat population when, one month before the elections, the Organisation for Security and Cooperation in Europe (OSCE) altered the election rules concerning the House of Peoples (*Dom naroda*) of the Federation Parliament, giving both Bosniac and Croat cantonal delegates the right to vote for Croat (and Bosniac) representatives, rather than having them chosen only by members of the same national group as had been the case up until then. The new rules, which were intended to dilute the influence of the nationalist parties, thus seriously endangered the future predominance of the HDZ among the allotted Croat members of this chamber.[25]

The HDZ subsequently attacked international organisations, accusing them of systematically disadvantaging Croats. The Croat emigration from Bosnia-Herzegovina in the 1990s, and the ensuing decline of this population was presented as part of the 'proof' of this. The HDZ's main election slogan during this campaign, '*Opredeljenje ili istrebljenje*' ('[Self-]Determination or Extermination'), illustrates the dramatic way in which this party projected its message to the Croat population. This slogan was combined with demands for the creation of a third, Croat entity in Bosnia-Herzegovina. While doing this, HDZ leaders continually drew attention to the fact that a similar entity had been given to the Serbs in 1995 and argued that Croats had no chance against the Bosniac majority in the

---

[25] The House of Peoples (*Dom naroda*), one of two houses of the Federation Parliament, reserves 30 seats for Bosniacs and 30 for Croats, the delegates for which are elected by the assemblies of the ten cantons forming the Federation. Until October 2000, representatives of each national group in the House of Peoples were elected by members of the corresponding group in the cantonal assemblies. On 10 October 2000, the OSCE decided that the representatives of both national groups would thenceforth be elected by all members of the cantonal assemblies, meaning that Bosniac representatives would have a say in the selection of Croat members, and vice versa. In the case of the Croat representatives, the new rules gave a clear advantage to the SDP and the small Croat political parties opposed to the HDZ, precisely as the OSCE had intended.

Federation without their own 'self-government' (*'samouprava'*). International organisations condemned the tone of the HDZ campaign as a serious misinterpretation of the situation in the country and accused them of openly working to undermine the peace agreement. The High Representative removed several candidates from the HDZ election lists and forbid them to run for office in the future. The banned politicians were accused of obstructing the return of refugees, discriminating against local minorities, and spreading ethnic hatred. The HDZ was successful, however, in publicising these decisions as further proof of discrimination against the Croat people.

Escalating tensions further, the HDZ organized a grouping of all 'patriotic parties and institutions' and, on 28 October 2000, a so-called *'Hrvatski narodni sabor'* ('Croat National Congress') was convened in Novi Travnik. This initiative was supported by most of the small Croat right-wing parties in Bosnia-Herzegovina like the Croat Party of Rights (HSP), but also by most of the Christian Democratic parties, such as the Croat Christian Democratic Union (HKDU), the Croat Christian Patriotic Rebirth (HKDP), and the Croat Demo-Christians (*Hrvatski demokršćani*). Associations of war veterans and other war-related groups, along with most of the Croat cultural societies,[26] also joined in support. Finally, the presence of the leaders of the Catholic Church was of particular importance, since this could appear as a signal for support to the HDZ and its policy.

In the weeks before the elections, the atmosphere became increasingly emotional in Herzegovina as well as in the Croat parts of central Bosnia. Election rallies in various towns of Herzegovina, culminating in a mass gathering in the football stadium of West Mostar, most often featured joint appearances by the leaders of the 'Croat National Congress' and attracted more people than expected. The well organized veteran groups and cultural societies close to the HDZ were also able to coordinate mass protests against the decisions of the OSCE and the High Representative. The appeal to stay *zajedno* was again combined with typically highly charged appeals to Catholic faith or war memories and allusions to the new 'threat to the Croat people' in Bosnia-Herzegovina. This 'patriotic' wave overpowered all earlier grievances against the HDZ and made it particularly difficult for those few Croat parties who remained in opposition to the HDZ and did not join the 'Croat National Congress' to gain larger support.

Finally, a 'referendum' was planned for 11 November 2000, the very day of the state-level official election, at which Croats were to support or reject the work and plans of the 'Croat National Congress'. In essence, the HDZ turned this into a 'profession of faith' and support for the Croat nation. Similarly, not voting for the HDZ or voting for a party outside the 'Croat National Congress' became a betrayal of the 'Croat cause'. International organisations strongly criticized the referendum

---

[26] In the 1990s, many Croat cultural societies were (re)established, such as the *Matica Hrvatska*, the Croat Cultural Society *Napredak* ('Progress') and the Society of Croat Writers. For a comparison with Serb cultural societies, see Maners 2000.

as violating the election law and the Dayton Peace Agreement, and threatened the HDZ leaders with dire consequences. Nevertheless, the referendum was held and the HDZ remained by far the strongest party among Croat voters, especially in Herzegovina. In the Herzegovina-Neretva Canton, the party won almost the same number of votes as it had in September 1998. In the Western Herzegovina Canton, its percentage of the overall vote dropped from 81 to 71 percent, as it did in the Livno Canton (from 71 to 62 percent). None of this endangered the power of the HDZ in the region, however. The tendency was similar in other cantons with large Croat populations. Despite this general success, however, some trends make it obvious that the HDZ's call for Croat national unity was no longer heeded as strictly as before. In Posavina, the NHI was again able to win a significant share of Croat votes (17 percent of the total vote), in central Bosnia the SDP seems to have attracted a portion of the Croat vote, and even in western Herzegovina the independent list *'Radom za boljitak'* won 8 percent of the votes. Yet what was even more striking than this limited success of a few opposition parties was that an increased number of Croat voters did not cast ballots at all. This reduced the number of votes for the HDZ, in some areas quite drastically.[27]

The 'Croat Crisis': The HDZ versus the International Community

In the months following the elections, the SDP and the SBiH, along with a few small Croat parties such as the NHI, the Croat Peasant Party (HSS), and the independent list *'Radom za boljitak'*, formed a new governing coalition called the 'Alliance for Change' (*Alijansa za promjene*). Despite its success among Croat voters, the HDZ had lost power at the Federation and state levels, as had the SDA, its former coalition partner which had suffered its second major electoral defeat in less than a year. HDZ leaders refused to acknowledge this situation, however, claiming that the new government was illegal because it was formed without the main Croat party, and therefore against the will of the majority of the Croat people. In addition, it accused international organisations of trying to manipulate the election results when the OSCE-led Provisional Election Commission dismissed some HDZ representatives from cantonal assemblies for having taken part in organising the referendum.

The HDZ subsequently called for a boycott of all state institutions and, on 3 March 2001 in Mostar, the 528 delegates of the 'Croat National Congress' proclaimed a temporary 'self-government' covering all areas of Bosnia-Herzegovina populated by Croats. The HDZ even managed to get Croat soldiers in the Federation Army to leave their posts until a compromise was found by

---

[27]   For comparison, the number (not the percentage) of votes for the HDZ at the cantonal level shows that, between September 1998 and November 2000, this party lost 6,842 votes (about 25 percent) in the Western Herzegovina Canton, 3,071 votes (14 percent) in the Livno Canton, and 1,905 votes (4 percent) in the Herzegovina-Neretva Canton.

promising them provisional salaries from the 'Croat National Congress'. In Posavina, central Bosnia, and Herzegovina, veteran associations occupied the barracks of Croat components of the Federation Army, and also organized street demonstrations and road blockades.

The proclamation of a Croat 'self-government' further intensified the conflict with international organisations. On 7 March 2001, the High Representative dismissed Ante Jelavić from the Bosnian Presidency, banning him from serving in any political capacity in the future. On 6 April, with the support of SFOR troops, the *Hercegovačka Banka* was placed under international control with the stated justification that the financing of the illegal Croat 'self-government', as well as some criminal activities, were being channelled through this bank. At that time, street violence in opposition to international organisations escalated in Herzegovina, or, more precisely, was organized on a large scale by Croat activists. Later, some Croat politicians who were members of the Alliance were targets of bomb attacks. All of these events contributed to a tense atmosphere in Croat Herzegovina.

At their peak, these initiatives garnered much support among the Croat population for the HDZ and its 'fight for Croat interests'. But as the situation calmed down, and in the course of the next months, a more differentiated attitude became evident in Croat public opinion. The idea began to take hold that the HDZ was encouraging isolation for the sole purpose of allowing dominant HDZ elites to maintain their profitable businesses. Even the HDZ Mayor of Mostar, Neven Tomić, publicly expressed this opinion. With a thinly-disguised hint to his own party, he stated in an interview that 'we have specific forces [within the HDZ] that cannot cope with a situation when there is normal communication, since they cannot function without conflict'.[28]

In the end, the HDZ attempt to mobilize the Croat population failed. One of the first and most important setbacks was the fact that the HDZ was not able to pay the Croat soldiers whom the 'Croat National Congress' had ordered to leave their duty posts. The blockage of all transactions via the *Hercegovačka Banka* played an important role in this context. Just a few weeks after the start of the Croat soldiers' rebellion, negotiations began for their return to regular command. First, the new Federation Minister of Defence from the Alliance, former HDZ member Mijo Anić, succeeded in convincing some officers in Posavina and central Bosnia to return to the Federation Army. After it became clear that the HDZ had failed to uphold the unity of all Croat military leaders, the Croat military in Herzegovina also returned to regular service. The HDZ further failed in its attempt to form a uniform front of Croat businessmen to support the plan for a Croat 'self-government'. Despite having declared themselves officially in support of the idea, most of them feared the consequences of being systematically isolated by the international community.

---

[28]   *Oslobođenje*, 19 June 2001.

The confrontation between the HDZ and international organisations also met with criticism from the government in Croatia, as well as from an increasing section of the Croat population in Bosnia-Herzegovina. Croats in many parts of Bosnia, where they formed only small local minorities, had felt uncomfortable with the idea of a 'third entity' from the very beginning. Even in central Bosnia, the project of a Croat 'self-government' was regarded as an impossible goal to realize in the face of opposition by the Federation Government and the international community, given that most Croat communities formed enclaves within territories inhabited by other national groups. In Herzegovina, too, popular support was increasingly fading. In the predominantly Croat western Herzegovina, with its relatively well-off economy, people increasingly feared that nothing could be gained out of this confrontation, and that the HDZ was only risking further deterioration in the standard of living, a trend that had began to be felt in that area. The idea of a Croat 'self-government' likely remained attractive the longest among Croat displaced persons settled in the formerly mixed municipalities of Central Herzegovina, south-east of the Neretva.

Conclusion

Several factors can help to explain the 'exceptionalism' of Croat Herzegovina. Some of them were rather short-lived, as for instance the relative economic prosperity in western Herzegovina or the power of the 'Herzegovinian lobby' in Croatia throughout the 1990s. Others reach further back into the past, like the great importance of the Catholic Church in Herzegovinian Croat community life, the political marginalization of western Herzegovina after World War II, and the development of a significant diaspora with roots in this region. In addition, this Croat Herzegovinian 'exceptionalism' has much to do, of course, with the concentration of HDZ strategic interests in this region. HDZ policy had deeply affected the social realities of Croat Herzegovina during the war and throughout the 1990s, as the region, in keeping with plans for a 'Greater Croatia', had de facto become attached to Croatia proper, both at the political and economic levels.

The 'Croat crisis' of 2000-2001 brought about a break in this configuration and resulted in a new kind of Croat political factionalism in Bosnia-Herzegovina. The HDZ could not prevent other Croat political parties from participating in the Bosnian and Federation governments and thereby gaining the support of the international community. Once in power, these parties were able to distribute material resources to at least portions of the Croat population and local power holders. This was particularly true for Croats living in Posavina and central Bosnia, which had been less of a priority in HDZ politics for years. In the months following the 'Croat crisis', therefore, the position of Ante Jelavić and his closest supporters became more and more awkward. New divisions came to the fore within the HDZ and, at the party convention held in October 2001 in Mostar, Ante

Jelavić officially announced the end of the Croat 'self-government'. Six months later, he relinquished the party leadership. The defeat of the HDZ during the 'Croat crisis' weakened the party's position and, as an indirect consequence, also reinforced the institutions of the Federation. Many Croat politicians, officers and company directors started to join the Croat political parties that belonged to the Alliance for Change, not only to continue ethnic quota politics under new circumstances but also to save their own 'armchairs'.

Against this background, Croat political factionalism was no longer expressed primarily through internal fights within a hegemonic HDZ but increasingly took place in public and between various competing political parties. A new constellation of outspoken, rather than hidden, political antagonisms became a common feature of everyday life. This transformation of Croat politics without question modified the political landscape in the Federation and in Bosnia-Herzegovina as a whole. It remained less accentuated in Croat Herzegovina, however. Here, the HDZ could still count on its control of cantonal and local administrations, its dense network of activists, and its economic power. Although defeated by the international community, it was still able to win over (or to 'buy') small Croat parties as strategic coalition partners, and to convince a major part of the local Croat population of the need to stay *zajedno*, whereas those expressing scepticism or discontent about their *foteljaši* were rather inclined to withdraw from any political (or electoral) activity.

Chapter 5

In Search of 'Decent People':
Resistance to the Ethnicization of Everyday Life among the Muslims of Stolac

Torsten Kolind

Introduction

This chapter explores the relation between war, violence and identities in the Muslim community of Stolac, a minor town in southeast Bosnia-Herzegovina.[1] When the war broke out in April 1992, the Muslims and Croats of Stolac together faced the same enemy, the Yugoslav People's Army (JNA), but one year later, the Croat Defence Council (HVO) suddenly turned its back on its former Muslim allies (see Grandits, this volume). In July 1993, the entire male Muslim population was placed in concentration camps (*logori*), the Muslim parts of the town were looted and destroyed, and women and children were deported to areas under control of the Bosnian Army. Ethnic cleansing happened both at the material and symbolic levels (Stolac Municipality 2001). After the war, when the first Muslims started to return, with the support of international organizations, many of the remaining Muslim houses were dynamited or burned as part of an attempt to prevent the return process. Due to these outbursts of violence, the Croat Mayor of Stolac was twice sacked by the High Representative, and the local police was placed under the close scrutiny of the International Police Task Force (IPTF). When I did my fieldwork in Stolac from September 2000 to April 2001, the violence had almost stopped and a large part of the Muslim population had returned.[2] The town was still divided at the

---

[1]   In 1991, according to the population census, the municipality of Stolac had 18,681 inhabitants (Muslims: 43.4 percent; Croats: 33.1 percent; Serbs: 21.0 percent), and the town itself had 5,530 inhabitants (Muslims: 62.0 percent; Serbs: 20.1 percent; Croats: 11.8 percent).

[2]   According to the daily newspaper *Dnevni Avaz* (8 December 2001), between 1998 and 2001, about 3,700 Muslim refugees had returned to the municipality of Stolac, and 1,700 to the town itself. During my fieldwork in Stolac, most of the Muslim returnees were confined to a few neighbourhoods in the eastern and southern part of the town that were heavily destroyed during the war.

institutional level,[3] but small islands of interaction had (re)developed in the private sphere.

My findings suggest that war has profoundly changed the landscape of cultural identities at all levels of social life. Ethno-religious identity (*nacionalnost*) has been lifted to the foreground in both the public and private spheres. It has become the most important mode of identification, determining or influencing nearly all others. This finding corresponds with other anthropological studies, which have shown the inherent potential of violence and war to create new identities (Appadurai 1998; Feldman 1991; Sorabji 1995). At the same time, however, other kinds of culturally informed categorizations still exist and, in some situations, are even more important. Furthermore, when ethnic categories and stereotypes are employed, they are often complex and situational. I would therefore argue for the existence of a counter-discourse which works in opposition to both nationalist propaganda and the actual political practices of ethnic separation.

The counter-discourse that I locate among the Muslims of Stolac persistently resists stereotypical labelling of ethnic others and keeps open the possibility for interaction between ethnic groups (*narodi*). It is not a predominant or a well-defined analytical discourse; it is not even possible to locate persons who can act as its pure representatives.[4] What characterizes everyday life in Stolac is, rather, a constant tension between a nationalistic discourse informed by war – excluding the ethnic other in general and arguing for the impossibility of future co-existence – and local modes of identification related to concrete situations – rejecting ethnic stereotypes and trying to facilitate co-existence and rebuild everyday life. This shifting between two attitudes is not a matter of truth or falsehood – that the Muslims of Stolac are lying in one situation and revealing in others how they really feel about the ethnic other. For this reason I refrain from simplistic use of the concept of 'resistance'. In a way it is possible to see the Muslim counter-discourse as resistance towards the hegemonic ideology and practices of nationalist exclusion. However, much anthropological literature alludes to resistance as expressions of real, genuine or sincere acts originating from an authentic inner core (Scott 1990). In contrast, rather than distinguishing between posturing and reality, I

---

[3]   At the time of my fieldwork, the municipal council was dominated by the Croat Democratic Union (HDZ), and Muslim counsellors were completely excluded from the local administration. Similarly, Muslim returnees were excluded from the local public health care and local public employment. Since the reunification of the cantonal police in the Herzegovina-Neretva Canton in June 2000, the local police station was officially multiethnic, but interethnic cooperation was in reality very rare. Since May 2000, Muslim school children have been permitted to attend the local primary school (until then, classes for Muslim children took place in private houses), but classes for Muslim and Croat children were still held separately. On institutional segregation in Stolac, see Revival of Stolac 2001.

[4]   Throughout this chapter I present the Muslims of Stolac as a more or less homogeneous group. This is naturally not the case. I do not have the space to elaborate on internal differences, though I want to mention that they primarily relate to age and place of residence during the war (see e.g. Povrzanović-Frykman 1997, 2001).

would see such conflicting practices as 'evidence of the coexistence of deeply felt yet contested discourses' (Gal 1995: 413).

What is often at stake at the local level for people living in traumatized societies like that of Bosnia is not primarily a matter of politics. People's lives have been unmade due to the violent erosion of their ontological security and the everyday taken-for-granted world (Nordstrom 1997; Scarry 1985). Remaking or rebuilding an everyday life both practically and meaningfully is therefore about being able to recontextualize the narratives of devastation and thereby generate new contexts through which everyday life may become possible (Das and Kleinman 2001; Maček 2000; Warren 1993; Zur 1998). I am therefore not arguing for the existence of an ideology of resistance to ethnic categorization but rather, as Veena Das and Arthur Kleinman put it in a discussion of similar matters, 'we are looking not necessarily for a grand narrative of forgiveness and redemption but for the small local stories in which such communities are experimenting with ways of inhabiting the world together' (Das and Kleinman 2001: 16). In what follows, I will examine three areas of such recontextualization which together form what I call a counter-discourse. These areas relate to 'politics', 'decent people' and, lastly, the complex use of the ethnic label 'Croat'.

Politika as Moral Category and Explanatory Device

Politika, or 'politics', is a central component in the lives of the Muslims of Stolac: during the last decade, the politics of the region and towards the region have had catastrophic consequences, among them the politicisation of many aspects of everyday life. Moving beyond the common understanding of politics as 'realpolitik', I will try to analyse *politika* as a category of moral action created and used by the Muslims of Stolac in order to resist the invasion into everyday life of ethnic categories, and to account for ungraspable aspects of life produced by the war.

Politicians and the field of politics in Stolac are associated with a specific moral (one should rather say immoral) universe, a universe sharply contrasting with the life and ethical standards of ordinary people. This is probably related to the lack of political modernization in Yugoslavia, where civil society as a mediating level between everyday life and state politics never seems to have really developed. As a result, large parts of the population did not relate to political decision making, and when they did it was through fixed patron-client relationships (Allcock 2000: 245-308, 351-76; Sunić 1998). It is my impression that this distance between the political realm and people's everyday worlds has grown larger throughout the war and post-war periods.

The Muslims of Stolac are very direct when talking about the moral universe of *politika*: politics are perceived as the pursuit of power for the sake of power and politicians are seen as people who think only of themselves; they are depicted as cynics, scheming and untrustworthy. *Politika* is also linked to other specific cultural types of blameworthy actions: corruption and criminality (see also Helms, Grandits, Armakolas, this volume). Politicians are often seen as not merely cunning but also involved in direct criminal activities such as fraud, bribery, smuggling, drug sales, and incitement to actual violence. All together, *politika* represents an ethically devalued universe consisting of immoral actions and immoral persons sharply contrasted with another category of persons I will come back to in the next section: *pošteni ljudi* (decent/honest people). When I asked Nermin,[5] one of my informants, about the meaning of the word '*politika*', he smiled a little, showing that there was much more to the word:

> *Politika* is something that is above you, something ordinary people do not understand or have any influence over. *Politika* is something being done by people far away, those who do not have to live with the consequences of their actions; it is cynical and egoistic acts. For instance our people [Muslim politicians] in Sarajevo are requesting people to return to Stolac, so when the year has passed they can say: 'Look, now a thousand Muslims are living in Stolac, now the Croats can no longer say that this is Croat territory.' But none of them ever come down here to see how we live, or just to talk to us. They do not care about common people, what we think or feel. We have a saying: '*politika je kurva*' ['politics is a whore'] – they are only doing it for themselves, like a whore is only doing it for money.

Using *politika* as an explanatory device is a withdrawal from using ethnic stereotypes and as such resists the dominance of ethnic identities created by war-related violence and the post-war political situation. In using the cultural category *politika*, the Muslims of Stolac insist on blaming not the Croat or Serb other, but the politicians: the war was not the result of an aggressive Serb mentality but of the actions of Slobodan Milošević, and it is not because of the Croats that they have suffered and still suffer, but because of Franjo Tuđman and his party, the Croat Democratic Union (HDZ). To put it simply, there is an element of resistance in merely avoiding ethnic categories as explanatory devices.

It is also possible, however, to find components of a more conscious critique of nationalist ideologies and practices that clearly and unambiguously maintain that Muslims, Croats and Serbs cannot live together due to differences in mentality. Contrary to the discourse of nationalism, the Muslims of Stolac assert that if it had not been for politicians and the forces of *politika*, ethnic identities would never have become a determining factor and the war would never have occurred (see also Helms, Jansen, Armakolas, this volume). They stress that politicians stir up ethnic divisions and fears in order to maintain power, that they manipulate people, and that, if it were not for the present politics, all the citizens of Stolac could easily live together again. They further say that society is not functioning due to a lack of political will, and that, if politicians would sit down together and work for the

---

[5]   All names in this chapter are pseudonyms.

future of Bosnia-Herzegovina, many of the present day economic, social and legal problems would be solved:

> Anvere: Before [the war], we had good relations with the Orthodox and Catholics. It is interesting that after this war, which was so terrible, we have come back to this city where Croats have occupied everything. And despite everything that happened, we still have contacts with our neighbours and we live and work together. We are a people who have lived together for a thousand years. Many of the politicians are to blame for what happened; they keep repeating that we cannot live together. They say that people cannot live together, but in spite of that, we do.

The Muslims of Stolac also talk about how it was politicians who forced the Croats or Serbs to participate in the war and in actual violent acts. In the same manner, they often state that the war and post-war violence and discrimination did not occur because people in general are mad or because ordinary Croats or Serbs are evil, it occurred because they were placed by politicians in situations beyond their control, in situations without choices. Again, ethnic difference is presented as a positive aspect of daily life that was manipulated by the politicians. Safet told me that when the Serbs occupied the Stolac area in 1992, every Serb capable of carrying arms was forced into uniform and those who did not turn up at the barracks were picked up. He continued:

> When the Serbs withdrew from Stolac they were on the hill just behind our house. At that time we were communicating with the Croats. We knew that the Serbs would withdraw in a couple of days, but just in case we armed ourselves so that they would not come down and hurt the women and children. Then my father came, whispering to me and Emir that if we saw Goran [a Serb friend forced in uniform] we should not shoot at him. But it was war and we were afraid to go out of the house. Even so he said that we should not shoot at him. Everything happened at night when you cannot see if someone is coming with a gun. Nevertheless my father said that we should be careful not to shoot Goran. This is how my father is, and this is the way he taught us to be.

Goran has returned to Stolac. He tills the soil together with Safet's father and they are still good friends. The use of *politika* as counter-discourse, however, should not be confused with actual practices of interaction. There are small islands of interaction but the Croats, Muslims and Serbs mostly keep to themselves and I am not sure this would change overnight if the political climate were to change. This does not mean that people's constructions and uses of *politika* are a pretence. Instead it should be seen as a part of the (new) world that people creatively try to (re)construct around themselves, a world that makes sense of a senseless past and present, and that offers guidelines for future behaviour. It is thus possible to say that the use of *politika* is also political. It is a social vision, an attempt to create a picture of a future Stolac rid of the immoral force of *politika*, a place where Muslims would have the same opportunities and rights as Croats, and where the different ethnic groups could co-exist as they did before the war.

The use of the cultural category *politika* represents a critique of the ethnicization of the world. Tension still exists, however, when Muslims state for instance that while politicians are all scheming power-seekers, 'their' politicians do this even more than 'ours' do, or when political parties are seen as in fact representing the mentality of the ethnic groups they claim to represent. In these instances the Muslims of Stolac suddenly identify with 'their' own political parties. In other cases, they say that people have been brainwashed and manipulated by nationalist politicians, but that Croats are much easier to manipulate and that 'they' are manipulated in many more spheres of life that Muslims are:

> Safet: In the Bosniac areas the SDA loses every time, so that the SDP, the SBiH and the others [non-nationalist parties] are getting more and more votes and SDA fewer and fewer. But in the Serb Republic the SDS gets the largest portion [of votes], and in the Croat areas HDZ gets most of the votes. … I am also in favour of those changes [against nationalist parties], but they [Croats and Serbs] are not. They think that national parties will help them, but if they could understand, they would see that the politics of nationalism are losing.

What we have here is a critique of politicians, and especially the nationalist ones who, as Safet says, do not really help ordinary people. But it is also an indirect critique of the ethnic other. It is an example of how ethnic categorization is at the same time resisted (by blaming the politicians and referring to the immoral state of *politika*) and also used as a framework for explaining the present lack of inter-ethnic interaction (because the Croats are not in favour of changes). It is exactly this ambivalence which is so characteristic of post-war Stolac.

Sometimes the use of *politika* as an explanatory device extends beyond the simply rational uses I have described so far and is established as an almost independent force or agent operating in the world. It is used to explain, or more correctly, to put aside events and feelings that are too radical to be comprehended. In such cases, *politika* is not necessarily somebody doing something. It is rather a free-floating autonomous power, by reference to which the unmaking of the world is given a conceptual place (see also Helms, this volume). This force is used to explain or grab hold of the unexplainable or the ungraspable. People have experiences – and here I am referring to both war traumas and present social and personal problems – that cannot find relief or expression through ordinary language. There are no public symbols or representations that could absorb or give meaning to them (see also Maček, this volume). Thus, people resort to existing cultural and moral categories, which they mould to function as some kind of representation of the disintegrated and unmade world. *Politika* is such a moral category externalising the madness in relation to everyday life.

By way of example, an old woman I visited a lot during my fieldwork often told me about the war, or rather tried to tell about the war, but it was as if she never succeeded in creating a story that could explain or give meaning to all the losses she had experienced. This is a short extract from my fieldnotes:

She is talking about life during the war, and it is obvious that it is sad, tears are running down her cheeks, and her speech is halting. The story doesn't have a clear line or structure; if there is one it is: we were expelled, we came to Jablanica to the refugee camp, we stayed there, we did not know what had happened to our men, fathers or sons, there were continuing bombardments, we only had a little food, it was hard, and then we returned. The war is told very personally, in total contrast to a political science analysis. *Politika* is continually evoked to account for this unexplainable element.

In this extract, I was trying to sketch a structure in the woman's account. Many other war stories similarly exhibit such discontinuity of events, memories and feelings. *Politika* is a way to link all these fragments, to give them some kind of framework and meaning. Abrupt flashes of memory are linked together, not by an overarching and coherent narrative, but by an abstract force creating havoc and escaping the understanding of ordinary people. Along these lines, it is possible to synthesize a structure representative of many of the stories I heard in Stolac, a structure with *politika* at its core: 'We were living happily together, then came this insane war, it could be so nice here, but – *politika!*'

Decency Rather than Ethnicity

On the moral scale adhered to by the Muslims of Stolac, *politika* is opposed to the category of *pošteni ljudi*. Whereas *politika* alludes to actions and persons existing in a separate and rather abstract sphere, the kinds of actions and persons referred to with *pošteni ljudi* are embedded in local and face-to-face relations. *Pošteni ljudi* means something like decent, honest and straightforward people. To behave decently is to be able to provide for oneself and one's family, to be honest and hard-working, to be self-sacrificing, to be considerate to others and to pay visits to them, and also to remain the same no matter what pressures or temptations to which one is exposed. It refers to an inner essence or character, and sometimes also to religious devotion, implying that if one is a true believer one is also a decent human being. As one woman stated: 'I only believe in God and decent people; money – one day you have some, the next one you have nothing.' This utterance came as she talked about how her daughter and son-in-law were to come to visit her from Germany but she did not have a bed or mattress on which they could sleep. She and her husband themselves slept on a bed without mattresses. Before the war her house had been fully equipped. What the woman meant, in other words, was that war can strip people of their material possessions but not of their decency.

With *pošteni ljudi*, as with *politika*, the Muslims of Stolac have an important tool that can be used to evaluate concrete behaviours without resorting to ethnic categories (see also Jašarević, Maček, this volume). One day, Muhamed, Mala and I were talking about Villa Ragusa, a house in a beautiful setting by the river, which before the war had been the local *dom kulture* (House of Culture) where young people enjoyed themselves on Saturday nights and where musical performances were held. During the war, a Croat family called Raguz rented the house very cheaply under some rather unclear circumstances and turned it in to a fashionable restaurant serving rich Croats and international personnel visiting Stolac. What was more, the Raguz family is one of the most influential families in Stolac, and they are said to have played a role in the destruction and looting of Stolac, as well as the deportation of its Muslim population. So the restaurant is perceived as a symbol of the destruction of the city, the humiliation of the Muslims, and the enrichment of local Croat politicians. As Muhamed explained:

> I knew Martin Raguz [6] when he didn't even have enough money to buy cigarettes. But a friend of mine has been to his flat in Sarajevo. It was stuffed with original paintings, and his daughter plays tennis. But in fact he comes from a village. They were not poor but certainly not rich. The only reason they have become rich is through criminality and corruption, because the wealth they have … cannot have been obtained by decent work, because you do not become rich by that. You cannot become rich by working with your hands. You can live well, sure. We have lived well. We have had food on the table, in the summer we were able to go to the seaside, I was able to build my own house, but we were not rich. Even if I had worked twenty-four hours a day we would not have been rich. You do not get rich through decent and honest labour. If I had been rich, I would have had someone to build my house for me. It took me seven years to build my house.

By referring to decency and, implicitly, to the category of *pošteni ljudi*, Muhamed was condemning the owners of Villa Ragusa. But everything they represented and all the actions they have been involved in were not explained by reference to an intrinsic Croat mentality but to their personal indecency, in sharp contrast to Muhamed's own work ethic.

During the war, many people experienced disappointment (see also Maček, Jansen, Armakolas, this volume). I heard many stories of how friends and neighbours, especially those of different ethnic background, had suddenly let people down, did not help when needed – neither during nor after the war, they failed to share surplus goods, and they did not even come to visit. Though such stories were common, former friends or neighbours were seldom criticized explicitly. Instead, the situation was outlined, leaving moral judgement to the listener. This aspect of moral judgement very often referred to values associated with the category of *pošteni ljudi* and the saying that people reveal their true nature during hard times.[7] Sefer's mother originates from a *mahala* (neighbourhood)

---

[6]   Martin Raguz is one of the leaders of the HDZ and one of the most prominent Croat politicians in Bosnia-Herzegovina. He was briefly appointed Prime Minister of Bosnia-Herzegovina between October 2000 and February 2001, and then, on 3 March 2001, became the 'coordinator' of the self-proclaimed 'Croat self-government' (see Grandits, this volume).

[7]   'One gets to know his friends in misfortune' ('*Čovjek upozna svoje prijatelje u nevolji*').

where many Croats had settled well before the war and where her *prvi komšija* (first neighbour) had been a Croat:

> We had a good relationship with their children. My wife went to gymnasium with their daughter, and we were *kumovi* [witnesses] at their wedding. We spent a lot of time together. They came here and we visited them. We were together at least every second or third week, but today we do not see each other. We haven't heard from them since the war. I know they are rich, they have an apartment in Jablanica and they drive a BMW. But we haven't heard from them. I am not going to contact them and, you know – it would be a little like apologizing – to ask if we are going to see each other again. But if they come to our place, they will be welcome; they will get everything they need. But they never called us or tried to help us even though they are rich.

The moral universe surrounding the category *pošteni ljudi* has direct bearing of the judging of war-related behaviours. Stolac Muslims accept that people were forced into uniforms, that soldiers shot at each other, in short, that there was immense pressure on everybody. *Pošteni ljudi* is used to categorize those people who behaved decently in such a situation. The day the male Muslim population was expelled from Stolac, some of the men escaped and others hid in the hills. For those who hid, it was terrible to watch helplessly as fathers and husbands were taken away, their children and grandchildren calling out desperately. It was equally unpleasant in the weeks afterwards to live in a state of uncertainty, knowing that the Croats could come back at any time. Nusret was one of those who hid himself. One day when Croat soldiers returned to his house, he knew he had to give himself up, as much as anything for the sake of his family:

> In front of the house was a Croat whom I did not know. He was from somewhere in [central] Bosnia. He made a lot of noise and wanted to shoot us. But there was another one with him, one of my former work colleagues, whom I had helped to build his house. When I recognized him I knew he was not going to hurt me. So I walked out of the house and talked to him. Then we smoked a cigarette together and he said to me, 'Nusret, nothing is going to happen to you or to your family, you just have to think carefully' [not to do anything rash]. Nobody touched me.

Nusret stressed that his former colleague 'did not touch him' and that they were smoking a cigarette together, implying that this man had had no choice, and did not enjoy the situation either.

The categorization of actions and persons in relation to decency and non-decency instead of ethnicity can also function as an important tool in facilitating interaction with people of different ethnic backgrounds. The category *pošteni ljudi* can go beyond ethnicity, not suppressing it but rendering it less important. An obvious case is with relationships among former friends and neighbours of different ethnic backgrounds. As in many other places, rumours and gossip are a very important source of information in Stolac. People generally know where their neighbours were during the war, whether they have relatives abroad and where, what their children do for a living, who their children's spouses are, and all kinds of other information conducive to good relations. Even so, people do not know everything, especially when it comes to Serbs who spent the war in the *Republika Srpska* or in Serbia, or Croats who remained in Stolac during the cleansing and looting of the city. Categorising those people as decent removes the uncertainty that always hangs over what they did during the war, where their sympathies lay then and now – in short whether one can trust them again as one did before (see also Armakolas, Jansen, Jašarević, this volume). Often when Stolac Muslims are talking about renewed interaction with friends and neighbours of different ethnic background, they unequivocally stress that these are *pošteni ljudi*. One can say that the category of decency fills in the hole of insecurity that has been left behind by the lack of social knowledge. In some cases, in a kind of reverse logic, the Muslims of Stolac state that the very fact that people returned shows that they are decent and that they did nothing wrong during the war.

After the war, ethnicity continued to pervade everything, including friendships and love relationships. Cross-ethnic relations are no longer unproblematic and must be clarified each time in a way they do not when Muslims interact among themselves. Against this background, the category of *pošteni ljudi* helps resume and legitimatize these *a priori* tense and problematic relationships.

Complexity in Ethnic Categorization as Part of the Counter-Discourse

I have argued that Stolac Muslims use non-ethnic moral judgements, that is, moral classifications and condemnations through reference to non-ethnic cultural categories. This is not to say that ethnic denunciation does not exist. Sometimes Muslims harshly criticize Croats in general. A central experience is, naturally, the feeling of betrayal. Once trusted friends and acquaintances suddenly let people down, either by participating in the violent expulsion of the Muslims or simply by failing to act, even to warn those they knew. Such deceit is difficult to come to terms with. Sometimes Muslims explain this shift in attitude by ascribing it to the Croat mentality, along the lines of, 'they let us down because they are that kind of people and we were stupid to trust them'.

> Salko: During World War II, exactly the same thing happened to the Serbs here in Stolac as happened to us now at the hands of the Croats. Croats caught the Serbs and threw them into big mass graves in the ground. They tied thirty people together, for instance, and threw them into these pits and that's why they fled from the Croats in this war.
> Salko's son: It happened in '41 and '42.
> Salko's friend: During World War II the Croats killed a lot of Serbs from the Stolac area. During this war they did nearly the same to us.

Today, distrust is very pronounced between Stolac Muslims and Croats. When I asked Muslims whether it was possible for the two groups to live together again, many responded that it was too soon. The feeling of not being able to trust Croats is one of the major obstacles to (re)building relations with them. Moreover, the Croats are perceived as being generally better off than the Muslims, taking all the jobs and controlling the local political scene. Despite this, Muslims say that Croats are always complaining of discrimination by the 'international community'. This is felt as a provocation by the Muslims of Stolac, since they consider themselves the ones who suffered and who still face severe discrimination.

Fierce statements based on ethnic stereotypes are often expressed when the subject is nationalism, war-related violence, or post-war political discrimination. The fact that a Muslim says, for instance, that 'all Croats are fascists', or that 'they will never change', therefore does not demonstrate anything. It is important to take such utterances into context and to know what the same person says about Croats under different circumstances. Sometimes Stolac Muslims state that all Croats are and have always been fascists, and at other times they insist that you cannot group them all together because only Croats coming from outside Stolac cause trouble.[8] This suggests that even though the war and war-related violence have clearly carved out different ethnic identities, these identities remain complex, fragmented, inconsistent, and very much related to the situation in which they are employed and in which they function as ordering devices.

The Muslims of Stolac clearly conceptualize several different categories of Croats, each with different moral values attached. Complexity, rather than uniformity, thus characterizes what is meant by 'being a Croat' in the eyes of the Muslims. This complexity attached to the Croat ethnic identity is part of the Muslim counter-discourse.

One of the categories of Croats in Muslim discourses is the '*Croats from Central Bosnia*'. The main issue associated with the presence of Croat displaced persons from central Bosnia in post-war Stolac is housing (see Grandits, this volume): I have met several Muslims in Stolac who live in a rented house or with relatives because their own residence is occupied by refugees. These Muslims obviously want the occupiers to leave, saying that they have no right to settle in their houses or flats. The Muslims of Stolac often say that it is precisely this group of Croats that is making trouble, burning down houses, beating up Muslims, blowing up Muslim cafés, and generally threatening Muslims in the hopes that they will give up the idea of returning and thereby reclaiming their property.

The line of reasoning is clear. Croats from central Bosnia were told that Muslims would never return. Suddenly, however, Muslims started to return and, even though the first step was to rebuild destroyed Muslim houses, it was clear that repossession of occupied houses would be next to come. Croats from central Bosnia occupying Muslim houses are therefore the ones who have the most to lose by the return process. Even so, many Muslims have a contradictory attitude toward

---

[8]   On similar reasoning in Sarajevo, see Maček, Stefansson, this volume.

them, feeling some pity for them as well. The Muslims can see the dilemma the displaced Croats are caught in, and say that the Croats have been betrayed.

Another arena of conflict is more cultural and relates to social knowledge. There is a feeling shared by all Muslims of Stolac that Croats from central Bosnia do not know the local culture and codes of behaviour. They lack the cultural competence necessary for living in Stolac; they simply do not fit in. Many Muslims think that a lot of the problems and tensions in the city would be solved if these strangers would only go back to their own villages, just as it would also be better for themselves to return to their place of origin. Stolac Muslims attach various stereotypical characteristics to the Croats from central Bosnia: they say they are backwards but sly at the same time, having left miserable central Bosnia for pleasant Stolac. The point is, however, that such stereotypes are related to specific situations and experiences and, furthermore, that the problem with these people in the Muslims' eyes is not that they are Croats, but that they are strangers and are occupying someone else's houses.

Sometimes Croats from central Bosnia are merged into a larger category, that of the '*Croats from the countryside*'. This is in turn linked to the central distinction between '*kultura*' ('culture') and '*nekultura*' ('non-culture'), one that had already been common in Bosnia-Herzegovina before the war (Bringa 1995; van de Port 1998). Muslims of Stolac often use this distinction to explain the war and make sense of their ruined lives, to condemn bad deeds and locate responsibility. The wartime violence, 'urbicide', and the present lawlessness are thus basically seen as a struggle between people from the countryside and people from the town. Croats from the countryside living in Stolac are therefore considered illegitimate occupiers of both Muslim private houses and the urban public space.[9]

> Mensur: In the villages around Stolac, people live in their own world, they never wanted to send their children to secondary school or university. They had their own world, which was different from ours, and there is hatred between these two worlds. We Stolac people [*Stočani*] take care of the town. Before the war, if somebody came from Europe or another place, he came here to see the *Begovina* [[10]] and all the old houses and antiquities, and people enjoyed seeing this. But these people who lived outside [of the town] Stolac, they did not like it, and this is why they did all these things.

The point to bear in mind is that, while this category of people constitutes a more or less well-defined class of Croats, their main characteristics relate not to their Croat ethnic identity but to a narrow-mindedness stemming from their lack of education and 'non-culture'. Its potential for resistance rests in its ability to disconnect ethnicity and bad deeds, and to make possible interaction with the

---

[9] On similar attitudes towards displaced persons of rural origin in Sarajevo, see Stefansson, this volume.

[10] The *Begovina* ('house of the bey') was a residential ensemble of substantial architectural and historic value dating back from the 19th century. It was set on fire in 1993.

ethnic other by blaming only some particular Croats for the war. In this way it constitutes an element in the Muslims counter-discourse.

'*Naši Hrvati*' ('our Croats') and '*naši domaći Hrvati*' ('our local/homegrown Croats') are expressions used about yet another category of Croats: '*Croats from Stolac*'. Local patriotism constitutes an important source of identification for the Muslims of Stolac, and the 'homegrown' is more or less the icon of this identity; it is by definition superior. Even though it is not always consciously intended, therefore, the utterance '*naši domaći Hrvati*' has positive connotations. The class of Croats from Stolac furthermore exists in definitive opposition to that made up of Croats from both central Bosnia and the countryside, who clearly are not 'homegrown'.[11]

Some consider that Muslims and Croats from Stolac have much more in common than Croats from Stolac do with Croats from Central Bosnia: people originating from Stolac want to talk to each other, they are glad to see each other again, and they want to hear what happened during the war. Some Muslims also emphasize a level of understanding and respect between themselves and Croats from Stolac which outsiders do not understand. When Muslims have good relationships with Croats, it is mainly with this group of Croats, whom they knew before the war.[12]

A common attachment to the town, which unites all 'true' citizens of Stolac, is also stressed when talking about Stolac Croats. The total destruction of the city is hard to grasp, and many Muslims express the idea that the wrongdoers must have come from outside. Some of them even consider that, if it were not for all the Croats from the countryside or from central Bosnia, the Croats who are originally from Stolac would return to their pre-war attitude and everything would be as it had been before. As Mensur expressed it, 'if we only had real Stolac people [*pravi Stočani*], people born here in Stolac, then we would not have any problem. These people come from outside'.

There is a dilemma embedded in such semi-romantic feelings, since Muslims also know that some of the Croats from Stolac participated in the expulsion of Muslims, and even in some of the atrocities, but they do not always know who did what and, more to the point, they do not know how the Croats feel about the expulsion of the Muslims. Did they support it or were they too afraid to stand up and oppose it? Croats from Stolac are therefore simultaneously seen as *pravi Stočani* who identify with the town and respect the Muslims, as well as the very people who let their former friends down. Some Muslims even speculate that the original Croats of Stolac accept the presence of Croats from the countryside and from central Bosnia since, without those fellow Croats they would once again be a

---

[11] On the notion of *domaći* as applied to agricultural products, see Jašarević, this volume.

[12] Some Muslims told me that the HDZ forbid the Croats to mingle with the Muslims, so that former Croat friends would not dare to pay visits in daylight; only at night did they go to their Muslim friends' houses and welcome them back.

minority and would thus have to face the consequences of their own misdeeds. Muslim attitudes towards Croats from Stolac depend on the situation, therefore. In my view, the category of 'good Croats from Stolac' is especially invoked in statements about the legitimate presence and property claims of the Muslims in post-war Stolac, and about the possible expulsion of all its non-native citizens.

The last category I will introduce is more consciously linked to resistance. It relates to the identification of '*good Croats*'. It struck me how many people had one or two stories about some 'good Croats' they knew. It was as if people collected such stories. I deliberately use the term 'stories' because they were commonly told in a clearly dramatic form. A typical story emerged one day as I visited Fatima and Safet. I was served some lovely and tasty white wine, which I commented upon. Fatima responded:

> Fatima: Yes, it is homemade, my aunt brought it. She got it from her neighbours. They are Croats! Yes! My aunt told that when she rode on the *Bregavatrans* bus [the Muslim bus company] two Croat women boarded the bus.
> TK: Was it the first time she saw Croat women in the bus?
> Fatima: Yes. And it was two women my aunt knew. One of them had been one of her good friends, but it was my aunt who had to make contact [*prvo zvala*], they don't do that. They hadn't talked for ten years and my aunt said, 'Come and sit!' and then they talked. ... Now it is difficult to make the first step, but one side has to do it. ... This woman and my aunt gave birth at the same time, they were at the hospital together, and then my aunt did not have enough milk in her breasts to give to her daughter, and so she was given milk by this Croat women. ... Yes that's how it was then, and you don't forget such things.

I do not dispute the correctness of the story. It seems as if people sometimes deliberately omit negative aspects, but this is not the point. People could still choose not to speak about 'good Croats', or they could read events differently. So when informants presented me with such anecdotal accounts I saw it as a more or less deliberate choice which served at least two functions. First, these stories work against the erosion of the moral world that the war and war-related violence have caused (see also Maček, this volume). They express the idea that good and righteous action still persists even in a world which seems to be completely morally flawed; it is still possible to believe in the goodness of a fellow person, even one of different ethnic background. Second, these stories resist the ethnic generalisations and stereotypes which I outlined in the previous section. The use of Croats' individual names have faded away after the war at the expense of the general expression 'they', a development some Muslims explicitly acknowledge. The narratives about 'good Croats' can be seen as working in the opposite direction, as attempts to reinstall the personal pronouns and personalize the relationship toward those Croats one still feels or wants to feel connected to. It is a strategy that attempts to personalize relations which the war related violence has depersonalized.

This section focused on the production by Stolac Muslims of various stereotypes of different categories of Croats. What this intra-ethnic categorization shows is an internal complexity full of contrasts and differences: there are 'evil fascists' on one side and 'good Croats' on the other; Croats of the city and the greedy and uncultured ones from the countryside. Even when Stolac Muslims make fierce and generalizing condemnations, these are rather specific and linked with discussions of violence or discrimination. It is therefore possible to view this complexity as part of a Muslim counter-discourse resisting ethnic categories: stated simply, the complex and fragmented way the Muslims of Stolac use the ethnic label 'Croat' is also an implicit denial of its very relevance.

Conclusion

Among the Muslims of Stolac, there exists today what I have labelled a counter-discourse which argues for the possibility of future existence among the different ethnic groups. The element of resistance in this counter-discourse is the shift away from ethnic categories towards non-ethnic cultural and moral categories in order to condemn actions, claim property, explain misfortunes and changes, or make the world predictable and possible to live in again. *Politika* is such a category through which an abstract and morally loaded class of people is constructed to account for the war. *Pošteni ljudi* is another cultural category, operating more at the local and everyday level, used for evaluating concrete actions and persons. Finally, the Muslims of Stolac distinguish between various kinds of Croats, identified with dissimilar values and mentalities. This very complexity breaks down any monolithic representation of the Croat ethnic identity.

This counter-discourse is not an ideological, deliberate or even fully conscious endeavour. It is more a steady reintroduction and reshaping of already existing cultural categories. Furthermore, it is impossible to fully separate those situations where categories like *politika*, *nepošteni ljudi* or, for example, 'Croats from the countryside' are used as a basis for implicit ethnic condemnation, and those situations where they are used as implicit critique of the ethnicization of the social landscape. This is not due to a lack of analytical tools, but it is because these two implicit, and sometimes explicit, tactics are interwoven and hard to separate, even for people themselves. Blame and exclusion of the ethnic other exist simultaneously with a desire for ethnic co-existence and dissociation from the exclusiveness of nationalist politics and rhetoric. This tension constitutes one of the central features of everyday life among the Muslims of Stolac in their attempts to make sense of the world, which the war and war-related violence have unmade, and results in a feeling of personal and societal confusion. People may appear and act in contradictory ways not because they are schizophrenic but because the social situation is (Mead 1967 [1934]).

A first possible partial explanation for the present counter-discourse among the Muslims of Stolac is the reality of everyday ethnic interaction before the war.

Though this has not been studied thoroughly (Beljkašić-Hadžidedić 1988), ethnographic works from before the war about Bosnia-Herzegovina show that ethnicity and religion did matter in many aspects of everyday life, but that it was only one among several important kinds of categorization (Bringa 1995; Sorabji 1992; Lockwood 1975). Gender, generation, work relations, and local networks were as important and sometimes even more so. Secondly, coexistence among the different ethnic groups often entailed a great deal of respect. Differences were not downplayed, as they are in Scandinavian contexts, for example (Gullestad 1992). They were consistently nurtured, but in a way that Georgieva has described in the Bulgarian context as 'familiarisation of differences' (1999: 66): the network of intertwined relations encompassed all levels of everyday life, eliminated otherness and changed it into familiar difference. The war then dislodged the practical nature of ethnic identities; they were separated from their context and took on new meaning (both political and concrete) through violence. Suddenly ethnicity was, or could easily become, a matter of life or death. This is reflected in the way in which many ordinary people were totally taken by surprise, not only when war started in Yugoslavia, but also when it came to their own place of residence (Bringa 1993; Maček 2000).

The existence of a counter-discourse articulated by Stolac Muslims must also be understood against the background of the post-war situation. Several years after the war, Stolac remains divided at the political and administrative levels, and there is only meagre interaction among members of different ethnic groups. Despite the politicization of ethnic identities, however, nationalist discourses do not completely permeate everyday life, and there is some space left for alternative identifications and interactions at the local level. Some islands of inter-ethnic interaction do exist and are growing: neighbours greet each other on the street and old acquaintances attend friend's funerals, children play football together in the schoolyard, Muslim teenagers use Croat cafés because they have a pool table, people use the same shops and sell different items to each other, and they sometimes travel on the same buses when their 'own' bus is cancelled or delayed. Through tangible interactions, a *modus vivendi* is developing between Croats and Muslims: the strategy people in Stolac use is to avoid talking about politics. As one woman told me, this is not easy at all because everything is so politicized. She found that the only things she could and would discuss with Croat colleagues were cooking and children. Nevertheless, I believe that through the interaction between Croats and Muslims in Stolac a 'working consensus' (Goffman 1990 [1959]: 10) is developing that in many ways supports or informs the Muslims' counter-discourse. Whether this working consensus will in time resemble the habitual integration of ethnic difference into everyday life before the war or will develop new patterns is still too early to say.

PART 2
Beyond 'Ancient Hatred'

Chapter 6

Commemorating Srebrenica:
Histories of Violence and the Politics of Memory in Eastern Bosnia

Ger Duijzings

> [T]hat which is sadly memorable is not easily commemorable.
> Robert Frank, *La mémoire des Français*.

Introduction[1]

With just a few thousand inhabitants and a couple of streets, the eastern Bosnian town of Srebrenica has acquired a global reputation. Its name has become synonymous with what is considered the worst atrocity in Europe after 1945: the massacre of approximately eight thousand Muslim men by Bosnian Serb forces after the fall of the United Nations 'Safe Area' of Srebrenica in July 1995.[2] The UN (with Dutch troops playing a dubious key role) failed to prevent this bloodbath, an outcome that has spawned a number of investigations and reports, starting with a UN document followed by major French and Dutch reports (United Nations 1999; Loncle 2001; NIOD 2002). I contributed to the largest Dutch inquiry carried out by the Netherlands Institute for War Documentation (NIOD). My task was to provide the anthropological and historical background to this event, and to focus on its local dimensions, in order to help answer questions such as why the massacre happened as it did, why local Serbs participated in it, and what role memories of previous conflicts played? Although it is too early to provide comprehensive answers to these questions, I nevertheless tried to shed light on

---

[1] This text is the outcome of an intensive and prolonged exchange with Elissa Helms and Xavier Bougarel. Many of their ideas and suggestions have found their way into the final version of the text, and they also provided me with important sources. Any mistakes or flaws in the analysis are mine.

[2] For the earliest accounts of the Srebrenica massacre, see Honig and Both 1996; Rohde 1997.

them by analyzing the local media, interviewing Muslims and Serbs from the region, and reconstructing events in this part of Bosnia at the end of the 1980s and beginning of the 1990s.[3] In my research, I took a wide historical angle, looking at the legacies of previous episodes of violence, particularly the memories of them, going back almost two centuries. My aim was not to write a conventional history but to examine the ways in which the past was remembered and represented as well as used and instrumentalized before and during the most recent Bosnian war (Duijzings 2002b).

It is clear that myths, collective memories, and commemorative practices helped to fuel the Bosnian conflict (see also Grandits, Bougarel, this volume). One cannot fully understand the war or specific events, such as the Srebrenica massacre, if one ignores the role that perceptions of the past played in people's interpretations of events. It was common among political and military leaders to make historical allusions in order to explain and justify their actions: it is sufficient in this context to point to the references made by General Ratko Mladić to the Battle of Kosovo (1389), during a speech he gave in the nearby town of Bijeljina just days before he started the attack on Srebrenica.[4] Similarly, when his troops entered Srebrenica, on 11 July 1995, Mladić presented the take-over of the town as an act of revenge for the defeat suffered at the hands of the Turks during the First Serbian Uprising (1804-1813): 'We present this city to the Serbian people as a gift. Finally, after the rebellion against the *dahije* [local janissary leaders], the time has come to take revenge on the Turks in this region'.[5] This imagery of past events, such as the Battle of Kosovo and the First Serbian Uprising, is of relevance for an understanding of the ideological context behind the massacre in July 1995, and the mindset of at least some of those who orchestrated and committed these crimes. It is indeed likely that Mladić's worldview was permeated by nationalist epic narratives romanticizing the fight against the Ottoman Turks. As he saw the taking of Srebrenica as revenge for a defeat suffered almost two centuries before, he might just as well have seen the massacre of Muslim men as a way of settling historical accounts with the (purported descendents of the) 'Turks'.

Nevertheless, in my history of Srebrenica (published as an annex to the NIOD report), I tried to avoid drawing a straight line of causation from nationalist myths to ethnic violence and genocide, as some authors have done (e.g. Anzulović 1999; Sells 1996). I developed an approach similar to Pål Kolstø's, who argues that myths do not function or 'act' in one way or another of and by themselves: it is people who employ myths, in more or less harmful ways (Kolstø 2005). In brief, I

---

[3]   Most interviews were retrospective in character, and did not focus on the post-war period. For this reason, I do not refer to them very much in this text.

[4]   He held this speech on *Vidovdan* (28 June), the anniversary of the Battle of Kosovo and the day of the patron saint's day of the Bosnian Serb Army. The local Serb newspaper *Naša Riječ*, appearing in the town of Bratunac, published the speech on its frontpage (*Naša Riječ*, 21 June 1995). The speech is also reprinted in Bulatović 1996: 154.

[5]   For images of Mladić's entry into Srebrenica, see Woodhead 1999.

argued that Serb collective memories of distant historical events (such as the Battle of Kosovo, the First Serbian Uprising and World War I) and the nationalist myths that grew out of them, fed into the living local memories of more recent events, such as the massacres carried out against Serbs by the *ustaše* during World War II and those perpetrated during Muslim attacks on Serb villages around Srebrenica in 1992 and 1993. This blend of nationalist myths, collective memories and localised personal memories resulted in a desire for vengeance among local Serbs, which was one of the key factors contributing to their willingness to participate in the massacre, even though it was planned and ordered from above.

The issue of collective memory after violence is crucial in the present chapter. Since the end of the war, certain Bosnian intellectuals have argued that if Muslims, Serbs, and Croats in Bosnia cannot reach agreement on how to remember events such as the Srebrenica massacre and fail to develop mechanisms to establish a shared narrative about the war, it is difficult to see how the country can continue to exist. I followed a similar line of thought when I wrote my history of Srebrenica, investing much time and effort in trying to weave an 'inclusive' narrative that would do justice to all sides, comparing Muslim and Serb sources, correcting the usual nationalist simplifications and merging various partial narratives into an overarching one.[6] My hope was that this would produce a story that would be acceptable to both Muslims and Serbs. I made a particular effort with regard to World War II, which was never properly dealt with in Yugoslav historiography due to the taboos imposed by the communists (see also Grandits, this volume). According to some authors, this was one of the main causes of the violence of the 1990s: the country's communist elite, and Yugoslav society in general, had never 'worked through' the bitter experiences and unrefined memories of that war (e.g. Denich 1994; Hayden 1994; Höpken 1999). By writing a history 'from below', that is from the perspective of a small town like Srebrenica, I hoped to demonstrate that World War II was more complex than nationalists wanted us to believe, that conflicts ran along and across various ethno-religious and political lines, that alliances shifted and people switched sides (sometimes *en masse*), but also, that people offered each other assistance and support despite being on opposing 'sides'. I wanted to show that nationalist accounts of World War II, in which each community remembers and commemorates from behind the safe walls of its own sanitized versions of history, are often at odds with historical facts and with personal memories. Although I was never very convinced of the idea that there is only one historical truth, I still believed that out of these partial, divergent and mutually exclusive histories it was possible to shape a 'more truthful' version of events.

---

[6]   The main Muslim sources I used were Ibišević 1999, Mašić 1996, Mašić 1999 and Orić 1995. From the Serb side, I used Ivanišević 1994 and Miljanović 1996.

Commemorative Arenas

In this chapter, I extend my analysis of war memories to the present: I look at the 'afterlife' of the Srebrenica massacre, that is the various ways it has been remembered and commemorated, and the effects this has had or may have on the process of reconciliation. I would like to make clear from the outset that, although I made several fieldtrips to eastern Bosnia between 1997 and 2000, this chapter is primarily based on published material which I collected after the completion of my fieldwork. Moreover, since the publication of the NIOD report, my position has evolved: I am now more sceptical about trying to write an 'accurate' and 'inclusive' history, since realities on the ground seem to resist such attempts, at least for the time being. Muslims and Serbs are reluctant, even hostile to attempts to come to a balanced and shared understanding of the past. Because the political will is lacking, a Truth and Reconciliation Commission has never been established. This chapter is an attempt to come to terms with these stubborn post-war realities, and to explore whether this, at first glance undesirable, situation of divided war memories might not perhaps have positive sides.

In my analysis, I apply some of the concepts and approaches used by Timothy Ashplant, Graham Dawson and Michael Roper in their introduction to *The Politics of War Memory and Commemoration* (Ashplant, Dawson and Roper 2000: 3-85). Their approach is useful, as it combines the political and the psychological, which they regard as the two main paradigms in the study of war commemoration. They distinguish between commemorating from above (with elites engineering and orchestrating these processes mainly for political reasons) and from below (where the focus is on the subjective and psychological needs of individuals), and between hegemonic (publicly articulated) and sectional (marginalized, subordinated, suppressed and/or oppositional) narratives. Yet, instead of drawing these distinctions rigidly, they show that there is a complex entanglement between public and private, official and personal, hegemonic and sectional. So, for example, individual experience is often rendered meaningful only through pre-existing 'templates', that is myths, tropes, and dominant narratives, including those of the nation-state. Similarly, grief, far from being 'outside' the sphere of politics, is often framed in pre-existing narrative forms. For this reason, it can be manipulated and mobilized with ease. The authors point out that the politics of war commemoration is also linked to issues of social exclusion and citizenship: sectional memories often demand inclusion and modification of the official regimes of historical truth, for example, through the creation of counter-monuments. The authors advance the idea of a 'commemorative arena', in which there are different issues at stake for those caught up in it, and where outcomes are not decided in advance. This also means that war events and their memories are 'managed' differently by the various actors, depending on their own war experiences, political objectives and interests. What is common to all these perspectives is that they are selective: they remember some episodes while concealing or forgetting others (see also Jansen, Kolind, Helms, this volume).

This approach is relevant for us. One of the characteristics of post-war Bosnia is that there is a wide gap in terms of how Muslims and Serbs perceive the war, which is underpinned by narratives produced by historians, journalists and politicians for 'consumption' within their own communities (see also Bougarel, Grandits, this volume). Though very similar in style and rhetoric, most Muslim and Serb accounts of the war tell completely different stories, documenting suffering among members of their own nation, while ignoring victims on the other 'side'. Apart from this, members of both communities have developed separate commemorative practices. The Muslim commemorations of the massacre taking place opposite the former 'Dutchbat' compound in Potočari and the Serb counter-commemorations organized in the nearby villages of Kravica and Zalazje seem to indicate that there is very little common ground, undermining any attempts to bring the two communities together. Yet, importantly, even though they involve separate Muslim and Serb 'sides', these commemorations also engage with divisions existing *within* each community, both at the local and national levels (see also Bougarel, Jansen, this volume). As is often the case in religious and other rituals, they are instrumental in overcoming these divisions.

Against this background of deeply divided memories, Srebrenica is much more than just a local problem. If wartime antagonisms are already difficult to overcome elsewhere in Bosnia, the brutality and scale of the Srebrenica massacre, the sense of denial among local Serbs, and the bitterness that exists among the families of those who were killed has made reconciliation very difficult if not impossible. Likewise, for Bosnia as a whole the massacre remains a controversial and divisive issue: its legacy rests heavily on the country, as the two most important war criminals sought by the Hague Tribunal, Ratko Mladić and Radovan Karadžić are both indicted for genocide in relation to the Srebrenica massacre and still remain at large. In the eyes of many Bosnians, peace and reconciliation will not be possible as long as the main instigators of the Srebrenica massacre have not faced justice (see Delpla, this volume). Some people including Jakob Finci, leader of the Jewish community and advocate of a Bosnian Truth and Reconciliation Commission, have suggested that the bitter memories of the massacre, and the Serb failure to face up to it and apprehend its perpetrators, will even affect Bosnia's prospects of becoming a 'viable state'.[7]

The post-war situation in Srebrenica is also characterized by a high degree of involvement by the so-called 'international community'. Some organisations, such as the International Commission on Missing Persons (ICMP), assist the victims' families to find and identify their relatives (see Delpla, this volume). Non-governmental organizations (NGOs) (including Dutch ones) provide assistance to Muslims who want to return to Srebrenica, trying to help them build up their lives and re-establish relations with the Serb population. Yet when it comes to shaping the memory of the Srebrenica massacre, the two most crucial players are the International Criminal Tribunal for the former Yugoslavia (ICTY) in The Hague

---

[7] NIOD interview, 24 October 2000.

and the Office of the High Representative (OHR). The ICTY performs an important role in establishing facts and qualifying the crimes perpetrated during the war, although its goals sometimes clash with the immediate needs of the families (Stover and Shigekane 2002; Delpla, this volume). 'Srebrenica' has been thoroughly investigated by the ICTY and several indictments have been issued, including one against the former commander of the Muslim forces in the enclave, Naser Orić. One of the most crucial legacies of the Tribunal is that the Srebrenica massacre has been classified by the court as a case of genocide, an outcome of the conviction of Radislav Krstić (former commander of the Drina Corps of the RS Army) (ICTY 2001). In the long run, this judgement is likely to have important political and judicial implications, affecting relations not only between the Federation and the *Republika Srpska* (RS), but also between Bosnia and Serbia.

The importance of the OHR, on the other hand, stems from its crucial role in shaping the commemoration of the Srebrenica massacre, resulting in the creation of a memorial site on the spot where most of the women of Srebrenica last saw their sons and husbands, the battery factory in Potočari (see Figure 6.3). In this chapter, I look closely at the ways in which the OHR has influenced the local commemorative arena, and what effects this has had on the process of refugee return. At the same time, I also describe how local Serbs have reacted to this increasing international involvement, and how they have tried to influence the ways in which 'Srebrenica' is remembered and commemorated. However, before doing this, I will first look at the historical trajectory of local memories, that is of how Serbs and Muslims in eastern Bosnia have remembered and commemorated previous wars, especially World War II.

Serbs and Muslims: Different Ways of 'Being in History'?

In his book *How We Think They Think*, Maurice Bloch has demonstrated how communities may engage with the past in fundamentally different ways, developing their own specific modus of 'being in history', depending on their social make-up, political position and historical experience (Bloch 1998: 67-84). In ethnically and religiously diverse societies such as Bosnia, this means that in spite of state attempts to impose 'official' versions of the past, communities will connect differently to these official histories, or to the past as such. In this section, I argue that because of their diverging historical experiences, Muslims and Serbs in eastern Bosnia and in the rest of the former Yugoslavia developed different ways of 'being in history', although I would also like to caution against perceiving these differences in absolute and essentialist terms. More specifically, the ways in which Serbs and Muslims were encouraged or discouraged to remember and commemorate crucial episodes from their history, especially World War II, affected the processes of retrieval of war memories at the end of the 1980s and beginning of the 1990s. In more recent years, we will observe that the Muslim way of 'being in history' has been changing and has started to more closely resemble that of the Serbs.

If we look at the Serb side, many authors (including myself) have pointed to the centrality of the past in Serbian nationalism (e.g. Bakić-Hayden 2004; Bieber 2002; Duijzings 2000: 176-202). In general terms, perceptions of perpetual and/or repeated suffering and victimization have been central to Serb mythology, expressed for instance in epic songs that describe the most important events in Serb history. Muslim identity, on the other hand, has been less defined by collective memories of victimization or by the past as such, but is based more on diffuse and implicit notions of a shared religious and cultural tradition. The main reason for this seeming indifference to the past has been that, for the greater part of the twentieth century, Muslims formed a minority in a state (Yugoslavia) that was largely dominated by non-Muslims who treated the Ottoman past with contempt. For Muslims, it was difficult to define their place in history since the Ottomans or 'Turks', as they were always identified, were usually presented in negative terms.

To be sure, events such as the expulsion of Muslims from Serbia during the 1860s and 1870s (which brought many Muslims to eastern Bosnia), the expropriation of land owned by Muslims during the Yugoslav land reforms of the 1920s, and the *četnik* massacres of World War II, left traces in Muslim memories. Yet they were largely private and hidden from the public sphere. As a result, Muslim memories remained rather inarticulate, and history was less of an ideological force than it was among the Serbs. During the first Yugoslavia, official memories were indeed predominantly 'Serbian' in outlook, meaning that Serbia's role in the struggle for independence and the sacrifices it made towards the creation of Yugoslavia were emphasized. In the story of how Yugoslavia came into being, Serbs were the main heroes and suffered the greatest losses, whereas Slovene, Croat and Muslim victims of World War I remained unacknowledged because they had mainly fought on the wrong (Austrian) side. Serbian 'hegemony' in the way World War I was remembered and commemorated was also visible in Srebrenica. In 1924, the Serbs erected a monument in the centre of the town, honouring a Serb volunteer unit led by Kosta Todorović that had suffered many casualties at the start of the war. Whereas Serbs revered him as a hero who had avenged Kosovo and helped to 'liberate' Bosnia, Muslims silently saw Todorović as a criminal who had killed hundreds of Muslims in the district of Srebrenica in 1913 and 1914 (Ibišević 1999: X; Mašić 1999: 15; Orić 1995: 9). The monument remained in place until 1941, when the *ustaše* forced local Serbs to remove it. After World War II the monument was not put back, with the communists eradicating all reminders of the previous 'bourgeois' order and suppressing all signs of interwar Serbian 'hegemony'.

Here, I will not describe World War II in detail, but only look at the ways in which that war was remembered and commemorated.[8] Yet, in order to do this it is

---

[8]   For a comprehensive account of local events during World War II, see Duijzings 2002b: 47-69.

necessary to at least mention some basic facts: Srebrenica was brought under *ustaše* control at the start of the war but then changed hands many times. A substantial proportion of the Muslim population in eastern Bosnia, especially in the villages, joined the *ustaše* movement, and between 1941 and 1943 *ustaše* units carried out several massacres against the local Serb population (among others one in Srebrenica in June 1943). In return, local *četnik* bands massacred numerous Muslims, regularly attacking and pillaging Muslim villages. Towards the end of the war (Autumn 1943) most *četnici* (but also some Muslims) joined the Partisan movement. They came to occupy positions in the administration and the police, in spite of the fact that it was a public secret that some of them had killed their Muslim neighbours. Even though the situation on the ground was extremely complex, massacres on an ethno-religious basis remained a central feature of the war in eastern Bosnia.

After World War II, the communists imposed a simplified and sanitized version of history, reducing the war to a clash between anti-fascist Partisans and fascist 'quislings'. No great emphasis was placed on the fact that this had also been a brutal civil war, which in eastern Bosnia was mainly fought along ethnic lines. Although *ustaša* massacres against the Serbs and *četnik* massacres against the Muslims appear in the post-war historical literature, they certainly were not central in the communist narrative of World War II, which put more emphasis on the heroic Partisan struggle. In addition, a kind of 'ethnic key' was observed when discussing these atrocities, balancing out massacres between *ustaše* and *četnici*. As Wolfgang Höpken argues, the communists carefully and persistently downplayed the war's ethnic dimension, reinterpreting the violence primarily in class terms. They described the war from the point of view of the Partisan victors, demonstrating little sensitivity to contradicting memories and different traumas that the war had caused among various groups (Höpken 1999, 2001; Grandits, this volume).

In and around Srebrenica, the monuments erected after 1945 to commemorate the victims of the war reflected that official history. They did not mention the ethnic background of those killed, referring to them as 'victims of fascist terror'. Yet, there was an 'ethnic' subtext to such monuments, which was obvious to those who knew the local conditions of the war. Most monuments did not list the names of victims, but some of them (such as in Srebrenica and Zalazje) did, and these were Serb names only. What's more, monuments were erected in Serb villages and in mixed towns such as Bratunac and Srebrenica, but no such monuments were placed in Muslim villages. Thus, even though they did not spell out the ethnic belonging of the victims, these monuments left the impression that the Serbs were the main victims of the war. For Muslims the message was clear: their victims remained unnamed because they had been on the 'wrong' side in the war, and for this they were being 'punished'. Serb victims were commemorated because the great majority of Serbs had been on the Partisan side at the end of the war, even though many of them had been *četnici* before and had participated in massacres against the Muslim population. Thus, despite the fact that many Muslims killed in these massacres had been civilians, with no link to the *ustaše*, there was virtually no public acknowledgement or public space for mourning and commemorating these victims.

Official memories under socialist Yugoslavia were therefore not as openly 'Serbian' as they had been during the 1920s and 1930s, but Serbs were still able to commemorate their victims, whereas Muslims had to forget theirs and were basically forced to turn away from the past, thus perpetuating the Muslim way of 'being in history' that had set in after World War I. Yet, the monuments of the communist period did not tell the whole truth even from a Serb perspective, as they silenced the fact that the perpetrators had been Croats or (local) Muslims (e.g. Miljanović 1996: 55). As the communists banned any discussion and reduced the complexities of the war to a simple conflict between Partisans and fascists, no real justice was done in the eyes of either Muslims or Serbs. Both sides felt that their own status as victims had not been fully recognized or truthfully represented, nor had the perpetrators been properly named and punished. In spite of socialist rhetoric, private and unofficial memories lingered on, perpetuating the hidden 'symbolic geography' that had existed during the war: some Serb villages such as Kravica continued to be regarded as *četnik* strongholds, while certain Muslim villages such as Potočari and Osmaće were still seen as *ustaša* strongholds.

While it was easy for Serb nationalists in the 1980s to revive feelings of perpetual Serb suffering, it took more effort to bring memories of Muslim victimization to the surface. Recognition for the Muslim victims of *četnik* terror came only in 1990 with the publication of the book *Genocid nad Muslimanima* [Genocide against the Muslims], which was at the time by far the most comprehensive treatment of *četnik* massacres against the Muslim population during World War II (Dedijer and Miletić 1990). Interestingly, even though it was published in Sarajevo, this book was part of a larger research project sponsored by the Serbian Academy of Science and Arts, investigating the genocide against the Serbs and other Yugoslav nations. It was written by two non-Muslims (Vladimir Dedijer, a Serb, and Antun Miletić, a Croat) who had both also published books on Jasenovac, the largest (*ustaša*) concentration camp on Yugoslav soil during World War II. As such the book exemplified a wider trend, not only in Yugoslavia but also elsewhere, to shift the attention from the 'heroes' of the anti-fascist and Partisan resistance to the civilian victims of the war, including those on 'the enemy' side.

Thus, it was after Serbian intellectuals and politicians started to revive the memories of genocide committed against the Serbs in the Independent State of Croatia (NDH), that the topic of Muslim victimization during World War II entered the public sphere. In the early 1990s, Muslim politicians, historians, journalists and intellectuals started to renew and elaborate these memories, although this process never achieved the same intensity as in Serbia. Journals close to the Islamic Community (*Preporod* and *Glasnik*) and the Party of Democratic Action, the SDA (*Muslimanski glas* and *Ogledalo*), but also former communist newspapers (such as *Oslobođenje*) published numerous articles, series, and special issues on the *četnik* massacres against Muslims during World War II. Part of this process was also the rise of a new culture of public commemoration: on 25 August 1990, for instance, in the midst of the election campaign, the SDA organized a mass meeting in Foča to commemorate the massacres of Muslims in the Drina valley during World War II. It is in this period that the key elements of a newly emerging Muslim 'genocide' discourse were laid down, most notably during a conference organised by the Muslim cultural society *Preporod* ('Rebirth') in November 1991. At this conference, prominent historians such as Mustafa Imamović, Smail Čekić and Šemso Tucaković proclaimed that the genocide that took place during World War II was only one episode in a long series of 'genocides' against the Muslim population that had started in the late seventeenth century and continued to the present day. According to them, during the twentieth century this continuous genocide has also taken the form of an economic genocide (with the land reforms after World War I) as well as a cultural genocide (with the attempts at cultural assimilation and secularization during the first and the second Yugoslavia, respectively). This narrative was further developed and elaborated in publications that appeared during and after the war, contributing to the process of Bosniac nation-building (see Bougarel, this volume).

From the Revival of Genocide to the Serb 'Liberation' of Srebrenica

By the beginning of the 1990s, both Serb and Muslim politicians were using World War II memories to mobilize their constituencies, but the extent to which they employed history as an ideological and political tool was different. As described above, on the Serb side, remembering and commemorating events such as the Battle of Kosovo, the First Serbian Uprising and World War II was a crucial aspect in the pursuit of war; it helped to camouflage the territorial, economic and political interests that formed a crucial impetus for the wars of the 1990s. There was also a strong warning on the Serb side that 'this time, we have to be ready [for war]', with open references made by political leaders to the need for military preparations. Also present was a deep-seated wish to take revenge for what had happened during World War II, and to claim back the territories that had been demographically 'lost' to the Croats and Muslims as a result of the *ustaša* genocide. Muslim leaders, on the other hand, did not openly call for military preparations but used World War II memories primarily to emphasise the need for international protection.

Also in the local Bosnian Serb press, important episodes in Serbian history were constantly commemorated and reiterated. During the war, *Naša Riječ* ('Our Word'), a newspaper appearing in Serb-held Bratunac was one of the main vehicles: along with local news, reports from the frontlines and interviews with Serb leaders, the newspaper covered local commemorations and carried articles on important local and national historical events. One finds reports about the annual *Vidovdan* celebrations, with references made to Kosovo and to Serb suffering in the past and present. The newspaper also provided space to local authors writing on either of the World Wars. Serb heroes from these wars were honoured with articles and poems, underlining their importance to the national cause. Then, as the war started to produce casualties among local Serbs, these new victims were fit into the already existing templates of Serb suffering. The frequent Muslim attacks on Serb villages around Srebrenica in the first year of the war contributed greatly to this development. Serb sources claim that Muslims attacked more than one hundred Serb villages and hamlets in the municipalities of Srebrenica, Bratunac, Vlasenica and Milići, and that more than one thousand Serbs were killed, three thousand injured and thousands of others expelled from their homes. Many of them took refuge in Bratunac (Ivanišević 1994: 40-2). *Naša Riječ* published reports about these attacks, followed by death announcements, obituaries and poems in decasyllabic 'epic' style commemorating those who had been killed or died a heroic death in defence of 'Serb territory'. For the Serbs in the region it was clear that history was repeating itself and that Srebrenica had again become 'an epicentre of genocide' – the Muslim attacks confirmed that Serbs had always been a 'suffering' nation threatened with extinction. In one of its last wartime issues, published shortly before the Srebrenica massacre, *Naša Riječ* all but embraced the Muslim attacks on Serb villages as confirming a higher Truth that had always accompanied the Serbs, a Truth that now carried the promise of redemption: on its front page, alongside Mladić's *Vidovdan* speech, it published a map of Serb villages and towns that had been attacked or destroyed by Muslims. The caption 'The terrible salvation-bringing truth' hinted at an imminent but still undefined catharsis that would put an end to all Serb suffering (see Figure 6.1).

With hindsight this may be read as an omen for the settling of scores that would occur in July 1995. Especially after the Muslim attack on the Serb nationalist stronghold of Kravica in January 1993, in which forty-six people were killed, local Serb feelings of humiliation ran deep and the call for revenge was strong. As one local Serb chronicler of the war wrote, Serbs were looking forward to the day of vengeance: '... in spite of the loss and sorrow, we encountered at every step an unshakable determination among people that the *balije* [derogatory term for Muslims] should be paid back for what they did. ... People lived for and believed in the day when they would be able to settle accounts...' (Miljanović 1996: 8). So when Mladić's forces took Srebrenica in July 1995, local Serbs celebrated this event as the 'liberation' of the town, expressing contempt for the Muslims who had been living in Srebrenica during the war. In the Bosnian Serb newspaper *Javnost* ('The Public'), the taking of the town was celebrated as the 'cleansing of a blot on the map', and as the erasure of the stench of Muslim backwardness.[9]

Yet the euphoria over having beaten 'the Turks' was mixed with feelings of grief for those who had died during the war. In the first years following the war, the annual celebrations of the 'liberation' of Srebrenica (11 July), were immediately followed by commemorations mourning the dead (12 July). In some Serb villages, monuments were erected and plaques were unveiled to honour the

---

[9]   *Javnost*, 22 July 1995, quoted in Čolović 2002: 42.

Figure 6.1 'The Terrible Salvation-Bringing Truth'

(*Naša Riječ*, June 1995)

victims. Zalazje, a tiny village on a hill overlooking Srebrenica, formed the symbolic centre of these commemorations: Muslim forces had attacked the village on 12 July 1992, killing at least forty local Serbs. The village had already once before been the site of a massacre, more precisely in June 1943, when ninety-six people were killed. On 12 July 1997, a monument commemorating the victims of the July 1992 attack was placed next to the existing World War II monument (see Figure 6.2). These monuments were part of a much wider effort to inscribe the new political order into the landscape: crosses were installed, new Orthodox churches were built and mosques were torn down. Streets, schools and villages were renamed. Through these changes, Serbs sent out a clear message that there was no place for Muslims in the RS. Local Serbs I talked to in 1998 either denied that the July 1995 massacre of Muslim men had taken place at all, or rationalized it away as deaths resulting from combat.

One of the most interesting symbolic acts of 're-appropriation' carried out by Serbs after the recent war was the re-erection of the Kosta Todorović monument, the small World War I monument mentioned earlier, consisting of two plaques, which local Serbs had been forced to remove at the start of World War II. As the story goes, instead of getting rid of this monument, a Serb peasant kept the two plaques hidden, only to take them out again in 1995.[10] What happened with the Todorović monument is a good example of how official history and public commemoration can be subject to revision, and how claims to the past that were silenced may be brought to the surface again even decades later. It also shows that the equations 'Serb memory = public' and 'Muslim memory = hidden' are too simplistic, and that not all 'Serb' memories (especially nationalist memories) were hegemonic after 1945. This case is a good example of how myths, memories of distant historical events and remembrances of more recent events blend together, and how monuments can be used to re-appropriate both time (history) and space (territory).

Polemics and Mourning: Muslims Coming to Terms with the Massacre

Likewise, Muslims have attempted, through commemorations and the creation of a monument, to re-establish their presence in Srebrenica and to symbolically 'undo' the results of Serb ethnic cleansing and genocide, most notably through the creation of the Potočari Memorial Centre. It should be stressed, however, that the initiative for the creation of this site came from the families of those killed, for whom it has served important psychological rather than political needs:[11] it is in Potočari where most women of Srebrenica saw their husbands and sons for the last

---

[10] Earlier requests to put the monument back, in the late 1980s, had been refused by the local authorities (see Duijzings 2002b: 42).

[11] For the important psychological functions of commemorative sites, see especially Winter 1995.

**Figure 6.2   Monument Commemorating Local Serb Victims of the War,
Erected in Zalazje on 12 July 1997**

(Photo by Ger Duijzings)

time, and where they want to bury their men's bodies. For them, a proper burial and the possibility of visiting the graves and mourning the dead at this very location are of enormous importance in trying to find closure (Pollack 2003b: 130-32; Delpla, this volume). They also see the Potočari Memorial Centre as a form of non-violent redress for what was done to them. It is a way of making the legacy of the massacre visible locally: Serbs are forced to live in proximity to the signs of a crime committed by them or in their name (Pollack 2003b: 133).

In this section, I will focus on how the Muslim community has come to terms with the Srebrenica massacre, describing first of all how the tragic events in July 1995 led to polemics about the responsibilities of the Muslim political and army leadership. These debates were later suppressed and the massacre was made into a shared and generic symbol of Muslim victimization. In the following section I will describe how the members of the family associations, predominantly women (who represent the overwhelming majority of those who were left after the massacre), were the main driving force behind the establishment of the site: the Potočari Memorial Centre only came into being after persistent lobbying by these family associations. In spite of all the obstacles and opposition, these proposals for a memorial site in Potočari were eventually realized with the support of the High Representative and the international community. In the course of this process, the Srebrenica commemorations acquired new political meanings especially for the international community. Finally, in the last section, I look at the reactions the Potočari Memorial Centre has provoked among the Serbs.

Until late in the conflict, Srebrenica was marginal in the story of the Bosnian war, except for the time in March 1993, when the Serbs almost completely overran it and Srebrenica was declared a UN 'Safe Area'. It is clear that 'Srebrenica' only became a symbol of Muslim victimhood after the massacre, but not before allegations and debates about the contested role of the Bosnian Army (ARBiH) and Government had been silenced. Immediately after the fall of Srebrenica, questions about the responsibility of the army leadership were raised in the Muslim press, especially in *Ratna tribina* ('War Tribune'), a Tuzla-based magazine run by displaced journalists from eastern Bosnia.[12] In the following years, former political and military leaders put forth similar allegations, denouncing the 'betrayal' and deliberate 'sacrifice' of Srebrenica by the SDA and the ARBiH: during the entire war, it was said, the Muslim forces in Srebrenica received little support from the Bosnian Government and Bosnian Army. The ARBiH was accused of pulling Naser Orić and other officers out in May 1995 to intentionally weaken the enclave's defences, and of ordering Muslim attacks on Serb positions and villages around Srebrenica (in June 1995) in order to support an attempt to break the siege of Sarajevo by diverting scarce fighting power from Serb forces besieging the city. This provided the Serbs with a clear pretext for attacking the enclave. President Alija Izetbegović himself was accused of knowingly sacrificing Srebrenica as part

---

[12]   *Ratna tribina – List za oslobađanje Podrinja*, 31 July 1995.

of a territorial swap between the eastern Bosnian enclaves and the Serb-held suburbs of Sarajevo.[13]

What is most relevant to my argument is that despite the fact that this criticism was voiced more than once by political and military leaders who were close to where the decisions had been taken, its echo among the relatives of those killed has been effectively muted. Initially, the women of Srebrenica were also critical of the role of the Bosnian Government and Army, venting their anger on various occasions. In February 1996, for instance, when they stormed the headquarters of the International Red Cross in Tuzla demanding better efforts in the search for their relatives, the women also threw stones at the building of the Tuzla Cantonal Government and demanded a meeting with Naser Orić, Alija Izetbegović and other Bosnian officials in order to hear why Orić and other officers had been ordered to leave the enclave two months before the Serb offensive.[14] In the following months, however, the SDA and Bosnian Army leadership effectively managed to silence the critics among the women of Srebrenica.

At the beginning of August 1996, on the eve of the first post-war elections, Rasim Delić, Chief Commander of the Bosnian Army and very close to the SDA, presented a report to the Bosnian Parliament responding to earlier criticism and essentially pinning responsibility for the fall of the enclave on its Muslim defenders. Delić claimed that between 1993 and 1995 the Muslim forces in Srebrenica had received more than sufficient quantities of weapons, that the fall of the enclave had been primarily caused by internal rivalries and not by lack of support from outside, and that Naser Orić had refused to go back to the enclave after he had left it in May 1995. On 6 August, the Bosnian Parliament passed a resolution acknowledging only minor 'weaknesses' in the ARBiH's performance, identifying the international community (the UN and Dutchbat) as the main culprit in the tragedy.[15] At about the same time, various actors close to the SDA were involved in nourishing the hopes of the women of Srebrenica that their men may still be alive, kept as prisoners in mines in Serbia and Kosovo. This was very effective in making the women dependent on the Bosnian leadership and the SDA to mediate on their behalf and put pressure on the Serb(ian) authorities to reveal the fate of their men. Thus, with the elections around the corner, the SDA succeeded in

---

[13]   Among the main critics of Izetbegović's policy towards Srebrenica were Sefer Halilović, first Chief of Staff of the Bosnian Army from May 1992 to June 1993 (see e.g. Halilović 1997: 105-10), Ibran Mustafić, a former SDA leader from Potočari, who left the SDA and became president of one of the family associations (see e.g. interview in *Slobodna Bosna*,14 July 1996), Hakija Meholjić, one of the commanders of Srebrenica's defence from the start of the war and one of the leaders of the local SDP after the war (see e.g. interview in *Dani*, 22 June 1998), and Esad Hećimović journalist and political analyst at the SDA Party Headquarters during the war (see e.g. Hećimović 1998).

[14]   *Ljiljan*, 7 February 1996; *AIM Press*, 5 February 1996, available at <http://www.aimpress.ch/dyn/pubs/archive/data/199602/60205-002-pubs-sar.htm>.

[15]   *Oslobođenje*, 3-4 August 1996 and 7 August 1996.

neutralizing the political threat the women of Srebrenica represented. Ever since, opening the issue of Muslim responsibility for the fall of the enclave has been perceived by the family associations as a danger to the achievement of other more important aims such as the clarification of the fate of their men, identification of bodies and their burial in Potočari, commemoration of the massacre, the arrest of Serb war criminals, and the prosecution of international actors deemed accountable for the massacre.

The Potočari Memorial Centre and the Role of the OHR

The commemoration of the Srebrenica massacre started on a small scale immediately after the war, with the mothers and wives of the missing men organising commemorative protests in Tuzla on the 11th of each month. The first anniversaries of the massacre led to both official as well as informal commemorations organised by the women and their families. The women also returned to Srebrenica as soon as that possibility arose with the first organised visit taking place in June 1998. As I witnessed myself, while the women visited a graveyard containing the graves of Muslims killed before the 1995 massacre, local Serbs, mostly refugees from other parts of Bosnia, jeered the unwanted Muslim visitors by displaying nationalist symbols and airing nationalist songs from the windows of their apartments. The first large commemoration of the massacre near the former Dutchbat compound in Potočari took place only on the fifth anniversary in July 2000. Among the estimated three thousand people who attended the ceremony was Alija Izetbegović, setting foot on RS territory for the first time since the end of the war. Representatives of the international community and ambassadors from Western and Islamic countries were also there. No representative of the RS attended the ceremony.

The next step in this process of re-establishing some form of Muslim presence in Srebrenica, of 'undoing' ethnic cleansing and defying Serb claims to the territory, was the creation of the Potočari Memorial Centre and the subsequent burial of the victims of the massacre. As early as 1996, the Srebrenica women had expressed their wish to bury their men, if found dead, in Potočari, where most of them had seen their men for the last time. In addition to the plan for a cemetery, the women and family associations also launched the idea to transform the former Dutchbat compound (the battery factory in Potočari) into a memorial complex with an educational centre and museum. Initially both the international community and the SDA opposed this idea as being either unrealistic or undesirable. The international community only started to accept and actively support these plans when the return process got going: they then began to see the Potočari Memorial Centre as an important tool in the process of Muslim return to Srebrenica, creating new physical and symbolic anchors for those who were contemplating going back (Pollack 2003c). Nor did the SDA at first encourage the idea of a cemetery and memorial in Potočari: SDA leaders were pressuring survivors to forget about

Potočari, because of its location in the RS, and to decide in favour of Kladanj, the nearest Muslim-held town in the Federation. In July 1998, the SDA organized a commemoration of the massacre near Kladanj, where it had already started building a monument; the ceremony was attended by the *Reisu-l-ulema* Mustafa Cerić and Alija Izetbegović.[16]

Despite SDA objections, however, the great majority of families were clearly in favour of the 'return' of the dead to Potočari. A poll organised by the association 'Mothers of the Srebrenica and Žepa Enclaves' showed that families did not wish to bury their loved ones anywhere but in Potočari (Pollack 2003a: 795; Pollack 2003c: 189). In April 2000, through their political representation in the municipal council of Srebrenica, the former Muslim inhabitants of Srebrenica succeeded in passing an ordinance mandating the creation of a burial site in the municipality. As a mixed commission of Muslims and Serbs could not agree on a suitable location – Serbs opposed the Muslims' preference for Potočari – the site for future burial remained unresolved (Pollack 2003a: 797; Pollack 2003c: 189-90). After its initial opposition, the SDA decided to support the proposals for Potočari, taking a U-turn in its policy with regard to eastern Bosnia out of fear that the party would suffer electoral losses if it did not support the return process.[17] On 25 October 2000, in the midst of the local deadlock over the site for the memorial, High Representative Wolfgang Petritsch issued a directive setting aside land for a cemetery and memorial complex in Potočari, pointing to the need for an appropriate place of mourning for the families and explicitly linking the burial of the victims in Potočari to the issues of return and reconciliation.[18]

In May 2001, Petritsch established the Srebrenica-Potočari Memorial and Cemetery Foundation, charged with overseeing the building of the complex.[19] On the sixth anniversary of the massacre, the site of the future memorial was marked by the installation of a three-ton marble stone with the inscription '*Srebrenica 11 July 1995*', and in 2002, a sample grave headstone was put in place and unveiled (see Figure 6.3). In October of that year, under the leadership of new High Representative Paddy Ashdown, the building of the Potočari Memorial Centre and Cemetery started, with donations from the US, the Netherlands, the UK and other governments. In March 2003, the first six hundred victims of the massacre (599

---

[16] Interview with Hakija Meholjić in *Dani*, 10 September 1999.

[17] *Dani*, 17 July 2000.

[18] OHR, *Decision on the Location of a Cemetery and a Monument for the Victims of Srebrenica* (25 October 2000), available at <http://www.ohr.int/decisions/plipdec/default.asp?content_id=219>.

[19] The Executive Board of the foundation is chaired by the High Representative. Other members are the US ambassador to Bosnia, the *Reisu-l-ulema*, the Head of Mission of the ICMP, and the Bosnian Minister of Human Rights and Refugees. There is also an Advisory Board, which consists of three (male) representatives of the families, one representative of the Islamic Community, and the (Muslim) Mayor of Srebrenica (see Salimović and Sekulić 2003: 2-3).

Figure 6.3 The Potočari Memorial Centre, with Open Mosque and Marble Stone 'Srebrenica, 11 July 1995'

(Photo by Ger Duijzings)

men and one woman) were buried there, and the following September, the memorial complex was officially opened by Bill Clinton. Moreover, not only the dead but also the living began to come back. Muslims began returning to their villages, while, in the town itself, some form of Muslim presence was re-established with the appointment of an imam, and the rebuilding of the White Mosque in the town's centre. As before, the High Representative played a crucial role in breaking local Serb opposition, by, among other things, halting the building of a new Serbian Orthodox church in Potočari.

Because of the genocidal dimensions of the Srebrenica massacre (which is by far the largest single war crime committed during the Yugoslav wars) and the close involvement of the international community in these events, as well as in the way they are being remembered, the Srebrenica massacre has moved to the centre of the official commemoration of the war in Bosnia. What's more, the Srebrenica commemorations have not only grown into demonstrations of Muslim survival and unity, symbolically and ceremonially dominated by the Islamic Community; they have also evolved into a platform for the ritual declarations of guilt and responsibility by members of the international community, who use it to express their regret at having allowed the massacre to happen. Through their strong political and financial support, the High Representative and other representatives of the international community have also made the Srebrenica commemorations, unlike other commemorations in Bosnia, into acts of remembrance meant for international consumption.

Serbs between Obstruction and Reluctant Cooperation

Serb reactions to the commemorations and the building of the Memorial Centre have oscillated between outright obstruction and reluctant cooperation. Locally, there has been fierce resistance to the (even temporary) return of Muslims. The fifth anniversary of the massacre in July 2000, the first large-scale commemoration to take place in Potočari, was accompanied by violent incidents: on the eve of the event, a house belonging to Muslim returnees was set on fire and on the day itself Serbs threw stones at buses carrying Muslims. Serb media described the commemoration as a deliberate attempt to invade 'Serb' territory and as a form of political manipulation. In utter denial of the massacre, the local leader of the Serb Democratic Party (SDS), Momčilo Cvijetinović, claimed that Muslims had no reasons to come to Srebrenica: they had never before really cared about their dead, he claimed in a conversation with me, and were using this event as an excuse to enter *Republika Srpska*.[20] When the decision to build the memorial in Potočari came down from the High Representative in October 2000, the Serb Deputy

---

[20]   See also *AIM Press*, 12 July 2000, available at <http://www.aimpress.ch/dyn/pubs/archive/data/200007/00712-003-pubs-sar.htm>.

Speaker of the Srebrenica municipal council Dragan Jevtić resigned in protest and called upon all Serb officials in Srebrenica to do the same.

Also in the following years, local Serbs continued to express discontent with the commemorations, jeering the arriving mourners, welcoming them with the three-finger Serb nationalist salute and holding up pictures of Mladić and Karadžić. In July 2001, as one American visitor wrote, a Serb party roasted pigs on a spit in front of the warehouse in Kravica (where probably more than one thousand Muslim men had been slaughtered in 1995) apparently set up and timed for the Muslims to see (Ruga 2001).[21] One extremist *četnik* group threatened to disrupt the laying of the foundation stone for the Potočari Memorial Centre, and on the day of the ceremony, a Muslim returnee was murdered in nearby Vlasenica. Much of the local Serbs' resentment of the changes brought about by the decision of the High Representative was directed at Srebrenica's Muslim mayor, whom they accused of trying to expel Serbs and destroy Serb monuments and heritage. At the level of the RS Government, however, Serb officials and the RS police have been increasingly cooperative in allowing and providing security for Muslim commemorations, even though the RS has been far less cooperative with regard to the arrest of those responsible for the massacre.

It is clear that in the years following the end of the war, the issue of 'how (not) to remember Srebrenica' has divided the Serb community and its political leaders at both the national and local levels. While some Bosnian Serb politicians have now acknowledged that the massacre happened, others still continue to deny it. The first official admission came in July 2000, from RS Prime Minister Milorad Dodik who acknowledged that a 'mass crime' had been committed in Srebrenica. Still, he did not attend the commemorations.[22] After Dodik's electoral defeat in November 2000, the new RS Government again played down and even denied the massacre. Since then, the reluctance to recognise what happened in Srebrenica has not disappeared: for Serb politicians, publicly acknowledging the massacre may very well damage them politically or seriously threaten their personal safety. It is likely that pressure from hardliners and threats from extremists has been one of the reasons why high RS officials have declined to attend the commemorations. Those who have attended the ceremony, such as the former chairman of the Srebrenica municipal council, Desnica Radivojević, have been labelled 'traitors'.[23] It was only in July 2003 that a high level RS official (Prime Minister Dragan Mikerević) attended the ceremony in Potočari for the first time.[24]

The most common Serb response to the commemorations in Potočari has been to demand recognition also for the Serb victims of the Bosnian war and to urge

---

[21] Needless to say, this was a provocation to the Muslims, most of whom do not eat pork for religious or cultural reasons.

[22] See *Balkan Crisis Report*, 18 July 2000, available at <http://www.iwpr.net/ ?p=bcr&s=f&o=247215&apc_state=henibcr200007>.

[23] See interview with Desnica Radivojević in *Slobodna Bosna*, 17 April 2003.

[24] *Oslobođenje*, 12 July 2003.

international organizations to take them into account as well. For instance, in July 2001, on the eve of the sixth anniversary of the massacre, the Speaker of the RS National Assembly, Dragan Kalinić, issued a statement paying tribute not only to the Muslim victims of Srebrenica but to all the other victims of the four-year conflict, 'which affected all three peoples'.[25] The dominant Serb discourse, which is also shared by moderate politicians, equalises Serb and Muslim suffering, drawing parallels, for instance, between the Muslims of Srebrenica and the Serbs of Sarajevo. In response to the creation of the Potočari Memorial Centre, refugee Serbs from Sarajevo demanded that a similar monument be built in Kazani (a deep mountain pit near Sarajevo where Serb inhabitants of the city were killed).[26] Deputy Mayor of Sarajevo Savo Vlaški criticized the initiative as being hypocritical and lacking respect for the victims of Srebrenica, adding that it is absurd to build separate monuments to Serbs, Muslims, Croats, and Jews.[27] Separate monuments may be senseless in the case of Sarajevo, but in eastern Bosnia it seems to be the only option possible. To underscore this, local Serbs have built 'counter-monuments' and organised 'counter-commemorations', such as in the villages of Kravica and Zalazje. When, in June 2001, the RS Justice Ministry made the provocative suggestion that the names of all Serb victims from the Srebrenica area also be added to the memorial in Potočari, Serb associations of war veterans and families of those killed protested vehemently.[28]

With the 11 July commemorations in Potočari becoming more and more established and institutionalized, 12 July, Petrovdan (St Peter's Day), has developed into the main commemorative date for local Serbs. On that date in 1992, Muslim forces killed several dozen Serbs in Zalazje and other villages nearby. This date has now become more important for Serbs in Srebrenica than 11 July, which they previously openly celebrated as 'liberation day', especially in the first few post-war years. Apart from growing embarrassment about celebrating Srebrenica's 'liberation' on the same day as the commemorations in Potočari, the shift in the Serb ceremonial calendar from 11 to 12 July, and more generally the growing emphasis put on Serb victimhood, are not only ways to counter the Muslim discourse and raise international awareness. They also serve to neutralise divisions within the local Serb community about how (not) to commemorate the Srebrenica massacre. 12 July has also been introduced as the day of commemoration for Serb victims in other localities such as Kravica: on 12 July 2001, Serbs unveiled a plaque there, marking the foundation for a monument to be built for the 1,300 Serbs of the area said to have been killed during the war. High RS officials, absent at the commemorations in Potočari the day before, did attend the ceremony in Kravica, declaring, in the words of RS President Mirko Šarović, that 'we have

---

[25]   *Tanjug*, 11 July 2001.

[26]   *Dani*, 6 April 2001.

[27]   *Hrvatska Riječ*, 27 August 2001.

[28]   *BiH Media Round-up*, 22 June 2001, available at <http://www.ohr.int/ohr-dept/presso/bh-media-rep/round-ups/default.asp?content_id=527>.

decided to let the truth free and tell the world that the truth also has another side, namely that on this spot a crime was committed against hundreds of Serb civilians'.[29] Some local leaders have suggested including in the Kravica monument the names of all Serb victims of the (wider) Birač and Podrinje areas, or even all Serb victims of World War II, in order to reach a figure comparable to the number of Muslim victims in Potočari.

Conclusion

This leaves us with a situation of divided memories and separate commemorations organised almost simultaneously in two adjacent villages, Potočari and Kravica, well-known Muslim and Serb nationalist strongholds, respectively, before and during the 1990s war. The Potočari Memorial Centre has received the strong political and financial support by the High Representative and the international community, without which it probably never would have been built on RS territory, while the Serb community has relied solely on itself for similar initiatives to commemorate the victims on their side. As discussed above, I call this a commemorative arena in which there are different issues at stake for all the actors and 'sides' caught up in it. For relatives of those that were killed or went missing, the most important thing is the fact that they can bury their dead in Potočari and go there to mourn, which seems to fulfil their most important needs. Their main concern is a proper burial for their loved ones: this helps them to arrive at some kind of closure. Most of the bereaved, nearly all of them women, are deeply traumatized and have many other urgent needs to solve (such as securing acceptable housing and a stable income), which has meant that in practice only a minority of them has become politically active, in one of the 'families' or women's associations. Because the number of experienced and educated female community leaders is small, male survivors have adopted a leading role in representing the families and in setting the agenda.[30] For some of them, the Memorial Centre is not just a way of coming to terms with the massacre, but also a powerful way of reclaiming space: it brings back the bodies that were meant to be removed and re-establishes a Muslim presence on land that is now occupied by the Serbs. Finally, the women's associations have used the commemoration of the massacre as a means to demand compensation, to 'leverage for economic and political support by the international community' (Pollack 2003b: 134), and call for the prosecution of the international actors they hold accountable for the massacre.

The Potočari Memorial Centre is also used to force local Serbs to acknowledge the massacre. As Craig Pollack writes, family associations and Muslim politicians are aware of the potential of the communal burial in Potočari to define past and

---

[29]   *B 92*, 13 July 2001.
[30]   On the various forms of women's organizations, see Helms, this volume. On victim associations, which are often dominated by women, see Delpla this volume.

present, and to shape the future (Pollack 2003b: 138). Serb recognition of the massacre potentially undermines the legitimacy of the RS and may help to dissolve Serb control over the region. The commemorative space thereby also becomes an arena for ethnic and nationalist politics, which may overshadow the important psychological role it plays for the bereaved families. Muslim leaders, as well as representatives of family associations, may indeed at times use this commemorative arena to promote a nationalist agenda. The same is of course true for the Serb side. Monuments and commemorations have become a tool to maintain control over constituencies, both for Muslims and Serbs (Pollack 2003b: 138-41). The approach developed by some Muslim politicians helps to conceal certain sensitive issues: the massacre is decontextualized and made into a generic symbol of Muslim victimhood, of a genocide carried out by the Serbs against the Muslims of Bosnia as a whole (e.g. Mihrović, Salihović and Kržalić 2002: 17, 127).[31] Yet, this representation of events helps to divert attention away from the fact that Srebrenica was an important centre of Muslim resistance. During the war, this was the first town that Muslim forces re-conquered. It was also a base for attacks on Serb villages, even after the enclave had been officially demilitarized. Further, this representation helps draw attention away from accusations that Srebrenica was 'betrayed' by Muslim politicians, the Bosnian Government and the Bosnian Army. The fact that SDA politicians are reluctant to use the term '*šehidi*' (martyrs who died in combat) for the victims is salient in this respect (see also Bougarel, this volume): although most of those massacred were unarmed civilians or prisoners of war at the time when they were killed, many of them had been active soldiers before, resisting the Serbian onslaught under extremely difficult conditions. Preferably for these politicians, the resistance element is blotted out from the story in order not to raise painful and controversial questions about the lack of SDA support and its indirect responsibility for the massacre.[32] In 1996, the Bosnian Government turned 11 July into the Day of Remembrance of Civilian Victims of Fascist Aggression (*Dan sjećanja na civilne žrtve fašističke agresije*): the Srebrenica massacre and the issue of responsibility were 'dissolved' into a commemoration of all civilian victims and a denunciation of (Serb and Croat) fascist aggression. The reluctance to use the term '*šehidi*' also has much to do with the high level of internationalization of the Srebrenica commemorations. Muslim leaders may want to downplay the military aspects of Srebrenica when talking to an international audience but praise its resistance when addressing a local one. And international officials are normally not very keen on the use of Islamic terms that refer to the victims as martyrs of the faith.

---

[31]   Here, my analysis is inspired by American historian Sarah Farmer, from whom I have borrowed the concept of decontextualization (Farmer 1999).

[32]   There may be an additional reason not to acknowledge these men as former soldiers. In the years following the war, 1,800 men from Srebrenica who had gone missing were removed from the army register, as a result of which their families lost the right to claim war pensions from the Federation Defence Ministry (see Mustafić 2001: 25, 34-5).

Serbs, on the other hand, through their counter-monuments and counter-commemorations, have tried to convince the world that the Muslim attacks on Serb villages are an indispensable part of the Srebrenica story. They claim that events are much more complex than the 'official' story, sanitized by the Muslims and supported by the international community, suggests. Even though most Serbs are blind to the fact that the Muslim attacks on Serb villages were a consequence of a ruthless Serbian campaign of ethnic cleansing at the beginning of the war, most of them no longer deny that the massacre happened, which can be seen as the beginning of a process of facing the past. Serb politicians try to balance Serb and Muslim guilt and suffering, placing the main emphasis on individual responsibility in order to 'depoliticize' the Srebrenica massacre and avoid undermining the very legitimacy and existence of the RS. Yet, the fact that Ratko Mladić and Radovan Karadžić are still at large will continue to thwart attempts to bring closure, for Muslims as well as Serbs.

For the international community, the support for the Memorial is a way of expressing its *mea culpa* about its role during these tragic events. It is clear that there would have been no international support for the Potočari Memorial Centre, or no memorial site at all for that matter, if the international community had not played such a key role in declaring Srebrenica a 'Safe Area' and then failing so miserably in keeping its promise to protect the population. Even though massacres occurred in other parts of Bosnia too, none of the commemoration practices taking place there are supported or sponsored by the international community. Pollack points to the ambiguity and contradictions of a situation in which the international community is indeed one of the main culprits in this tragedy and at the same time makes the families dependent on it for the realization of the commemorative site they desire (Pollack 2003a: 799). What's more, in supporting the Potočari memorial, the OHR has adopted a version of events that is close to the official Muslim version, decontextualizing the massacre and presenting it as an irrational Serb act, as a warning that this is what might happen if 'a nation loses its head and forgets about the values of tolerance'.[33] The international community's approach does not recognize that within Bosnia, among its communities, the events in Srebrenica are highly contested. They mean different things to members of different communities, or for that matter to members within the same communities, and the international community is imposing its version of what Srebrenica represents and how these events should be commemorated. Clearly, there is a danger that the way in which the commemoration of the Srebrenica massacre is shaped by the international community at the same time undermines its attempts to keep the country together.

Instead of regarding divided memories and commemorations as necessarily detrimental to the creation of a shared understanding of Bosnia's recent history, I argue that they can be seen as an understandable legacy of the war. Instead of

---

[33] Speech held on 31 March 2003 by the High Representative Paddy Ashdown, reproduced in Salimović and Sekulić 2003: 13-14.

imposing an official narrative from above, a mistake made in Yugoslavia after World War II, it seems better to give free reign of expression to these contrasting memories. Of course, it is highly unlikely that a completely shared understanding will ever be possible, particularly when talking about such turbulent and violent episodes: as the 1990s have shown, reminiscences of and perspectives on World War II are very different among those who went through that war, even fifty years later, because experiences of violent conflict are often very personal and subjective. What we need to recognize is that a plurality of voices and perspectives is normal in such situations. Open expression of differences will hopefully lead, at some stage, to the creation of a shared public space (which is not the same as a homogenized public space) in which different perspectives and views will be discussed and tested. Monuments and commemorations may split communities and solidify divisions, and even fuel future conflict, but they can just as well help to overcome the losses and traumas of war if designed and managed properly. Instead of triggering memories of ethnic or national victimization, as political and religious leaders may feel tempted to do, monuments and commemorations can assist in bringing closure for the people most concerned.

Chapter 7

Death and the Nationalist:
Martyrdom, War Memory and Veteran Identity among Bosnian Muslims

Xavier Bougarel

Memory issues have played a crucial role in the Yugoslav crisis. In particular, communist narratives of World War II have been replaced by new official ones that rehabilitated the main nationalist forces of that period and denounced as a myth the Titoist insistence on 'Brotherhood and Unity' among the South Slavs (e.g. Höpken 1999; Duijzings, Grandits, this volume). In the late 1980s, these new 'politics of war memory' (Ashplant, Dawson and Roper 2000) led to the reopening of mass graves (e.g. Bax 1997), to outright competition over the commemoration of real or alleged genocides (e.g. Denich 1994; Hayden 1994), and later to the neglect or destruction of monuments celebrating the Partisans, the erection of new monuments dedicated to local 'quislings', and the reburial of some of them – all practices Katherine Verdery terms 'the political life of dead bodies' (Verdery 1999).

However, if the political life of the dead bodies from World War II has been explored, the same does not hold true for those related to the more recent wars. This observation applies especially to fallen soldiers. Some social scientists have scrutinized related issues such as the heroic male characters mobilized during the Yugoslav wars (e.g. Čolović 1993; Senjković 2002; Žanić 1998), while others turned their attention to the figure of the victim and its gendered nature (e.g. Spasić 2000; Žarkov 2001; Helms, this volume). But fallen soldiers as such have remained almost unnoticed, despite a few precursory works dealing with Croatia (Rihtman-Augustin 1993; Roćenović 1993). This fact reveals another flaw in the analyses of post-war Bosnia-Herzegovina: in spite of the fact that they constitute about two-thirds of the adult male population in this country, war veterans are rarely taken into account as a new and specific social group produced by the war.[1]

---

[1]   Both Natalija Bašić and Ivana Maček have insisted on the specificity of the war experience of veterans, but their rise as a socially distinct and politically active group

Against this background, I would like to focus on the way in which the memory of fallen soldiers is commemorated by Bosnian Muslims. Such an examination of the rise of a new public cult of *šehidi* (religious martyrs[2]) not only sheds light on the transformations of Muslim national identity, but helps to understand how these changes are related to other issues such as controversies over the meaning of the war (see also Duijzings, Maček, this volume), and the reshuffling of various social divides and normative hierarchies within the Muslim community.[3]

Reislamicization, Militarization and the New Cult of *Šehidi*

In the 1990s, Muslim fallen soldiers were referred to with increasing frequency as *šehidi*. This is particularly obvious in the case of official institutions: in 1993, the Party of Democratic Action (SDA) set up *Fatma*, an association dedicated to 'the care of children of *šehidi* and fallen soldiers' (Fatma, 2003), and, a year later, the Foundation for the Families of *Šehidi* and War Disabled. In both cases, the honorary president of these SDA-affiliated organizations was party and state President, Alija Izetbegović himself. In March 1994, the Islamic Community (*Islamska zajednica*) turned the second day of the festivities marking the end of Ramadan (*ramazanski bajram*) into the Day of *Šehidi* (*dan šehida*). But this shift was perceptible among the population as well; during the war, the expression *'preselio se na ahiret kao šehid'* ('went over to the world beyond as a *šehid'*) became more and more frequent in the death notices that were published by local newspapers or pasted to community buildings and trees.

To be sure, the cult of *šehidi* in itself is nothing new in Bosnia-Herzegovina: its origins date back to the Ottoman period (Palavestra 2004: 491-5; Popović 1996). In the late 1980s, Tone Bringa noted that some *šehid* graves were still being venerated in rural central Bosnia (Bringa 1995: 171-7). Such practices, however, were linked to the magical powers of these *turbe* (mausoleums) rather than the heroic military feats of the dead. It is also clear that, at the time of Bringa's study, a majority of Bosnian Muslims ignored the very concept of *šehid* or considered it obsolete and devoid of any practical importance. Its rapid spread during the war thus does not constitute a mere 'awakening' of tradition, but rather one aspect of the nation-building and reislamicization processes initiated by the SDA and the *Islamska*

---

remains at the margins of these analyses (see Bašić 2004; Maček 2001, 2005). For a study of veterans as a new social group produced by war, see for example Kriger 2003.

[2]   From the Arabic word *'shahid'*: witness of the Faith, martyr fallen while fighting on God's Path. On the cult of *shahids* in the Muslim world, see among others Brown 2003; Adelkhah 1998: 122-7; Mayeur-Jahouen 2002.

[3]   This chapter is based on material I collected during dissertation fieldwork in the 1990s (Bougarel 1999a, 2001b, 2002), and on interviews with veterans and representatives of veteran organizations I conducted in 2001 and 2002 as part of a research project on local level institutions in Bosnia-Herzegovina (World Bank 2002).

Figure 7.1 'The Division of Muslims before and after the War'

(*Muslimanski Glas*, 13 April 1993)

zajednica. The reintroduction of the word '*šehid*' into Bosnian political discourse can in fact be dated to the ceremony organized by the SDA in Foča on 25 August 1990, which commemorated the massacres perpetrated by *četnici* against the local Muslim population in August 1942 (see also Duijzings, this volume).

In order to better understand this new cult of *šehidi*, one has to keep in mind the main features of the reislamicization policies initiated during the war in the Muslim-held territories of Bosnia-Herzegovina. First of all, these were mainly 'top-down', authoritarian policies, in which political and religious leaders strove to impose their own conception of Islam and definition of Muslim national identity upon a largely secular population (see also Maček, this volume). At the same time, the SDA tried to take over the role previously played by the League of Communists and to turn Islam into the new ideological criterion for the selection of political and military elites (Bougarel 1999a, 2001b). These policies were not only pursued in war-time circumstances, but rested on a deliberate attempt to islamicize the meaning of the war. For example, the slogan promoting the idea that the Serb and Croat genocidal projects or Western indifference to the plight of the Bosnian Muslims were 'just because we are Muslims' ('*samo zato što smo muslimani*') was already present in speeches held by political and religious leaders on the eve of the war (Bougarel 1995), and remained one of the key elements of the war rhetoric aimed at the local Muslim population.[4]

In April 1992, the *Islamska zajednica* started labelling Bosnian Muslims who had been killed fighting the Yugoslav People's Army (JNA) and Serb paramilitaries '*šehidi*', and some imams or local warlords brandished this word in order to stress their religious motivation. It was only in 1993, however, after the last Yugoslav *Reisu-l-ulema*, Jakup Selimoski, had been removed and former officers of the Bosnian Territorial Defence had been marginalized, that the SDA was able to wield extended control over both the religious and the military apparatuses (Bougarel 1999a; Hećimović 1998; Hoare 2004). Despite the resistance put up by some officers and ordinary soldiers, the Army of the Republic of Bosnia-Herzegovina (ARBiH) became the site of various reislamicization practices, as illustrated by the almost compulsory character of the ceremonies linked to the main religious holidays, the appointment of imams as assistant officers for morale and religious issues, and the formation of distinct religious units such as the famous 7th Muslim Brigade based in Zenica. More and more, Islam began to serve an ideological function similar to that of 'Brotherhood and Unity' in the Yugoslav People's Army. However, in a sort of reversal that appears quite frequently in SDA rhetoric, party leaders cast reislamicization practices as simple respect for tradition and justified the use of the army as a place for religious re-

---

[4]   At times, SDA leaders even stated that the war had happened 'only because we are *bad* Muslims'. In October 1994, for example, Alija Izetbegović told the soldiers of the 7th Muslim Brigade that 'we had to endure this inferno to return to the right path, to remember who we are and what we are, to remember that we carry the legacy of faith, the legacy of Islam, and that we have the duty to protect it in these regions' (Izetbegović 1994).

socialization with the argument that the army should 'resemble its own nation' (Izetbegović 1995a: 44).

A turning point in this instrumentalization process occurred in January 1994 at a seminar dedicated to the role of Islam as the 'spiritual force of the defence' (Press Centar ARBiH 1994), which brought together high-ranking officers and *ulema*s (religious scholars). On this occasion, Fikret Muslimović, recently appointed as the new head of the Department of Morale (*Uprava za moral*), criticized the outdated anticlerical attitudes of some officers, as well as the illusory desire to depoliticize the Bosnian Army, stating:

> It is desirable that commanders, and especially those holding key responsibilities, adapt their behaviour to the religious tradition of their own nation during events expressing patriotic feelings, and that they support the main objectives of the liberation struggle (at official gatherings), or when tribute is paid to the *šehidi* (at burials, for example). In such circumstances, in which respect for the victims of genocide is expressed with strong emotion, officers should show that they are aware of the fact that the genocide against our nation is conducted *precisely with the purpose of eliminating our religious traditions*. (Muslimović 1994: 93-4; emphasis added)

Of course, the term '*šehid*' is not the only one that gives meaning to the struggle and death of Bosnian Army soldiers. In poems and songs written during the war, living and fallen soldiers alike are described as 'knights' ('*vitezovi*') and 'heroes' ('*junaci*'), bound to the epic tradition of the Ottoman Empire ('*gazije*') and the Partisan movement ('*heroji*') (Žanić 1998). This image of a male hero defending his nation and his family is often complemented by that of the passive and powerless female victim (*žrtva*) (see Helms, this volume), and therefore represents a typical example of gendered nationalism (e.g. Goldstein 2001; Moser and Clark 2001; Yuval-Davis 1997). However, in Bosnian Muslim wartime art and poetry, the figure of the *šehid* remains by far the most important, since it joins together heroic behaviour, religious motivation, and ultimate sacrifice. Muharem Omerdić, author of the first *fatwa* (legal advice) labelling Muslim fallen soldiers *šehidi*, issued on 28 April 1992 (Hodžić 2003: 19-21), emphasizes that *šehidi* are chosen by Allah among the best believers, that they occupy a privileged place in Heaven and, therefore, should not be considered dead (Omerdić 1997).

In official speeches and documents, the most frequent expression is '*šehidi i poginuli borci*' ('*šehidi* and fallen soldiers'), the second term referring to non-Muslims and non-believers who fought in the Bosnian Army. In both cases, however, the latter term remains secondary, or even derogatory, in comparison to the first one. In November 1998, on the sixth anniversary of the 7th Muslim Brigade, Alija Izetbegović addressed its soldiers in the following terms: 'I came to recite with you the *fatiha* [the first surat of the Qur'an] for the *šehidi* of the Seventh, for all the fallen soldiers [*pali borci*] and for all the innocent victims [*nevine žrtve*] of the recent war' (Izetbegović 1999b: 146). In this sentence, *šehidi*, fallen soldiers and civilian victims form three distinct, concentric and hierarchic circles. What is more, the idea that the *fatiha* can be recited for 'all the innocent victims' of the war suggests that, in Bosnia-Herzegovina, all of them are Muslims.

In wartime circumstances, Islam was expected to bolster the fighting spirit of the Bosnian Army and to broaden the primarily local motivation of its soldiers. According to Muharem Omerdić, 'the day when the ideal of religious martyrdom was awakened in the hearts of Bosnian boys and girls, victories over the enemy started to accumulate' (Omerdić 1997: 5-6). After the war, the cult of *šehidi* has remained a central element in the commemorative practices of the SDA and the *Islamska zajednica*, its main function being to cultivate the remembrance of fallen soldiers and to influence the character of nascent war memory:

> The *šehid* cemeteries that have spread all over Bosnia, across its devastated cities and villages, are the guarantee of our future and a testimony to Bosniac invincibility. They are the roots out of which an even stronger Nation, Faith, and State are growing. ... The *šehid* cemeteries are and should remain at the centre of the memories of all Bosniacs, and not only of the families [of the *šehidi*]. (Omerdić 1997: 5-6)

The importance attached to the cult of *šehidi* is not only reflected in official speeches, popular songs and death notices. Many streets and squares have been named after prominent *šehidi*, and the public space has been increasingly occupied by *šehid* cemeteries (beginning with the most famous one at Kovači in Sarajevo – see Figure 7.2), by monuments and fountains dedicated to local *šehidi*, and by commemorative plaques affixed to school and university buildings, public service offices and workplaces.[5] Since 1994, the Day of *šehidi*, at the end of Ramadan, has been devoted to visits to the graves of *šehidi* and to *šehid* families.[6] The memory of the *šehidi* has been evoked on many other occasions, such as the reburial of war victims excavated from mass graves, anniversaries of the founding of military units, celebrations of important battles, and the inauguration of rebuilt or brand new mosques. In this way, the cult of *šehidi* structures both space and time for the Muslim community, closely following the extent of its territory, emphasizing the imprint of war on its recovering social life, drawing new boundaries between profane space and sacred space, Islamic time and secular time.[7]

---

[5]   By the early 2000s, there were 154 *šehid* cemeteries in the Sarajevo Canton (Fond kantona Sarajeva 2001: 6) and, in the municipality of Sarajevo Centar alone, 779 plaques have been put in place to celebrate the memory of soldiers killed during the siege of the city (Općina Centar 2003).

[6]   Visiting cemeteries during the festivities at the end of Ramadan (*ramazanski bajram*) is a tradition predating the war, but these visits have been transformed from a private ceremony into a patriotic gathering attended by politicians, army officers and delegations of veteran associations. Moreover, the institution of the Day of *Šehidi* is also aimed at commemorating the beginning of the war on 6 April 1992, which was the second day of *ramazanski bajram* in 1992.

[7]   On similar 'politics of war memory' in Serb- and Croat-held territories, see Duijzings, Grandits, this volume.

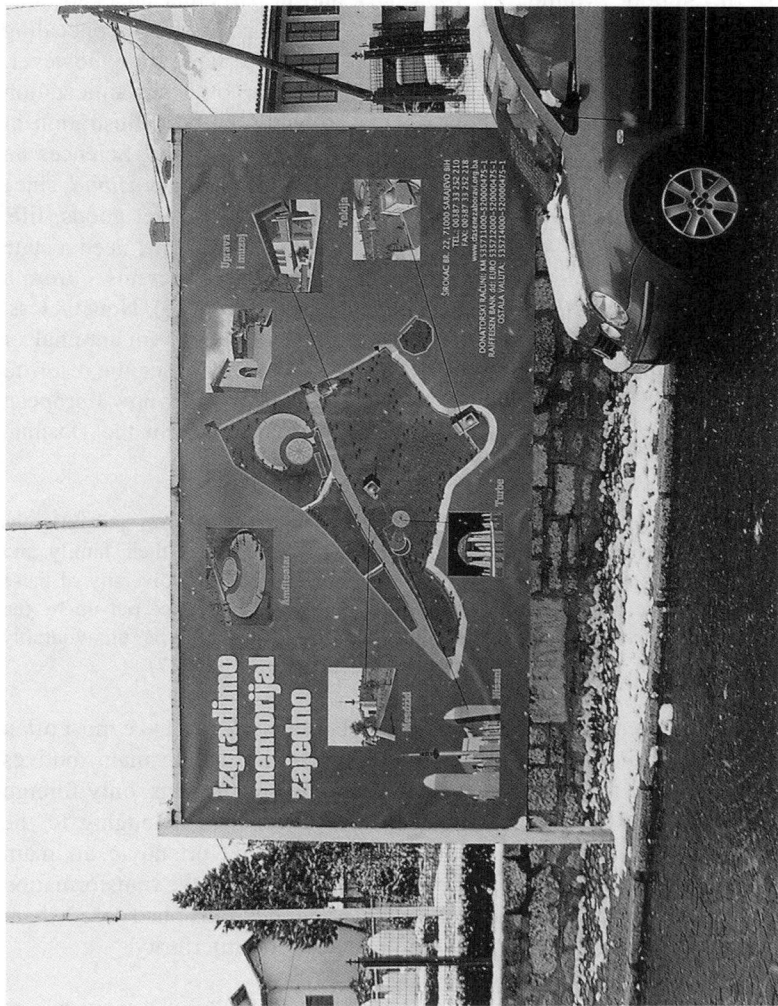

Figure 7.2   Plan of the _Šehid_ Memorial Complex at Kovači

(Photo by Xavier Bougarel)

Polysemy and Paradox Surrounding the Cult of *Šehidi*

The purpose of the seminar organized by the Department of Morale in January 1994 was not only to make reislamicization activities in the Bosnian Army official, but also to gain firmer control over them. Participants deplored the anarchic use of religious symbols, which 'ranges from mere kitsch or bad taste to the crude and improper use of religion' (Muminović 1994: 84), and in particular attacked units 'in which the ostentatious display of religious symbols is used for concealing criminal greed and activities' (Muslimović 1994: 92). At the same time, however, they had difficulties in defining the exact content of their own reislamicization policies. The issue of *džihad* (*jihad*, holy war) is probably the best illustration of their dilemmas. Enes Karić, professor at the Faculty of Islamic Sciences in Sarajevo, asserted, for example, that the Bosnian Army was waging a *džihad*, since it was fighting to 'safeguard the free expression of Islam, to protect goods, life, honour, and dignity' (Karić 1994: 75). According to him, 'if Muslims need a state in order to defend these values, then the building of this state represents – from a religious point of view – a *džihad* par excellence!' (Karić 1994: 76). Nonetheless, he recommended careful thought about 'which rhetoric to choose for internal or external purposes, in the short or the long run' (Karić 1994: 77), since the resort to *džihad* could be used by Serb and Croat propaganda to stir up 'European islamophobia' and could also give rise to strong resistance within the Bosnian Army itself:

> Some soldiers [are fighting] out of patriotism, others out of patriotism and religious inspiration, still others out of courage and heroism, or to protect their family and property, etc. For this reason, it would not be advisable to crush the diversity of these motivations that make up the mosaic of the heroic Bosniac resistance put up by the Bosniacs, and especially not by imposing something that could be unfavourably received by soldiers, or at least by some groups of them. (Karić 1994: 77)

Throughout the war, references to *džihad* made by Bosnian *ulemas* have most often remained implicit, as for example through the enumeration of the main motives that can justify resorting to *džihad*. Outside the religious institutions, only foreign volunteers coming from the Muslim world and local soldiers belonging to the religious units defined the ongoing war as a *džihad*. Suljeman Kurtanović, an imam fighting with the 7th Muslim Brigade, for example, declared that the transformation of Bosnian Muslims into a 'nation of *mudžahidi* [*mujaheddins*]' had freed them from their political immaturity, from their feeling of cultural inferiority:

> The time is gone, inch'Allah, when my people were '[nationally] undetermined', or 'Serbs of Islamic faith', or 'Croats of Islamic faith', '*poturice*' ['half-Turks', derogatory term for Muslims], traitors to the faith of their ancestors. … The time has come when we have proven that we really have sound foundations, that all of us, or at least a large majority of us, are *mudžahidi*, that *džihad* is our path and our choice, our destiny, the creator of our destiny. … No child will believe any more in the toy called 'Brotherhood

and Unity', in a community shared with perpetrators and murders. The young generations have seen and understood who our open or covert enemies are. The lesson of *četnici* and *ustaše* has been taught to them by the tenacity of the *mudžahidi* and the graves of the *šehidi*. (Kurtanović 1993)

Within the general Bosnian Muslim population, however, it was rare to find anyone who considered the war a *džihad*, or who saw a clear link between the concepts of *šehidi* and *mudžahidi*. In the media and in everyday conversations, the term '*mudžahid*' referred first of all to foreign volunteers from the Muslim world, and often carried a negative connotation (see also Maček, Stefansson, this volume).[8] In contrast, the most frequent terms used for labelling the war – 'resistance to aggression', 'struggle against fascism' – originated in international law or Titoist rhetoric. As for the Bosnian authorities, they defined the war as external aggression, rejecting any interpretation that would frame it as a civil or religious war. In this case as well, the rare hints at *džihad* were only meant for a selected audience. In March 1994, Alija Izetbegović urged the SDA Convention to prepare for peace and, following the Prophet's example, to switch 'from a small to a big battle' (Izetbegović 1995b: 78). This phrasing alluded to the distinction existing in Islam between the small, worldly and military *jihad*, and the big, inner and spiritual *jihad*.

This de-linking of the related concepts of *mudžahidi* and *šehidi*, *džihad* and *šehadet*[9] helps to explain why, at the same time as the term '*šehid*' has been gaining currency, it has also partly lost its religious meaning, to the point where it has begun to encompass all defenders of the national cause. This nationalist dimension is perceptible even among the *ulemas*, as shown by the writings of Sulejman Kurtanović. It is even more obvious among other segments of the Bosnian Muslim population, where references to *šehidi* can appear against a completely secular backdrop and are sometimes more reminiscent of the Titoist epic tradition than of the Ottoman or early Islamic ones.[10] A clear sign that the term '*šehid*' has been undergoing a process of secularisation are the graves marked '*Bosanski šehid*' ('Bosnian *Šehid*') that can be found in parks and other public places (see Figure 7.3). In this case, the title '*šehid*' is given to an unknown person whose personal beliefs and motivations, and possibly even religious identity, remain a mystery.

---

[8] During the seminar held in January 1994 on Islam as the 'spiritual force of the defence', Fikret Muslimović himself denounced the '[foreign] emissaries who endeavour to modify the traditional religious and ethical values of our nation, ... contributing in this way to sowing the seed of new divisions' and, 'at the international level, to providing our enemies with arguments [against us]' (Muslimović 1994: 92).

[9] From the Arabic word '*shahada*': testimony, martyrdom (Brown 2003).

[10] See for example the countless books and brochures published with the support of municipal authorities and other local sponsors, which contain hagiographies, poems, and other materials dedicated to local *šehidi*.

Figure 7.3   Grave of an Unknown Bosnian *Šehid* in Sarajevo

(Photo by Xavier Bougarel)

More generally, as the term '*šehid*' has become widespread, there has been a growing fluctuation in both its definition and uses. During the war, SDA leaders endeavoured to apply this term to all Muslim war victims. In his opening speech of the first *Bošnjački sabor* (Bosniac Assembly) in September 1993, for example, the writer Alija Isaković defined as *šehidi* all those 'who went over to the world beyond as soldiers or as civilians, from the children in the incubators of our maternity hospitals to the centenarians in our old people's homes', for 'all have borne witness to the truth with their lives and in this way have earned God's blessing' (Isaković 1994: 378). A similar use of the term '*šehid*' was apparent after the war, especially during religious ceremonies dedicated to the victims of wartime massacres. When used in such a comprehensive way, the concept of *šehid* not only loses its religious meaning, but also its role in the building of new boundaries and hierarchies between soldiers and civilians, men and women, heroic martyrdom and passive victimhood (see also Helms, Delpla, this volume).

The secularisation and polysemy surrounding the cult of *šehidi* also explain why certain rituals attached to the burial and veneration of *šehidi* have not always been followed. According to Islamic teachings, *šehidi* must be buried in the clothes they wore when they died and without being washed, since they have already been purified by their own blood (Omerdić 1997: 10). However, the journalist Šefko Hodžić notes in his diary that 'the first *šehidi* [of Sarajevo] were not buried at Kovači in a common grave, as had initially been planned, but in individual *mezar*s [graves] that had been dug for each of them. This [was] because it had been insisted upon by the families, and because some prominent Sarajevans were also hostile to [the idea of] a common grave. It is also important to note that the first *šehidi* were washed and that their blood was thus removed. The director of [the funeral service] *Bakije*, Fuad Šehbajraktarević, says that they started to bury the *šehidi* without washing them or changing their clothes only after they got the *fatwa* issued by Muharem ef. Omerdić [on 28 April 1992]' (Hodžić 2003: 20).

Later, the adherence to Islamic rules regarding the burial of *šehidi* was relatively quickly and smoothly ensured, as this was a task taken on by funeral services and by the army itself. Such was not the case with funeral monuments. According to early Islamic traditions and to fundamentalist interpretations of Islam, the graves of *šehidi* should not be indicated by any sign, their very imperceptibility stressing the unselfishness and modesty of *šehidi*. In Bosnia-Herzegovina, however, graves of *šehidi* dating back from the Ottoman period display various markers of prestige (double gravestones, turbans on top of the headstones, specific epitaphs and symbols) and are often surrounded by a fence or turned into a *turbe* (mausoleum) (Bringa 1995; Popović 1996). During and after the war, many of the *nišani* (gravestones) placed over *šehid* graves have followed still different styles: many families of the dead have chosen *nišani* with pictures of the deceased and other non-Islamic symbols, or in the shape of a stylized lily, the Bosnian national symbol. These practices reflect the adoption of Christian or atheist death rituals, a phenomenon that predates the war and has been a source of anxiety for the *ulemas* since their appearance during the communist period.[11]

Political and military leaders of the Muslim community have themselves expressed ambiguous attitudes on this issue. During the war, they encouraged giving greater visibility to the graves of *šehidi*. During the SDA Convention held in March 1994, for example, Alija Izetbegović declared:

> We will not allow these mounds [of earth] to be flattened, to disappear rapidly. They have to be seen. Of course, we will not put expansive monuments on them, but we have to erect *nišani*. All of Bosnia-Herzegovina is dotted with these mounds of earth, with these mounds of fresh earth. … We will slightly change the tradition and erect *nišani*, so that we remember and so that, when children visit them during future *bajram*, they will recite the *fatiha* and remember these people and events. They must not be forgotten. (Izetbegović 1995b: 74-5)

It therefore appears that the cult of *šehidi* has been simultaneously diffused and transformed through the manifold ways in which people have accommodated it to their own beliefs and needs. Against this background, the official promoters of the concept of *šehid* have been compelled again and again to delineate its boundaries and regulate its uses, to rank its beneficiaries and symbolic retributions. Especially after the war, Bosnian *ulemas* have insisted that there are several categories of *šehidi*, and that the only ones that can be considered 'first-rank *šehidi*' are the soldiers who died in battle and whose motivation was purely religious. Those who died defending their family, their honour or their property, as well as all the people who died a violent death in non-combatant roles (including hostages and prisoners of war who were executed), are 'second-rank *šehidi*'. Only those in the first category should be buried in the clothes they wore when they died and without being washed; only they are absolved of all sins and will be fully rewarded in the world beyond.[12] In making this distinction, the *ulemas* are also reinforcing hierarchies, between soldiers and civilians, heroes and victims, men and women,

---

[11]   A booklet dealing with Islamic death rituals that was first published in the early 1990s and reprinted in 2001 deplores the fact that, 'in this domain as well, Islamic traditions and customs have largely ceased to be respected, which has led to the present situation where cemeteries are to a great extent a display of bad taste, kitsch, neglect and – what is the most unfortunate – a place for obviously non-Islamic epitaphs and symbols. … Today our *nišani* are often very expansive, excessively luxurious, with pictures and all kinds of personal designations, which is contrary to Islamic rules that call for extreme modesty and simplicity' (Bevrnja and Strik 2001: 68-9).

[12]   This distinction between various categories of *šehidi* was already present in the *fatwa* issued in April 1992 by Muharem Omerdić (Hodžić 2003: 20-21) but gained importance after the war (Omerdić 1997: 19-23).

that had sometimes threatened to break down in the course of the war, as illustrated by the case of Srebrenica (see also Duijzings, this volume).[13]

Of course, the *ulemas* admit that it is impossible to know with certainty the inner motives of the soldiers, and that only Allah can recognize the true *šehid*. The insistence on the religious motivation of 'first-rank *šehidi*', however, bolsters their own attempt to reinforce the ranking power of the status of *šehid*, as well as their own monopoly over the awarding of this status. A similar insistence on the normative dimensions of the cult of *šehidi* can be found at the level of ritual: since 1997, state institutions have embarked on a project to replace the makeshift wartime *nišani* with more permanent, standard marble *nišani* so that all are properly aligned and have the same form all over Bosnia-Herzegovina.[14] This standardization policy has enabled many destitute families to provide their relatives with a permanent grave marker, but it has also met with some resistance: in the Sarajevo Canton, for example, between 5 and 10 percent of the families have expressed a desire to keep or put up a *nišan* that is different from the official one. In such cases, according to its president, the Fund in charge of the maintenance of military cemeteries paid the families a lump sum equivalent to the price of the standard *nišan*.[15]

Tensions that pit the relatives of *šehidi* against political or religious authorities have taken many other shapes. They were bluntly expressed when, in the immediate aftermath of the war, the father of a young fallen soldier addressed an open letter to Alija Izetbegović, in which he denied Izetbegović the right to talk about his son as a *šehid*:

> Why are you associating the religious term '*šehid*' with the first name of my son and of so many other courageous fighters for the Bosnian cause? My son is not a *šehid* and I do not allow anybody to refer to him this way. In my language there are a thousand non-religious and non-partisan words to describe his sacrifice for Bosnia. ... Why are you reciting the *fatiha* for those who have been killed? I am not reproaching you for doing it as a private person, as a believer. But you are the official representative of a state and,

---

[13]   Most of the men slaughtered by the Bosnian Serb Army after the fall of Srebrenica on 11 July 1995 were Bosnian Army soldiers. However, the term most frequently used in public commemorations is 'victims' (*žrtve*). In 1996, the Bosnian authorities designated 11 July as the Day of Remembrance of Civilian Victims of the Fascist Aggression (*Dan sjećanja na civilne žrtve fašističke agresije*), thus implicitly classifying the men of Srebrenica as civilians, and enshrining their deaths into Western time (11 July), whereas the sacrifice of the *šehidi* is related to Islamic time (2 sevval). This semantic shift underscores the fact that the men of Srebrenica were slaughtered after their surrender and facilitates the presentation of the massacre as part of a genocidal project comparable to the Holocaust.

[14]   The only information inscribed on these *nišani* is the name, year of birth and year of death of the *šehid*, as well as the Qur'anic verse 'And do not say about those who died on God's Path: "They are dead". No, they are alive, but you do not feel it' (Qur'an, 2:154) and a lily, the symbol of Bosnia-Herzegovina (see also Figure 7.3).

[15]   Interview with Emir Zlatar in *Preporod*, 1st September 2001.

moreover, of a multinational Bosnia [*multinacionalna Bosna*]. As for my son, I would request you to remain silent. It is better not to say anything than to use a language that neither he nor I understand. (Tica 1996)

Most often, however, these tensions have remained implicit. Such is the case, for example, when religious newspapers rail against the lack of respect for *šehid* cemeteries, whereas independent media mock the incompetence of the institutions in charge of them. Such accusations are partly a reflection of the wider climate of distrust and bitterness prevailing in Bosnia-Herzegovina. However, denouncing breaches of the respect due the *šehidi* is also a way of talking in their name and, indirectly, using their memory to bolster one's own agenda. Therefore, seemingly petty polemics surrounding the new cult of *šehidi* can reveal deeper conflicts and changes experienced in the Muslim community.

Šehidi and the Controversial Articulation of the Meaning of War

Recurrent debates surrounding the cult of *šehidi* testify to its importance in the articulation of the meaning and memory of war. During the war itself, when open criticism of the SDA's reislamicization politics was made difficult by political pressures and self-censorship, an implicit denunciation was still possible through the rejection of the new cult of *šehidi*. This reality was quite obvious in Tuzla, an industrial city in north-eastern Bosnia governed by the Social Democrats (see Jansen, this volume). There, local newspapers criticized the use of the term '*šehid*' as conducive to discrimination against non-Muslim soldiers within the Bosnian Army, to artificial divides between them and their Muslim brothers in arms, and to a gross manipulation of Islam (Alispahić 1996: 66-9; 225-7).

Sometimes, this kind of polemic went far beyond newspaper columns and invaded all of local public life. On 25 May 1995, during the celebration of Youth Day, a holiday dating from the communist period, a Serb shell fell into the centre of Tuzla killing 71 people, most of them teenagers. In the following days, the municipality decided to bury all the victims in the same place and without any religious markers. Yet, whereas the local imams and priests supported this idea, the *Reisu-l-ulema* Mustafa Cerić insisted on separate burials. In the end, the choice was left to the families and 48 of the 71 victims were buried together in the Slana Banja Park, where the Partisan cemetery is also located. A year later, commemoration of the incident gave rise to new debates. *Ljiljan*, a Sarajevo weekly close to the SDA, accused the Mayor of Tuzla, Selim Beslagić, and other 'Muslims full of inferiority complexes [*iskompleksirani Muslimani*]' of having authorized the use of candles, 'a Christian symbol', during the funeral ceremony and, in so doing, of leading the Muslims into 'political slavery', 'cultural powerlessness', and 'idolatry' (Latić 1996). This comment, taken up by the SDA-controlled local newspaper *Zmaj od Bosne* and the cantonal TV station, provoked a sharp reply from the victims' families:

Instead of showing devotion to the dead, instead of the compassion felt by the city for the anniversary of this tragedy, these two media outlets led by the journalist V[edad] Spahić are busy insulting and humiliating not only the relatives and friends of the victims, but the whole city that has commemorated with dignity the biggest tragedy of its history. [In their eyes], we are guilty of wanting our children to rest together, the way they died, of refusing to divide them along national or religious lines, as they were not divided during their short lives. We are guilty of disobeying the *Reis* who came to Tuzla the day after the tragedy to tell us that it would be *haram* [illicit] to bury our children side by side. We are guilty of remembering our loved ones, as has been done for centuries on Bosnian soil, we are guilty of lighting candles for the souls of our dead, as people light candles in front of *turbe*, churches and mosques, and this since Bosnia has been called Bosnia.[16]

In Bosnia-Herzegovina, death and its representation have played a key role in the articulation of the meaning of war (see also Duijzings, Grandits, this volume). Against this background, the dead can also be conjured up to silence the living. That *šehidi* were being used in this way was obvious in January 1995 when, for the first and last time during the war, Bosnian legal institutions were consumed by the sensitive issue of the war's true meaning. After Alija Izetbegović and the Iranian ayatollah Ahmad Jannati attended a parade of the 7th Muslim Brigade in Zenica, the five opposition party members of the Bosnian Presidency denounced the 'ideologization of faith' in the Bosnian Army, reaffirming that this army 'must be secular and multinational, beyond political influences and rivalries'.[17] The next day, Alija Izetbegović and Ejup Ganić, the two Presidency members from the SDA, retorted that the Zenica parade had only been 'an expression of faith, and the right to express one's own faith exists and will exist everywhere, including in the army'. They further stated that 'the emphasis put on faith in some of our army units … is often a spontaneous reaction to the destruction of religious symbols', and that these units 'have protected the population from genocide, without ever committing genocide. Their religious inspiration did not prevent them, but rather encouraged them to protect the weak, their lives, their honour and their property, without first asking them their first names. Moreover, their cry of "God is great!" is the source of their courage and strength in the face of dangers implied by this long and difficult struggle'. And they conclude:

Let us count the graves! The fate of this country will be decided by those who are fighting, acting and dying for it! [18]

This propensity by the SDA leaders to use the war dead to homogenize the Muslim community and to claim a monopoly on the interpretation of the war itself has been apparent in various forms on many other occasions. During the war, these leaders

---

[16] Press release quoted in *Naša borba* (22 June 1996).
[17] Press release quoted in *Oslobođenje*, European weekly edition (2 February 1995).
[18] Press release quoted in *Oslobođenje*, European weekly edition (9 February 1995).

readily referred to 'ultimatums' sent by the *šehidi* in order to justify their own strategic choices, as for example the acceptance or rejection of peace plans. During and after the war alike, 'counting the graves' and conjuring up the SDA's *šehidi* also enabled the party to underscore its contribution to the war effort, to brush aside embarrassing questions about its own responsibility for the outbreak or outcome of the war, and, last but not least, to mobilize voters against 'traitors' (*izdajnici*), 'deserters' (*podrumaši* – literally: those who hid in basements) and all those who 'do not recite the *fatiha* when innocent victims and soldiers are buried' (Izetbegović 1999a: 98).

Just as Bosnian legal institutions were circumvented in the use of the army as a tool of reislamicization, they were again deprived of any sort of control over death and its interpretation: representatives of the *Islamska zajednica* took over the central role in ceremonies commemorating the war dead, and in Sarajevo, the most famous defenders of the city were buried on the grounds of the Ali Pašina mosque, next door to the Presidency, rather than in a military cemetery. Moreover, the construction of a new official memory was also aimed at undermining the communist and Yugoslav memory of World War II, which was still influential at the beginning of the war, both in state institutions and among the population. In 1994, for example, Deputy *Reisu-l-ulema* Ismet Spahić justified the introduction of the Day of *Šehidi* by stressing the need to put an end to veneration of the Partisan movement and, more precisely, to the commemoration of the battle of Sutjeska.[19]

New official memories, however, are far from uncontested (see also Duijzings, Kolind, Jansen, this volume). In the post-war period, the apparent unanimity of the Muslim community on war-related issues has crumbled, the independent media has inquired into the SDA's mistakes and misdeeds, and some opposition forces have once more been tempted to blame the three main nationalist parties *en bloc*. The international organizations present in Bosnia-Herzegovina have also endeavoured to rid the local mass media and schoolbooks of bellicose language and have joined in the criticism of nationalist parties. The SDA and the *Islamska zajednica* have responded to all of this by rejecting the equation of victims with their executioners:

These days I have been watching some electoral spots on television, whose authors or sponsors are international organizations or, to be more precise, some individuals within these organizations. These spots insult those in power and openly support the other side. I don't know what gives them the right to do this, but I know how they do this. Most often [it's done] in an impudent way: for example, they suggest to the population and to the citizens of Bosnia that all sides in the war were equal, that there is no aggressor and no victim, that we are all equally guilty. We, who fought to defend freedom and, quite

---

[19]   Quoted in *Ljiljan*, 23 March 1994. In July 1943, in the gorges of the Sutjeska River (eastern Herzegovina), thousands of Partisans broke through enemy lines after having been surrounded by German forces. This battle, at which the death toll was very high and which is considered the greatest armed feat of the Partisan movement, was duly commemorated during the communist period and remains a site of commemoration attracting people from various parts of the former Yugoslavia.

simply, our own lives, are worth nothing more than the SDS [Serb Democratic Party] and the *četnici*. ... We have protested, but opposition leaders remain silent – this situation suits them – they hope that, in this way, they will get a few more votes. They accept the exchange of votes for a state of amnesia. But amnesia will not get through. We will turn ourselves towards the future, we will teach people to forgive, whenever it is possible to forgive, but we will not forget. We would have to be idiots to forget, and we are not idiots. The time of innocence is gone. (Izetbegović 1999a: 100)

The SDA's attempts to reshape war memories to its own advantage have not always been successful: when, during the local election campaign of 2000, the party reminded voters that '[We have spent] the ten most difficult years together', the slogan backfired, since it could be interpreted as a recognition of the SDA's own share of responsibility in the hardships voters had endured during and after the war. Furthermore, the defeat of the SDA in the local elections of April 2000 and the general elections held seven months later triggered a shift in the balance of power underlying the way in which war memories were expressed. Inevitably, as the Social Democratic Party (SDP) and the Alliance for Change (*Alijansa za promjene*) rose to power, the narrative of the war that had until that time been promoted by the SDA was increasingly called into question.

At the legal level, this period brought the first indictments against high-ranking officers of the Bosnian Army by the International Criminal Tribunal for the former Yugoslavia (ICTY), while at the same time, several SDA leaders who had occupied key posts in the military and secret services were prosecuted for embezzlement or terrorist activities. At the discursive level, onslaughts against the war memory promoted by the SDA intensified. In April 2001, the new state-level Prime Minister, Božidar Matić, asserted that 'Bosnia-Herzegovina does not have an army, but three political phalanxes set up by the three nationalist parties'.[20] Predictably, this statement provoked strong reactions. Rasim Delić, the former head of the Bosnian Army, protested on behalf of 'all those who fought, died, sacrificed their health and parts of their bodies for a unified, independent, multiethnic and democratic Bosnia-Herzegovina and not for whatever political party'.[21] He also became the leader of an Association for the Protection of the Legacy of the War of Liberation (*Udruženje za zaštitu tekovine oslobodilačkog rata*). Newspapers close to the SDA, for their part, denounced what they termed the subjugation of the Muslim community to an 'aggression of amnesia'[22] and 'serial humiliation'.[23]

At the same time, the conflict between the Alliance for Change and veteran associations over the reform of war pensions brought the concept of *šehid* back to the centre of political life. In order to understand the place of this concept in the

---

[20]   Interview with Božidar Matić in *Večernji list*, 3 April 2001.
[21]   Press release reproduced in *Jutarnje Novine*, 7 April 2001.
[22]   *Preporod*, 15 April 2002.
[23]   *Ljiljan*, 12 August 2002.

political and social crisis of 2002, however, it is first necessary to consider how it has contributed to the political construction of the veteran population (veterans, war disabled, and families of fallen soldiers) as a specific social group enjoying a specific material and moral status.[24]

Šehidi as Cornerstone of the Veteran Identity

As early as in the first months of the war, the Bosnian Presidency subsumed Bosnian Army soldiers under the jurisdiction of laws dating back from the 1980s that applied to members of the Yugoslav armed forces as well as veterans of the Partisan movement. Due to the institutional chaos of this period, however, material aid to Bosnian soldiers and their families became the de facto responsibility of municipalities, the largest public companies, and myriad diaspora networks and humanitarian organizations. The SDA and the *Islamska zajednica*, for their part, focused from the outset on war widows and orphans. The material aspect of these efforts to promote the concept of *šehid* was reflected in regular visits and the distribution of humanitarian and financial aid to the families of *šehidi* by the local Muslim charity *Merhamet*, the association *Fatma* and various foreign Islamic NGOs.

Once again, it was only in 1993 that the Bosnian authorities were able to set up nation-wide social assistance mechanisms adapted to war circumstances. At that time, Fikret Muslimović, head of the Department of Morale, warned that the 'resolution of the social and statutory problems faced by the soldiers, the families of *šehidi*, the disabled and the wounded' was an urgent necessity since, 'if we maintain our present way of operating, problems will keep accumulating, the discontent of the soldiers, their families, and the families of *šehidi* and the disabled will grow [and] the fighting spirit will deteriorate' (Muslimović 1993: 42). A few months later, a participant at the seminar dedicated to Islam as the 'spiritual force of the defence' established a clear link between the symbolic importance of the *šehidi* and the material care to which their children are entitled:

> We, the living, have a burning obligation towards the orphans of this war, an obligation we have no right to ignore because they are the children of our soldiers ... and the Prophet has said: 'The one who takes care of the family of a *šehid* is elevating himself to his level.' If we cannot bring back the son, the father, the brother, or the husband war has taken from them, we can at least, through our care, through grateful attention and receptiveness, stop their tears and breathe a bit of happiness into their souls. In so doing, we are not only accomplishing a deed that is pleasing to God, but are providing more security to our soldiers and reinforcing their fighting spirit. (Muminović 1994: 84)

---

[24] On Croat veteran associations, see Grandits, this volume. On civilian victim associations, see Delpla, this volume.

In the following years, free housing, access to basic utilities as well as various social benefits have been granted to the war disabled and the families of *šehidi* and fallen soldiers, while the salaries owed to all army members were compensated for by the distribution of privatisation vouchers (Purišević 2000). In this way, a new social welfare system has slowly replaced the one inherited from the communist period. Furthermore, the purpose of this residual welfare state was not only to bolster the fighting spirit of the Bosnian Army: against the background of the collapse of the production economy, it has cushioned the impact of widespread impoverishment (see Maček, Jašarević, this volume), alleviated tension between a destitute population and a minority of *bogataši* (*'nouveaux riches'*) and *ratni profiteri* ('war profiteers'), and facilitated the coalescence of new social groups produced by the war. A World Bank report noted that in 1999 in the Muslim part of the Federation there were 80,140 war veterans, 33,149 war disabled and 87,803 recipients of pensions for the relatives of fallen soldiers. According to this same report:

> If one considers extended family members, at least one third of the population is directly affected by veterans' affairs. Politically, it is a powerful lobby group, and well organized. ... Socio-culturally, vet[eran]s are viewed as having 'saved' their respective ethnicity. They are distinguished as ones that stayed rather than fleeing as refugees. Finally, their sacrifice, by life or limb, is recognized by the population as something which should be compensated for, recognizing that full compensation is impossible. (Gregson 2000: 3)

In the Muslim part of the Federation, *šehidi* are at the heart of this new social welfare system, as shown by the relatively high sums paid by state institutions in pensions to families of *šehidi* and fallen soldiers,[25] as well as the SDA's establishment of a Foundation for Families of *Šehidi* and War Disabled. More generally, *šehidi* and their families represent the cornerstone of the financial, institutional and symbolic constructs that are buttressing veterans' collective identity. The ultimate sacrifice of the *šehidi* not only occupies a central place in the memory of their brothers-in-arms but also serves to call attention to their own losses: amputated limbs and disabled bodies, ruined professional ambitions, months and years spent on the frontline. Against this background, *šehidi* are invoked by veterans in order to remind society of its indebtedness to them, to justify their privileged legal and moral status, as well as the additional material and symbolic retributions they demand for themselves.

At the same time, reference to the *šehidi* is also used by state authorities in order to segment, rank, and control the veteran population. As early as August

---

[25] At the beginning of 2002, in the Muslim part of the Federation, the monthly war pension granted to widows of *šehidi* and fallen soldiers ranged from 257 to 572 KM (129 to 286 €), depending on the number of children. At the same time, the average salary in the Federation was 459 KM (230 €), and the average pension 170 KM (85 €).

1992, a Veterans' Union (*Unija veterana*) was founded in Sarajevo with the aim of providing 'moral and material assistance to all those who need it, above all to the families of fallen soldiers and war disabled'.[26] Two years later, this union was converted into a state-wide United Soldiers' Organization (*Jedinstvena organizacija boraca*, JOB), which covered all segments of the veteran population and was partly influenced by the SDP. In order to defuse the threat presented by this initiative, the SDA first encouraged the foundation of separate associations for war disabled (the Union of War Disabled, *Savez ratnih vojnih invalida*) and families of fallen soldiers (the Organization of the Families of *Šehidi* and Fallen Soldiers, *Organizacija porodica šehida i poginulih boraca*), before launching its own Alliance of Demobilized Soldiers (*Savez demobilisanih boraca*) in 1998.

Finally, reference to the *šehidi* has fed other forms of statutory discrimination which, despite their lack of legal foundation, have had great practical impact. The dual institutional and legal constructs that are so characteristic of SDA power practices can also be found in the social assistance mechanisms set up for the veteran population. In particular, the material support that *Merhamet*, SDA foundations and Islamic NGOs have granted only to the families of *šehidi* (as opposed to those of fallen soldiers) have contributed to the establishment of a two-tier social welfare system which benefits the SDA's political clients (see also Maček 2000: 192-3). Between 1996 and 2001, the inability of the Federation Parliament to pass a law on the 'rights of soldiers, war disabled and families of *šehidi* and fallen soldiers' and the ensuing legal void has thus benefited the SDA.[27]

In November 2000, the rise to power of the Alliance for Change destabilized these social assistance mechanisms inherited from the war and led to an open conflict between the new Federation Government and the veteran population, whose growing frustrations had actually been one of the factors leading to the electoral defeat of the SDA. In July 2001, the World Bank and the Office of the High Representative (OHR) demanded drastic cuts in veteran-related state expenditures, which were seen as the major contributor to the budget deficit.[28] Two months later, the Minister for Veteran Affairs, Suada Hadžović, presented a new draft law that discontinued all pensions for able-bodied war veterans, partly disabled war veterans (up to 50 percent disability) and relatives of fallen soldiers who held paid employment.

---

[26] Statutes of the Union of the Veterans of the Resistance Movement of the Republic of Bosnia-Herzegovina (*Unija veterana pokreta otpora RBiH-e*), partly reproduced in *Ljiljan*, 16 May 1994.

[27] This state of affairs, however, was mainly due to obstruction from the Croat Democratic Union (HDZ) which has been preoccupied with upholding its own system of parallel war pensions for veterans of the Croat Defence Council (HVO) with the financial support of Croatia (see Grandits, this volume).

[28] In 1999, The World Bank reported that veteran-related expenditures in the Federation amounted to 210 million KM (105 million €), that is 26 percent of the overall Federation budget (Gregson 2000: 10).

Although this draft law foresaw a substantial increase in the pensions granted to the most severely disabled war veterans and the poorest relatives of fallen soldiers, it met with strong protest from veteran associations and the SDA. The latter saw this crisis as a good opportunity to take revenge on the Alliance for Change. The showdown between the Federation Government and the veterans reached its peak during street protests organized on 1 March 2002, the tenth anniversary of Bosnian independence. When the Federation Prime Minister Zlatko Lagumdžija tried to address the crowd of thousands of veterans gathered in Sarajevo, he was taken to task by a group of protesters. A few weeks later, the government withdrew the draft law and began new talks with the veteran associations, in spite of the pressures put on it by the World Bank and the OHR. Munir Karić, representative of the Party for Bosnia-Herzegovina (SBiH), a member of the Alliance, and head of the War Veterans Commission, then submitted his own draft law to the Federation Parliament, a law that would have been much more profitable for the veterans, but the costs of which would have exceeded... the total budget of the Federation! Against the advice of the government, this law was passed on 25 September 2002. Ten days later, the nationalist parties won the general elections, and the whole debate on veterans' issues was brought full circle.

The importance of war-related social benefits to the survival of many households is sufficient to explain the strong resistance to the proposed cuts in veteran benefits. Yet the crisis of 2001-2002 must also be placed into the wider context of the crisis of veterans' collective identity. Since the end of the 1990s, the veteran population has experienced a rapid decline in its material and moral status. At the material level, war veterans have been directly affected by an economic crisis that has left half of the working population unemployed (see Jašarević, Jansen, this volume). Delays in the payment of pensions accumulated and the privatisation vouchers distributed at the end of the war lost 97 percent of their value within a few years. Following the new property laws passed by the OHR in 1998, private houses and socially-owned flats that had been allocated to veterans were returned to their pre-war owners, leading to awkward situations where war disabled or war widows were expelled to make way for people considered 'deserters' in the case of Bosnian Muslim refugees coming back from abroad, or 'traitors' and 'criminals' in the case of Serb and Croat returnees (see also Stefansson, Armakolas, this volume). This restoration process gave rise to numerous protests, with the sense of injustice reaching a peak in December 2001, when the Court for Human Rights ordered the restoration of socially-owned flats to their former, pre-war occupants: officers of the Yugoslav People's Army.

Coupled with challenges to the official narrative of the war, this decline in veterans' material status nourished the feeling among veterans that their prestige was rapidly vanishing and that wartime normative categories and hierarchies were becoming blurred. In 2001, the debate over the draft law on war pensions further deepened this identity crisis: the law no longer based pension amounts for veterans and their closest relatives on wartime sacrifices and merit but on actual, present material need. The new law thus devalued their wartime status: it reversed the relationship of indebtedness linking veterans to society as a whole and exposed their difficulties in earning a legitimate income, caring for their families and building a new social status under post-war circumstances. In short, it turned war heroes into social misfits and powerless family heads. What was more, by placing veterans of the Bosnian Army, of the Croat Defence Council (HVO) and former supporters of Fikret Abdić[29] into one pension fund, the new law further blurred the categories and hierarchies inherited from the war.

Against this background, veterans' protests crystallized rapidly around two symbolic issues. The first was the very personality of the new Minister for Veteran Affairs, Suada Hadžović. In the eyes of many veterans, the reversal of their status was embodied by the fact that a woman was now in charge of 'their' ministry, whereas Sefer Halilović, the first head of the Bosnian Army (and a man), had been appointed as Minister of Social Affairs, an area of government activity typically associated more with women (see Helms, this volume). Veterans thus put forth repeated demands for Hadžović's resignation and denied her the right to speak in the name of the veteran population, in spite of the fact that she was herself a war widow.[30] Hadžović also became the target of violent attacks in the media close to the SDA. After she denounced the misuse of female bodies in advertising campaigns during an unrelated initiative, *Ljiljan* accused her of disrespecting the (male) bodies of the war disabled and the *šehidi*:

> This time, Minister [*ministrica*] Hadžović showed that she has an opinion about bodies exposed on billboards. She was very constructive. For other bodies, which were long ago exposed under the fire of shells and the view of snipers on the front lines of defence of the state of Bosnia-Herzegovina, the Minister was not really so understanding. ... More precisely, the Minister has thrown [the term] families of *šehidi* out of the Law, purely on a stylistic level one would say. But it's not only style [that is at stake]. The new Ministry will once again settle accounts with the *šehidi*, and then will throw out those used and mutilated bodies not onto billboards, but onto the street. Recently a real reckoning with those who got pensions as soldiers and war disabled has started. All souls, then, who survived with some sort of body parts or remnants are being freed of any income and thrown out onto the street. They would be better off naked on a billboard. (Omeragić 2001)

---

[29] In September 1993, after the Bosnian Parliament had rejected the Owen-Stoltenberg peace agreement, an uprising led by the local strongman and Bosnian Presidency member Fikret Abdić resulted in bloody fighting with the Bosnian Army in the Cazinska krajina (Bihać area). Abdić's supporters were regarded by the *Islamska zajednica* as *murtadi* (apostates) and thus denied a religious burial.

[30] Suada Hadžović's husband, an influential local politician in the Sarajevo suburb of Ilidža, was murdered by the Serbs at the very beginning of the war. Asked whether she would consider her husband a *šehid*, Hadžović replied: 'My husband was a Social Democrat and he had his own ideological opinions. I consider that I would offend him by calling him a *šehid*. ... He was not a believer but he respected people who sincerely believed in God.' (interview in *Oslobođenje*, 12 January 2002)

As shown by this quotation, the other issue of concern to the veterans' organizations close to the SDA was the wording of the new law, in which the term 'war military disabled' (*ratni vojni invalidi*) was replaced with 'military disabled' (*vojni invalidi*), and all references to *šehidi* had been removed. The veteran crisis of 2001-2002, together with this battle over terminology, therefore centred around the concept of *šehid*. On 17 December 2001, the Day of *šehidi*, the *Reisu-l-ulema* himself added a dramatic dimension to this issue by stating that 'the right of the *šehidi* to be called '*šehidi*' is established in the Qur'an. This right has also been established by the Prophet, it was not invented in Bosnia. ... At stake here are our human and religious rights. What is put into question is the honour of our faith. Consequently, whoever attacks this right is attacking our faith and our honour' (Cerić 2002). In order to better underscore the universal dimension of the issue, without undermining the specific status enjoyed by the *šehidi*, Mustafa Cerić also resorted to a rarely used distinction between *šehidi* (martyrs) and *šahidi* (witnesses):

> It seems that some people still don't know what a *šehid* is. We who are alive are *šahidi*, and those who gave their lives on God's Path are *šehidi*. If someone denies the [concept of] *šehid*, he is also denying the [concept of] *šahid*. The attempts to deprive us of our right to call those who have sacrificed their lives '*šehidi*' amount to attempts to deprive us of our right to testify. What is at stake is not only the denial of those who are *šehidi*, but the negation of us, the *šahidi*, the witnesses to what took place [in Bosnia-Herzegovina]. (Cerić 2002)

Three weeks later, when Hadžović was asked by the Congress of Bosniac Intellectuals to present the new draft law, members of the audience demanded that she first utter the word '*šehid*'. When she began to respond by saying that 'the nature of the war has not yet been defined', the same people interrupted her and ostentatiously left the room shouting: 'Get up, families of *šehidi*!'[31] A few days later, in an interview given to the daily newspaper *Oslobođenje*, Hadžović accused the SDA of having orchestrated the incident to put her on the spot. She also clarified her interrupted remark on the nature of war by saying that she had ongoing international legal proceedings in mind:

> If we state that there has been an [external] aggression, and so we do, since we who stayed here were directly affected by it, then terms like '*šehid*' and 'family of *šehid*' unnecessarily reopen the question of the nature of the war: was it aggression, or was it some kind of religious war?[32]

This terminological and symbolic struggle reached a new peak in the aftermath of the street protests held in Sarajevo on the 1st of March 2002. Taken to task by some protesters, the Federation Prime Minister Zlatko Lagumdžija compared them

---

[31]   *Oslobođenje*, 6 January 2002.
[32]   Interview with Suada Hadžović in *Oslobođenje*, 12 January 2002.

to the Serb hooligans he had been faced with a year earlier in Banja Luka.[33] Immediately, the SDA demanded that Lagumdžija publicly apologize for this 'shameful statement' – through which, they said, he had 'liken[ed] the legitimate discontent of the defenders of Bosnia-Herzegovina to the orgy [of violence] staged by the *četnici* during the opening ceremony for the rebuilding of the Ferhadija mosque in Banja Luka' – and called for his resignation.[34] Lagumdžija countered by asking the SDA to apologize to the veterans, 'to whom it has lied for years, and whom it has led into distress and misery', before denouncing an attempt at 'transforming their legitimate anger into a cheap [bit of] political manipulation'.[35] A few weeks later, however, the Federation Government changed the wording in the draft law and, out of a lack of solutions to the material difficulties faced by the veteran population, filled it with flattery. The official formula used in the title of this draft (as submitted by Munir Karić to the Federation Parliament) was: 'soldiers, war disabled, families of *šehidi* and fallen soldiers of the war of defence and liberation'.

It is difficult to know how far the prediction made by some veteran associations, that the parties of the Alliance for Change 'will attend their own [electoral] burial in October [2002] if they do not use the word "*šehid*"',[36] has proven to be true. It is obvious, however, that the intended reform of the war pension system, conceived by the World Bank and the OHR merely as an adjustment to 'objective' financial constraints, called into question normative categories and hierarchies inherited from the war and, in the process, stirred up certain social tensions and political conflicts running deeply through the Muslim community. Beyond just the veteran crisis of 2001-2002, the way a new cult of *šehidi* has developed in Bosnia-Herzegovina suggests that the violent transformation of ethno-national identities in this country cannot be explained without taking into account their links with other social and cultural categories dating back from the pre-war period or produced by the war. In order to homogenize the Bosnian Muslim population, the SDA has not only resorted to nationalist and religious rhetoric, but has also integrated into its own power practices some patriarchal and militaristic values, as well as some social welfare practices inherited from the communist period. The conflicts surrounding the cult of *šehidi*, for their part, show that this homogenization process is neither complete

---

[33]   On 7 May 2001 in Banja Luka, thousands of Serb protesters violently interrupted the opening ceremonies for the rebuilding of the Ferhadija mosque (destroyed in 1993), compelling a few hundred attending Bosnian Muslims, along with official representatives of the international community and the Federation, to take refuge inside the building of the *Islamska zajednica*. During these riots, one Bosnian Muslim was killed and dozens of others were injured.

[34]   Press release quoted in *Oslobođenje*, 3 March 2002.

[35]   Press release quoted in *Oslobođenje*, 4 March 2002.

[36]   Kasim Memić, president of the Organization of Demobilized Soldiers in Ilidža (Sarajevo), quoted in *Oslobođenje*, 6 January 2002.

nor unchallenged. The term '*šehid*' reflects specific interpretations and memories of the war, as well as new social divides and normative hierarchies within the Muslim community. Its formal acceptance by a majority of Bosnian Muslims has been accompanied by regular tensions between political authorities and bereaved families, and funeral practices emphasizing the individual dimension of death and grief.

Chapter 8

Remembering with a Difference:
Clashing Memories of Bosnian Conflict in Everyday Life

Stef Jansen

Several years after the signing of the Dayton Peace Agreement, the situation in Bosnia-Herzegovina[1] is still far from stable. Nevertheless, the war that propelled the country into the global media spotlight is slowly becoming 'history' now. This means, among other things, that different actors on the domestic and international front, in their attempts to represent the war in historical terms, aim to impose their version of these events as the only true one. These official and semi-official narrations of the recent violent past are in turn adopted and instrumentalised in a variety of ways by Bosnia's citizens. In an experimental way, this chapter puts the use of memories of the war in everyday life into critical perspective.[2] It describes and analyses one particular event during my ethnographic fieldwork in Bosnia: the first post-war encounter of a trio of ex-colleagues in Tuzla. The chapter offers a reconstruction of that evening's conversation, full of personal and political tensions, and contextualises it within post-war Bosnian realities.

Whilst my method may be unconventional, the aim of this ethnographic exercise is nevertheless straightforward: I hope to deploy the critical impact of a vivid description of one specific event against the sterile simplification that often comes with the more sweeping journalistic and scholarly accounts of contemporary Bosnian life. I believe that many such accounts tend to underestimate the complexities of everyday life, while overestimating the importance of national identities at the expense of other (non-national) factors. Thus, this detailed reconstruction of a perhaps unrepresentative but nevertheless significant encounter

---

[1] For reasons of brevity, I use the term 'Bosnia' to refer to the state of Bosnia-Herzegovina.

[2] I have explored similar issues with regard to post-war Croatia in Jansen 2002.

of four men – three Bosnians and myself – indicates the need to challenge such dominant frameworks of understanding.[3]

One

In the year 2000, the first day of October was a Sunday, and even in post-war Bosnia that day had remained a day for rest and social occasions. But as unemployment was over fifty percent, large numbers of people always seemed to be involved in some *biznis*, even on Sunday. It was therefore not a surprise when, on that day, two visitors, unknown to me, arrived separately, knocked on my door and asked for my landlord Samir.[4] I referred them to the upper part of the house, where Samir lived with his wife Lejla and their daughter Jasna.

A few months earlier I had arrived in Tuzla to start my fieldwork on experiences of 'home' and displacement. In the heat of the summer, the atmosphere was very different from the one during my latest visit, which had been in the middle of winter. The tiny traffic-free centre of the sun-baked town was buzzing with life, streets were packed, and even though most people were simply parading up and down the *korzo*, the outdoor terraces were virtually unable to contain the crowds of people sipping coffee. Later I understood the seasonal character of Tuzla's vibrancy, as many of the people on the streets had been *Tuzlaci* who were now living in Western Europe. They had come for a summer visit and it was possible to pick them out on the basis of their cars and clothing. In many cases, the smaller kids, running around in front of their parents, spoke German, Dutch or Swedish amongst themselves, while adults stuck to Bosnian.

Like many people in Tuzla, Samir and Lejla had been keen to rent out a part of their house to a foreigner. I received the keys of their small flat downstairs, which they normally used for themselves during the summer. The two adjacent houses belonged to Samir's mother and to his absent sister, who had married a German citizen and moved to Germany three decades ago. During the 1970s and 1980s, Samir himself had also spent some time in that favourite *Gastarbeiter* destination, sometimes engaging in small on-and-off jobs. In 1990, when most people still considered a war in Yugoslavia to be an impossibility, Lejla was offered a job as a cook in Germany. Partly because of the effects of the economic crisis on his firm, and partly out of a sense of adventure, Samir resigned from his job and followed his much younger wife. Their daughter Jasna was born in Germany and it was

---

[3]   This chapter deploys ethnographic representation in order to evoke rather than to analyse. For a more theoretically embedded argument, see Jansen 2005.

[4]   All personal names in this article are pseudonyms. I use 'national' equivalents for the originals: Hasan, Samir, Edin, Suad, Safeta and Lejla are considered typical Muslim/Bosniac names, Đorđe and Rade typical Serb names. Jasna is used by all. Željko and Goran are fairly neutral but mostly used by Serbs and Croats. Robi is a nickname borrowed from English.

there that she learned to read and write. Samir's frequent trips back to Bosnia came to an abrupt end when the war started, which also resulted in the family now being categorised as refugees. In the late 1990s they returned to Tuzla, just before they were to be forcibly repatriated by the German Government. This was a matter of pride on Samir's part, who argued that since they had come to Germany out of their free will they had also wanted to leave voluntarily.

Although Samir had started building the houses in the early 1980s, even in 2000 the work was still very much in progress. This reflects a common pattern in former Yugoslavia, where house building is a long process, sometimes lasting a lifetime. And sure enough, Samir, unemployed now, carried out construction work in and around the houses almost on a daily basis, depending on cash flow and a multitude of other factors. Lejla, a professional cook with experience in several hotels in Bosnia and Germany, was now relying on an unsteady job in a small roadside restaurant in town. Monthly salary: 300 Deutschmarks. Social insurance: none. Necessary nonetheless.

Two

When the two visitors arrived, Lejla was still at her job. While I was at work in my flat, I could hear Samir and the guests upstairs breaking into the *rakija* (a strong and popular homemade spirit, usually made of fruit). It was only a matter of time before my landlord would come down and invite me to join them for 'a quick drink'. Despite my belief in professional work ethics and my strict timetable I accepted the invitation. The upstairs room was large and chilly, with a mattress on the floor and a television set playing soundlessly in the corner. Dishes were drying in the kitchen sink while a washing machine was running in the background. A large glass door opened to the balcony that offered a view of the Tuzla skyline. Even though I had arrived only shortly after the start of the drinking session, the smoke was already thick. In the middle of the room: a table with four chairs.

With my arrival, there were now four people around the table. Samir, just over fifty, tall and strong, tanned from his outdoor work was dressed in his usual worn-out tracksuit bottoms and a striped shirt. As a counterpoint to this workman-like appearance he wore a pair of round 'intellectual' glasses, giving him the air of a libertarian soul in a very seventies way. Next to Samir was a man of similar age in a shiny black and white tracksuit. His greying hair was meticulously taken care of by his wife, a hairdresser by profession. The third person was a slightly older man, dressed in a turtleneck sweater and fake brand-name trousers. Then there was me, a twenty-nine-year-old in trousers and T-shirt, who spent most of his time trying to refute his landlord's joking allegations that he was a CIA spy.

Four men, a table and a bottle of *rakija*. That could be it, but this was Bosnia. Although I am reluctant to refer to 'national' statistics, post-1992 writing about Bosnia seems to require just that, as the numbers game became a crucial weapon in the hands of the 'ethnic cleansers', and, in different ways, of the so-called 'international community' and scholars (Jansen 2005). So here we go: in the last pre-war census, Tuzla registered just under 132,000 inhabitants, with no absolute majority of any nationality (*nacionalnost*). Forty-eight percent of the inhabitants declared their nationality as Muslims, sixteen percent as Croats and fifteen percent as Serbs. The town counted a large number of 'mixed' marriages and a high rate of persons who declared themselves 'Yugoslavs or others' (twenty-one percent of the population, the highest proportion in all of Bosnia).

'Hasan is our neighbour', Samir told me, pointing to the tracksuited man. Upon hearing the name I knew that he was the person that Samir and the other neighbours usually referred to as '*hodža*'. His father had been a *hodža* – a Muslim minister – and he himself was known as a practising Muslim. Samir himself was also a Bosniac by national background, but in terms of political orientation he was a Yugoslav and secularist. His father had been a Partisan and a communist and Samir never tired of telling me that, despite his *very* Muslim name and surname, he was not a believer. 'And this is Robi', said Samir, and then laughing, 'he is an international friend, from our neighbouring country'. He then introduced me to the others as 'Stef, a Belgian or a Dutchman, depends which day it is, a Westerner, but to me it seems like he is actually from these Balkan areas'. Hereby the tone was set. Right from the start Robi's Serbian origins were the target of jokes by Samir and by Robi himself. Similarly, Samir, who had a habit of greeting me in the morning with a cheery 'How're you doing, occupier?', relentlessly referred to me as the representative of all things Western.

Importantly, Tuzla as it was in 2000 was unimaginable without its enormous foreign presence. People from all around the globe, but particularly from Western Europe and North America, worked in numerous international organisations and NGOs. Often easily recognisable by their large, white four-wheel drive vehicles, 'foreigners'[5] were an integral part of the landscape: they frequented the shops, visited reconstruction projects, sat in (their 'own') cafés and ate in (their 'own') restaurants. Many upmarket flats were targeted at foreigners and their owners earned more than double the amount of what they would receive from local tenants. Thus, apart from their role in post-war reconstruction and conflict resolution, foreigners constituted a crucial element in the local economy through consumption and employment. A man from the Tuzla employment agency estimated – there were no official data – that around thirty percent of all officially employed *Tuzlaci* worked for an international organisation or NGO.

As a result of this pervasive foreign presence, citizens of Bosnia rarely saw their everyday experience in isolation from the activities of the so-called 'international community'. In combination with the previously mentioned seasonal influx of Bosnians from the diaspora, this meant that a 'Western' element was part and parcel of the present context. As we shall see, some discourses associated with 'the West' (those promoting European-ness, modernity, multiculturalism and

---

[5]   The lingo of these organisations spoke of 'nationals' and 'internationals'. Bosnians sweepingly referred to the latter as 'foreigners' (*stranci*) (see Coles, this volume).

tolerance) framed the political situation, not only through the activities of the 'international community', but also because they provided a source of inspiration for similar local interpretations (see also Coles, Delpla, Helms, this volume). In any case, I had grown used to the fact that, whenever a conversation touched upon the role of 'foreigners' – usually ironically – all eyes focused on me. On this particular evening, such instances of mockery took place in a very relaxed manner but, interestingly, Hasan did not join in. Only later did it dawn on me that the humour had served partly as an attempt to defuse potential trouble.

Three

My three drinking buddies were ex-colleagues, engineers in a large state company in Tuzla for almost twenty years. Robi and his wife, like many others, had moved there from his nearby hometown in Serbia in 1973. Samir had come from a neighbouring town in northern Bosnia at about the same time. Hasan, born and bred in Tuzla, had started working in the firm in 1975. The men soon embarked on a conversation about ex-colleagues. Yet again I found myself listening to a discussion in the post-Yugoslav 'past tense' conversation mode (Jansen 1998). So many things had changed due to the war that most experiences those individuals had in common were definitely past. Many of the people they mentioned during their conversation had left Tuzla and hardly anyone worked in their old firm anymore.

A regional centre in Ottoman times, Tuzla had grown into a main industrial hub during the Austro-Hungarian and Yugoslav eras (e.g. Alispahić 2000; Kožar 1998; Trifković 1981, 1983, 1988 and 1990). Always mixed, its mines and heavy industries attracted many more people from various backgrounds and the town became associated with workers' resistance and socialist solidarity (Antonić 1979, 1984 and 1987). In 2000, the industry, once the town's trademark, performed on a fraction of its capacity due to outdated equipment and the disintegration of the Yugoslav market. Unemployment was soaring and even only a short walk through town made clear that Tuzla's infrastructure was falling apart at the seams. Add war damage and the pressure of some 40,000 displaced persons (Wubs 1998: 38), and it is clear that most *Tuzlaci* lived in very difficult conditions.

When I asked Robi what brought him to Tuzla, he said he had a job in town. 'Where?', I asked. 'In the same company where I worked before', Robi replied dryly. The bizarre truth was that, of those present, he was the only one who was working in that firm now. Almost a decade after his departure, the new boss had called him up in Serbia and had invited him to come back to work. To make things even more unlikely, Robi had not known the man, who was a Bosniac who had recently migrated to Tuzla from… Serbia. Unsurprisingly, I found out later during my fieldwork that Robi was only planning to stay in Tuzla in order to repossess his flat ('socially owned' by the firm). That was also the reason why he had taken up his job. According to a law much maligned by Serb refugees and displaced persons, he had to demonstrably live in his flat for two years before he would be able to buy it off. Then he would sell it and return to Serbia. In the meantime he worked long hours and took weekends off to join his family in the parental house in Serbia. Their Tuzla flat, of course, had been stripped bare by its wartime occupants. This repossession-without-permanent-return strategy caused much concern amongst international organisations and local pro-return activists. However, some months later Samir matter-of-factly suggested that it was the best scenario for Robi and his family. Most Serbs did it, he said. What could they do? There was nothing here for them anymore. Whether desirable or not, repossession with the aim to sell was indeed a dominant trend amongst Serbs from this part of Bosnia.[6] Official statistics of 'returnees' are therefore inflated.[7]

Four

Interrupting my questions, Hasan intervened, asking Robi if he did not think it shameful to come from Serbia to take a job in a town with such high unemployment rates. Robi did not react, but this was the first of a long series of little ripples. At this point Samir took his responsibility as a host to heart and tried to bridge the gap by changing the subject. In fact, the first part of the evening was relaxed with much joking precisely about Serbia, Bosnia and 'the West' – all targeted at the 'representatives' around the table. Samir, for example, argued sarcastically that while he had spent the war in the rich West, they had been fighting their dirty Balkan war. And now, he complained, the other two were well-off and he had nothing. Robi laughed but Hasan was not amused. He simply noted that Samir had only himself to blame. Later on in the conversation, Hasan referred several times to his own financial well-being and his success as a private entrepreneur, but when I asked him what he did for a living he smiled and said: 'All kinds of things.' Later it became clear that he had been involved in several kinds of 'business' during the war. He nonchalantly mentioned his arsenal of weapons: he kept five hundred stabilisers for landmines and two hundred and fifty grenades in a warehouse. In case he needed them again.

During the 1992-95 war, Tuzla was continuously controlled by a local alliance of the (nationally mixed but Bosniac-dominated) Bosnian Army and the Croat Defence Council (HVO). The town suffered shelling by the Bosnian Serb Army and an estimated three hundred civilians died in these attacks (Alispahić 2000: 30; Komisija za prikupljanje 1996; Pašalić 1995). The war brought about drastic

---

[6]   On the case of Sarajevan Serbs, see Armakolas, Stefansson, this volume.
[7]   Genuine 'minority return' figures are small amongst all groups, with Bosnian Serbs even less likely to engage in it than Bosniacs and Bosnian Croats. On 'minority returns' in eastern Bosnia, see Andrade and Delaney 2001; d'Onofrio 2004; UNHCR 2003; Wubs 1998. For updated figures see the statistical packages issued by the UNHCR (available at <http://www.unhcr.ba>).

changes in Tuzla's population structure as many people sought refuge abroad or in other parts of Bosnia. With regard to the national composition of the town it virtually erased Yugoslav identification – at least on the public level: many 'Yugoslavs' became Bosniacs, Serbs or Croats instead. The war also resulted in a clear majority of Bosniacs, partly as a result of Serbs and Croats having left the town and partly due to the influx of Bosniac refugees. Some of the latter arrived directly from nearby Serb-controlled areas whereas others were repatriated from countries in Western Europe (Germany in particular) where they had fled during the war. Rather than move back to their previous places of residence, now under Serb control, many Bosniacs had relocated to Tuzla.[8]

Having said this, a large number of *Tuzlaci* liked to emphasise their town's unusual history of resistance and its multi-national character. Part of this was due to memories of World War II, when Tuzla was incorporated in the Independent State of Croatia (NDH), a fascist puppet-state, but became the largest liberated city within occupied Europe at the end of 1943. More importantly, however, it occupied a specific position during the 1990s, being the only Bosnian town with a consistent electoral majority against the three main nationalist parties.[9] After the war, Tuzla still housed a larger proportion of national 'minority' groups than any other urban centre in Bosnia.[10] What is more, non-Bosniacs continued to play a role in local administration to a degree that was unthinkable in other parts of Bosnia. Hence, despite the trend towards homogenisation in the national composition of the town, many *Tuzlaci* still represented it as a bastion of multiculturalism.[11] Let me add that, in conversations involving myself and other foreigners, it was clear that we all did indeed feel that Tuzla was somewhat different from the rest of Bosnia.

---

[8] For a comparison with Sarajevo, see Armakolas, Maček, Stefansson, this volume.

[9] Throughout the war the Tuzla municipal authorities remained oppositional to the Bosnian Government led by the Party of Democratic Action (SDA). Combining its pro-Bosniac agenda with a pro-Bosnian one, the SDA had engaged both before and after the war in a *de facto* policy of cohabitation with Croat and Serb nationalist parties, allowing all three to rule in their own presumed national territory. During the war, in 1992-93 and 1994-95, it did so with the Croat Democratic Union (HDZ) (Bougarel 1996; Hoare 2004).

[10] According to UNHCR estimates, more than a third of Tuzla's population has a background other than Bosniac (Wubs 1998: 37). As indicated before, this figure is probably inflated because of the inclusion of non-permanent returnees.

[11] Apart from the fact that this was supported by statistics, other elements also played a role in this self-representation of Tuzla's inhabitants, such as the previously mentioned leftist tradition, a sense of urban pride, sentiments of '*jugonostalgija*' and the comfort of occupying a special, foreign-supported niche in the post-Yugoslav political landscape.

Five

The conversation now evolved into an increasingly tense plot, its main ingredients
being: lack of information and rumour, *rakija*, choice and force, and defence and
attack. Latching onto the occasion of my presence and my questions to Robi,
Hasan looked hard across the table and asked Robi when he had left town. There
was no explanation for this inquiry. 'When did you leave town?' was simply a
repeat of one of the most common questions that Serb returnees were (often
implicitly) being asked in Tuzla. It referred to the exodus of many Serb *Tuzlaci* on
the last days before the outbreak of violence there. The underlying question was
always: *why* did you leave? Robi answered in full detail: 'I left by bus on 15 May
1992 at seven in the morning.' He repeated the exact date and time several times.
Hasan immediately cast a sharp look across the table at Robi and cried, '15 May,
ha! Why is it always 15 May? How did you all know?' He referred to a common
acquaintance, Đorđe, who had left at noon on that very same day, and then fired
off his next, rhetorical question: 'And when did hell break loose in Tuzla? When
did the first shells fall? At one! One hour after he left!' Robi replied quietly that he
did not know how or when Đorđe had left and made clear that he had nothing to
do with the man. He insisted that he could only talk about himself. But Hasan
ignored his plea and loudly exclaimed: 'But why is it that you all knew?'[12]

At this point, Samir intervened. Laughingly addressing the two as 'comrades',
he stated that he had known *everything*, and long before anyone else in the room
for that matter. That, my landlord joked, was why he had left for Germany in
1990, almost two years before the war. Hasan, unfazed by Samir's irony, repeated
his question to Robi: why was it that almost all Serbs had known what was going
to happen before it actually happened? He claimed that the previously mentioned
Đorđe had actually received a phone call on that day from Rade, another common
acquaintance of all three men. Rade had told Đorđe to pack his stuff, save his
children and get out of Tuzla. The Muslims, so he had warned him, were about to
slaughter them. So, Hasan concluded, Rade and Đorđe and other Serbs had *known*
when the shell attacks on Tuzla by Serb forces were going to take place and they
fled in time. Robi again attempted to bring the conversation back to his personal
story and to the circumstances in which he had left, but Hasan interrupted him and
named yet another example of a Serb who had 'known'. However, the man in
question, married to a Croat and father of several children, had stayed on in Tuzla,
for which Hasan expressed his appreciation. Robi, growing tired of the allegations,
said he would explain the exact events of those days on one condition: Hasan had
to take his word for the truth. Otherwise, Robi said, he would not bother. Hasan
nodded but the situation had grown tense now. I kept my head down while Samir
was visibly nervous, watching his two old colleagues but keeping quiet.

---

[12] On the widespread opinion among Bosniacs that 'the Serbs knew' what would
happen, see also Maček, Armakolas, this volume.

Six

What follows is a reconstruction of the discussion that emerged. By evoking as much as possible of the lived experience of the evening, and placing it in its context, I aim to provide the reader with an insight in some complexities of Bosnian post-war everyday life.

> Robi: Okay, we all know how things were those days. The situation was getting completely out of hand. We were sitting in that bar down there, what's it called again, *Palm Beach*, and we could hear the detonations in Živinice [a small town near Tuzla]. We all heard them, didn't we?
>
> Hasan: Yes, sure, we heard them. But we didn't think that such trouble was going to come to Tuzla! We never believed that!
>
> Robi: No, exactly, I didn't think that either. We never believed it was going to happen in Tuzla! I am sure you remember, just before that I had crashed my *Yugo* and I ordered a roof to replace the old one. Željko was taking care of that for me, so I was waiting. On the evening of 14 May, I called Željko and I asked him, 'What's going on? Is there a roof coming for me or not?' He said: 'Are you out of your fucking mind, Robi? Have you not been into town at all? I was just at the bus station. Everything is blocked, man. There's soldiers everywhere. Instead of worrying about a fucking roof, you better get out of here before it is too late.' And, sitting on the benches outside of my building, I found that everybody was talking about it. There were barricades, they said, and loads of shit going on. Safeta, my neighbour, who is married to a Catholic, told me about it. My wife and children had left the day before – on 13 May. They got a lift with Goran. So I asked Safeta to take care of my flat and to water the plants. The next morning, at seven, I left Tuzla. That is the story of how Robi left Tuzla, and there is nothing more to it. So don't go all heavy on me and tell me that all Serbs knew what was going on... They didn't, and anyway, the things that I knew, other people knew as well.
>
> Hasan: But why did you leave if you didn't know that Tuzla was going to be attacked just after? Everybody always says, 'We didn't know!' Nobody knew anything, but they all left! There's something fishy about that story, Robi. If you didn't know, why would you leave? Why didn't the Muslims leave? If somebody had told them about what was going to happen... Of course, later, many of them left as well. They abandoned this country when it most needed them. They sneaked out... It's a disgrace.

Raising his voice, Hasan increasingly phrased his opinions as accusations, pointing at Robi over the table. Samir was distressed as well, partly because he was the evening's host and partly because he had just been indirectly accused of abandoning his fellow countrymen to their fate by moving to Germany. Robi, slightly angry as well now, attempted to keep his voice down. Playing the card of 'reasonability' he tried not to engage with Hasan's provocative questions. He maintained that he had not known anything special and appealed to Hasan's honesty and humanity to accept his word for it. Hasan did not buy it.

> Robi: Why would I want to betray the country where I lived for nineteen years? I have said this to many people, and I say this to my own people in my town in Serbia as well:

I spend the best years of my life in Tuzla! I have been treated very well by Bosnia, and I will never say a bad word about it. Of course, I am talking about the people, not about the state. I am not talking about Alija [Izetbegović].

Hasan: No, of course not. Fuck Alija's mother. Fuck Karadžić's mother. Fuck the state. We are not talking about that. They are not important. But what is important is that we were left here, we were attacked from all sides and we were left to our own devices! We didn't have a choice. You guys knew and you left!

Robi: (smiling a smile of desperation) Okay, okay, believe what you want to believe, but remember that I said that I didn't know anything that you didn't know. If you don't take my word for it, what can I say? What I don't understand is how you can say that when you know that I love Bosnia. You know I have spent nineteen years here. You know I feel at home here, in my soul. Okay, I have one homeland where I belong, where I was born and grew up, where my people belong. But I have another one as well. In all the years I was in Bosnia, I can tell you, I never experienced any trouble. In fact, only *one* person ever treated me with disrespect here. Only one person, Suad, whom you know very well.

Hasan: Suad is an asshole, we know that. He's always been an asshole.

Robi: He is the only person in Bosnia who has ever insulted me. I had been here for at least fifteen years and we worked together a lot. I had nothing against him, and certainly not because he was a Muslim. I just didn't get on with him because...

Samir: ...because he was an asshole. He was always trying to seek out the best for himself.

Robi: Yes, he was. He was smart and he wasn't a bad man, but he was high up in the Party, and he was taking advantage of his connections all the time.

Samir: (laughing) Ha ha! But tell me honestly now, which of the two of you was not in the Party? Tell me! I want to know!

The two muttered some objections but their sideways looks at me, the resident international observer, left no doubt about it. As for Samir, even though his father had been a Partisan soldier in World War II, and a Communist Party member and a director of a state firm afterwards, he himself had never joined the Party. This led to an ironic situation: in the present company the only person who had never joined the Party was by far the most pro-Yugoslav of the three and not reluctant to occasionally spell out his Titoist sympathies. But let us not see the Party issue in strictly ideological terms...

Robi: It's not just that Suad was in the Party. He was the kind of guy who would always try and be on the director's good side. You remember how he got this flat from the firm and I didn't? So I was renting for some more years, but, okay, later I got mine as well. Anyway, not long before the war Suad took me aside and said: 'Robi, we know very well that you didn't just come all the way from your town in Serbia to Tuzla for no reasons at all.' That really hurt me. He really insulted me – as if I had lived here for all those years, worked with you for all those years, spent time with you, and there was some plan behind all this. As if I was here for some political reasons, just because I came from Serbia! That was the only time I ever experienced any trouble like that. Now, don't get me wrong, those kinds of things also happened in Serbia. When we got there in 1992, I moved into my family house. That property has been in my family for many generations, so I can really say it is mine. I was born there and I grew up there. We attended some funeral and I heard someone say: 'They are not our people [*naši*]. They are refugees.' On my own land! So that hurt too. But here in Bosnia, apart from that one time with Suad, I have always been treated very well. You know, I am now staying with Edin – remember him? Long ago, I used to rent from them before I got my flat. They are very correct with me. It is not easy for them, you know. Their son was sent to the front in Brčko and he was killed. Honestly, I wonder if my son was killed by a Serb shell, would I be able to treat a Serb with so much respect? I don't know if I could do that… All credit to them! They are good people.

Seven

The smoke in the room was so thick now that it could be cut with a knife and regular rounds of *rakija* supplied the fuel for the discussion. Some time around this point my landlady Lejla entered the room and immediately saw that something was not right. After some light-hearted remarks aimed at defusing the situation, she sat down on a stool next to Samir. My own role in the conversation had been minimal up to then. I had mainly served as a sounding board for the odd comment about 'the West' and as a supposedly neutral outsider whose confirmation was sought for some 'objective, generally accepted' statements. But the discussion did not end there. Clearly, Hasan was not prepared to let things go. He directly confronted Robi and, indirectly, his host Samir. He contrasted the circumstances in which they had lived during wartime with his own: while Samir had been 'sitting on his ass and drinking beer in Germany' and Robi had been 'living well in Serbia', Hasan argued, he had been under fire from Serb shelling for years. For him, he shouted, it had not just been TV. He had been mobilised and sent to the front. For him, forgetting was not as easy as for them.

By now it was clear that Samir was building up a ferocious anger. So while Robi more or less kept his calm and tried to laugh about it, it was Samir who exploded. Through a series of twists the discussion thus seemed to come full circle. Hasan vented his war experience on Robi, the Serb in the company, but as the conversation went on, the actual target of his stories seemed to become Samir, his fellow Bosniac who had lived abroad during the whole conflict. In response, starting off his usual style, joking and cursing his way through his argument, Samir launched a tirade driven by anger, frustration, used-up patience and alcohol. Interestingly, he mainly addressed his words to me now, explaining things to the only foreigner in the company. However, the obvious audience was Hasan, with whom he directly engaged towards the end.

Samir: Listen, I was in Germany since 1990. This was very different from your lives, I agree. But that also means that I could see things in another light. I can tell you: I did not change over the years. I have been Tito's scout [*Titov izviđač*] since I was five and I have not changed since then, and living in Germany did not change that either. I might have lived outside of these Balkan events, but I remained who I am. I know what is mine. Mine is the forest. Mine is not Bosnia, or Croatia or Serbia. Mine is not Islam, or Christianity. Mine is the forest. When I see a tree or a bush, or a path up the mountain, I know that that is mine. And I know that, ever since I was five, this has been the truth. And I am saying this now and I have said it before, and I will say it again. There is no person, no country, no state, nothing I would fight for. Only fools die for ideals [13]. I would never fight for anything. And, because I know the forest is mine, and I know every tree and every rock, I can't see how they could get me to fight. Before they would have been at my door, I would have left through the back of the house.

Hasan: You wouldn't have. You couldn't have. There was no choice.

Samir: I would be in the forest. My forest. There…

Hasan: You wouldn't be. No way. They would be on your door, they had their ways. You wouldn't escape.

Samir: I would, Hasan, I would. The only way they could ever make me fight in their dirty war was to tie me up and drag me to the front. And you know what? Then I would turn around and make my way back. I would not fight. No fucking way.

Hasan: That is what we all said, my man. That is what we all said before. But when it is war, it is war. You wouldn't say that anymore!

Samir: I would. I know that there is nothing in the world that could make me fight [14].

Hasan: But your own dad was here. Surely you cared about him?

Samir: Of course I cared about him. But only because he is my dad. I don't give a fuck about what he believes in or not. I always said, fuck your Party card, dad. Fuck all that. It doesn't mean anything. You know, even my own mom, here next to us, she is a Muslim, but what she believes or not – I couldn't care less. I would never even consider fighting for something like that. All those years, I have remained the same. All that crap doesn't mean a fucking thing to me. Nothing whatsoever. It makes no sense at all to speak about nations and parties and faiths and all that. I believe only in myself. I am only my own [*samo svoj*]. I live with Lejla for thirteen years, and I live with Jasna, my child, for twelve years. And even they can't change me. So surely, nobody else could ever change me.

Robi: He's right about one thing at least. There are only individuals who can be good or bad. How can you talk about whole groups of people being good or bad? That's nonsense. Only persons can be good or bad.

Hasan: You guys simply don't understand. It was war. There were people being shot and we were living in fear and we had nothing to eat. There was no time for such considerations. It was easy for you. You just switched off the TV and had another beer and that was it. Bosnia was far away. But not for me, it wasn't!

Samir: Hasan, listen, I'll be honest with you. This whole war of yours, this war of Balkan peoples, of Muslims, of Serbs, of Croats – Hasan, it doesn't mean a fucking thing to me. It is your war, not mine. I don't want to have anything to do with it. I have nothing to say about it. There is no way that you can pull me into it. And you know

---

[13]   Samir was paraphrasing well-known song lyrics by Beograd rock band *Riblja čorba*: '*Za ideale ginu budale.*'

[14]   In a conversation months later, Samir effectively inverted Hasan's reasoning in order to support his own argument. The people who blamed him for not having been there, he said, always claimed that they simply had to go fight, that they had had no choice. Therefore, Samir concluded, they confirmed exactly his point: they did not believe in it either. They just fought because they had to, not because they wanted to.

what, I am always very open to other opinions. I believe in tolerance. That's why I don't see the fucking point of the whole war of you Muslims, you Croats, you Serbs. I don't give a fuck about it, because I only care about myself.

Hasan: There we have it, that's what we need in this country, my man. You don't give a fuck, do you? You only care about yourself. Me, and only me! That's what we need!

Samir: Yes, for fuck's sake. That's it. That whole war of yours was completely fucking useless. Pointless, Hasan. It doesn't mean anything to me, and I don't want anything to do with it. I am tolerant, but in that way, yes, for fuck's sake, I am absolutist. I believe this. I only care about myself. I am God, for fuck's sake. I am God!

Hasan: (getting up from his chair) Very well. You care about yourself. And only about yourself.

With these final words Hasan made his way to the door. He did not greet anyone. Lejla quickly followed him and let him out with some whispered words of goodbye. For a while, a silence came down over the table. Samir, Robi, Lejla and I sat uneasily and turned to the easiest solution at hand. More cigarettes. More *rakija*.

Eight

After a brief pause, Samir and Lejla turned to me. They explained to me, the foreigner, and indirectly to Robi, what had happened. Lejla said she had known it was going to happen all along. She had been watching Samir and she had seen he was boiling inside. This had not been the first time, she said. Hasan and others like him really resented people who had left. It was difficult for Samir, Lejla argued, because they had spent all these years in Germany, and some people in Tuzla simply did not understand what their situation had been like there. Especially for a man, she added, this was difficult. Then Robi intervened. Perhaps he should have reacted differently, he said, but with a man like Hasan it was impossible to argue. Lejla vehemently shook her head and told him that this was not Robi's problem. It was Hasan who should have known better. Samir agreed and added that Hasan's real problem had been the presence of a Serbian guest in the house. That was what he had been unable to stomach. And that was why it had to end as it did, Lejla continued. You could not go to someone's house and start causing such trouble because of the nationality of another guest. It just was not on. If Hasan had a problem with them having a Serbian guest, he should have excused himself and dashed off home. This was their house, Lejla said, and they could invite any guests they wanted.

Turning to me again, she explained that it was often thought that Bosnians who spent the war years abroad had not suffered at all. Those who stayed behind then now often expressed strong resentment and blame towards them. 'Where were you when it was the hardest for us?' they asked.[15] That was so ironic, Lejla exclaimed, because they would have been out of Bosnia themselves if they had had the slightest opportunity, all of them! They simply could not imagine that people abroad had also suffered because of what was going on in Bosnia. They did not see that they had been helping the country in many different ways. Or what about all those truckloads of arms, food and money? All Bosnians abroad had helped; if no one else, at least their own family!

In reply I suggested that it was nevertheless understandable that people felt such resentment and anger. Also I thought that there was some truth in the fact that 'we' (and this time this meant the four of us left around the table), as relatively far-away spectators, could hardly imagine the conditions in wartime places. Given my own background I gave the example of the NATO air strikes on targets throughout Serbia. Samir now joined the conversation again, arguing that there were many ways of dealing with differences, and that tolerance was the only real solution; but, he said, tolerance in a European way, in a democratic way. Ironically, this was the same Samir who never let slip an opportunity to criticise 'the West' or 'Europe' (and me as its unwilling representative) for getting it all wrong. This is how the topic finally disappeared from view: Samir, Lejla and Robi, to a certain extent, assured me and each other that everything was fine and that Hasan was the one with the problem. The conversation thus soon became a series of mutual affirmations, including mine, of the need for respect, the inadequacy of generalisations based on national categories, and the like.

Nine

This text has dealt with the first post-war encounter three ex-colleagues, with different characters and convictions, as well as different personal backgrounds and experiences during the war. Clearly, it is not an event that we would expect to see replicated frequently and therefore its potential for generalisation is limited. However, it seems fair to say that almost every situation in post-war Bosnia is bound to contain peculiarities of a similar nature. In conclusion, then, let me very briefly highlight some critical insights that emerge from the evening described above. Perhaps they could serve as modest reminders of the complexities of Bosnian realities.

Firstly, national affiliations and (current or remembered) territorial attachments, while crucial to any understanding of contemporary Bosnia, are not nearly as clear-cut as is often assumed. While the military violence that occurred during the war was surely aimed at bringing about processes of national un-mixing, I am alarmed by the willingness or even enthusiasm amongst locals and

---

[15] This rhetorical question, '*Gdje si bio kad nam je bilo najteže?*', has turned into a common catch phrase in post-war Bosnia, both in mundane contexts and in the political rhetoric of the SDA (see also Maček, Stefansson, this volume).

foreign observers alike to exercise parallel acts of symbolic violence: the retrospective national disambiguation of the past (Jansen 2002; Jansen forthcoming). Ambiguities with regard to nationality *did* exist in the past and, while sometimes forcibly suppressed, they persist in the present, not only through so-called mixed marriages but also in the reminiscences and reminders of Yugoslavness, and the demographic realities that were shaped by a long history of migration. Furthermore, the relevance of forms of identification is often dependent on context. If we limit ourselves to territorial identification, in the Bosnian conversation above, the term 'we' alternately refers to those who spent the war period in Bosnia, to a national group, to *Tuzlaci*, to citizens of Bosnia, to all post-Yugoslavs, or even to all 'Balkan people' (see Herzfeld 1985).

Secondly, the example of Tuzla shows that every locality in Bosnia has its own peculiarities in terms of history, demographic composition, geography and politics. This local specificity highlights the problematic nature of making sweeping generalisations about 'the Bosnian war'. Quite simply, there was not *a* war, but rather many wars, which were shaped by local power patterns and coloured by local allegiances. This is not just to say that people experienced and remember the wars in subjective ways, relying on their embodied experience of them (Povrzanović-Frykman 1997). It also means that it is imperative for scholars and judicial institutions alike to study the local anatomy of conflict, including its build-up, in order to come to a balanced picture of the events (e.g. Duijzings 2002b). While national and international factors played a crucial role in the violence, these worked differently in different local contexts.

Thirdly, even though the war was waged overwhelmingly along national lines of division, nationality is clearly only one amongst several major fault lines in Bosnian everyday life. Given the current relative paucity of national 'Others' on the local level, which was the objective and the desired result of 'ethnic cleansing' campaigns, these alternative (non-national) fault lines are slowly coming to the surface again. The evidence presented in this chapter demonstrates how, in everyday life, national 'unity' is sometimes undercut by diverging political allegiances, by unequal socio-economic opportunities and access to resources, by gender divisions and the issue of (non-)participation in military operations and local defence, and last but not least, by the different individual histories of displacement, of taking refuge elsewhere or of staying behind (Jansen 2002; Jansen forthcoming). Other ruptures, not specifically addressed in this text, include the urban/rural divide, which itself is strongly linked to hierarchies of cultural capital. Importantly, many of those divisions based on non-national principles were already present prior to the war.

Finally, this case shows that individuals engage actively with the official histories they encounter, incorporating some elements in their personal narratives, while ignoring others. Nationalist versions of the past are frequently sanctioned as the only true ones, but there are other discourses at hand, for instance those based on ideas of common European-ness or multiculturalism. Again, people's engagement with such discourses depends not only on their nationality, but also, among other things, on their personal experiences during the war and on their current circumstances. The three colleagues in this text are men of about the same age, of comparable education, and of similar lifestyle. Two of them share the same national background. Yet their encounter shows that the making of memories – of fairly recent events by those people who were involved in them or affected by them – has to be approached as a situationally embedded and contested process. This sheds a critical light on the ways in which recent history works on the ground. The three men remembered, but they did so with a difference.

PART 3
Beyond 'Protectorate'

Chapter 9

In the Midst of Injustice:
The ICTY from the Perspective of some Victim Associations

Isabelle Delpla

Introduction[1]

International criminal justice is aimed at a common humanity in the name of universal values. Beyond general principles, however, it remains to be evaluated whether this kind of justice actually addresses this part of humanity over which it has jurisdiction. What are the local effects of the International Criminal Tribunals? More specifically, do these tribunals meet or inform the sense of justice held by the local populations? Given the grave internal dysfunctions of the International Criminal Tribunal for Rwanda (ICTR), and the break which occurred between this institution, on one hand, and the Rwandan Government and victim associations which first supported it, on the other hand, the answer to these questions is likely to be negative.[2] No comparable divorce has occurred between the International Criminal Tribunal for the former Yugoslavia (ICTY) and the Government of Bosnia-Herzegovina or the victim associations which most supported the Hague Tribunal at its start. The effects of the ICTY in post-war Bosnia are more difficult to assess. What do Bosnians mean by 'justice', do their concepts of justice overlap

[1] Due to my poor knowledge of Bosnian, the study on which this chapter is based would not have been possible without the friendly support and the translating skills of Aida Muratović, Dževad Osmanović and Slađana Milunović. I am also grateful for long conversations over the years with Emir Suljagić, Irham Cećo, Marianne Costa, Jean-Louis Fournel, Isabelle Wesselingh, Agnès Lejbowicz, Elizabeth Claverie, Sara Liwerant, Vesna Miloš, Nusreta Sivac, Jasmin Odobašić and Amor Mašović. All my warm thanks go to all those who kindly took their time to help this study whether on a personal or more official level in the work of their association. This chapter has greatly benefited from the sharp comments of the editors and the writing skills of Rachel and Peter Burk.
[2] In January 2002, the main associations of Rwanda survivors, *Ibuka* ('Remember') and *Avenga* ('Association of the widows of genocide'), launched a boycott of the ICTR, thus blocking the ongoing trials for lack of witnesses.

with those embodied in the functioning of an international criminal tribunal and, if so, how? I did not find the answer to this question in most analyses of the Hague Tribunal, most of which have been written from the perspective of legal studies, political science or journalism. These analyses are primarily devoted to legal procedures, the institutional functioning of the ICTY, or its role in the 'progress' of international justice from the ICTY and the ICTR to the International Criminal Court (ICC). Aside from a few notable exceptions (Fletcher, Stover and Weinstein 1999; Fletcher and Weinstein 2002; Neuffer 2001; Wesselingh and Vaulerin 2005), they do not enable us to see whether or not the ICTY matters to Bosnian people, beyond its place among international organizations that oversee the country and the stances of Bosnian political parties. One can alternatively claim either that international criminal tribunals are convened in the name of and for the victims, or that they are designed more for the sake of international lawyers than that of victims: a lack of data means we cannot weigh in favour of either claim.

I first went to Bosnia to teach philosophy at the University of Sarajevo in 1996 and 1997. I was struck then by the deep rejection of revenge and the calls for justice expressed by Bosnian people and, later on, by a relative lack of concern about the ICTY. I then wondered how to characterize this discrepancy, which amounted neither to an adequacy nor to a rupture between the perspectives of the locals and those of the ICTY. I therefore started a study of the effects of the ICTY in the day-to-day lives and social relationships of ordinary Bosnians, using a 'bottom-up' approach. I came to this anthropological perspective, not as a specialist of the Balkans, but as a philosopher who pursues research on international ethics and justice and who has long worked on the relationship between philosophy and anthropology and the norms of translation.

This chapter relies on fieldwork that was carried out in The Hague in September 2002 and in Bosnia between April and July 2002: the Bosnia research was mainly in Sarajevo and two of its suburbs, Hadžići and Vogošća. I also made shorter trips to Banja Luka, the capital of *Republika Srpska* (RS), to Ključ and to Sanski Most, two municipalities located in the western part of the Federation, near Prijedor. This fieldwork on the local reception of international ethics and justice consisted mainly of interviews with the main partners of the ICTY in Bosnia, including the ICTY's Outreach Programme, 'internationals' in charge of the supervision of local trials and of the reform of the local judiciary system, the International Commission on Missing Persons (ICMP), and governmental organizations such as the Federal Commission for Missing Persons or the Commission for Gathering Facts on War Crimes in Bosnia-Herzegovina. Those interviews extended to NGOs that follow the ICTY's work or support the project of a Truth and Reconciliation Commission.

The primary focus of this fieldwork was on victim associations, associations of displaced persons (DPs) and returnees, and on individual victims whom I met inside or outside associations, DPs, and returnees, some of them witnesses at the Hague Tribunal. I combined two approaches in my work with victim associations: a comparative approach consisting of meetings with several victim associations of different types in the same place (Sarajevo) and of the same type in different places, and a more qualitative approach in which I followed the activities of a few associations and some of their members over the course of interviews, informal conversations over coffee, meetings in the association office or with international organizations, public events such as conferences, exhibitions, ceremonies, and exhumations. All of these associations are often in close contact with each other.[3]

While the ICTY remains of little concern for the greatest part of the Bosnian population, for those associations it is not solely a distant institution, since they are in close contact with it and follow its work in various ways. Such close connections are much less obvious in the case of Serb victim associations in the RS, reflecting the refusal of the authorities there to cooperate with the ICTY. For this reason and because most civilians victims of war crimes were Bosniacs,[4] I will focus in this chapter on the predominantly Bosniac associations. I will, however, refer to the concerns of Bosnian Serb victim associations where possible.

Those predominantly Bosniac associations in some cases consist only of Bosniac members, as in the associations of women of Srebrenica; for others, the living members are Bosniacs but they are also searching for the dead from other national groups (*narodi*) as is the case for the association *Izvor* ('Source') in Prijedor; still others are made up mostly of Bosniacs with a few Croats, as in Hadžići, or with some Croats *and* Serbs (along with others such as Jews and Roma) as in the Association of Civilians Victims of War in Sarajevo.[5] The national structure of these associations directly reflects the make-up of the victimized population. In the cases I am focusing on, Bosniacs, sometimes together with other groups, were victims of Serb forces.[6] The distinction between Bosniac and Bosnian

---

[3]   This more qualitative work was focused on the Cantonal Association of Civilian Victims of War in Sarajevo, and on the small world of interrelations between the International Commission for Missing Persons, the Federal Commission for Missing Persons, the Federal Union of Camp Inmates and some associations of families of missing persons (especially the Association of the Mothers of Srebrenica and Žepa), all of them being in close contact with ICTY representatives.

[4]   Roughly 85 percent of the missing persons in Bosnia-Herzegovina are Bosniac, out of a total of more than 21,000 according to the International Committee of the Red Cross and out of more than 27,700 according to the Federal Commission for Missing Persons.

[5]   The exact name of the associations of families of missing persons I will refer to are: Association for the Missing Persons of the Hadžići Municipality; Association of the Families of Missing Persons of the Vogošća Municipality; Association of Women from Prijedor *Izvor* ('Source'); Association of the Mothers of Srebrenica and Žepa Enclaves, located in Sarajevo; Association of the Families of Missing Persons *Višegrad 92*, located in Sarajevo.

[6]   Bosniacs (and Croats) were ethnically cleansed from suburbs of Sarajevo like Hadžići and Vogošća in 1992. In Prijedor, Sanski Most and Ključ (north-western Bosnia), massive numbers of Bosniacs and Croats were killed, expelled or detained in camps, the most infamous being those near Prijedor (Omarska, Trnopolje, Keraterm). At the end of the war, the Bosnian Army recaptured Sanski Most and Ključ, but Prijedor remained in the RS.

is therefore tenuous in this context, all the more so because individual Serbs and Croats might share the views predominant among Bosniacs.

Different Phases in the Reception of the ICTY in Bosnia

I propose to distinguish three phases in the reception of the ICTY by Bosnian citizens. Over the course of the first phase (1993-1997), around the time of the creation of The Hague Tribunal and the first trials of Dušan Tadić and Dražen Erdemović – both considered to be 'small fish' – the ICTY raised both scepticism as well as great hope, mainly among Bosniacs. It was then primarily the incarnation of the ideal summarized in the motto 'No peace without justice', an ideal that has been promoted by international jurists and NGOs, both local and international, in their 'fight against impunity'. In contrast, Bosnian Serbs in the RS generally opposed the Tribunal, seeing it as political and biased against Serbs.

Over the course of a second phase (1998-2002), the one dealt with in this chapter, the Tribunal became a reality, an institution functioning with its own set routine. A large number of indictments were made public, more arrests were made, and several trials of highly placed leaders like Slobodan Milošević, Momčilo Krajišnik and Biljana Plavšić[7] got under way. Some defendants were tried and convicted in this period, among them General Radislav Krstić, who was sentenced in August 2001 to 46 years of prison for genocide in Srebrenica (ICTY 2001). The early trials of Tadić and Erdemović might have led many victims to expect that the ICTY would also bring to justice those war criminals who had personally victimized them. As time passed, however, the limited number of indictments and arrests has aggravated the distance between the ICTY and victims' expectations. In 1999, with the awareness that the Hague Tribunal remained distant and of little concern to the populations of the former Yugoslavia, the president of the Tribunal at that time, Judge Gabrielle Mc Donald, created an Outreach Programme to inform the local populations about the ICTY and its activities.[8]

In 2002 and 2003, the ICTY initiated a completion strategy to bring its activities to a close by 2008 and to transfer the remaining cases to courts in former Yugoslavia. It began concentrating its efforts on 'big fish' and encouraging guilty pleas. Their number increased after Plavšić was sentenced to eleven years of

---

Prijedor represents a noteworthy case. There, the ICTY has indicted one of the largest numbers of suspects and most of them have been arrested and tried. Prijedor is also one of the places where a great number of Bosniacs have returned to the RS. On the situation in Prijedor, I refer mainly to Wesselingh and Vaulerin 2005.

[7]   Both Krajišnik and Plavšić were key political figures in the RS during and after the war. They were indicted for genocide, crimes against humanity and violations of the laws of war by the ICTY (see <http://www.un.org/icty/cases/indictindex-e.htm>).

[8]   See <http://www.un.org/icty/bhs/outreach/outreach_info.htm>), as well as Cibelli and Guberek 1999.

incarceration in February 2003.[9] This new strategy of the Tribunal, which became manifest in Bosnia with the Plavšić trial, led to a change in its reception: many Bosniacs have opposed the closing of the Tribunal and have become increasingly critical of its sentences. This, in turn, has contributed to the ICTY's belated questioning of its own lack of a coherent sentencing policy. Some Bosnian Serb victim associations, who fear the transfer of cases to Sarajevo and hope that more crimes against Serb victims will be judged, have also started opposing the closing of the Hague Tribunal.

According to its 1993 statute, the ICTY takes primacy over states and their national jurisdictions. Moreover, in order to avoid trials based on political biases and flimsy cases, the 'Rules of the Road' procedures established in 1996 stipulate that no local trials for war crimes can take place in former Yugoslavia without the agreement of the ICTY. The Bosniac part of the Federation has closely cooperated with the ICTY, arresting and delivering indicted Bosniacs to the Tribunal. By contrast, the RS has refused to cooperate and has not handed over a single indicted suspect. Similarly, in years that followed, some local trials took place in the Federation, including in Herzegovina, but not in the RS. Those trials face difficulties that stem from the current Bosnian judiciary system, particularly concerning the protection of witnesses. Given the difficulties of transferring cases to existing national courts, the ICTY has favoured establishing a special state level war-crimes chamber in Sarajevo, to which some of the ICTY cases would be transferred.

The 'Top-Down' Approach and Its Limitations

During my fieldwork in 2002, some effects of the Hague Tribunal were already observable in Bosnia. However, most publications available at that time on the ICTY were still a reflection of its first phase or were focused on the progressive establishment of the Tribunal as an institution (e.g. Cigar and Williams 2002; Hagan 2003; Scharf 1997). Accordingly, its impact in terms of its purported contribution to peace and reconciliation has been extrapolated rather than observed. It has mainly been derived from other historical experiments, such as the Nuremberg trials, for its alleged pedagogical value,[10] or the South Africa Truth and Reconciliation Commission, for its supposed reconciliatory effect.[11]

---

[9]   This was the first time that a Bosnian Serb leader pleaded guilty. Most famously, Biljana Plavšić acknowledged that 'many thousands of innocent people were the victims of an organized, systematic effort to remove Muslims and Croats from the territories claimed by Serbs' (see <http://www.un.org/icty/transe3940/021217IT.htm>). The ICTY considered this as a major achievement. To many Bosnians, however, the sentence appeared very light.

[10]   Concerning the pedagogical value of this kind of trial, see among others Osiel 2000.

[11]   Such an interpretation is manifest in the appointment of Richard Goldstone as the first president of the Hague Tribunal.

A second difficulty is determining what should count as effects of international justice. As Gary Bass (2000) has rightly emphasized, none of the predicted effects of the ICTY can be shown to have been entirely confirmed or refuted. Contrary to the expectations of 'realists', who oppose the normative role of international law in international relations, the activities of the Tribunal neither provoked a resumption of the conflict nor a nationalist backlash in Bosnia. The predictions of ICTY advocates, who promote Kant's idea of international peace through law, were not clearly fulfilled either. According to them, the ICTY was supposed to prevent further conflicts, establish truth, prevent the stigmatization of entire groups by ascribing individual responsibility, and bring peace and reconciliation.[12] For example, the goal of establishing truth is more clearly achieved through the amount of evidence collected, especially the exhumation of mass graves or the examination and cross examination of witnesses (Bass 2000: 284-310). However, judiciary truth established in The Hague is far from achieving public acknowledgement in Bosnia. One year after the Krstić conviction for genocide, a report published by the RS authorities stated that 2,000 Bosniacs had been killed in July 1995 in Srebrenica, mainly in combat (Bureau of Government of RS for Relation with ICTY 2002), an account which obviously contradicted the ICTY forensic evidence showing that many victims had their hands tied behind their back and/or were blindfolded.

Overall, the gap between expectations and reality is difficult to interpret. Given the paucity of indictments and arrests as compared to the magnitude of crimes and the obstruction by many national and local authorities, it is difficult to decide whether justice and truth do not have the supposed effect or whether there is simply too little justice and too little truth for them to have an effect, the lack of effect being proportional only to the weakness of causes. This difficulty is accentuated by the ambiguity of the goals publicly ascribed to the ICTY by its promoters – goals that come from various theoretical sources and historical analogies but without clear coherence. Accordingly, their supposed effects are unclear. For example, what should count as reconciliation: the ending of armed conflict? A decrease in nationalist votes? An increase in DP returns? Forgiveness? Expecting a direct effect from criminal justice proceedings according to such criteria would be naïve, both theoretically and empirically. Therefore, a top-down assessment of the place of the ICTY in post-war Bosnia tends to lead to negative conclusions and primarily highlights the relative absence of the predicted effects.

Such are the limitations of the major study led by the Berkeley Human Rights Center (Fletcher, Stover and Weinstein 1999; Fletcher and Weinstein 2002; Stover and Weinstein 2005), which argues that many justifications for the ICTY are flawed when applied to the Bosnian situation. However, this study does not take adequate account of the political context and the presence or absence of local mediations likely to hinder or facilitate ICTY actions. Hence, the study tends to reproduce the belief of ICTY advocates in a direct and decontextualized effect of

---

[12]   For a more complete analysis of the reasons why these different criteria do or do not obtain, see Delpla 2004b.

justice as a panacea for all evils. Such justifications for the ICTY lead first to an overestimation of its possible impact on social reconstruction, and later, due to the relative failure of such predictions, to an overestimation of the gap between the ICTY and Bosnian society. However, it does not prove that the ICTY's actual practices conform to those *a priori* claims, and that the ICTY does not produce other effects than those expected.

Concluding that the ICTY has no effect because of the failure of such grandiose claims would, therefore, primarily express the disappointment of its advocates and overlook a more modest, but nonetheless significant, place for the ICTY in Bosnian society. On one occasion, in Sarajevo, during a conversation with a Bosniac friend of mine who had been driven out of Foča, his hometown, and did not want to go back there, I expressed my own sense of discouragement, wondering whether this tribunal was of any use in Bosnia. Referring to one of the indicted figures from Foča, this friend remarked: 'Well, thanks to the arrest of this criminal, my parents could go back to Foča and sell our apartment.' And this sale had helped them build a house in the suburbs of Sarajevo. Instead of starting from *a priori* theorizing in a top-down study, such an unpredicted effect of the ICTY shows the relevance of a bottom-up approach for assessing its place in Bosnia. This assessment calls both for empirical description and for conceptual redefinition of the relevant criteria of justice in the Bosnian context.

The 'Bottom-Up' Approach and Its Difficulties

Granting a great deal of importance to international justice does, however, also have its roots in Bosniac expectations. The claim 'We want justice and not revenge' can frequently be heard among Bosniacs, be they DPs from the countryside, ordinary Sarajevans, victim association representatives, academics, or politicians, such as Alija Izetbegović. To what does this strong call for justice correspond? Depending on the speaker, it can express a staunch denunciation of impunity, a personal attempt to forgive, or both, since the two stances can be compatible. It corresponds to a personal refusal to use violence, which is deemed painful and useless ('There has been enough pain', or 'It [vengeance] won't bring back the dead'). Whether it is forgiveness or a simple refusal of violence, such pronouncements are underlain by an attempt to draw the line between the perpetrators and oneself ('We do not have the genetic code to kill') and by a sense of moral worthiness or even superiority ('If I had hit him [when seeing him after the camp], I would have been like him'). For some, this claim corresponds to a religious quest for inner peace and the consolation offered by ultimate divine justice. Nonetheless, such feelings extend beyond religious significance, given how widespread they are among atheists and believers alike. In this context, justice is not an intermediate category situated between vengeance and forgiveness;[13] rather it is placed in opposition to vengeance and can also include forgiveness.

Such a deeply rooted demand for justice has often been interpreted by jurists, human rights activists, and researchers as support for the Hague Tribunal. Such an interpretation is put forth in Sabina Subašić's movie, *Viol, une arme de guerre* [Rape, a War Weapon] (2001), and Elizabeth Neuffer's book, *The Key to My Neighbour's House* (1998). These two share a narrative construction that alternates between scenes of trials in The Hague and those of people in Bosnia watching these trials on TV, expectantly following their findings and results; or, in the case of the book, descriptions of the development of international law in parallel with individual fates in Bosnia and Rwanda. The way the book and the film have been crafted suggests that the fate of the victims and the work of the ICTY share a common development, as if transformations of post-war Bosnian society could be read through the lens of the progress of international criminal justice.

But interpreting this local call for justice solely in the light of the ICTY would be misleading. It was expressed with as much force during my fieldwork in 2002 as in 1996 and 1997, and by people who were not necessarily referring to the ICTY. Furthermore, with few exceptions, the Hague Tribunal was rarely a spontaneous topic of conversation, although people regularly denounced the fact that Radovan Karadžić and Ratko Mladić are still at large. In early 2002, Sarajevans were much more likely to express their opinions about Danis Tanović's Oscar winning film, *No Man's Land*, rather than about the on-going trial of the Serb General Stanislav Galić.[14]

More generally, a deep and widespread sense of injustice creates a gap between a justice-oriented perspective and the viewpoint of ordinary Bosnian citizens (see also Jašarević, Armakolas, Bougarel, this volume). During my first visit to the Cantonal Association of Civilian Victims of War in Sarajevo, I indicated that I was studying international justice in Bosnia. The president, Senida Karović, who lost her leg in the shelling of Sarajevo, commented that I was drinking black coffee because I had a rosy life, whereas Bosnians were drinking sweetened coffee because they had a bitter life. She added that I was 'interested in international ethics and justice, but next time we will talk about immorality and injustice'.[15] In a similar way, when I asked Munira Subašić, president of the Association of the Mothers of Srebrenica and Žepa Enclaves, what she thought about international justice, she answered back, 'But which justice?' After I specified that I meant the Hague Tribunal, she replied, 'But there have been only four arrests', meaning that

---

[13] In opposition to the title of Martha Minow's book, *Between Vengeance and Forgiveness: Facing History After Genocide and Mass Crime* (Minow 1998).

[14] Galić was the commander of the Sarajevo-Romanija Corps of the Bosnian Serb Army, and was indicted in March 1999 for the campaign of shelling Sarajevo during the siege.

[15] Interview, Sarajevo, 6 May 2002.

this was close to nothing with respect to the magnitude of the crime.[16] In light of these remarks, studying post-war Bosnia through the lens of the ICTY and international justice amounts to filtering injustices that one does not want to face through a reassuring prism, an approach that seems all but indecent considering the horrifying wartime experiences and post-war difficulties of the victims themselves.

Starting from the sense of injustice shared by many Bosnians would diminish this gap but would entail enormous difficulties. Injustice is at the very root of the claims of many Bosnians when they denounce war and post-war evils. Faced with what amounts to an ocean of injustices, it might be arbitrary to select the ones that the ICTY deals with. A focus on wartime crimes, from a distant, international standpoint, can overshadow post-war impunity in places where attacks and threats have continued, though to a lesser extent (see Duijzings, Kolind, this volume). What's more, the impunity of suspected war criminals is considered deeply scandalous by many Bosnians, but so is the impunity of corrupt politicians or '*mafiaši*' ('mafiosi') (see also Grandits, Helms, Kolind, this volume). There is also a feeling of injustice in reaction to growing disparities of income, unemployment, and housing problems, and there is an overall sentiment of having lost the collective and personal living conditions and status that people had under Tito (see also Maček, Jašarević, Stefansson, this volume). Against this background, a bottom-up approach faces the difficulty of getting lost in a maze of injustices.

A second major difficulty is the elusiveness of the ICTY. From a local perspective, it is meaningless to study the role of the ICTY in the development of international criminal law or the internal functioning of the Tribunal as an institution, even if its own complexity, internal divergences and conflicts are kept in mind. The ICTY does not have an obvious presence in Bosnia, and the object 'international justice' is not a given but has to be built from diverse events and actions. The trials take place in The Hague. The Outreach Programme, with a staff of two people located in the UN building in Sarajevo, is rather inaccessible to ordinary citizens. No Bosnian newspaper had a permanent correspondent in The Hague until 2002, when the weekly newspaper *Dani* sent the journalist Emir Suljagić there.

The three most obvious phenomena are the interactions between the ICTY and other international institutions present in Bosnia, the decisions and public statements of government officials and political parties in regard to the ICTY, and the media coverage of the trials. But this public presence does not reflect the actual role of the ICTY in Bosnian society. Investigators remain discreet in their groundwork and avoid publicity, especially in their relationships with potential witnesses, which are sporadic. The Bosnians contacted by the Tribunal remain vague about those contacts if they talk about them at all. Moreover, as a legal institution, one of the main effects of the Tribunal is a negative one: the 'Rules of the Road' procedures prevent unfair local trials. Since what it produces is an absence, its effect cannot be directly observed.

---

[16] Informal conversation, Sarajevo, June 2002.

The other local partners of the ICTY are less publicly visible. These include judiciary professionals, witnesses, the governmental commissions for missing persons and some victim associations. Except for a few lawyers who defend individuals indicted in The Hague, most legal professionals have no direct experience with the ICTY's work. Moreover, judges and prosecutors are dependant on their own government authorities. Thus, studying the ICTY from this standpoint tends to deliver disappointing and predictable results, reflecting the official statements of those authorities.[17] More than legal professionals, the Bosnian citizens who play a key role in the ICTY's procedures are the witnesses, without whom no trial could take place.[18] However, witnesses constitute a very particular and limited segment of the population likely to give more importance to the ICTY than the average Bosnian citizen. They also remain scattered, without a visible place in Bosnian society.[19]

Many witnesses, however, are members or representatives of the victim associations upon which I focus this study. There are three main reasons for focusing on the concerns of these associations. First, proponents of the ICTY claim that international justice is carried out in the name of and for the victims. Second, some victim associations are direct interlocutors of the ICTY. Third, they represent a large segment of the population and have a public role.

Victim Associations and their Relations to the ICTY

It is difficult to evaluate how representative victim associations are. On one hand, individuals might formally register as members of an association in order to be eligible for present or future material benefits but without participating in any of its activities (this is especially the case with civilian victims associations). On the other hand, some associations led by a small group of activists can have much wider influence.[20] For example, only a small number of women are regularly active in the Association of the Mothers of Srebrenica and Žepa Enclaves. However, this association claims more than 8,000 members; 10,197 Srebrenica survivors answered its inquiry to decide on a place of burial for the dead (83 percent chose burial in Potočari) (Pollack 2003a: 795), and thousands of Bosniacs, whether members of the Srebrenica associations or not, have attended the 11 July commemorative ceremony, which has been organized by these organizations since 1996 (see also Duijzings, this volume).

---

[17]   Such is the case of the results of a survey of Bosnian judges and prosecutors led by the Berkeley Human Rights Center (see Fletcher, Stover and Weinstein 1999).

[18]   Elizabeth Neuffer (2001) follows a few of them in their personal experiences, offering thus both narrative coherence and ontological clarity.

[19]   In the ICTY statute and procedures, as in the Anglo-Saxon legal tradition, victims have no other status than that of witnesses.

[20]   On DP and veteran associations, see Bougarel, Grandits, this volume.

Not all victim associations share the same status and goals. We could limit our definition of victim associations to those comprised of civilian war victims.[21] Indeed, only civilian war victims (unlike former camp inmates, for example) are granted legal status under Bosnian law, allowing them certain benefits. It can also extend to associations of displaced persons and returnees, all the more so because, at the local level, some victim associations are entirely made up of DPs. I will leave aside DP associations, however, because not all refugees, DPs and returnees were victims of war crimes. Victim associations can be divided into three main types, according to the way in which they categorize victims:

- The Union of the Associations of Civilian Victims of War (*Unija udruženja civilnih žrtva rata*) was created in 1971 for the victims of World War II and later extended its activities to include the victims of the 1992-95 war in Bosnia. This Union is made up of several cantonal associations that are in closer contact with their members than the Union itself. In order to become a member of this type of association, one first needs to have been granted the status of civilian victim by a governmental commission according to two criteria, regardless of one's nationality: physical disability such as the loss of a body part and/or loss of a close family member. The civilian victims receive a pension that these associations deem quite meagre in comparison with the pensions of war veterans. Civilian victim associations try to garner support for their members, for instance, by helping them get humanitarian aid or scholarships. They deal mainly with the material, social and economic consequences of the war, as it reduced many victims to poverty.

In Sarajevo, the Cantonal Association of Civilian Victims of War reports 3,470 members. Its representatives denounce the aggression against Bosnia-Herzegovina and against civilians as well as the institutional division of the country. They complain that, as a result of this division, civilian victims cannot return to their home or are afraid to do so, that they lose their pensions and their status of civilian victim if they return to the RS. They consider it both scandalous and telling that the 1993 RS law on civilian victims was signed by Krajišnik, a Hague Tribunal indictee. Although some members from eastern Bosnia testified in The Hague, the associations of civilian victims are not, as such, in contact with the ICTY.

- The Union of (Former) Camp Inmates of Bosnia-Herzegovina (*Savez logoraša Bosne i Hercegovine*) was created in 1996 and brings together several cantonal associations which try to garner material and psychological support for their members. In Sarajevo, for example, the cantonal association organizes regular meetings where women victims of rape can talk about what they endured in the past and about the problems they confront in the present. Former camp inmates do not have a specific legal status. At the individual level, they can be considered either as war veterans or as civilian victims. If, as civilians, they were abused and raped in camps, without major and permanent physical consequences, they are not recognized, as psychological trauma and moral suffering is not enough to be granted the status of civilian victims of war. Against this background,

---

[21]   On war veterans and families of fallen soldiers, see Bougarel, this volume.

representatives of these associations assert that a specific status should provide the former camp inmates public recognition and certain social rights.

According to the 1949 Geneva Conventions, the definition of camps and places of detention includes private houses where people where detained against their will. The Union of Camp Inmates counts 618 places of detention. In response to criticisms of its loose categorization, the Union works on establishing a formal list of all detention places and criteria for membership.[22] It also gathers information and testimonies through its Centre for Investigation and Documentation, publishes books and organizes commemorations.

Because many witnesses in The Hague are former camp inmates, the Union of Camp Inmates claims to be one of the ICTY's main partners. Its representatives have testified several times in The Hague in the name of the association, for instance in the trials of Plavšić (on a total of only nine witnesses) and Milošević.

- The associations of families of missing persons were created after the war, in order to search for the missing and, as hopes of finding them alive waned, to recover their bodies for proper burial. They try to gather information to locate the mass graves and identify the corpses. This search for the missing is first organized at a local level, by the families, and in close connection with the Federal Commission for Missing Persons, the agency in charge of the exhumations. These families have also been fighting to obtain legal status for the missing, since the lack of such status leaves them faced with significant administrative problems, notably in regard to inheritance. Unlike the camp inmates who consider themselves victims because of their personal experiences, the families of missing persons consider that the true victims are the 'missing' rather than the survivors, who define themselves on the basis of their family relationships with the missing. The women of Srebrenica, for example, consider themselves primarily as mothers and widows. They have formed their associations not out of feminist concerns but because the men in their families were killed.[23] In several of these associations, the important role of women and of ordinary members who express their views directly, contrasts with the formal organization of other victim associations in which official representatives and men tend to monopolize the floor. Without the supervision of a formal federal union, these local associations are less 'politically correct' in their public protests (see also Duijzings, this volume).

These associations are first of all memorial associations where people come to talk about what is sometimes not even mentioned at home because it is too painful. They publish books that aim to individualize the missing: each page is dedicated to a missing person, with his or her name and picture when available, or to 'N.N.' (for 'Non Nominatus') in the case of corpses buried without identification. They organize commemorative ceremonies, such as those held on 11 July in Srebrenica

---

[22]   After such a survey, the number of members dropped from more than 100,000 in 1996-98 to 10,000.

[23]   On women's NGOs, see Helms, this volume.

for the anniversary of the massacre. These are attended by representatives and members of other similar Bosniac associations, who express their solidarity.

The associations of families of missing persons that I met are or have been in direct and indirect contact with the ICTY. Access to the mass graves located in the RS often depends on the exhumations carried out by the ICTY in cooperation with the Federal Commission for Missing Persons. When mass graves are located within the Federation, the ICTY remains a necessary intermediary for gathering information on their location or for indicting and trying the accused, either directly or indirectly through the 'Rules of the Road'. In Hadžići, near Sarajevo, the association of families of missing persons could neither locate the remaining mass graves nor hope for the arrest of those suspected criminals who were beyond the reach of Federation authorities. Its representatives had met with ICTY investigators but did not know the results of those contacts, especially since the ICTY can and does seal some indictments.

As has been rightly emphasized, the families were initially disappointed when they found out that the ICTY investigations did not reveal the identity of the dead (Stover and Shigekane 2002). Indeed, the ICTY's goals and the claims of the victims diverge with respect to the bodies. The judiciary logic seeks the causes of death and not the individual identity of the dead. Group identification by age, gender, or clothing is sufficient for qualification of a war crime against civilians, a crime against humanity, or genocide against a national group. Such a divergence should not lead us to oppose two senses of justice – an international one, focused on trials, and a local one, focused on the identification and the burial of the dead. The associations of families of missing persons first want to find the missing, but they also want to see criminals tried. The fact that the ICTY investigations granted access to most of the mass graves in Srebrenica and Prijedor is of great importance for the local associations of families of missing persons. This fact, however, did not diminish the frustration of the Association of the Mothers of Srebrenica and Žepa Enclaves over the small number of arrests, while the association *Izvor* in Prijedor expressed a greater satisfaction due to the number of ICTY indictments and arrests in this municipality. Moreover, by the second phase of the reception of the Tribunal, associations of victims' families had realized that, in the majority of cases the Tribunal would not identify bodies. On this issue, they began to revise their expectations towards the ICTY and henceforth turned their hopes to the International Committee of the Red Cross (ICRC) and later especially to the International Commission on Missing Persons (ICMP). The latter has launched a massive DNA identification program and works in connection with the ICTY.

What these three types of victim associations have in common is their denunciation of the effective impunity afforded to suspected war criminals and the small number of arrests of those who victimized them; they do not complain that the ICTY is geographically distant but that it does not try more perpetrators. Unlike Serb victim associations from the RS, however, who tend to attribute this state of affairs to the ICTY's partiality against Serbs, the Bosniac associations are more lenient and tend to attribute those facts to the ICTY's lack of means or power.

Overall, the disappointments towards the ICTY should not be overestimated, especially as compared to the situation of the ICTR vis-à-vis Rwanda. As disappointed as they might be, Bosniac victim associations have never refused to cooperate with the Hague Tribunal. Serb victim associations protest that the ICTY does not pay enough attention to Serb victims and ask for more indictments. Moreover, victim associations are not in a one-way relationship of dependence towards the ICTY. They expect information on the missing and the arrest of criminals but, in return, they support the investigators by providing information and testimonies.

The ICTY is not, however, the primary concern of victim associations. The foremost concerns of the representatives and members of these associations are widespread in post-war Bosnia: concerns about the material difficulties of everyday life, the meagreness of pensions and salaries, the dire straits of DPs expelled from their war-time lodgings, the difficulties of return. They campaign for a legal status that would grant them specific rights, including financial compensation and social benefits. Victims frequenting those associations are often those who suffered most in the war, who feel that 'we lost everything, when before the war, we had everything'. They tend, more than others, to view post-war Bosnia through categories inherited from the war. International justice appears as a post-war epiphenomenon rooted in an overwhelming presence of war and its aftermath, a war that Bosniac victim associations commonly denounce as aggression and genocide against Bosnia-Herzegovina. There is an asymmetry between denunciations of injustice and direct reference to justice. Most Bosniacs denounce the impunity of suspected war criminals but, once these criminals are arrested, their trials attract less attention. Therefore, direct references to the ICTY's achievements remain limited and scattered, which makes it difficult to fully contextualize them. After all, the victims' call for justice also includes material and financial aspects that would in theory fall under the aegis of civil courts or some other apparatus for granting reparations, or depend on a global system of distributive justice. Nonetheless, their call for justice, as opposed to revenge, refers specifically to criminal justice.

In which context *do* representatives and members of those associations refer to the ICTY? Most references are made in relation to the arrests of criminals who victimized an individual or close members of his or her family, especially when they are missing. When I visited the Cantonal Association of Civilian Victims in Sarajevo, its president Senida Karović told me that she considered the judgment of criminals a precondition for reconciliation; she did not, however, regularly follow the trials on TV, not even that of Galić.[24] Muzaref Teskeredžić, secretary of the same association, indicated that he was in Sarajevo during the war, but then focused on the fact that his father and sister were killed in Višegrad by a former pupil of his sister's, Milan Lukić, who had been indicted by The Hague and was still on the run. He insisted on the need for criminal justice and mentioned the

---

[24]   See note 14.

Hague Tribunal when talking about his father and sister and vice-versa. The more the ICTY investigations and trials concern suspected war criminals who are directly known or seen by victims, the more those investigations and trials are important. Thus, they particularly matter in places where there was face-to-face violence, as in Višegrad, Foča or Prijedor, more than in Sarajevo, where the artillerymen and snipers generally remained anonymous and unseen.

People who have been in direct contact with the prosecution teams express various degrees of frustration, fear, satisfaction, or relief according to whether their testimony has been requested, put aside, or delayed. Thus, the transcripts of the ICTY judgments do not give an adequate picture of the relationships between victims and the ICTY. Instead, they show only the public part of the investigations. More generally, for Bosniacs originating from what is now the RS, the ICTY matters, both symbolically and practically in their daily life, in the various forms of return ranging from settling back home to returning only to reclaim and sell property. Many displaced persons from eastern Bosnia feel that not enough arrests have been made for them to return. In contrast, returnees in Prijedor state that the arrests that happened in this municipality facilitated return (Wesselingh and Vaulerin 2005). Impunity is not an abstract concept and, in post-war Bosnia, it refers to empirical, local situations in which victims encounter former neighbours who attacked them during the war and who continue to threaten violence upon the victims' return (see also Duijzings, Kolind, this volume).

This focus on arrests and impunity is significant. It might be argued that the victims only want a non-violent 'elimination' of the criminals from civic life rather than formal trials. In that case, an indictment without an arrest, which often amounts to the disappearance of suspects from the public scene, should satisfy them. Mere indictments, however, clearly do not satisfy the victims. In the best scenario, indictments are viewed as a public acknowledgment of the crime. In the worst case, they are perceived as additional proof of the weakness or hypocrisy of the international community: failed attempts of NATO troops at capturing Karadžić and Mladić are depicted by Bosniacs as a scandal and as a 'farce'. Given that indictments without arrests are deemed unsatisfactory and that trials do not attract major attention, I argue that the ICTY concerns Bosnian citizens mainly through arrests and sentences. What is expected from international criminal justice is primarily to put a material and symbolic end to impunity and to past or ongoing injustices. Victims might disagree on a positive and 'thick' concept of justice, but they agree on this 'thin' but core meaning of justice (Walzer 1994). The fight against impunity thus reveals both a closeness and a discrepancy between victims who emphasize the importance of sentences and ICTY advocates who argue that trials themselves set an example and pay little attention to sentences.

Legal Categories, ICTY Achievements and Victims' Search for Recognition

Overall, the ICTY as embodiment of international justice occupies a specific position for Bosniacs between a strong call for justice and morality, and a massive denunciation of the 'international community'. The ICTY is evaluated against the background of a deeply rooted rejection of international politics, which it leaves unchanged. Its credibility depends on whether or not it succeeds in distinguishing itself from such politics. This particular position of the ICTY among Bosniacs is reflected in the idea that 'the Hague Tribunal brings us only a little justice, but other institutions do not'.[25] It also appears indirectly through the fact that most of the widespread criticisms towards international organizations or NGOs are not addressed to the ICTY. I never heard that the ICTY was 'making money on our backs' or that the ICTY's budget would have been better used for other purposes, as was said about other international institutions and organizations. Likewise, even when members and representatives of predominantly Bosniac victim associations are puzzled by the selectivity and opacity of its policy of indictments, or frustrated by the impossibility of accessing the results of its investigations, they did not criticize the ICTY for being a power without accountability, criticism which is frequently addressed to the OHR and other international organizations.

The background of this very negative perception of the international community has, however, significant consequences for the Hague Tribunal in Bosnia. To various degrees, foreign politicians are deemed responsible for the war in Bosnia, especially for the siege of Sarajevo and the massacre of Srebrenica. Therefore, the importance of the ICTY is diminished by the widespread belief that this tribunal does not judge those who are truly and primarily responsible for the war, like the French, the American or the Dutch governments. Expressing an opinion that can be heard among Serbs and Bosniacs alike, a Sarajevan stated with reference to the ICTY: 'The international community is cleansing itself, because it knew very well who Milošević was and because it supported him nonetheless. It is the same for Saddam Hussein; all that is a circle.' Such a background also partially explains some of the differences among Bosniacs in their attitude towards international justice: the more the war took place under 'international control', as in Sarajevo and Srebrenica (and unlike in Prijedor or Višegrad), the more victims denounce the 'international community' and demand the judgment of those who are 'really' responsible, and the less the ICTY is likely to fulfil their call for justice.

The ICTY also occupies a specific position for Bosniacs between their call for justice and morality, on one side, and their distrust of national politics and institutions, on the other (see also Helms, Kolind, this volume). Such distrust is directed at the judiciary system, at the media, and even at some victim associations. In 2002, for example, women and human rights associations, as well as victims in

---

[25] Jasmin Odobašić, vice-president of the Federal Commission for Missing Persons, informal conversation, Sarajevo, 20 June 2002.

private conversations, expressed their criticism towards the book *I Begged Them to Kill Me*, a collection of testimonies from women victims of wartime rape published by the Union of Camp Inmates (Šaćirbegović, Malešević and Ajanović 2000). They saw it as an appropriation of women's voices by men: the women did not participate in the promotion of the book, which primarily benefited men, and women's stories were rewritten in a sensational style, without respect to their wishes. An even greater sense of outrage was produced when, on 29 March 2002, confidential documents arriving from the Hague Tribunal through the 'Rules of the Road' procedures, were published in the daily newspaper *Jutarnje Novine*. These documents released the names of suspected war criminals and 'protected' witnesses, including several women victims of rape. Such a violation of confidentiality cast serious doubts on the ethics of the journalists and politicians who were at the source of this leak. In such a context, however critical victims might be towards the ICTY, they express a confidence in the Hague Tribunal that they do not express towards most other international or national institutions. The ICTY's rules for respecting witness protection and anonymity, though imperfect, stand in clear contrast to the lack of protection or the lack of respect by national institutions towards individual witnesses who might be threatened or mistreated in Bosnia. The Tribunal's practices end up appearing to some as a norm, or at least a reference, in comparison with which local practices are considered even more immoral and difficult to cope with.

Can we go further and claim that the categories of international law are, or have become, a reference for the victims and victim associations? This is clearly the case concerning the status of civilian victims, or the rights claimed by the families of missing persons, which are framed in accordance with international humanitarian law. The description of the war as an aggression against civilians also draws on the distinction between combatant and non-combatant, which is the very basis of this international humanitarian law and of the legal classification of war crime. Likewise, descriptions of crimes as being organized, systematic and planned, more or less correspond to the criteria for qualification as crimes against humanity and genocide.

Beyond that, the impact of legal categories and of ICTY goals is much less obvious. In May 2002, during a meeting at the Cantonal Association of Civilian Victims of War in Sarajevo, I asked whether the Hague Tribunal could contribute to establishing truth. The immediate answer of several victims was: 'But we already know the truth.' The truth of the victim derives from personal experience so that 'the truth is something that trials can acknowledge, but not something that legal processes are needed to discover' (Fletcher and Weinstein 2002: 589). Such a conflict between the truth of the judge, that of the historian, and that of the eyewitness is not specific to Bosnia.[26] However, particularly for victims who were besieged in enclaves, the truth sought is also that of international responsibility,

---

[26] On a similar conflict in France, see among others Rousso 2002; Wieviorka 1998.

which remains outside the scope of the Tribunal's competence, thus deepening the gap between the truth of the victim and that of the judge.

A similar remark applies concerning the ascription of responsibility. While the ICTY judges only criminal responsibility, the victim associations tend to see only degrees of responsibility in criminal politics but do not deem relevant the difference between moral, political and criminal responsibility. Srebrenica associations request not only the judgment of Mladić, but also of the Dutch 'blue helmets' present in the enclave and of the French, Dutch and UN officials 'who wanted this genocide'.

Finally, one might be puzzled to hear representatives of victim associations claiming that the aggression and genocide against Bosnia-Herzegovina have not been recognized. In such a claim, they use the vocabulary of international law while they neglect the ICTY's achievements: the Tadić judgment concluded in July 1999 that the war in Bosnia-Herzegovina was an international conflict, Milošević was indicted for genocide in Bosnia in November 2001, and Krstić was convicted of genocide in August 2001. Although these achievements match some victims' expectations, they seem to remain without effect. How are we to understand this discrepancy? It can first be interpreted as a gap, common in Bosnia and elsewhere, between legal categories and lay categories, especially when they are as symbolically and politically loaded as genocide. This discrepancy might reflect the aforementioned asymmetry between injustice and justice, between impunity perceived as scandalous, on one hand, and the end of impunity perceived as a return to a more normal state of affairs, which remains quite gloomy for most Bosnians, on the other.

This discrepancy can also be interpreted in terms more specific to the Bosnian situation. The criminal trials are of individuals; they leave the power relations and institutional structure in Bosnia more or less unchanged. After general Krstić had been condemned for genocide in Srebrenica, Hakija Meholjić, president of the association *Srebrenica 99*, stated that 'all those who committed crimes must be judged, but those trials are of no use to us at all if what they did remains'.[27] The recognition that Bosniacs expect from international justice is both individual *and* collective. They expect both personal recognition of their victimization by their former neighbours and colleagues – people who abused them or let them down – and public recognition at the level of local or RS authorities. Victims hope that the establishment of truth in The Hague will lead to its recognition in Bosnia itself and they are disappointed that the ICTY's work prevents neither the denial nor the celebration of the crime in public monuments in the RS.[28]

The expectation of such a double effect from the trials expresses the victims' ambivalence towards the process of justice and, paradoxically, their disappointment shows how close they are to the ICTY's stance. The ICTY claims

---

[27] *Nezavisne novine*, 3 August 2001.

[28] On the public denial of the camps in Prijedor, see Sivac 2004; Wesselingh and Vaulerin 2005.

it can contribute to peace and reconciliation, a claim which supposes that the judgment of individuals will bring about collective change. Such views of the relationships between the individual and collective levels differ from those expressed by political parties. RS political leaders insist that ICTY trials and judgments are only those of individuals and not of institutions, so they have no institutional consequence. In contrast, according to representatives of the Party of Democratic Action (SDA), the main Bosniac political party, ICTY judgments reveal the illegitimate and criminal nature of the RS, founded on aggression and genocide, and help to support the suit that Bosnia-Herzegovina filed in 1993 against Yugoslavia for genocide at the International Court of Justice.

Contrary to Serb political leaders, Bosniac victims and representatives of victim associations do not consider that those judgments concern only individuals. But, contrary to the SDA reading in political terms, they refer to the ICTY judgments primarily in a personal context and do not view the Tribunal as an arbiter of state to state relations. The representatives and members of the missing persons associations and of the civilian victim associations never mentioned the Bosnia-Herzegovina law suit against Yugoslavia at the International Court of Justice in my presence. They did not expect a revision of the RS statutes in connection with the ICTY's work, even though they are among those who are living most in the memory and shadow of war, and they commonly blame RS institutions for favouring impunity or for the victims' fate. The Union of Camp Inmates is closer to the SDA. In partnership with the local association of camp inmates, the Union held a conference in Ključ in May 2002, entitled 'Aggression and genocide against Bosnia-Herzegovina', that was meant to support the 1993 lawsuit for genocide against Yugoslavia. However, the ICTY, as a specific topic, was not brought up during this conference, although a few participants protested against the weakness of certain sentences.

I argue that Bosniac members and representatives of victims associations, even when they denounce the RS and support the ICTY, still differ from the SDA stance. With the exception of a few representatives of the Union of Camp Inmates, most Bosniac victims support the ICTY, not as part of a political calculation, but as an expression of vital moral norms. The ICTY is evaluated in the context of a sharp opposition between morality and politics: politics, both domestic and international, amounts for most Bosnians to immoral deals, dirty deeds and corruption (see also Grandits, Helms, Kolind, this volume). In line with this division, while most Serbs in the RS blame the ICTY for being political, Bosniacs look to the ICTY to provide proof that 'evil cannot win' and to contribute to the restoration of the moral order shattered by the war. With this faith in justice, victims share with ICTY promoters a quasi-magical and messianic conception of justice as something that is able to act from a distance without tangible mediation (Teitel 1999). More generally, they somehow share a concept of post-war justice founded on truth and the exhumation of mass graves, along with a belief that the reconciliation achieved by communist

Yugoslavia after World War II was illusory and unsatisfactory because it relied on the concealment of truth and on the closure of mass graves.[29]

International Criminal Justice and the Idea of a Common Humanity

The relative disappointment or indifference of victims towards international justice, once rendered, can also be interpreted as a discrepancy between the recognition that the Hague Tribunal claims to offer to the victims and the recognition that they actually get in Bosnia following the trials and judgments. The promoters of international criminal justice claim that international justice restores a humanity attacked by crimes against humanity. This idea of a common humanity stands as mediation, on the international scene, between the judgment of individual perpetrators and the public and collective recognition of the victims. I would argue, however, that such mediation is almost absent for the victims in Bosnia: the ICTY does not release them from the isolation of suffering and injustice, either at the international or the national level.

From a Bosnian perspective, the ICTY does not bridge the gap of a humanity divided into states, or rather into those whose lives count and those whose lives do not, according to the state they come from. The feeling of having fallen in the hierarchy of humanity is widespread in Bosnia. It differs from the feeling of dehumanization brought about by the experience of violence, and is rather related to the international presence during the war. Before 1992, being a Yugoslav citizen amounted to belonging to a country that counted on the international scene, belonging to 'civilized Europe'. The experience of the war, the absence of international military intervention, and the lack of protection provided by the UN 'blue helmets', whose lives were deemed more important than those of the locals, undermined the feeling of belonging to that part of humanity where one's life matters (Delpla 2003). Such a representation of the value of humanity constitutes the background against which international justice is evaluated. The Holocaust of European Jews and the Nuremberg trials remain the main point of comparison by which Bosnians express their claim for justice (Živković 2000). By contrast, the genocide in Rwanda and the ICTR are hardly ever mentioned. As for the Hague Tribunal itself, it is partly judged according to whether it is seen as reflecting or rejecting the disdain of the international community for Bosnian and especially Bosniac lives.

This sense of a fall in humanity which prevails in the Bosnian reception of international intervention, such as humanitarian aid, was absent from the general evaluation of the ICTY. It has increasingly appeared, however, in the reception of

---

[29] For an expression of beliefs shared by some Bosnians and internationals concerning the relationship between justice, memory and reconciliation, see the testimony of Carl Bildt, former Swedish Prime Minister and first High Representative in Bosnia-Herzegovina, in the Plavšić trial (available at <http://www.un.org/icty/transe3940/021217IT.htm>).

some sentences. For some representatives of victim associations, like Džemil Sijerčic, president of the Union of Former of Camp Inmates,[30] the fact that a sentence was pronounced at all is more important than its severity. Others, like Amor Mašović, president of the Federal Commission for Missing Persons, judge the fairness of sentences by calculating the ratio between the number of years of incarceration and the number of victims: for example, he considers that Plavšić's sentence of eleven years amounts to 2.5 minutes per victim.[31] Representatives of families of missing persons see in such a ratio the divergence of law (*pravo*) and justice (*pravda*). Sentences, then, are evaluated according to the principle of proportionality with the crime and not according to the principle of individualization of responsibility, which is the basis of criminal law.

Such calculations reflect the price-of-life hierarchy in which the life of the locals is worth nearly nothing as compared to that of internationals. The following statement, heard in Sarajevo, expresses a common feeling: 'In the United States, you kill two people and you end up on death row. Here you kill several hundred and you get by with a few years.' While international criminal justice aims at restoring a common humanity, several ICTY sentences worsened the feeling of an international divide running through humanity,[32] or, at best did not succeed in bridging it.

A similar remark applies to the idea of a common humanity inside Bosnia. One might expect that trials of crimes against humanity and genocide would provide public recognition of victims' suffering. The French historian Annette Wieviorka contrasts the historical value of the Nuremberg trials, mainly based on documents, with the social effects of the Eichman trial in Jerusalem, based on eye-witness testimony. That trial, she claims, opened 'the era of the witness' (Wieviorka 1998).[33] In the years following World War II, the death camp survivors were silenced in favour of soldiers and heroes of the resistance. The Eichman trial in 1961 opened the way to an acknowledgment of the victims as such, to the social recognition of their suffering. In West European countries, Israel, and the United States, the 'era of the witness' also elevated Holocaust victims to nearly sacred status (e.g. Chaumont 1997; Novick 1999; Segev 1994). Gathering witness' testimonies then becomes a task of utmost moral importance. Such attitudes inform the thinking of many international promoters of the ICTY.

The social effects of the Eichman trial are, however, generally absent in Bosnia. The trials in The Hague do not bring about a shared recognition or an improvement of the social and symbolic status of victims. After paying lip service to the terrible

---

[30] Interview, Sarajevo, 22 May 2002.

[31] *Oslobođenje*, 1 March 2003.

[32] Although this feeling was not predominant in 2002, it has become so following several convictions in 2003, especially those of Plavšić and Galić sentenced to eleven and twenty years of imprisonment, respectively.

[33] This focus on witnesses and victims was harshly criticized by Hannah Arendt (see Arendt 1994 [1963]).

fate and suffering of Bosniacs from Srebrenica or Foča, Sarajevans typically shift quickly to talking about the victims from rural Bosnia as illiterate and uneducated peasants who are out of place in an urban setting (see also Stefansson, this volume).[34] The ICTY trials do not bridge the barriers of a humanity divided into states, regions, and social classes. According to psychological interpretations, victims are locked in their suffering as they suffer from trauma. Such a reading of the situation of Bosnian victims misses the point.[35] The barriers are more sociological than psychological: the social status of victim is not prevalent enough to overcome the social disdain that certain victims endure. Neither does the ICTY modify this state of affairs, nor do victims from eastern Bosnia expect the ICTY to do so.

This situation raises the sensitive issue of 'the competition of victims' (Chaumont 1997), which refers to the fight for recognition among victimized groups (see also Duijzings, Grandits, Bougarel, this volume). The category of genocide particularly crystallizes such a struggle (Denich 1994), which is also a claim for certain rights. Are we to conclude that, in Bosnia, the ICTY fuels or tempers such competition? It is certainly too early to resolve this matter. It is worth emphasizing, however, that the competition among victim associations is if anything fuelled much more by the competition for humanitarian donations and the conditions put on NGOs for obtaining material support than it is by the ICTY. Admittedly, the ICTY trials bring a sense of recognition to victims, which is all the greater when those trials have accompanied social changes such as the return of Bosniacs to Prijedor (Wesselingh and Vaulerin 2005). Beyond the Prijedor case, however, it remains to be seen whether the ICTY provides a common language through which the conflicting claims of victims can be not only expressed but also heard in Bosnian society.

Furthermore, the solidarity of victim associations belonging to the same national group (*narod*) does not suffice to account for the sense of injustice and the denunciation of impunity. The fact that there were several judgments for the crimes committed in Prijedor and Foča does not diminish the sense of outrage felt by Srebrenica associations. The level at which impunity is most vehemently denounced is neither that of Bosnia-Herzegovina as a whole, nor that of the national group (Bosniac versus Serb) or region (eastern versus western Bosnia), but that of the municipality. The 'we', which representatives of the local association for missing persons used in Hadžići, for instance, refers to the Bosniacs and Croats of this municipality, and not to the Bosniac nation or to Muslim believers in general. Except as concerns Karadžić, Mladić, and a few others, impunity is not a concept applied to suspected war criminals in general but refers to the freedom of movement of some locally known individuals who are therefore not the same from

---

[34]   I did not, however, hear such derogatory comments among members of victim associations.

[35]   For a criticism of psychological categories as applied to political violence, see for example Humphrey 2002: 105-24.

one place to another. In Hadžići and Vogošća, the associations of families of missing persons did not mention Milan Lukić, a war criminal from Višegrad; the local association from Višegrad, in turn, did not refer to Milomir Stakić, who was talked about in Sanski Most and Prijedor. The fact that there had been many arrests in Prijedor but none in the neighbouring town of Ključ even left some people in the latter place with the feeling that they had been forgotten, despite the fact that many of the men from Ključ shared the same fate as those from Prijedor in camps such as Manjača.

National divisions certainly correspond to degrees of adherence to or rejection of international justice, but they are insufficient to understand the ICTY's impact if they are not combined with the effects of municipal boundaries. During the war, municipal authorities played a key role in the implementation of ethnic cleansing.[36] The municipal level is the level at which individuals consider themselves as more or less direct witnesses of atrocities, and at which war criminals can be identified individually by way of pre-war social relationships. Therefore, in conversations with victims or representatives of victim associations, the individuals most frequently pointed to as criminals were local public figures like the former mayor or chief of police.

This importance of the local dimension has two consequences relative to impunity. First, some human rights activists or promoters of a Truth and Reconciliation Commission for Bosnia criticize the tendency of Bosnian citizens to request and approve justice only when their own national group is the victim. Such a criticism is accurate but it is still too general. While individuals and associations tend to focus on crimes committed against their own group, they are most concerned with crimes that took place in their region or municipality against their national group or against others who where victims of the same perpetrators.

Second, the primarily local character of the outrage over impunity means that Bosniac victims are not satisfied by the indictments and arrests of suspected Serb or Croat war criminals who victimized other Bosniacs in other municipalities. Such a state of affairs makes it difficult to reconcile the ICTY's claim that it brings justice to the victims with its policy of selective indictments, a practice that is unavoidable due to the number of the crimes.[37] The reconciliation of this claim with the policy rests on the assumption that victims could and should be satisfied by indictments and arrests that might not concern them directly. Such a supposition amounts either to considering victims to be disencumbered cosmopolitans or to attributing to them such strong belief in the collective guilt of Serbs or Croats that the arrests of some of them should matter to all victims of Serb or Croat perpetrators. A certain localism of victims and victim associations tends to show that they are not cosmopolitans so detached from their community that they can adhere, without accessible mediations, to the idea of a common humanity.

---

[36] On the decentralized features of ethnic cleansing in Bosnia, see Sorabji 1995.

[37] On this policy of selective indictments, see Bass 2000: 297-301; Fletcher and Weinstein 2002: 580.

However, this localism also reveals the limits of national and nationalist categories: even when adherence to the categories of aggression and genocide corresponds to a sentiment of collective victimization, victims' minds are not so enmeshed in collective 'ethnic' thinking that they define being a perpetrator, being a victim, or victims' relationships to their perpetrators as national collective phenomena.

The victims' sense of injustice and related expectations combine personal, national and geographic dimensions. They reflect the pattern of crimes organized on a national basis and at the regional and local levels, as well as the importance of the local dimension in the pre-war social and political organization of communities. Further, paradoxically, they reflect the achievements of the ICTY itself. International justice claims to oppose adherence to national categories through the individualization of responsibility and the targeting of a common humanity. The impact of the ICTY, however, cannot be evaluated solely on the basis of *a priori* claims, but should be assessed in the actual context of the international and local mediations present or absent in Bosnia and on the basis of the actual practices of international criminal justice. In fact, the ICTY policy of indictments seems to follow both a national[38] and a geographic logic of scattered indictments throughout the territory of former Yugoslavia without a clear connection among them, thus potentially reinforcing the victims' localism. It remains to be seen whether this overlap of personal, national and geographic dimensions of victims' expectations will remain a durable feature of the reception of the ICTY in Bosnia or whether it is likely to evolve over time. Such a development could result either from further indictments and trials likely to overcome this localism or from the convergence of victim associations in their growing protests against both the ICTY sentencing policy and its completion strategy.

---

[38]   The ICTY explicitly relies on national categories in its definition of genocide and crime against humanity and in its attempt at revealing the pattern of crimes. It also implicitly relies on such categories in its policy of selective indictments in which one or a few individuals stand for a larger group of perpetrators. In addition, this policy aims at indicting suspects from all national groups out of a 'concern about evenhandedness of prosecutions' according to the 'premise that the judicial credibility of the ICTY needed to be upheld by the equal prosecution of all parties' (Humphrey 2002: 136).

Chapter 10

'Politics is a Whore':
Women, Morality and Victimhood in Post-War Bosnia-Herzegovina

Elissa Helms

> A young woman is hanging out by an SFOR [NATO] base in Sarajevo practicing the world's oldest profession. An older man from the community comes to her and says, 'Why are you doing this? You're young and fit, you're a Bosniac – surely you can find other things to do. Why didn't you choose instead to get an education?
>
> The girl replies, 'I have an education, I finished university.'
> Old man: 'Well, there must be another job you can do.'
> Girl: 'But I'm not a member of the party.'
> Old man: 'Why don't you join the party?'
> Girl: 'Are you kidding, my mother barely let me do *this*!'
>
> – joke recorded in Sarajevo, 1999

In the summer of 1999, a group of Bosnian women politicians and leaders of local non-governmental organizations (NGOs) were gathered in the city of Tuzla under the auspices of the Bosnian League of Women Voters (*Liga žena glasača*) to discuss strategies for increasing women's participation in formal politics. Senka Nožica, a member of the civic opposition in the Federation and one of the most prominent women active in Bosnian politics, held forth on the superiority of women politicians over men:

> Women are naturally responsible because of our duties towards our children. There are so many small details we have to think of and take care of, and we have no choice, we have to do these things. They are things that can't be put off, they have to be done everyday. We can't stay in the *kafana* [café-bar] for another drink like men can.

Several months later, Irena Soldat-Jovanović, a parliamentary representative from *Republika Srpska* speaking on Bosnian television lamented the dramatic fall in the number of women in formal politics which had accompanied the dissolution of socialist Yugoslavia. While the socialist system had required women's participation through quotas, the multi-party elections of 1990 did away with such requirements (although quotas for ethno-national representation were stipulated), and only 4.9 percent of those elected in those pre-war elections were women (Ler-Sofronić 1998: 91).[1] Soldat-Jovanović therefore concluded:

> Very few women were in politics [then] for the reason that women didn't even have the opportunity or the chance to shape Bosnia-Herzegovina. Had women had a higher degree of participation in 1991, maybe it would not have even come to this war, maybe we would have found, in some peaceful way, a compromise in which women were very prominent, and through which the family would be preserved.

Both of these women were appealing to popular notions of gender and politics circulating in post-war Bosnia-Herzegovina. Politics itself is often gendered through the common phrase, *'politika je kurva'* ('politics is a whore'), which is used to emphasize the corrupt, fickle, and immoral nature of political deal-making (Jalušič 1994; Grandits, Kolind, this volume). While politics is in this way feminized, it is nonetheless understood and portrayed in everyday and official discourses alike as a male arena where women, especially respectable women, have no place.[2] Since the end of the war, however, women have increasingly been active in a variety of capacities in the public sphere, engaging issues of political importance, as well as directly in the realm of formal politics.[3] In fact, a broad-based, multi-ethnic group of women NGO activists and politicians from a range of political parties, with substantial backing from the 'international community', has formed a movement of women calling for increased participation of women in politics and attention to a variety of 'women's issues'.

This activity directly clashes not only with local conceptions of 'politics', but also with gender constructions that place men in the roles of warrior and political actor (see Bougarel, this volume), and women as passive (war) victims, mothers and nurturers – objects rather than subjects of political processes. Women serve as symbols of the nation's moral purity and as such must be protected by the nation's

---

[1]   In 1986, women made up 24.1 percent of representatives to the Parliament of the Socialist Republic of Bosnia-Herzegovina and 17.3 percent of municipal council representatives in this republic. In 1990, when quotas for women were dropped, 2.9 percent of the republic's parliamentary seats and 4.9 percent of municipal seats were held by women (see OSCE 1998).

[2]   On the appointment of female politician Suada Hadžović as Minister for Veteran Affairs and her rejection by male war veterans, see Bougarel, this volume.

[3]   It should also be stressed that women were publicly active during both the wartime and socialist periods, engagement that could easily be described as political. On the socialist period, see Denich 1977; Woodward 1985.

men from defilement by the enemy (again, assumed to be men) (e.g. Mostov 1995; Verdery 1994; Yuval-Davis 1997). Indeed, the widespread acceptance in the region of such gendered logic gave power in the first place to the use of rape and sexual violence as tactics of 'ethnic cleansing' during the war (e.g. Hayden 2000; Korać 1998; Žarkov 1999). In post-war Bosnia, women raped, displaced and bereaved during the war have become the symbol of each nation's victimization and innocence, especially among Bosniacs. This is especially underscored by representations from outside of Bosnia in which the first, and perhaps only, image which springs to mind when one utters the phrase 'Bosnian women' is that of Muslim (Bosniac) women raped and forcibly impregnated by Serb forces. Bosniac women have thus become the archetypal victim of wartime rape in Bosnia, despite the fact that other women, as well as men, were also raped and sexually assaulted, albeit in smaller numbers.[4]

Within Bosnia, the treatment of wartime rape has been somewhat different. Although the subject is not a common public topic, it is invoked from time to time in Bosniac nationalist discourses, which depict the wartime rape of Bosniac women as symbolic of both the nation's innocence and suffering and of the barbarism of their enemies (Serbs and Croats). Women's own public self-representations generally avoid direct association with rape, although they position women as passive victims of male-led politics and military campaigns – victims of other sorts of suffering (see also Delpla, this volume). Still, in all of these discourses, the category of 'woman' is defined and affirmed by wartime events. Victim images have come to stand for all of Bosnian womanhood, leaving little space for women to construct identities other than as ethnicized, passive victims of enemy men.

In this chapter, I explore the discursive strategies women activists and politicians use to gain support and justify their involvement in the male-associated sphere of the political. I argue that women's self-positioning vis-à-vis 'politics' must be seen in the context of gendered meanings and a political climate in which moral purity is based on war-associated victim identities (see also Delpla, Duijzings, Bougarel, this volume). While notions of respectable womanhood exclude women from political participation, the moral purity associated with such constructions in fact bolster women's claims to legitimacy as political actors. They must, however, overcome strong resistance to the idea of women politicians, including the idea that a woman in politics is morally (sexually) suspect. To maintain their respectability, then, I argue that women must continue to be perceived *as women*, and moral women at that. It is this imperative which underlies

---

[4]   As a result of this and of the near exclusive focus on Muslim women, images of rape in Bosnia have taken on an Orientalist quality. Such depictions imply that Muslim communities, especially rural ones, are by definition more controlling of women and therefore sure to ostracize raped women to a degree that non-Muslims would not. Such assumptions, however, reveal more about Western images of Muslims than about the actual situation in Bosnia (see Helms 2004; Žarkov 1995).

the self-presentation strategies of politically active women and which determines the extent to which they are able to invoke and/or reject feminized victim identities, including that of wartime rape victim. Finally, I seek to demonstrate how examining Bosnian political processes through the lens of gender categories illuminates many of the otherwise hidden ways in which power and identities are being contested and shaped in the post-war period. My analysis is based on over two years of ethnographic field research (1997, 1999-2000) among women NGO participants and political party candidates in the Bosniac majority town of Zenica, and at gatherings of women activists from all parts of Bosnia.[5]

'Politika je kurva'

Images of female victimhood lie just below the surface when women are mentioned in public discourses. When they do appear, it is more often as a homogeneous group or category ('women') rather than in reference to individual actors, and primarily when the subject turns to righting injustices from the war or to problems of children, health, and unjust economic suffering. In other words, women are overwhelmingly the objects of 'politics' rather than political subjects in their own right.

Ordinary Bosnians generally view politics with a large dose of scepticism, except often in cases when they see party policies as supporting their interests. Politicians are derided as corrupt schemers, only out for personal gain and engaged in dark deals and morally compromising activities (Jalušič 1994; Grandits, Kolind, this volume). Since the dissolution of socialist Yugoslavia, politics have also been reviled for producing the politicized ethnic hatred which preceded and fuelled the war and which continues, in the eyes of many Bosnians, to underlie obstacles to the (re)establishment of peace and prosperity. Of course, there is no consensus on *which* politicians are guilty of this obstruction, as members of one ethno-national community are likely to regard the politicians representing perceived rival ethno-national groups as the worst nationalists rather than 'their own' politicians (see also Kolind, this volume).

Despite such negative associations, however, when the question arises as to whether women should or can be effective politicians, it becomes clear that politics is nevertheless regarded as a source of prestige and power, and one meant primarily for men. In a typical example, delegates at the opening session of the Federation Parliament in early 1999 were deadlocked after having elected a Bosniac from the dominant Bosniac party (the Party of Democratic Action, SDA) and a Croat from the main Croat party (the Croat Democratic Union, HDZ) for two of three executive parliament positions. When a prominent Bosniac politician

---

    [5]   The research was funded by the International Research and Exchanges Board (IREX), The Institute for the Study of World Politics, the Council for European Studies, and a University of Pittsburgh FLAS Fellowship.

suggested that the third post be given to a woman, the delegates burst into laughter. The few women representatives present chuckled nervously but said nothing and when the laughter died down, parliament got back to business and elected a man for the post.[6] Despite the serious political differences between the two ethno-nationally based parties, they were in perfect agreement that the only serious candidates for positions of power and prestige were men. As Senka Nožica, the politician quoted above, observed, 'a woman in politics today isn't a rarity, she's an incident'.[7]

It is said that women have no place in politics, not only because they lack men's strength of character necessary to endure its demands but also because women's role is in the home raising children and keeping house. This view is not necessarily incompatible with the general acceptance, among both men and women, of the considerable presence of women in the public realm of paid employment, even in positions of authority, which has been the rule since the socialist period (Denich 1977; Woodward 1985). Working women still care for the home and their children and are thus seen as respectable, while politics is nevertheless seen as too demanding and 'dirty' for women.

For women, this dirtiness implies not only dishonesty but also sexual immorality. Monika,[8] a nineteen-year-old political activist and candidate for the Zenica municipal council, told me that her boyfriend was now resigned to her involvement in politics but that, 'at the beginning he would make [critical] comments, he thought it wasn't right. You know, they say politics is a whore and a woman in politics is therefore a whore'. In this very common formulation, politics is feminized, but as a disreputable, immoral female – the whore. 'She' corrupts good men, compelling them to engage in immoral acts. Politicians are similarly cast as prostitutes who sell themselves and their moral principles for personal gain. The masculinity of male politicians, however, is not damaged through their participating in politics. Indeed, they engage in some of the most quintessentially masculine arenas: the public and the political. Even metaphorically, men's masculinity (virility) is enhanced rather than diminished through their association with a 'whore', through the sexual double standard (Simic 1983a). Thus, politics as a whore does not feminize or emasculate male politicians so much as point to the corruption and immorality of their profession. Women, however, are doubly excluded from this realm, both because they are not male and because, as females, association with such immorality calls their own moral reputations into question.

---

[6]   While the male politician's suggestion was reported briefly and without comment in the press, the reaction of the delegates was described to me by a Bosnian woman media analyst who had witnessed the event.

[7]   Interview with Senka Nožica in *Žena*, 29 October 1999.

[8]   This is a pseudonym, as are all other names in this chapter given as first names only. Where first and last names are given, these are the real names of public figures quoted in public forums.

As the concern of Monika's boyfriend suggests, politics is clearly no place for morally respectable women.

The connection between politics and women's sexual immorality is further underscored by comments aimed at women politicians, especially those who have risen to positions of prestige. Sabina, a woman in her mid-thirties and a member of the Federation House of Representatives, told me that when she was first elected to parliament, the men in her party 'questioned my abilities, my authority and knowledge. They said, "if I were your husband I would have found another woman by now", or "how does your husband let you do this?"' Later, Sabina told a gathering of women activists,

> I know one man who commented, 'if I had known my wife would go into politics I wouldn't have married her. A woman talking on the same level as a man about politics?! And being gone from home so much?!' But women make good politicians. *Women are more sensitive to questions of family, children. We are the pillars of our country.* (emphasis added)

A woman who spends a lot of time away from home, especially in the company of other men, is often seen as sexually suspect. By the same token, an unmarried and/or childless woman is also less respectable. This does not make her fit for politics, however, as the many remarks I heard about two prominent single women politicians attest. One acquaintance told me that Amila Omersoftić, the leader of the Women's Party (*Stranka žena*) and a former highly ranked member of the SDA, is 'in politics because she doesn't have children or a family, so she has nothing else to do and she decided to meddle into politics'. The only woman politician to have served in a major office in the post-Yugoslav period, former President of the RS and member of the pre-war Presidency of Bosnia-Herzegovina Biljana Plavšić, was also derided for not having children or a husband. In fact, many Bosnians of various political orientations found reasons for her failings in the fact that she is unmarried and childless.

These notions are beginning to change somewhat as women, especially those seen as respectable, have increasingly become visible actors in both political discourses and formal politics. Still, the idea that politics are incompatible with female identity remains strong, even among politically active women themselves. For this reason, Sabina countered her male colleagues' derogatory remarks with an appeal to women's moral purity based on their domestic roles (in italics above). Politically active women are caught in a contradiction. They want to retain the moral purity ascribed to women who conform to their roles as passive victims and keepers of the home and family, yet they also seek to be taken seriously as political *actors*. To manoeuvre themselves through this dilemma, women have sought to reshape both the definition of politics, as well as that of respectable womanhood.

NGO Women: Humanitarian, Not Political

Women who are publicly active yet not part of any formal political structure are arguably engaged in 'political' pursuits, as their activities seek to influence the direction of society. Many of the numerous women's NGOs that have sprung up since the war period easily fit this description, though those involved often insist that there is nothing political about their activities. At a workshop in 1997 for NGO women from all over Bosnia held on the subject of 'Women and Politics', two women political party members (educated urban professionals) tried to convince a room of mostly working class women from small towns that their women's clubs and income generating projects were in fact part of a more broadly defined 'politics'. Most of the women looked sceptical and adamantly repeated that they wanted nothing to do with politics in any form.

To be sure, the NGO sector is a relatively new phenomenon in Bosnia, and considerable confusion exists over the place of NGOs in relation to the state and government. In other words, any consensus on how political NGOs can or should be is still pending.[9] For NGO women, though, the gendering of the political sphere as male even more easily allows them to claim distance from 'politics'. Instead they portray their activities as 'humanitarian' and are eager to stress that they have no ties to any political party. Indeed, such assertions are often included in NGOs' official literature, in self-presentations in the media, at public gatherings and in interviews with outsiders.

Many participants in women's NGOs use the fact that they are women, mostly mothers and only work with other women to emphasize the humanitarian, apolitical and therefore noble character of their work.[10] During my fieldwork, they stated over and over that they did not 'meddle' in politics, reinforcing the idea that this was an arena in which they had no place. Furthermore, they wanted to make it clear that they did not even have any desire to engage in such a morally compromising activity which is all the more morally suspect for women than it is for men. For many NGO women, merely the fact that they are women, especially mothers, was presented as evidence that they are not political. As Zahida, the leader of one women's NGO explained, she works only with women because if they tried to engage men, 'then it would be political'. Male activity is, in this formulation, political and diametrically opposed to female activity, which is not.

Zahida's organization was made up of Bosniac women working to return to their former homes in eastern Bosnia, site of some of the worst massacres and 'ethnic cleansing' of Bosniacs by Serb forces during the war. The goal of return is,

---

[9]   See note 12.
[10]   Women are not the only NGO activists to claim moral purity on the basis of their humanitarian, non-political activities, but their gender position affords them an additional layer of authenticity in this role which is not available to men, the elderly, or youth in the same way.

of course, decidedly political, as it challenges the political control held by Serb politicians over the territories they conquered and populated with Serbs during the war. Of course, the twinkle in Zahida's eye as she told me that she and the members of her organization 'supposedly [*kao fol*] aren't political', shows she is well aware of the political nature of her activities. In fact, she continued:

> You have to deal with politics sometimes. You're going to come up against points of politics and you have to solve these things. You have to deal with the darkest, worst politicians. ... They say that politics is a whore but it's not everyone's place to prostitute oneself [*kurvati se*] with her. But we have to prostitute ourselves sometimes. ... We're not politicians. We just want to have our houses back and live in our town. But you have to get into politics at some point because it *is* political.

Again, politics is a realm of dark and terrible dealings and associated with the immoral and detestable female figure of the whore/prostitute. But even while Zahida and other women's NGO activists freely admitted the political nature of their activities to me and to each other, this was not stressed in public forums. The public persona, and ultimately the success, of these groups depend on their remaining apolitical, especially in the case of Zahida's group which hopes to achieve their goals of return through alternative channels, outside the male realm of formal politics. This involved behind the scenes pressure being brought to bear by women on husbands and male relatives who did hold formal positions of power.[11] All of these concerns required the women to maintain an apolitical and respectably female image.

Again, these attitudes are reflected in popular opinion. Women's NGOs are judged in their communities by their success in performing 'humanitarian' services for others.[12] This presents both an opportunity and a dilemma for women's organizations conscious of the political nature of their goals. On one hand, they are able to retreat into claims of apolitical humanitarianism and 'women's issues'. However, such a position in some ways ensures their political marginalization. When these NGO women take a more political stance – expressing their opinions in public, demanding legal changes or insisting on increased participation by women in the formal political sphere – they are more likely to be derided in the same gendered terms as women politicians are, dismissed as unqualified, nosy women meddling into an area where they do not belong. Several people told me that NGO women engaged in political activities were 'just sexually frustrated women with bad marriages' who only 'sit around and gossip over coffee'. One

---

[11] For further discussion of the strategies of Zahida's organization, especially their use of affirmative gender essentialisms to access an alternative (female) channel of power as a means of achieving their goals, see Helms 2003a.

[12] NGOs in general are judged by this standard, reflecting both popular sentiment as well as the trend to depoliticize humanitarian work, providing a cheap means of service provision for which the state can then avoid responsibility (see e.g. Smillie 1996; Stubbs and Deacon 1998).

acquaintance complained to me that the 'humanitarian services' of a local women's NGO were good, but that the women working on political issues in the same organization 'don't do anything. They just act important and pocket foreign money'. Others dismissed the public statements of women activists as unqualified and 'talking off the top of their heads' (*'govoriti na pamet'*) because, they said, the women do not hold government functions, academic posts, or other positions of authority normally associated with male public actors. Although some male NGO leaders were also dismissed as greedy tools of foreign donors who did not represent grassroots opinions, they were not derided in the same gendered terms as were women. Women were ridiculed for presuming to act within the public, 'male' sphere on issues of political importance, whether they had the right 'qualifications' or not.

Women Politicians in the Male World of Politics

Although the idea that women should participate in the political process is gaining some acceptance, men still hold the overwhelming majority of decision-making positions. Women are becoming more and more visible in formal politics, in large part due to the efforts of women's NGO leaders and foreign donors and officials. Indeed, the Organization for Security and Cooperation in Europe (OSCE), the body charged with organizing and monitoring elections and one of the most powerful international bodies which de facto govern post-war Bosnia (see Coles, this volume), was instrumental in increasing both the quantity and quality of women's participation in politics through its Women in Politics program, part of its Democratization Department. The program organized training for women in political skills, regular gatherings of women parliamentarians to cultivate solidarity across party lines on 'women's issues' and meetings of women politicians and NGO women designed to foster cooperation among women and communication across all levels of government and communities.

OSCE was also the main force behind the implementation of several versions of quota rules in place since the elections of 1998. This has dramatically increased the percentage of women in all representative bodies, from municipal councils to the state parliament, to 18 percent from a low of 2 percent during the period without quotas for women.[13] It is interesting to note that the participation of

---

[13] The quota rule mandated that 30 percent of candidate lists, including three out of the first ten, be 'members of the minority gender', that is women except in the case of the Women's Party. In the elections of 2000, however, a system of open lists was instituted, allowing voters to choose individual names from one party's list. Women activists feared that many voters would skip over women's names even though they appeared evenly distributed throughout the lists. In the end, only 18 percent of those actually elected were women.

women in politics was not new to Bosnia, as quotas for women had been in place in the socialist system.[14] Women's participation never exceeded 17 percent during this time, however; very few women served in high level positions and women's participation nearly disappeared with the decline of socialism and the rise of nationalist parties to power in 1990.

Other foreign donors have also been instrumental in funding efforts to increase women's political participation. Just one example was the League of Women Voters,[15] a Bosnian NGO founded after Swanee Hunt, the former American ambassador to Austria and a frequent advocate for women's issues in Bosnia, had described the American League to a group of NGO women in Sarajevo and suggested they start a similar organization. The Bosnian 'Liga' was locally run, though sporadically financed from abroad, and, in contrast to the American League, it specifically encouraged women to vote, and for all voters to vote for women candidates.

Many women activists were worried that this participation will render women little more than cosmetic dressing, or *ikebane* (flower arrangements), for the table where men continue to call the shots. In November 1999 in Zenica, I attended an OSCE-sponsored training session for women politicians, entitled '*Žene to mogu*' ('Women Can Do It'). The Bosnian facilitator told the participants that once they got to parliament, 'you're not there to be silent. If you are, they'll think you're a good *woman* but not a politician. You'll just be an *ikebana*'. On another occasion, three women politicians were scheduled to speak at an evening *tribina* (symposium) following a day-long meeting of the League of Women Voters and an afternoon hike. When the hike took longer than planned and it became clear that the group would have to go straight to the event in our hiking clothes, the three women speakers decided they could at least make their faces look presentable, and they proceeded to put on makeup and fix their hair as we waited in a meadow for the rest of the group. 'Look what politics demands of us!' joked one. 'But we are real women!' countered another.

While they seek to avoid the role of *ikebana*, female politicians and their supporters also express concern that women politicians 'remain women'. A woman activist ended a television program on women in politics with the words: 'To the women of Bosnia-Herzegovina I especially recommend that they do not under any circumstances cease to be women, that they remain women exactly the way they are – gentle, mothers and wives, but that they don't stop fighting [for their interests

---

[14]   See note 1.

[15]   Ironically, the Bosnian name, *Liga žena glasača*, is formed with the *masculine* plural of the word 'voters'. Some Liga activists later decided this was a mistake and expressed a desire to change their name to *Liga žena glasačica*, in order to conform to a new trend among women activists towards using feminine grammatical forms, or 'female language' ('*ženski jezik*').

in politics].'[16] Women must walk a constant line between being taken seriously as politicians and being perceived as unfeminine or 'some sort of feminists' (meaning, presumably, the standard stereotype of the radical, man-hating lesbian demanding that women dominate men).[17] Most importantly, though this was not explicitly expressed, to retain their moral authority they must continue to be seen as women rather than as following the model of aggressive, uncompromising, corrupt male politician they so firmly reject.

This dilemma was discussed regularly by women politicians and activists. Amela, a woman who led her small party's candidate list for the Cantonal Assembly, admonished her fellow women at a public presentation of female candidates gearing up for local elections in 2000 saying: 'Don't just use the refined influence of women over men – sons, brothers, husbands. Startle them. Go for real male behaviour. You won't lose any of your femininity that way. Show them how professional and capable you are, how much you know.' Later, Amela explained to me that women can do men's jobs, such as politics, but in a better way because they are women. A women needs to behave, 'not like a real man with boots but as a person with opinions'.

Velida, a League of Women Voters leader, expressed to me her frustration at the way in which female politicians were presenting themselves. We had just attended another of the many round table discussions organized by the League on the subject of women in politics. Senka Nožica, a Sarajevo lawyer who has long been a prominent public figure, had spoken. While Nožica is generally recognized as elegant and articulate, Velida found her *too* much of an elite, refined 'lady' to be appealing to Bosnian voters:

> Women in Bosnia have to decide what kind of woman politician they want, what model they have in mind. Do we want a Margaret Thatcher? I don't think so, that's just following a male model. But I don't think we want the model that Senka Nožica and [another female politician] follow either. This is so sweet and charming, nice, proper. That's not what Bosnian women are like. Senka may be nice to look at and I think a lot of men like to talk with her because she is pretty and eloquent. ... You can like her but in the way you like a Barbie doll, not a serious politician. This model of a woman politician may work in the West but not here. Senka is an elite woman and has always been presented that way, that's how people will always see her. But she has nothing to

---

[16] An unidentified woman's voice in the OSCE sponsored television special on women in politics.

[17] Amila Omersoftić, president of the Women's Party, during a televised candidates' debate devoted to women candidates, broadcast 26 October 2000, on the Open Broadcast Network (OBN) just before general elections in November 2000. Omersoftić repeated several times that she and her party were 'not some sort of feminists', until the moderator pointed out that neither he nor anyone else in the studio had mentioned the word. 'Feminist' continues to carry very negative connotations in Bosnia (Cockburn 1998: 189-92), as in the rest of the formerly socialist world (e.g. Gal and Kligman 2000; Occhipinti 1996).

offer the average woman – or man. They see her and don't see how she can identify with them, represent them. ... Bosnian women aren't like that – they are tough and direct and practical. We need a model of a style of woman politician who is still feminine but effective and who can represent Bosnian women.

These comments should not be read entirely as a reflection of class or rural/urban differences, as Velida herself, though not from Sarajevo, is a prominent lawyer in her own city and an 'elite' woman. Indeed, she does not dispute that Nožica is both feminine and an effective politician. Rather, Velida is bothered by Nožica's image as too dainty and not sufficiently aggressive. Being feminine and distinct from male politicians is thus important, but female politicians also needed to be assertive and to play a significant role in the political process (and to be 'Bosnian').

Women Politicians and Discursive Strategies

In keeping with these aims, women politicians expressed their motivation for getting involved in politics as an outgrowth of their identities as women and mothers and of the extraordinary conditions of the times. The war had forced 'politics' into everyone's lives in a way they could not ignore. With this claim, women infused their actions with a sense of moral duty, denying the possibility that they had any preconceived aspirations for personal power or engagement with the disreputable realm of the political. As one woman candidate put the frequently stated assertion, 'I started engaging [*baviti se*] in politics because politics was engaging with me!' One woman who was an SDA parliament member when I first spoke to her in 1997, stressed that her political engagement was only temporary. 'This is a time of crisis', she explained, 'a fight for survival of the Bosniac nation ... With the coming of the war I saw that politics wasn't just about power [*vlast*] but it now had a life dimension [*životna dimenzija*] ... You couldn't say anymore that you're not interested in politics.' She was answering the call of duty to her nation but when the danger passed, she said she planned to return to devoting her full attention to her children and home life – her feminine duties. Sure enough, when I looked her up in 1999, she had taken her name off the candidate list for parliament saying that politics was not as important as her family and her work. Interestingly, she had not mentioned the importance of her job as a university professor when she first discussed her duty to the nation, but only after she had retired from politics and was devoting more time to her work.

Others cited injustice, by which they meant the abuses of the war and the economic inequalities of the post-war period which are perceived by many as the product of inept, corrupt (male) politicians. Edisa, a member of the Zenica Cantonal Assembly who had been displaced into Zenica during the war by ethnic cleansing tactics, explained:

I didn't choose politics, politics chose me. Politics started messing with my life. People in politics, that is, people making decisions in the name of others. It was a reflex for me to get involved – to defend myself. This reflex was not to be an outside observer ... Now I'm in politics out of need because some other people took my life *and the lives of my family* and threw it in the air like a leaf into the wind. Our lives are now without security. I don't mean physical insecurity but the ability to plan for the future for us *and our kids*. (emphasis added)

This was a time of extreme crisis which warranted extreme measures in which the normal rules of social organization could be bent. Things were so bad that *even women* were feeling the need to get involved in politics.

What was worse, even those politicians in power who were supposed to be protecting the people were widely seen as incompetent or simply uncaring, pursuing their own personal interests instead (see also Grandits, Kolind, this volume). Amela explained to a group of female candidates why she had entered politics:

For years I thought that a woman like me, a doctor by profession who does a highly sophisticated job and also a mother and wife, has no need to enter into politics as a classic male pursuit. But when I saw what kind of jerks [*kreteni*] were passing certain laws, which led to certain changes and brought me and those closest to me into the situation where we have to endure hardship because they're either not responsible or not intelligent, then I decided and I said I'm not going to just talk at home or over coffee about how our salaries are small, how we walk along the street with three centimetres of mud on our shoes, how there's nowhere to go to hear some music, how there aren't anymore festivals here, the school curricula are pathetic, my child is dissatisfied, etc., not to mention all the other problems you all know about already. I decided, I'm going [into politics].

Amela makes it clear that she has been living up to her role as a respectable woman. It was the men who have failed to live up to the duties of *their* gendered role as defined in this view.

In keeping with women's emphasis on their female respectability, politically active women justified this extraordinary engagement through their roles as mothers and nurturers, again in an effort to 'remain women' and in opposition to the model of dirty, egocentric male politicians. As Edisa's comments reflect, rather than a bid for personal status, power, or gain, the impetus for women's involvement in politics is a noble sacrifice made on behalf of children and their future. In this way, they have rooted their political presence in traditionally womanly roles, especially the familiar figure of the sacrificing, morally pure mother (Simic 1983a).

Comments to this effect were offered by women politicians and activists in many settings – in televised debates, at public meetings, in small groups of activists, and in conversations with me. As one woman politician speaking on television put it: 'Women always think first of their own families, so women would have the right perspectives and priorities in politics. They're thinking about the future of the country.' A candidate from the Women's Party told a gathering of women politicians:

> Motherhood was and has remained the strongest argument for women to engage in politics, because she has a natural advantage in opting for and working towards creating conditions for a better and more prosperous future for the generations [of children] she brings to the world.

And a *male* political leader from Zenica (from a small opposition party which won very few votes) declared on local television: 'I advocate the equal participation of women in politics ... because women have endured the trials of giving birth and raising children for 18 years until they are adults, if they don't know something about life, who does? Women, mothers, know the needs in society.' The implication was not only that all normal women become mothers, but also that only women whose children have grown should enter politics.

These assumptions rest on essentialist characterizations of both men and women (Helms 2003b). Women claim to have their own unique 'female diplomacy',[18] to be interested in dialogue and a greater good. According to Sabina, 'women are more honest, have more soul, and are more open in conversation. They're not as arrogant. It's easier to communicate with women'. 'Bosnian women have a better feeling for justice', claimed a woman member of another party, 'so women would be more honest. They *are* more emotional, but this is good. They will have more feelings for others.' These characterizations implicitly, and often explicitly, portrayed men as incapable of dialogue or compromize, more interested in personal gain and in one-uping their fellow male politicians. 'Men are constantly insulting and degrading each other in public, in the parliament', asserted a woman candidate in a televised debate with other women candidates. Another debate participant agreed: 'Women always put general interests first – common interests – while men are in it for personal interests.'[19]

Women's abilities managing the home, especially in dealing with children, husbands, in-laws and neighbours are cited as good training for women to be successful politicians: 'We know how to rule/take charge [*vladati*] because we do that at home, too', declared a prominent leader in the Women's Party. Edisa pointed to men's and women's ways of getting things done: 'I don't give myself tasks, or take them on, if I'm not sure I can carry them out. Men do this all the time, but women finish one task to the end before taking on another one ... With

---

[18]   Mediha Filipović, prominent figure in the Party for Bosnia-Herzegovina (SBiH), speaking in front of other women activists and politicians at a round table sponsored by the League of Women Voters.

[19]   Mira Štic (Social Democratic Party, SDP) and Amila Omersoftić (Women's Party) during the October 2000 OBN debate (see note 17).

men it's often the case that they take on many jobs and don't follow through with any of them.' As is reflected in the quotation which begins this chapter, women portray themselves as morally superior as well as more efficient and responsible because they fulfil their duties at home, raise and nurture their children, and thus have more noble things to do than 'stay in the *kafana* for another drink like men can'. What's more, the *kafana*, like politics, is a place for men and profane (immoral) women – out of bounds for respectable women (Simic 1983a; Cowan 1991).

In these scenarios, men begin to sound like carefree, undisciplined children who need a mother or teacher around to take care of necessary tasks, to think responsibly, and to keep them on their best behaviour. Indeed, Sabina, a school teacher by profession, told me that when male politicians behave badly toward her, she says nothing but in her head, 'keep[s] giving them minuses, like in school'. Mensura, another teacher by profession, was famous in the Cantonal Assembly, where she was a representative, for admonishing the male politicians for their bad behaviour. As she explained proudly: 'I get up and say "shame on you all for not being able to agree!" Just like that, like to small children. ... I actually educate men in parliament. And I'm not there to attain some position of power at the top.' Whether to themselves or to the public, women politicians consciously place themselves in the role of mother to justify their involvement in politics and to retain their respectability.

'Votes for Women: A Force for Change'

During the local elections of April 2000, the League of Women Voters held a public forum in Zenica at which women candidates from all parties presented themselves and their ideas. The theme of the event was 'Votes for women: A force for change'. The League and many of the women candidates were promoting women as new faces who would change the dirty nature of male-dominated politics. This was not only for the reasons outlined above – that women are moral, nurturing, more capable of dialogue, more attuned to the needs of society – but also out of an un-stated assumption that women are less nationalistic. Coming at a time when nationalist parties still held undisputed control over the areas in which their ethno-national group was in the majority, any suggestion of voting for change meant voting out the ruling nationalist parties. In Zenica this meant the Bosniac nationalist party, the SDA.[20] Most people who wanted 'change' were eager to vote

---

[20] For reasons which are beyond the scope of this chapter to enumerate, the international community was also pushing hard for nationalists to be voted out of power. Indeed the OSCE's publicity campaign to get out the vote featured the slogan *'Glasajte za promjenu'* ('Vote for Change'), which Bosnians generally understood as a not-so-hidden endorsement of non-nationalist parties (see Coles, this volume).

the SDA out, whether they were bothered only by its corruption, its focus on Islam, its nationalism or a combination of these.[21] Again, this aspect of the political climate offered women a space in which their social position as non-combatants and victims in the war, and as non-participants in political corruption, granted them moral superiority.[22] Not only had women not been among those who waged the war and now obstructed the peace, this reasoning went, they are also less susceptible to the virulent ideologies which produced these terrible conditions in the first place.[23]

For politically active women, the greatest piece of evidence for this was their success in building cooperation among NGO women and female politicians across ethno-national and party lines. Most of this activity involving politicians had been initiated by foreign donors, especially OSCE, which tend to encourage the idea that women are less nationalist, aggressive, and violent than men (Helms 2003b). Once the women representatives were brought together, however, their cooperation proved to be quite successful, despite the antagonistic political views held within this group. What made this possible was also what enabled NGO women to work together to find common issues, namely, the women's identity as women. As we have seen, the construction of female gender roles leaves women out of the category of significant political (or military) actors. Women could therefore cross politicized ethno-national boundaries more easily and sooner after the end of the war than men could. Their political activity is also not taken as seriously, and is therefore less of a threat to the established male political leaders. What's more, because women came together to discuss 'women's issues', their cooperation across ethno-national and party lines was not as difficult. Sabina, a Bosniac participant in these meetings marvelled that, 'many people at the beginning took this cooperation with a great deal of scepticism ... However, it was shown that women understand each other very well, even without opening their mouths'. Female solidarity, she implied, is almost instinctual and based on their common bond as women, mothers and wives. She continued:

> With women it's a breeze [*sa ženama je pjesma*]. There are no problems with women of any age. The last Friday of each month we have our women's meetings with [OSCE]. Women of all parties are there, even from the SDS [Serb Democratic Party]. We're still talking about our common interests but there are lots of these – the labour law, maternity leave, social security, protection of children, etc. But other laws will come along, and we'll find agreement on that, too.

---

[21]   On similar trends within the Croat community, see Grandits, this volume.

[22]   Young people, who share with women the morally superior position of not having waged war or engaged in political corruption, were also promoted by those advocating a change from nationalist parties. Indeed, the League of Women Voters also urged voters to vote for youth as a 'force for change.'

[23]   On the parallel loss of moral prestige of male war veterans, see Bougarel, this volume.

The tight working bonds and many sound political initiatives dealing with 'women's issues' which these women have developed are remarkable, especially given the overwhelming failure and refusal by male politicians to come to agreement across party and ethno-national lines. Outside of these working sessions, however, the women still harbour many fundamental differences in ideological outlooks, especially on the question of ethno-national relations and the character of the Bosnian state. These are, after all, the main sticking points which prevent the male politicians, who nevertheless hold the most significant positions of power, from cooperating. At the end of the day, no matter what the women agree on, they must also follow the directives of their parties. Sabina acknowledged in private that there were many of these basic differences, but she insisted: 'Women have to get together, help each other change their opinions, get to know each other and understand each other, to *talk*.' It is on the basis of this belief that the women representatives have come as far as they have.

Conclusion

The discursive strategies of politically active women and the way they are received by the rest of their communities reveal much about the cultural construction of both gender roles and 'politics' in post-war Bosnia. When women (or men) cross the line of accepted behaviour, basic common assumptions about gender and the political sphere come into view. Because of women's significant presence in higher education and employment outside the home, many Bosnians (both men and women) insist that women have been 'emancipated', that they are perceived exactly the same by society (just as socialism claimed to have achieved). However, examination of how categories of gender and politics are negotiated reveals a strong association of women with domestic roles and patriarchal concern for women's sexual purity. Women's working outside the home is generally accepted, but their longer absences farther from home and assumption of positions of authority are much less desirable. Indeed, the commonly heard view that it is fine for women to enter politics once they have raised their children to adulthood points to a strong concern with the control of female sexuality. Women past their reproductive years can more easily step into male roles and mix with men other than their husbands.

As the materials I present here should make clear, assumptions about gender permeate and even drive constructions of a variety of political subjectivities on the levels of groups (ethno-national, urban) as well as individuals (politicians, public figures). However, this analysis also uncovers aspects of how social and political processes are being shaped in post-war Bosnia, aspects which might be less visible if gender were not taken into account. As Susan Gal and Gail Kligman have argued for the case of post-socialist Central and Eastern Europe, 'attending to gender is analytically productive, leading not only to an understanding of relations between men and women, but to a deeper analysis of how social and institutional transformations occur' (Gal and Kligman 2000: 3). In the Bosnian case, it reveals some of the less noticed ways in which power is contested and asserted. The power of the international community (and the assumptions foreign actors bring to their interventions – see Coles, this volume), notions of masculinity and femininity, ideas about the relationship between politics and society, understandings of public and private realms, and categories of morality and victimhood all play significant roles in social and political transformations in Bosnia. Notably, ethno-national classifications and nationalism may intersect with these elements but they are not the only stakes upon which political debates turn. This contrasts sharply with what is implied by most depictions of Bosnia since the break-up of Yugoslavia.

This examination of women public actors further makes evident the importance of moral purity to public identities. Specifically, we see the power of the victim identity as perhaps the only morally acceptable persona in post-war Bosnia (see also Delpla, Duijzings, this volume). To be sure, women do not hold a monopoly over claims to victimhood. Indeed, the politicized ethno-national identities which have driven social and political processes in Bosnia for the past decade have been heavily based on claims to victimhood, at the hands of other ethno-national groups and/or Western interventions and other foreign influences. However, women are more readily associated with victimhood due to the construction of female roles as apolitical, passive objects (victims) of male action. This construction, in turn, means that victim identities are all the more acceptable for women to embrace, as they pose little challenge to common expectations for respectable womanhood. Thus, the women I have discussed here cast themselves as innocent bystanders to war and nationalist chauvinism, as outsiders to the corrupt world of politics, and as the noble, self-sacrificing mother whose only wish is to protect her children and create for them a more peaceful world.

It is nevertheless interesting to note that these women do not stake much claim to the ultimate victim image, that of the female rape victim, in marked contrast to the way in which Bosnian (especially Bosniac) women are depicted outside of Bosnia. While the women often invoke the burdens faced by women during the war, they more readily emphasize women's suffering through displacement, loss, and having to support families under conditions of hunger, danger, and insecurity. In the first place, such predicaments are more common and much more visible in the post-war period. More importantly, however, there remains a considerable social stigma against victims of rape, even wartime rape, despite official appeals to the contrary, public recognition of raped women as national martyrs, and efforts by women's organizations to raise awareness about the plight of rape survivors in general. The moral purity which politically active women achieve through their identification as respectable women, therefore, may be jeopardized by an association with the rape victim identity. Furthermore, as we have seen, women in politics strive to be seen as decisive, effective leaders – the opposite of what the common image of the defeated, dishonoured, passive and weak victim of rape implies. The discursive strategies of politically active women allow them to walk the fine line between morality and corruption, purity and impurity, weakness and strength, actor and victim. They aim to 'show the dignity of Bosnian women to the world', as Mensura, a leader in the Women's Party, declared, adding: 'We're not just old peasant women like the world media showed.' Evidently, one could surmise, rape victims and rural women lack dignity. Mensura's point, however, as an educated urban woman, was to counter the image of weak, passive victim which 'old peasant women' implies, and to make known women's significant contributions to all aspects of public and domestic life (Mertus 1994).

In sum, politically active women must balance their public images between respectable femininity and being taken seriously as political actors. Their very presence in formal politics, and as participants in political processes, challenges established gender ideals, yet their need to retain the moral status attached to their identities as women leads them to utilize elements of more conservative female roles and limited victim images. It remains to be seen whether women will succeed in shifting the public persona of 'Bosnian women', of gender ideals and of perceptions of politics. Much will depend on whether women can distance themselves from the image of passive (rape) victim and concern over women's sexual purity to create new identities rooted in their present activities rather than the events of the war period.

Chapter 11

Ambivalent Builders:
Europeanization, the Production of Difference, and Internationals in Bosnia-Herzegovina

Kimberley Coles

Introduction[1]

A colleague of mine, new to the United States but familiar with former Yugoslavia, recently confessed that he had mistaken one of my Bosnia-Herzegovina maps as being of 'somewhere in America because of all the [English] road names'. What he had seen was in fact an 'international' mapping of the road system in Bosnia-Herzegovina, an overlaid organizational system created and maintained by the Stabilization Force (SFOR) and used by the 'international community'. For example, the main Sarajevo-Mostar road is labelled Route 17 on Bosnian road maps. However, it is also known and mapped as PacMan, its SFOR given name. PacMan, the name of a popular 1980s video game that had a 'PacMan' eating pellets and avoiding killer ghosts in order to survive, has become a major supply route for the NATO troops, providing nourishment and the means to avoid troublesome 'ghosts' in its own way. All major thoroughfares as well as some secondary and dirt roads have SFOR names, such as Sparrow, Corbieres, Gull, Aurore, Hornblower, and Arizona. The names of these roads, interesting in

[1]   An earlier version of this chapter was published under the same title in *Political and Legal Anthropology Review*, 25/1 (2002): 1-18 (© 2002 by the American Anthropological Association; used with permission). Research for this paper was funded through the support of an Institute on Global Conflict and Cooperation Dissertation Fellowship and the School of Social Sciences at University of California, Irvine. It would also not have been possible without the professional and collegial cooperation of the OSCE. I am indebted to all my election colleagues in Bosnia-Herzegovina for their patience and contributions. The paper has benefited from the keen commentary of Bill Maurer, Caroline Brown, the SAE 2001 and APLA 2001 Paper Prize Committee Members, and Andrew Gilbert. Christina Schwenkel, Karen Leonard, Rhonda Higdon, and Kyriaki Papageorgiou also contributed to earlier drafts. I am also grateful to Jim Ferguson and Teresa Caldeira for their intellectual assistance, and to two anonymous reviewers for their constructive suggestions.

themselves, are linked to the nationality of the military division in charge of the area: routes in the French sector are more likely to be French in origin, many routes in the US sector are named after American states and bird and animal names are common in the British sector.

These roads, used by international military convoys and patrols, are designated as safe, mine-free, and through-routes. Although a road may be pocked with potholes and in general disrepair, it will provide a route without destroyed bridges or other obstacles. The SFOR system is generally well-marked throughout the country. Small yellow signs (affixed to traffic sign posts, telephone poles and the like) note the road name and direction every 500 to 1000 meters. During my fieldwork, civilian internationals kept to these roads and often referred to them by name when they were giving directions or relating a story. Thus, while a Bosnian may give directions by telling a person to take the road up to the town of Jablanica, then toward Prozor and Gornji Vakuf, an 'international' is more likely to get to central Bosnia – on the same road – by relying on the small yellow signs marking routes Pacman, Opal, and Gull. This organizational system and its referent map take a Bosnian actuality and create a separate and parallel structure for international aid and relief workers than that used by Bosnians themselves.

In this chapter, I focus on the creation of separate spaces for the 'international Self' and the 'Bosnian Other' by the mostly European members of the international organizations that have, since 1995, been charged with the task of building a democratic Bosnia-Herzegovina. I refer to these people as they referred to themselves during my fieldwork (1997-2000), as 'internationals'.[2] Set within a political and social framework of Europeanization, I describe shifting processes of essentialization and representation at work in post-war Bosnia-Herzegovina. On the one hand, mechanisms of exclusion and differentiation undermine the goal of integrating Bosnia-Herzegovina into an idealized and imagined 'Europe'. On the other hand, the tensions between integration and exclusion combined with practices reinforcing hierarchy illuminate the debates and dynamics of the categorization and creation of that 'European' ideal.

In the following, I argue that, while enveloped in a discursive and institutional space of union and integration, the on-the-ground practices of internationals create difference and exclusion. Of course, all processes of inclusion simultaneously entail processes of exclusion. What makes it interesting in Bosnia-Herzegovina is that the subjects of inclusion and exclusion are the same. Furthermore, the mechanisms of exclusion are being created in relation to structures of state- and self-governance rather than other common markers of difference. This occurs in at least two ways: through the voluntary self-separation of internationals from the

---

[2]   John Carlane argues that the key division in Bosnia-Herzegovina is not, as he expected, between 'governmental' and 'non-governmental' organizations, but between 'local' and 'international' ones (Carlane 2000). This distinction marks interesting new divisions and territories in governance in a globalized world (see Ferguson and Gupta 2002).

Bosnia-Herzegovina state apparatus, and the exclusion of Bosnians from an imagined European-ness.

Bosnia-Herzegovina and the Idea of Europe

The openly formulated goal of the international community is to touch and change the political, social, and economic life of Bosnia-Herzegovina as a state and Bosnians as people in such a way that the country and its citizens become modern, democratic and capitalist with regard for human rights and the rule of law. With this in mind, international organizations have embarked on ambitious programs of change with the intent of rebuilding the country in a new image, that is, a new 'European' image. The Dayton Peace Agreement is discussed as a 'blueprint', and 'road maps' are created to help Bosnia-Herzegovina along the path to Europe. Besides SFOR, there are three major international organizations in Bosnia-Herzegovina: the Office of the High Representative (OHR), the Organization for Security and Co-Operation in Europe (OSCE), and the United Nations. Along with hundreds of international non-governmental organizations, they penetrate and intervene in practices governing Bosnians (see also Grandits, Duijzings, Helms, this volume). International activity ranges from running elections, lending money through micro-credit programs, rebuilding houses, assisting trauma victims, de-mining land, creating state symbols such as the flag, training nurses and doctors, supplying hospitals with equipment, to reforming legal and financial institutions. Internationals – the employees and volunteers of international organizations – are the 'experts' that design and implement these state-building and society-moulding strategies. In large part, internationals are professional managers and technicians, although in my own research, this varied remarkably from field to field. The electoral and human rights fields, for example, employed a wide range of professionals including teachers, lawyers, ex-military officers, diplomats, bureaucrats and managers. Many internationals, especially the younger ones (a large portion of the international community) were attempting to 'get into' international work and hoped their experience in Bosnia-Herzegovina would propel them into longer-term international employment.

Through their aid projects and programs, internationals consciously attempt to integrate Bosnia-Herzegovina and Bosnians into their 'rightful' place in a newly unified Europe. However, in conducting research on democratization among internationals in Bosnia-Herzegovina, I found that they were highly ambivalent about the Europe enlargement project they worked towards: they were simultaneously drawn to and repelled by the process and idea. They viewed Bosnia as geographically 'in' Europe and explicitly worked towards the goal of political, social, and economic inclusion into a common, unified, post-Cold War Europe, yet constructed boundaries that maintained difference. Boundary shifts kept the Bosnian categorically separate, as non-European (or as not yet fully European) and as lacking, in some cases inherently, certain requisite features of a cosmopolitan pan-European mentality. While the aid projects I researched mostly focused on the institutions Bosnia-Herzegovina lacked but needed in order to join a 'modern' Europe and become a 'functional' sovereign state, complaints and frustrations related to me by internationals highlighted the different capabilities (skills, attitude, ethics) of Bosnians. As an electoral logistician for the last four elections told me, 'Well, they aren't really European, are they? They have a completely different attitude!' Concurrently, the lack of participation by internationals in the Bosnian state or Bosnian public sector introduced a dichotomy between 'those-confined-by-the-state' (that is, Bosnians) and 'those-not' (that is, internationals), which in turn created a further differentiation based on governance. The nation-state, still crucial in and constitutive of the world-system (e.g. Malkki 1994, 1998), was for some relegated to a secondary status in the wake of globalization. The nation-state remained primary for some, but for others it was fast becoming a relic – a precious and valued relic, but a relic just the same. Exclusionary sentiments and parallel practices such as those described above, came into being through and in response to the daily living and working conditions of international, mostly European, aid workers and served to reinforce and maintain Bosnians as different and distinct.

Bosnia-Herzegovina has a history of being 'part of Europe'. Through its occupation by the Austro-Hungarian Empire in 1878 and annexation in 1908, Bosnia-Herzegovina became increasingly attached to Europe. Austro-Hungarian infrastructure investment in its newest province included roads, a railroad network, operational industrial plants, and factory buildings. Societal and political changes accompanied the change in government and the following industrialization (Donia 1981; Sugar 1963). Later, Yugoslavia had associations with the European Community and was much more 'open' to Western markets and assistance, global trade and financial institutions, and labour migration than other socialist states (Woodward 1995b). However, these historical connections, while making understandable election posters in 1998 proclaiming 'We Do Not Want War! We Want to Be in Europe *Again*. Think About That in September' (emphasis added), were relegated to the background for the rank-and-file internationals living and working in Bosnia-Herzegovina.

The Balkans have been objectified since at least the beginning of the 20th century. While Milica Bakić-Hayden and Robert Hayden treat 'balkanism' as a variant of 'orientalism' (Bakić-Hayden and Hayden 1992; see also Bakić-Hayden 1995), Maria Todorova sees them as substantially different rhetorics which speak to similar issues of discourses of power. Noting the Balkans as historically and geographically concrete (as opposed to an intangible Orient), Todorova places the Balkans as inextricably linked with Europe rather than opposed to it: 'Unlike orientalism, which is a discourse about an imputed opposition, balkanism is a discourse about an imputed ambiguity' (Todorova 1997: 17).

This ambiguity was produced through continually reinvented legacies and perceptions of the Ottoman Empire, processes of modernization or 'Westernization' in the 19th and 20th centuries, and the placement of the Balkans in between the West and the Orient. The Balkans, a region conceived out of contradictions and transitions, are seen as a European alter-ego. Following Todorova, I argue that the relationship between 'Europe' and 'Bosnia-Herzegovina' is janus-faced. Exclusion can not easily be opposed to integration. Rather, they are conjoined processes, sharing the same source (for example, the practices of international aid workers) and both relying on reductionist representations of 'Self' and 'Other'.

The Balkans have been primarily linked with a static ethnic essentialism, with secondary status given to the more traditional essentialist representations of fragmentation, barbarism, tribalism, or reversion to pre-civilization. Much post-World War II academic literature dealing with Yugoslavia focuses on the 'problem(s) of co-existence'. The importance placed on ethno-religious identity not only leads to erroneously homogeneous ethnic categories but also sets up a priori interpretations of Balkan behaviour and events. These processes of essentialization framed many political and social analyses of the latest Balkan war and the 'dissolution of Yugoslavia'.[3] As widely reported, then-President Clinton relied on the 'age-old ethnic hatred' descriptions in Robert Kaplan's political travelogue *Balkan Ghosts* (Kaplan 1993) in framing his non-interventionist foreign policy toward the wars in Croatia and Bosnia-Herzegovina. As the back cover explains, Kaplan 'deciphers the Balkans' ancient passions and intractable hatreds for outsiders'. This made it easier for American and European policy makers to view intervention as futile and unproductive (Malcolm 1994a).

Among my international informants, the historically and ideologically constructed nature of ethnicity and identity was clear; many had heard, for example, testimonies from local colleagues who had not realized they 'were' Serb or Muslim until after the war began. With this in mind, internationals often attempted to nullify ethnicity as a salient category. Some purposely avoided learning the ethnicity of 'local' colleagues; others referred to the now distinct languages as the 'local language',[4] or (along with many Bosnians) ridiculed the cultural politics distinguishing coffee into three ethnicized coffees – Serb *kafa*, Croat *kava*, and Bosniac *kahva*. Internationals' negotiations with Bosnian identity politics are complex, varied and a large enough topic for another paper. Here, I only wish to emphasize that the conscious avoidance of ethnic marking does not liberate Bosnian peoples from dangerously reductionist representations. Rather, the conviction that Bosnia-Herzegovina should be a single nation-state may also further the solidification and maintenance of singular representations.

While it is evident within my ethnographic data that 'otherings' based on past 'communism', 'war' and 'balkanism' influenced the representation of Bosnians by

---

[3]   For accounts that critique these processes of essentialization, see for example Bowen 1996; Campbell 1998; Woodward 1995a.

[4]   In socialist Yugoslavia, the official name of the language spoken in Bosnia-Herzegovina was Serbo-Croatian. As the country broke apart into territories based on national distinctions, there was a concurrent move toward linguistic differentiation and three 'new' languages emerged: Bosnian, Croatian and Serbian.

internationals, they were not primary. Instead, I suggest that Bosnians, already different under these various conceptualizations, were more readily fit into new or modified oppositions. Essentialist representations held by internationals were produced through daily experiences and relationships. The 'Other' and the 'Self' were not created through media accounts, travel stories, World's Fairs, or propaganda (Mitchell 1989; Said 1978; Todorova 1997). The process of differentiation did not have distant exoticism or spectacle as its source. Rather, the 'othering' was a consequence of the daily shoulder-rubbing of internationals with their Bosnian hosts (see also Delpla, Jašarević, this volume). The production of difference was rooted in those daily activities and the residence of internationals in Bosnia-Herzegovina, which, in turn, constituted explicit attempts to bring this country into Europe. Therefore, in this case, attempts at inclusion produced exclusion. From one perspective, the coupling of integration projects with practices of exclusion undermines the success of such projects. A different perspective, however, holds that the coupling is indicative of the complexity of integration (a link between integration and equality should not be assumed), and also of the myriad of ways difference is produced and located, even under and through formalized and universalized statements of equality (or integration) (Foucault 1995 [1977]). In this case, difference is not primarily located in identity, but in relationships with governing and regulating institutions such as the nation-state.

Europe within the Electoral Law

Europe, what it is and what it should be, has been debated for centuries, although the latest dominant discourses trace it to the formation of post-World War II institutions, de-colonization, and immigration. The gradual and conflict-ridden formation of the European Union is merely one aspect of the question of who and what constitutes Europe. Other debates have centred on immigration from Eastern Europe, Africa, and the Middle East and yet others on East/West distinctions, 'common' ideologies, and religious trajectories. 'Europe' is increasingly a 'dominant symbol' (Turner 1970 [1967]: 30-32) in the 20th century, 'an icon that embraces a whole spectrum of different referents and meanings' (Goddard, Llobera and Shore 1994: 26). It is by no means a stable object. Rather the edges of 'Europe' change when considering particular historical, social, political or institutional interactions and processes. Thus, 'Europe' is best viewed as a 'configuration of knowledge', debated, disputed and experienced differentially through space and time. While recognizing diverse, heterogeneous and dynamic Europes, it would be foolhardy to discount the competitions for conceptual hegemony in the political and social arena: some narratives are more dominant than others. 'Europe' is increasingly a political ideal and a mobilizing metaphor associated with EU neo-liberal institutions, multiculturalism and civil liberties. In Bosnia-Herzegovina, the narrative is deployed as a strategy calling Europeans to identify with a particular definition of Europe. The call – a promise of future benefits and prosperity – reaches out to both Bosnians and internationals. The later relate to this narrative through self-representation; they are promise-benefactors as well as promise-holders. Bosnians, by contrast, are entreated to accept the call, to sign up for tutorials in modern state- and self-governance. The invocations of 'Europe' call for Bosnia-Herzegovina to conform, reform, and introduce particular standards, unmarked but surely neo-liberal in character (see also Jašarević, this volume). The unmarked, unlabeled, and thus unquestioned, deployment of 'European' traits acts to depoliticize and naturalize powerful definitions of 'appropriate' economic policy, 'expertising' them rather than to leaving them open to debate and contestation (Ferguson 1994, 1995). Further, 'Europe' takes on a superlative essence and symbolism. European internationals use this dominant representation of 'Europe' as a form of identification and as a bribe for wary Bosnians.

The most visible project explicitly linked with European-ness and Europeanization during my fieldwork was the 1999 and 2000 election law campaign.[5] Lasting over a year, this project incorporated legal drafting, public opinion surveys and forums, lobbying and marketing. The drafting officially included international lawyers, Bosnian lawyers from each ethnic group and political party, as well as various technical and legal consultant-experts. During the drafting process public opinion was solicited via numerous local roundtables, web questionnaires and chats, media discussions and opinion surveys. This campaign, labelled 'Say Clearly What You Want in Your Election System', concluded that Bosnian citizens wanted more accountability from elected officials, women's participation and effective representation. Discussion of Europe and European standards was largely absent during the drafting period, instead surfacing during the subsequent lobbying and marketing efforts.

The High Representative and Western ambassadors urged Bosnians to support the proposed election law and to ask their politicians to adopt it without delay. It was repeatedly stated that the country would not be fully sovereign, functional, or European until it had a permanent election law. In a speech, the High Representative Wolfgang Petritsch stated unequivocally that the adoption of this law was a 'prerequisite for any deepening of relations between Bosnia-Herzegovina and the European Union, its accession to the Council of Europe as well as for the functioning of the state of Bosnia and Herzegovina'.[6] The advertising campaign for the law relied heavily on European imagery, counting on the draw of Europe to garner popular and political support. Despite heavy international pressure, both cajoling and coercive, the election law was not passed when it was first brought before the Bosnian Parliament in October 1999. Nor did it pass in multiple introductions, despite concessions and changes to the law, and

---

[5]   The prior post-war general elections had occurred in accordance with the 'Rules and Regulations' of the Provisional Election Commission, which derived its authority from the OSCE's mandate to organize elections under Annex III of the Dayton Peace Agreement.

[6]   *OHR Press Release*, 12 May 2000.

continuing appeals and invocations of Europe, as shown by the ads of the 'Say Clearly What You Want' campaign (see Figures 11.1 and 11.2).

These ads textually and symbolically evoke the possibility of connection to 'Europe'. Figure 11.1 links signing the election law with entrance into the ring of Europe, symbolized by the twelve stars of the European Union. Figure 11.2, more evocative, has Europe-the-saviour, symbolized this time by a halo of EU stars, holding the election law as a book (or commandments?) and showing it to a dapperly dressed Bosnia-Herzegovina. The ads also place responsibility and accountability on Bosnians: 'The way into Europe depends on *You*.' This slogan neatly condenses the ideas of 'ownership' and 'nationalization' that the international community tried to bring to state-building and reconstruction projects. That is, Bosnians should participate in and control their own social, economic, and political affairs. They could, after all, write their destinies themselves with the new writing instruments that the election law provided.

The appeal of Europe was not strong enough to overcome opposition by political parties and members of parliament. Was it that Bosnians rejected their place in 'Europe'? Not entirely. Some of the opposition rested on perceived discrepancies between the draft law and existing European human rights standards. Much of the remaining reluctance focused on how centrally ethnicity should figure in the designation of the House of Peoples (*Dom naroda*) and of the collective Presidency.[7] However, an international heading the lobbying effort for the law told me: 'I don't think any law would have passed; their [Bosnian politicians] unwillingness to cooperate supersedes all other factors and desires.' International campaigning clearly overestimated the power of European symbolism and misunderstood the stakes for Bosnian politicians, not European membership but maintaining power and the status quo.

Internationals' self-understanding of their role in Bosnia-Herzegovina relies on two concepts: helping this country to recover from the war, and assisting it to take a place in a unified Europe. As a raison d'être, the international community necessarily relied on the idea of Europe as a goal, a benefit, and a marketing strategy for Bosnia-Herzegovina; even when it failed to deliver, they continued to use it. Other instances of bringing Europe symbolically into public debate and consciousness relied on images of the Eiffel Tower, the European Map cut into puzzle pieces with Bosnia-Herzegovina being placed into the almost complete puzzle, and the omnipresent EU's circle of stars. These invocations of Europe were one strategy for constituting a new inclusive, imagined community (Anderson 1983; Shore 2000).

---

[7]   The permanent election law was finally passed in August 2001 by both houses of the Bosnian Parliament, nearly two years after its first introduction, and after huge pressures of the High Representative.

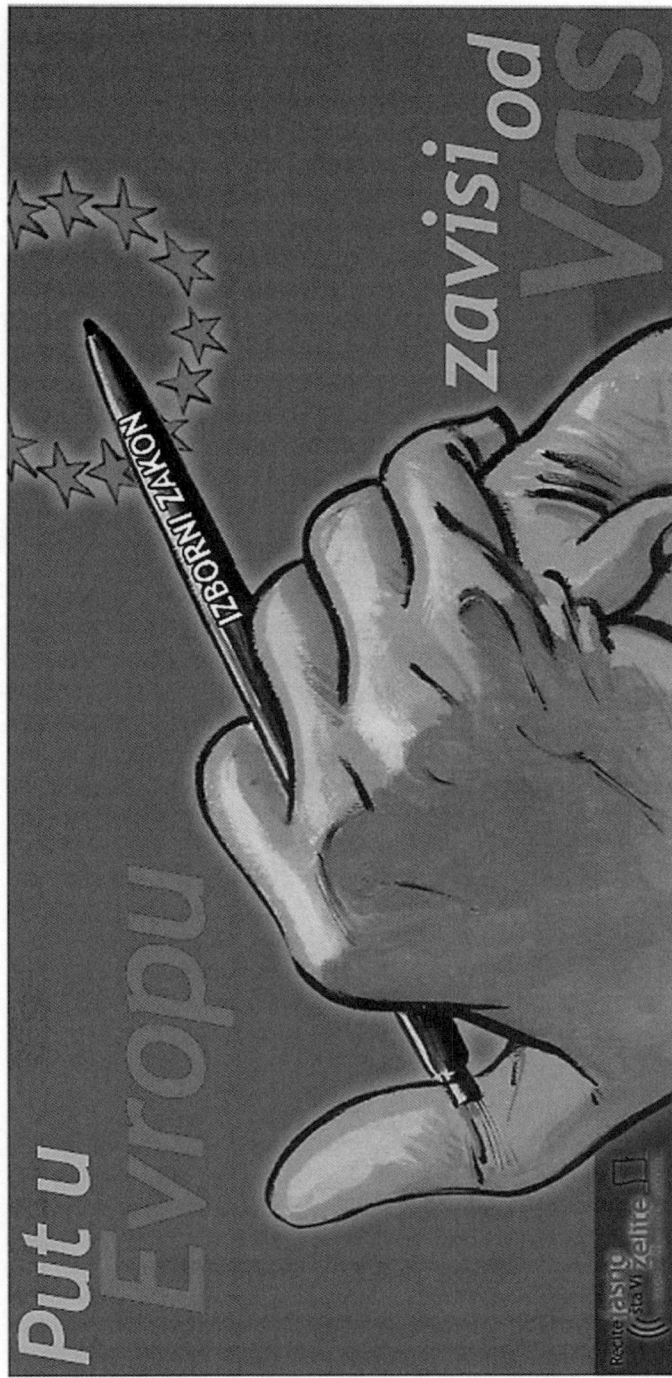

Figure 11.1 'The Way into Europe Depends on You' (pen: 'Election Law')

(© OSCE Bosnia-Herzegovina)

Figure 11.2 'The Way into Europe Depends on You' (book: 'Draft Election Law')

Mechanisms of Exclusion (1): International Self-Separation and Supra-Nationality

Interacting with the Europeanization efforts are various on-the-ground interpretations, representations, and actions vis-à-vis Bosnia-Herzegovina as a state and Bosnians as a people that suggest that internationals have highly ambivalent and complex attitudes toward Bosnian inclusion in the idea of Europe. These mechanisms of exclusion work on at least two fronts: 1) international's self-distance or exclusion from Bosnian state and society (such as the creation of international road names and maps); 2) exclusion of Bosnians from a self-essentialized European-ness. These mechanisms, based in daily experience and contact, construct a new aura of distinction and difference and ultimately have important political implications. First, Bosnia-Herzegovina does not fit into the new world order as conceived and experienced by a highly mobile and cosmopolitan professional elite. Increasing globalization, privatization, and the displacement of state governance and public space seem at odds with the emphasis placed on turning Bosnia-Herzegovina into a viable state (see also Jašarević, this volume). Second, Bosnians were viewed by many internationals as lacking the proper discipline or self-governance techniques that successful 'Europeans' were thought to hold.

Internationals, on the whole, were marked by the lack of deep roots and local integration in Bosnian society. Similar to accounts of other expatriate communities, such as diplomat or development circles, internationals felt alienated from their Bosnian hosts. Even in Sarajevo, which came the closest to welcoming its international guests (rather than openly despising them or complaining about their presence), many internationals agreed that 'they'd never feel at home here'. Chris Shore notes that this style of tight-knit community, isolated from their larger residential context, exists among expatriate EU civil servants in Brussels and is well-documented among people who are displaced or uprooted (Shore 2000: 161-4). He also comments on how this alienation forges stronger senses of common identity and, in the Brussels case, European-ness. How then does this well-documented societal separation play out in everyday experience and what can it tell us about the larger relationship between internationals and Bosnia-Herzegovina, and the changing role of state regulation? Globally, the increasing expatriate residential patterns of elite foreigners suggest profound changes to governance particularly within the realm of sovereign authority. In the case of Bosnia-Herzegovina, internationals existed above and beyond the Bosnian state, and outside Bosnian society.

Although my interviews included internationals married to Bosnians, entrepreneurs with no thoughts of leaving, and several who declared an affinity for Bosnia-Herzegovina and Bosnian society, statements such as, 'Sarajevo is my all-time favourite European city', and 'We love it here; life is so fulfilling', were in the minority and did not necessarily suggest any conscious attempt at integration or involvement. In these interviews, Bosnian 'culture' was being consumed but not incorporated, much like those who delight in 'ethnic' food but register no affinity for 'ethnic' people themselves. There was little evidence of willingness to become involved with the 'Other'. Those willing to search beyond international circles for genuine friendship were few and far between and popularly viewed as brave, unusual and often 'biased'. 'Bias' and the preservation of 'neutrality' were key concerns among internationals and their employers. In one case a long-term aid worker recounted how superiors reprimanded him for being 'too friendly' with local Croats. This aid worker, vigorously denying the allegation, said he was friendly with local Serbs and Bosniacs as well. Neutrality and unbiased-ness were associated with lack of involvement. Other alternatives, such as unqualified friendship or engaged professionalism, were less a part of the scope of 'neutrality'.

Internationals were not heavily engaged or involved with the Bosnian state, despite their professional work in creating and reforming state institutions through such practices as running 'democratic' elections, privatizing the economy or training police officers. That is, internationals generally did not partake or participate in Bosnian state services or Bosnian society, nor, in many cases, were they subject to its regulatory mechanisms. Their activities and presence transcended national boundaries, authorities and interests, even while their presence and activities defined Bosnian nation-state boundaries, authorities and interests. This disjuncture between building the Bosnian state and not participating in it has serious side effects. If the persons building and reforming political and civic space do not engage with state institutions, what message is being transmitted to Bosnians about the place of the state in modern society?

Internationals are supranational vis-à-vis the Bosnian state. The issues here are actually two-fold. On the one hand, internationals do not partake or minimally partake in the services provided by public and private Bosnian institutions (such as identification services, banking, healthcare and hospitals, transportation), and they were not always subject to Bosnian state regulations (such as border controls, taxes, traffic laws). On the other hand, international organizations often provide replacement services to their international employees, either individually or in consortium.[8] These acts of replacement signal growing comfort with the privatization and other displacements of state control and regulation. Increasingly, governance contests sovereignty through shifts into private or corporate and supra-state regulation. In post-war Bosnia-Herzegovina, this process can be illustrated by examining two of the most central domains of the modern state: currency and border access. As with the previously cited example of international over-mapping of the Bosnian state road system, the relationships described below describe

---

[8] At the same time, many internationals – particularly employees of intergovernmental organizations – are also legally and financially separated from their own nation-state. They work for organizations that are either international or supranational in scope. They may sign statements pledging loyalty to the organization rather than their nation or national interests. They may not be subject to national taxation due to long-term foreign residency, tax treaties, offshore accounting strategies, and/or the politics of payment.

parallel systems of governance for Bosnians and for internationals. Parallel systems also exist in banking, security, healthcare, transportation, and even, in some cases, shopping.

State Currency

The Bosnian Convertible Mark (*Konvertibilna Marka*, KM), introduced in June 1998, was one of the first institutions and symbols of Bosnia-Herzegovina to be accepted across the entire country. Pegged to the Deutschmark (DM) and then to the Euro, the KM is extremely stable. As shown by Eric Helleiner, unique national currencies became a part of state building and unifying projects starting in the mid-nineteenth century. It was felt that linking territoriality and currency affairs would strengthen collective national identities (Helleiner 1999). Following this logic and despite the growing official use of foreign currencies inside domestic territories (as in 'dollarization'), the OHR and the Central Bank of Bosnia-Herzegovina created a territorial Bosnian currency. This unique and single currency was expected to replace the multiple currencies in use during and immediately after the war, and to consolidate a Bosnian identity through common and shared usage. The KM notes attempt to avoid overtly political overtones. In particular, artists and writers are pictured on the front of the notes and artistic or architectural elements are featured on the backs; however, notes issued in the *Republika Srpska* feature Serb writers and those issued in the Federation feature Muslim and Croat authors. The 5 KM bill is the only one which shares the same author, Meša Selimović, a novelist both Serbs and Bosniacs consider as belonging to 'their' literature. The notes use both Latin and Cyrillic scripts and are signed by the Governor of the Central Bank (at the time of my fieldwork, a New Zealander, Peter Nicholls).

Despite international backing and leadership, international organizations were slow to fully participate in the Bosnian currency regime. For example, several large organizations did not begin using the KM in their financial transactions (such as salary payments) until mid 2000. This was partly due to discontent from both national and international staff about being paid in KM, the official currency of the country. Two months after the KM's introduction, a prospective polling supervisor, worried about being paid in KM instead of the 'normal' DM, informed me that, 'having to exchange KM in Canada will mean a financial loss that would, for me, make this mission to Bosnia totally senseless'. Concerns revolved around stability, convertibility and convenience: the KM wasn't easily convertible to other currencies, so there would be commission charges. However, this money was mainly marked for use in Bosnia-Herzegovina as money that internationals lived on while in the country. Furthermore, most internationals (excluding Germans) would have to convert their savings anyway upon their departure. It was also illegal for banks to charge commission on KM-DM conversions.

The KM, introduced and designed by internationally led organizations, is the official currency of the sovereign Bosnian state, but three of the four residential groups (Serbs, Croats and internationals) used separate money. The Yugoslav

Dinar was in widespread use until 1999 and the Croatian Kuna was still, as of late 2000, popular in majority Croat areas such as western Herzegovina. Interestingly, international authorities considered the use of the Kuna and the Yugoslav Dinar by Bosnians a mark of non-cooperation with Bosnian state structures. What then can we say about the resistance to the KM on behalf of internationals, despite the commitment of their organizations to this currency? The lack of interest in supporting these new Bosnian institutions in daily life jeopardized their state-building projects and called into question their own commitment to these projects. Internationals continued to work towards building Bosnian institutions and civil society, and assisting in the mental, physical and social recovery of Bosnia-Herzegovina while not living or wanting to live within those same structures. Like the governing elite's disinterest in national currencies in the 18th and early 19th centuries described by Helleiner (Helleiner 1999), the increasing preference by internationals for convenient currency rather than sovereign currency demonstrates displacements in sovereign authority and salience.

Border Access

Borders are the delimiting lines of sovereignty and all countries control or attempt to control the movement of objects and persons in and out of their marked territory. Internationals, depending on their own affiliations (United Nations, UN partner agencies, OHR, OSCE, SFOR or similar organizations), were not subject to the same border protocols as other persons passing into or out of Bosnian territory. These internationals only had to display their organization ID card to the border agent, rather than handing over their passport for scrutiny. The ID card, an organizational artefact, replaced the passport as a marker of foreign and legal identity (as the passport acts as a substitute for national identification mechanisms – citizens carry national identification, foreigners carry passports). This was not something just accepted and taken as part of the 'natural order of things'. Rather, stories abounded about the thrill of being able to use one's ID card rather than a passport and of successfully refusing to produce a passport. Most people I spoke with carried their passports with them when travelling to the Croatian coast but actively strategized about only showing the border police their ID card, just to prove that they could. Also, ID cards were used instead of passports when checking into hotels. I used mine to open a bank account. The organization ID card not only replaced state-issued and state-accepted (foreign or local) legal identification but also granted privilege.

At borders, the ability to pass through with non-state sanctioned identification meant that on a practical level there was no need to wait in the omnipresent queue of cars at the border.[9] Here, supra-state identity became a form of privilege. I interviewed only two internationals who declined to register their private vehicles as 'international'. One woman specifically registered her car with the appropriate

---

[9]   This was not necessarily true when arriving at an airport on a commercial flight.

Bosnian service as a political and social statement against international privilege and segregation. Another couple simply kept the still-valid registration the car had come with. Later, they decided to renew the Bosnian registration because they 'didn't like to stand out' and had strong feelings about what they term 'the abuse' of international status, such as not waiting at border crossings: 'It doesn't make the Bosnians like you better when you cut the queue at the border [just because you can and they can't]! Who the hell do they think they are? Why are we so special that we deserve to get to our vacations before Bosnians?' This is in contrast to another colleague who, while agreeing that it was rude to cut the border queue, admitted doing it from time to time.

The interactions and experiences of internationals with sovereign control suggests a blurring of governance mechanisms. Living above the 'real' and 'sovereign' Bosnia-Herzegovina with authoritative and regulatory borders, policemen, taxes, banknotes, road systems, hospitals, banks and public transport, internationals have an ambivalent relationship with state institutions. They are increasingly comfortable with governance from supra- or non-state institutions. This suggests a reconfiguration of the place of governance in the lives and minds of internationals. As it is through representatives and objects of state power that people have relations with 'the State' (Gupta 1995), it is noteworthy that internationals may be sabotaging their own attempts at state-building through state displacement. How important is 'the State' if the very purveyors of the idea of the importance of viable state institutions act in ways that minimize or displace its authority? Furthermore, as I have suggested, having two sets of governing ideas and institutions creates an order which separates and distinguishes internationals, primarily European, from their Bosnian-European counterparts.

Mechanisms of Exclusion (2): Exclusion from an Imagined European-ness

Concurrent with processes of international self-separation from Bosnian state regulatory practices are other mechanisms of exclusion which act to keep Bosnians out of an imagined common European-ness. These boundaries of exclusion rely less on previous East-West distinctions of the Cold War – socialism vs. 'free' capitalism – and more on perceived differences in attitude and behaviour. They are born out of the process of bringing 'them' in, out of frustration at 'Europeanization' not happening on the prescribed timetable, if at all. This frustration, for its part, appears to be rooted in the perceived inability (or lack of will) of Bosnians to put the war in the past, and to do the 'things' necessary to join Europe and be European (that is, modern). The dominant narrative is that Bosnians simply do not have the 'proper attitude'.[10] During my fieldwork, this narrative was

---

[10]   Whether Bosnians could acquire the 'proper attitude' is mostly an unspoken debate amongst internationals. I argue that most internationals believe that through teaching and example-setting, Bosnians can change. Explicitly or implicitly, the dominant mode of

most visible in workplace interactions between Bosnian and foreign employees of international organizations, and within the larger context surrounding the promotion of 'ownership' and 'nationalization'. Emerging from the idea that Bosnians should take ownership of their 'own' social, economic, and political affairs, these efforts aimed to transfer to Bosnians the responsibility of state-building activities such as elections, human rights monitoring and law drafting.

Statements promoting 'ownership' and 'nationalization' were not incompatible with representations of Bosnians as dependent and passive. Complaints about their inability to foresee problems, engage in 'forward thinking' and create solutions were ubiquitous. Although internationals, when pressed, sometimes acknowledged that most jobs open to Bosnians were low-skilled and low-responsibility, and that many were trained in other professions but needed the money, in general this knowledge faded in the face of daily struggles to accomplish tasks. Additionally, the 'obstructionist' behaviour of the main political parties (see Armakolas, Grandits, this volume) continued to taint the representation of all Bosnians. Surprisingly little attention was given to the 'legacies' of socialism, whether at the institutional or personal level. Although internationals blamed the socialist system and mentality for a variety of ills, such as dependency, low tolerance to risk or legal obstacles to market economy, this rationale was de-emphasized in daily life. Rather, the 'negative qualities' of Bosnians perceived to hamper their progress into the modern capitalist arena were naturalized and taken out of their historical context (see also Jašarević, this volume). Of course, 'good workers' existed as well and were highly valued and sought after. But they were considered something of an anomaly, of exceptional (and non-Bosnian) character.

On the ground, the process of 'nationalization' showed the ambivalence of internationals and the bureaucracy of the main international organizations towards Bosnian 'ownership' of their own governance structures. As a colleague confided to me: 'In order for Bosnia-Herzegovina to take control, the international community must be willing to cede some!' In 1998, the OSCE began a nationalization program with a goal of having each department consist of at least 50 percent national staff. This was, on the surface, successful in many cases. For example, by the end of 1999, most election officers were nationals who without exception had attended an intensive electoral course at Essex University. However, these institutional changes toward more national responsibility led to on-the-ground resistance. A three-time election worker defiantly asked: 'How can there be free and fair elections if the nationals are in charge?' This remark, in response to seeing a chain-of-command chart showing her position under a national officer, pinpoints the agony and frustration felt in the spring of 2000 by internationals and nationals alike as short-term electoral internationals found themselves reporting to national staff for the first time. The changes in the scope of international participation – from active to more passive oversight – also produced a fair amount

---

international intervention is pedagogical. This does not mean that statements verging on biological determinism can not be heard.

of frustration. The losses in both authority and responsibility brought to light judgments on Bosnians' capabilities; they were considered incapable of professional neutrality and as lacking in the skills needed to independently manage polling and counting procedures.

During the next election period, in the fall of 2000, in response to the difficult time many national staff had with international subordinates, short-term internationals were pre-warned that they were going to report to a national and that under no circumstances were they to think of themselves as above this national election officer. Training for international supervisors now specifically mentioned the 'chain of command', marking who was international and who national, and reassuring the internationals, used to feelings of authority, that the national officers were indeed competent. Similarly, time during a staff meeting was reserved for discussion on how national staff could prepare and manage the international ego and condescension. Long-term internationals explained that they knew their Bosnian colleagues could do the work satisfactorily but that the short-term staff was ignorant of the capabilities of Bosnians because they didn't have the benefit of working with them for extended periods. That is, short-termers tended to come into the country with particular expectations and assumptions and, 'unfortunately', act accordingly. However, nothing is clear-cut. The decision to bring in these short-termers was made by long-termers who, while appreciating individual Bosnian colleagues, continued to construct the Bosnians in general as inadequate for the tasks at hand.

Counter examples attest to the complexity of integration politics. Some are as mundane as a refugee lawyer consciously cutting back on his legal cases in order to pass them to his 'assistant', whom he self-consciously treated and considered an equal colleague, or a logistician hanging out with Bosnians because he liked them better than his international colleagues. The story of Maja may be particularly salient. Maja, a Bosniac woman living in Sarajevo and working for an international organization, had her apartment robbed. She called the police, and they came to investigate. The next day, as normal, she went to work. As detailed above, many international agencies offer proxy services for some services traditionally organized through the state, such as banking. These services are generally reserved for international employees. Thus, I was surprised but ultimately pleased to learn that an international colleague working in security, Susanna, was upset that Maja had not informed the organization's security department of the theft! I did not think it unusual that Maja had called the police – as could be expected by a Bosnian citizen, or truthfully, any citizen or foreigner in any country. Susanna's argument was that the security department should also have been called (actually they should have been called first!); they should have been present at the crime scene to assist the police (who were already assisted by UN police officers). She repeatedly said: 'We serve all agency personnel, not just the international ones!' This is an uncommon sentiment in international circles, in whose eyes Bosnian institutions serve Bosnian citizens, and internationals are served mostly by international or foreign institutions. This small story is both a positive statement on the possibility of inclusion and equality for Bosnians and on the depth of international exclusion from (and intrusion into) sovereign state institutions.

Conclusion

Bosnia-Herzegovina is full of Europeans, Bosnians as well as internationals. However, the meanings attached to the notion of a common post-Cold War Europe juxtapose territory and people in such a way that Bosnia-Herzegovina can be Europe even while its state and its people are not (yet). East and West may be less salient categories than during the Cold War, but Europe is still categorically, hierarchically and, as it were, temporally divided. Moreover, the very processes of integration produce categorical shifts in the idea of Europe and European identity. At the same time, in Bosnia-Herzegovina, internationals negotiate the tricky world of state-building in a context saturated with challenges to the nation-state, and create a hyper-Bosnia of and for their own use. Hyper-Bosnia illustrates recent transformations in state governance characterized by privatization and displacement, and further emphasizes the gap existing between internationals and Bosnians. The fact that the very persons engaged with creating one of the world's newest nation-states are those most disengaged with the 'traditional' services and regulations of nation-states only demonstrates that, in Europe as elsewhere, two separate spaces exist: one for those 'stuck' in/with the nation-state form, and one for those with the 'ability' to rise above and beyond it.

Chapter 12

Everyday Work:
Subsistence Economy, Social Belonging and Moralities of Exchange at a Bosnian (Black) Market

Larisa Jašarević

Introduction

At the Arizona black market, nothing extraordinary happens. Bright-yellow Pokemon dolls hang off the stands. T-shirts billow in the wind, folding and unfolding an image of Eminem giving the finger. Stray dogs adopt corners and stands to mate, sleep or hang out. Wheelbarrows wheel in fast food, newspapers, and CDs. Gypsy children walk with huge, striped shopping bags for sale. Swarms of shoppers, families and couples look for bargains, dressed in their best because it is a family affair. Or because looking good makes them look out of place at the market where the alleys end in the smell of urine and hawking attracts as many people as do the signs announcing brand names: Levi's, Lacoste, and Lancôme. Between, behind and beside the stands, vendors gather around circular coffee trays.

Located in north-eastern Bosnia, in the neutral District of Brčko and on the Tuzla-Orašje highway linking Bosnia to Croatia and Serbia, Arizona spans over 45 hectares and draws a daily crowd of 20,000 shoppers from all over Bosnia, ex-Yugoslavia (mostly Croatia), and the rest of Europe.[1] Available for purchase is

---

[1] The market takes its name from NATO's code name for the Tuzla-Orašje highway. Throughout the war, the municipality of Brčko was divided by the frontline and split into three ethnic municipalities. The town itself, predominantly Muslim before the war, was held by Serb forces. It was the site of massive 'ethnic cleansing' in 1992 and was settled by Serb DPs in the following years. In December 1995, the Dayton Peace Agreement postponed the resolution of the final status of this highly contested area. When the market appeared in the spring of 1996, just a few months after the signing of the peace agreement, it was located within the territory of the self-proclaimed 'Croat municipality of Ravne-Brčko', and within the four kilometre wide Zone of Separation that ran along the Inter-Entity Boundary Line (IEBL) and was monitored by NATO's Stabilization Force (SFOR). Both the Croat

everything imaginable, from mundane household accessories to the stuff of forbidden pleasures: drugs, arms, and sex slaves. Contrary to the market's reputation, most goods sold there are neither shabby nor flawed and the 'vice commodities' are not so easily obtained. With an estimated 3,500 stalls in June 2002, Arizona is reputedly the second biggest black market in Eastern Europe.

Arizona is also the site of one of the biggest foreign capital investments in Bosnia, as well as the largest meeting place of Muslims, Serbs, and Croats in the region since the recent war. As such, the market has been in the limelight of contemporary regional discourses on the post-socialist and post-war 'transition'[2] to a neo-liberal economy and a multicultural society (see also Coles, this volume). Whether exaggerated or straightforward, claims about Arizona oversimplify its cluttered reality and conform to preconceived models of traditional (peasant) culture or transitional inevitabilities. But what does the market look like from within? What kinds of moralities of exchange are relied upon at Arizona and why?

I suggest that Arizona, as a site of extremes, brings into focus some issues that have pervaded the whole country after the war: the real, everyday ambiguities about the new realities of work in a post-socialist era and people's attempts to order social relationships at the market, which is neither traditional nor transitional, within the customary boundaries of what is moral and meaningful.[3] From within the black market of Arizona, the work appears uneventful and uncertain, and social belonging is negotiated from day to day.

Mico the trader tells me at one point: 'All this is illegal.' I respond (thinking he is talking about the traders): 'How come? They pay taxes.' Mico: 'What taxes? The poor pay taxes, but those on the top?'[4]

---

municipality of Ravne-Brčko and the Zone of Separation disappeared (at least officially) in March 1999, when the pre-war municipality of Brčko was turned into a neutral District. The District of Brčko belongs to no entity, has its own legislation and is headed by an international supervisor appointed by the High Representative.

[2]   The troublesome part of thinking about post-socialism in terms of 'transition', suggest Michael Burawoy and Katherine Verdery, is that it implies a '*process* connecting the past to the future. What we discover, however, are theories of transition often committed to some pre-given future or rooted in an unyielding past' (Burawoy and Verdery 1999: 4). By projecting a normative future, 'transition' prescribes a quick and radical break with the whole compromising (socialist, underdeveloped, irrational) past. Put in the terms of 'transition', the ideology of subsistence, long the basis of the Bosnian economy, particularly since the recent war, is hopelessly obsolete (see also Verdery 1996).

[3]   For other accounts of market and morality in post-communist countries, see Hann 1992; Mandel and Humphrey 2002.

[4]   All quotations come from my notes taken during a month of fieldwork at the Arizona market. During this time I assisted with sales at one stand (Miralem and Safet's) and shuttled between four others, running errands for and taking coffee breaks with vendors and their associates. Additionally, many quotes come from my conversations with taxi drivers and passengers on the way to and from Arizona.

On another occasion, at Zlata's stand, the traders tell me of a recent loss. The goods they bought in Hungary were confiscated at a customs station in Banja Luka (a major city in western Bosnia, capital of *Republika Srpska*) when the police arrested the trucker and the customs officials for evading customs laws. One of the arrested customs officials, Huso tells me, sported a Rolex watch worth 10,000 Convertible Marks (KM) (about 5,000 €). The traders usually reimburse the transporter for customs duties after the delivery: 600 KM (300 €) for each cubic meter of imported goods. If the transporter manages to avoid customs, he keeps their money. Zlata concludes (as others laugh): 'He skims off the cream' ('*Ubire kajmak*'). The metaphor refers to the making of a homemade dairy spread, *kajmak*, in which the valuable cream collects on the surface of cooked milk: the one who collects it leaves others with plain milk.

Mico and the traders at Zlata's stand tell tales about the relationship between the market and the society. What is at stake at Arizona is not primarily a negotiation of (multi)ethnicity. Nor is it a distinction between the formal, neo-liberal, and the informal, traditional or transitional trade of petty vendors, or the morally condemned, criminal networks that underlie the market. Rather, it is the differentiation between subsistence and an unchecked accumulation of profit. The former imagines work within presumed, normative boundaries of income sufficient to sustain one's family and allowing others to do the same. It references the egalitarianism of the industrial, socialist past and reinvents the normative subsistence of the agricultural peasant tradition. Inscribed in the traders' tales is the value of work as limited and inherently social: subsisting, not 'skimming off the cream'.

Arizona is also a case study of more general social uncertainties and negotiations surrounding the self and work that haunt Bosnia in the face of economic and social changes after the war.[5] The traders and shoppers from all segments of society now depend on a form of trade that has historically been (and outside of Arizona still is) marginalized and ambivalent. On the one hand, the open-air market offers the cherished *domaće* (homemade) products associated with the authentic peasant – the producer. On the other hand, it displays the cheap, *šverc* (contraband, illegal) commodities and their equally stigmatized vendors – Gypsies and 'transgressional', or non-producing peasants. The traditional distinctions operating within such markets, between the peasant producers of *domaće* goods and informal traders of *šverc* commodities, are complicated and contested, but also reinvented and reused in the ordering of everyday life at Arizona. There, the ethnic Gypsy and the peasant-producer are the fewest in numbers, but they are the most stable and most frequently invoked categories in the social imagination of the remainder of shoppers and vendors engaged in the circulation of contraband commodities. While the producer is formally displaced to the (economic) periphery, the categories of peasant and peasant production surface at the very centre of everyday discourses on work and the self. The *domaće* metaphor

---

[5]   On similar issues during the war, see Maček, this volume.

describes the ideal of work as production for subsistence, qualitatively recognizable and social, and helps redraw larger national, international and global schemes within comprehensive limits of right and wrong. The category of peasant, whether the productive or the transgressional type historically associated with the open-air market, is refused and confused at Arizona as the traders posit themselves across the normative terrain of the market and against the transgressing interests of other traders, the state, and non-state agents.

This chapter offers an insight into the everyday machinations of work at Arizona against the background of national and global developmental policies aimed at the market. By no means does it exhaust the range of meaning in the everyday lives of the traders; nor does it complete the story of Arizona at the macro level. It only approximates the reality that I glimpsed and invites further study and interpretation. I therefore present it as such; as a series of events and encounters surrounding the meanings of work and categories of social belonging that extend beyond the market into contemporary Bosnia.

'The Peasant has been Killed'

My research started as a quest for migrant peasant-traders at the market but ended as a study of the categories of peasants and work, themselves migrating and unstable in the changing realities of Bosnia. The categories, I found, are neither urban nor rural, but just like the market itself, mixed and mobilized across social lines. Locating the peasantry at the market, however, and in contemporary Bosnian society in general, is not a straightforward matter of theoretical definition or ethnological description,[6] but rather an on-going process of recognition and self-recognition across shifting markers of culture, subsistence, and residence.

In a landmark study of peasants and markets in Bosnia, William Lockwood posits rural residence and agricultural subsistence as two clear markers of a 'viable peasantry' in the Bosnia of the 1960s (Lockwood 1975: 9). The markets, Lockwood further suggests, embodied peasants' economic and cultural dependence on the dominant urban economy and society.[7] Situated within the town, the *čaršija*

---

[6] To date, the only attempts made in Bosnia at studying the peasantry have been catalogues of peasant material culture and customs, as previously published by the Provincial Museum (*Zemaljski muzej*) of Bosnia-Herzegovina, the Department of Ethnology at the Sarajevo Faculty of Philosophy and other centres for ethnological research. This tradition of taxonomic and static study continues in more recent texts on Bosnian culture. The exceptions are occasional articles in the local media that combine both the historical legacy and contemporary issues surrounding the peasantry in the region.

[7] A series of reforms in the early 1950s ended the erratic attempt to control private peasant land, promote cooperative farming, and yet retain peasant support for the communist regime, which had been established during World War II by an army overwhelmingly dominated by peasants (see Bokovoy 1998).

(market) played host to a meeting between the village and the town, 'the two poles of the traditional Balkan society' (Lockwood 1975: 7-8).

Even during Lockwood's fieldwork in the 1960s, however, socialist industrialization was beginning to blur the distinction between the village and the town and to merge industrial employment and agricultural occupations (Denich 1974; Lockwood 1973; Simic 1973, 1983b). After World War II, rapid urbanization left the ties between the village and the town sinuous and strong; the majority of urban dwellers maintained a weekend home in a neighbouring village and a place in the village genealogy. Many also grew vegetables, collected fruit, and produced their own brandy and preserves on country estates. *Domaće* products remained a source of family pride for the producers, referencing their work on the land without marking them as peasants.

Since the recent war, the dichotomy between village and town has formally disintegrated. The displacement of populations, both urban and rural, and the dispersal of income opportunities away from (both agricultural and industrial) production towards the informal sector of trade and services, has made the traditional markers of peasanthood obsolete. The village is no longer obviously the 'peasant's world' as Lockwood once described it. Miralem, another Arizona trader, is exceptionally straightforward when he says: 'All of us here, we are from a village.' Most of my principal informants come from villages around the town of Srebrenik, one of the five municipalities surrounding the market. But the village as the only viable location of the peasantry is now contested, as its residents have been displaced either from or to the cities (see also Stefansson, Kolind, this volume) and many commute to urban centres for employment, education, and entertainment. Additionally, since the war, many impoverished urban families have resorted to cultivating nearby land for subsistence, further confusing the category of peasant as the original producer of *domaće* products.

Agricultural subsistence is an equally ambiguous criterion for delineating the peasantry in post-war Bosnia. At the time of Lockwood's study, Bosnia was 'a rather typical peasant society, although ... caught up in rapid change to an industrial society' (Lockwood 1975: 7). Until the recent war, heavy industries presented peasants, predominantly small landholders, with income opportunities that never obviated household reliance on labour intensive agriculture and husbandry.[8] Post-war deindustrialization has reversed this trend, although the transition to the 'open market' and a negligent agricultural policy now render domestic food production extremely expensive and primarily subsistence oriented. Market sales are minimal and limited mostly to livestock products.

When I tell Mico that I came to study peasants at Arizona, he gets angry:

---

[8] With the industrialization of Bosnia after 1945, increasing numbers of peasant men found employment in industry. Peasant-workers often worked odd hour shifts which freed up time for agriculture and husbandry that continued providing both family subsistence and surplus for the market. Most peasant women remained in the village tending to the house, children, and land (see Lockwood 1973; Šivrić 1982).

The peasant has been killed [*ubijen*]. Whoever here claims to be a peasant is lying – he isn't. He didn't survive to come here and work. Who [among the peasants] came here? The destitute came here, the lowest, the dirt comes to sell me a litre of *domaće* milk for a Mark. Who else would come for such [little] money? No peasant has survived.

Mico concludes: 'The peasant is not protected. Today there is no one to work the land. No one plants. Who would?' Miralem still plants food ('I am accustomed to planting, besides, just in case, you never know') though he acknowledges, in the face of common sense, that produce is very cheap and cultivation is costly (and manual; machines are scarce). In contrast, a taxi driver on the way to Arizona, tells me: 'No one wants to work the land now. Ten marks in the shade is better than a hundred working. Only the older ones will work on the land. These younger ones will not walk cattle.' Mico blames the negligent state, while the taxi driver blames the moral corruption of the peasants; the two are common explanations for the decline of production by peasants after the war. The taxi driver maintains that peasants, many of whom are refugees, are unwilling to return to working the land, that they entertain urban, non-productive aspirations instead (see also Stefansson, this volume). Mico and Miralem, on the other hand, speak for many critics of Bosnian agricultural policy, which encourages unlimited importation of foreign produce and discourages local production. With an estimated two thirds of the necessary food imported and less than half of the arable land cultivated, critics describe the current agricultural policy in Bosnia as a 'very successful means for destroying agricultural production'[9] and an attempt to 'rid the country of the peasant strata – that source of conservatism that flirts with the right'.[10]

The peasants, however, are not at the economic periphery where students of 'transition' usually place them but rather in the midst of the current economic reordering, fully participating in trade (the staple of the Bosnian post-war, 'open market' economy) and maintaining, to varying degrees, subsistence plots and residence in villages. Located along highways and at the markets, in other words at the points of local and regional communication, these new sites of employment blur the boundaries between urban and rural.[11] No longer spatially contained, Lockwood's two poles of Bosnia are now (dis)integrating at the market. The peasant, whether a producer, ex-producer, or a category defined entirely by culture (idealized or ridiculed at that), is constantly invoked to order both emerging and

---

[9]   *Oslobođenje*, 17 June 2001.

[10] *Oslobođenje*, 4 February 2001.

[11] Based solely on fleeting observations, I would suggest that there has been a major spatial reconfiguration of the job market in post-war Bosnia. Refugees, the unemployed, and the temporarily unemployed (*na čekanju,* meaning on stand-by, literally 'on waiting') find jobs at open air markets and in the service activities supporting them such as transportation and catering. Most of the new markets in the region are now at the edges of towns, whereas before they occupied the town centres (as for instance in Tuzla, where the downtown market is now marginal), or at regional crossroads (as for example, Arizona and Nevada markets – the latter located on another major highway in eastern Bosnia, near the city of Bijeljina).

familiar positions in contemporary Bosnian society (see also Stefansson, Armakolas, Kolind, this volume).

Begajeta, a trader I find having coffee at Kada's stand, introduces herself as a retired teacher in special education and tells me: 'You will see everything here. Perhaps not doctors, but there are engineers, workers from everywhere. A need forced them, people are surviving [*ljudi preživljavaju*].' What Begajeta tells me is that Arizona is not an ordinary market and that many vendors, as professionals and urbanites like herself, traditionally do not belong there. Selma, Kada's assistant, once an accountant in a Srebrenik company, explains: 'It's hard [working] like this. Especially if you are schooled, this is like death to you.' Miralem disagrees: 'I did *this* before the war, too. This is not new to me. That's why it wasn't hard getting used to *it*.' (emphasis added) I find that vendors rarely name the work at Arizona, referring to it instead in vague terms. They rarely even use the word '*šverc*' (from the German word '*Schwarzhandel*': black market), an otherwise widespread and thus readily available term describing the informal, open-market trade in contraband, cheap commodities which has been common in Bosnia since at least World War II (Lockwood 1975: 156-9). A Gypsy woman in the corner of what is called the *buvljak* (flea market), musing over my note taking at an abandoned stand, makes explicit the historical comparison: 'This [work at Arizona] is not hard, we always did this.'

Traditionally, and presently also outside of Arizona, the trader at a Bosnian market either sells the products of family labour, as do the peasant and the farmer,[12] or sells mass-produced commodities, as does the *pijacar* (literally: one who lives off of the market, usually reselling products of someone else's labour) and the *švercer* (smuggler, contrabandist, or bootlegger of items produced by others). All traders are clearly divided spatially and distinguished by the items in which they trade. The word '*švercer*' is often used interchangeably with '*pijacar*', although the latter is more widely associated with the retail of agricultural produce. The *šverceri* (pl.) themselves are conventionally either (transgressional) peasants, or Gypsies.[13] The assumed illegal, cheap, and flawed nature of *šverc* commodities

---

[12] The difference between the *seljak* (peasant) and the *poljoprivrednik* (farmer) is palpable both in the production and consumption of their produce. Unlike the peasant who subsists off the land, the farmer produces for the market, under contract with agricultural cooperatives or processing factories. Furthermore, the farmer cultivates large scale plots of land, runs automated livestock facilities and generally uses the tools of mechanization and scientific technology (artificial fertilizers, pesticides and the like). In contrast, the peasant's produce, by virtue of being produced by labour intensive, time consuming, and low technology means, is deemed more natural, tastier and healthier – in short, more valuable, as expressed in the higher prices expected for *domaće*, peasant produce.

[13] The place of a Gypsy in the regional imagination is well captured by Marko Živković: 'perceived by most Yugoslavs as being at the very bottom of the hierarchy, Gypsies are often used at all levels to metonymically stand for the lower end of dichotomies. This conforms to a general tendency in interethnic perception to cast both oneself and others in terms of extreme contrasting terms' (Živković 2001: 25).

extends to the character of those who trade in them; such people are reputed to be morally corrupt, vulgar, and ignorant. Furthermore, the stigma envelopes the act of buying and particularly wearing *šverc* commodities, rendering a visit to the *šverc* market an embarrassment. In studying markets in western Bosnia, Lockwood notes that the 'derogatory epithet' of *švercer* is extended to 'all those who sell products not of their own production' (Lockwood 1975: 156). Juxtaposed against *domaće* products of peasant (hard) work, *šverc* denotes the open market trade in dubiously obtained commodities and farm produce, turning out easy, and therefore unearned, profits. Unlike *šverceri*, whose subsistence is fully dependent on the cash economy and the commodity form, the peasant-producers merely supplement their subsistence or income with market sales of their own produce (dairy, livestock, herbs and traditional medicines, tobacco and, more rarely, handicrafts and tools). The market exchange thus never confuses *domaće* goods with commodities. *Domaće* products enter the market and yet, by the particularity of their production, they resist being assimilated into homogenized value and straightforward exchange. In the midst of the commodity trade they retain the mark of a particular worker, along with a sensuousness quality of this work that eludes money exchange. Thus, a peasant woman is said to be clean, honest and hardworking if her sour cream is deemed good or else unclean and sly if the cream is watered down. The unassimilated value is registered by the participants in the exchange but is really acknowledged outside of it, within the realm of consumption. In this light, *domaće* goods are sold alongside identical items produced in farms or factories, at similar prices but with the distinctions of quality, taste and nutritional value that both peasants and consumers accord to the former. *Domaće* ultimately refers to the particularity of one's work as well as the person associated with the product.[14]

With the exception of a very few elderly peasants selling *domaće* goods, and a very few ethnic Gypsies engaged in small scale trade, the traditional distinctions between items of trade, relationships to the market, and the categories of peasant, *švercer* and Gypsy have been collapsed at Arizona. On the one hand, the majority of sales there are in commodities that are to varying degrees illegal. On the other hand, the market employs migrant traders from all ethnic and social groups, all equally displaced from the production economy and desperate for income. While in the past *šverc* was aimed at poorer buyers, the Arizona market figures as an average family's major shopping source in a region where the costs of formal trade make regular shops prohibitively expensive. A host of peasant-producers as well as urban, professional and semi-professional workers who have joined the trade confuse and refuse the existing categories of market work and market traders. I came to the market to study peasants, having in mind the classic markers, also used by Lockwood, of agricultural subsistence, rural residence and (in)dependence on the market, but found that the category is shifting in ways that reinvent and mobilize the traditional and transgressional images of the peasant. Furthermore, while the traditional producing peasant is cherished and vulnerable, though at the

---

[14]   On the notion of *domaći* as applied to people, see Kolind, this volume.

same time also a dangerous figure, recognition of the transgressional peasant is invoked in self-defence: it is always someone else.

On a slow day, while arranging bathing suits for display outside a store, I overhear the vendors at a neighbouring stand teasing Safet: 'What's that beard of yours for? [Safet has a sliver of a beard, a line running along the edge of his jaw] You look like a peasant, which is what you are.' Safet replies: '*Vela havle* [a popular phrase invoking Allah in wonder over something], it's the fashion now.' They: 'The fashion where? Up on your hill?!!' Safet: 'No, downtown.' They: 'Downtown where? In Sladna [another village near Srebrenik]?!!'

Earlier that day Safet himself recognizes a peasant. Motioning to a confused customer he says: 'Brother, what a peasant!' ('*Joj seljaka, braćo draga*') 'How come?' I ask later. Safet shrugs: 'Well, just like that. A peasant. Stupid. He doesn't know.'

Safet recognizes a peasant 'just like that' and is then experienced as one of them in a ubiquitous market exercise, the placing and displacing of the self within the popular Bosnian dichotomy of 'the asphalt' (*asfalt*) and 'the hill' (*brdo*). This variant of Lockwood's binary pair of the market town (*čaršija*) and village (*selo*) is no longer bound to a place and as such reflects the contemporary instability of the dichotomy. Now that asphalt runs through most villages, location is no longer a relevant distinction, but the new mobility makes the dichotomy all the more important. In the popular imaginary, peasants are noted for their illiteracy, dialects, dress and, in light of the recent history, for their nationalism and radical religiosity, all cemented in their persistent voting support for nationalist parties. Peasants appear as the origins of all the trouble in the region; having been seen to have started the war and invaded the city, they are now said to be profiting from the post-war disorder. A common, desperate lament on the asphalt is that 'peasants have come to power', 'peasants have seized the money' or 'peasants are getting university educations'. New politicians, businessmen, and other officials are ridiculed for their (peasant) dialects, despised for their (peasant) ignorance, and criticized for their (peasant) nationalist affiliations (see also Stefansson, Kolind, this volume). Neither wealth, nor new occupations or even university degrees can save peasants from recognition nor spare them from being laughed at. Laughing at perceived peasants, however, is also a privilege readily available for anyone to claim. At Arizona, I found that the exact location of 'the asphalt' is negotiable and the category of peasant (whether the genuine but ambivalent producer or the transgressional one) is necessary to mark one's own position at the market.

Lacking an unambiguous marker, the transgressional peasant is not the Other, but merely always another. Elusive, unstable, constantly available and thus threatening, the wielding of the category of peasant becomes a social skill. To spot a peasant – the menace, the embarrassment among us – is a relief; it is the comfort of knowing that it is not oneself who is being laughed at but someone else. Unlike traditional producers, peasant traders work on the asphalt, transgressing, confusing and mixing the categories of urban and rural. Safet's beard may look like a 'downtown fashion', but for those at the neighbouring stand and for Miralem, this claim falls apart. Miralem therefore says about Safet: 'He too is a kid from a village. That's not saying anything bad [*ružno*, literally ugly] to me. But some see an insult in it.' Miralem thus refuses the aesthetic exercise of locating the peasant away from oneself, aesthetics being used here in the original etymological meaning of a sensory experience of cognition. Others remain on the lookout for the transgressional form; for them appearances need probing and testing.

The consumers of *domaće* products, those who used to produce them (Safet, Kada, Mico), or those who are still active part-time producers now fully engaged in trade (Miralem, Safet, Zlata and her partners) carry to the market the notion of morally valued work once embedded in the consumption of *domaće* products and now also in the metaphoric use of the term. I argue that it is this notion of work as subsistence bounded within normative limits of work and gain which order the self, others and the state. It renders meaningful the work that preserves the record of the individual worker and recreates a social contract between workers related by friendship or kinship.

Like Lockwood, I started my study by following peasants from a particular village to the market (five of my informants came from the village of Gornji Srebrenik). But regardless of how closely I followed them, 'the peasant' kept disappearing and reappearing in forms that made my pursuit appear misguided, outlining instead a social imagination of meaningful work and workers that transcend the bounds of the urban/rural dichotomy. At Arizona, the *domaće* product is marginalized, reduced to meagre sales off a dirt road, and the producers selling it there carry a dual metaphor of exile: of the producers, indignant and utterly poor but, due to the 'naturalness' of their productive activity, genuinely human (thus of 'the people'), and of the ideal type of work – threatened but subsistence oriented and egalitarian ('surviving').

Market and Non-Market

In post-war Bosnia, the 'transition' from a centrally planned economy to a neo-liberal, global market economy is pursued with a vengeance. For local and international observers, the Arizona market embodies the tropes of the coming age of neo-liberalism and multiculturalism (it is commonly described as a 'thriving centre of business' or a 'multi-ethnic laboratory'[15]). But Arizona is not merely a break with the past as is typically attempted in a 'transition', nor a continuation of a regional black market form that traditionally stood for criminality and cheapness ('a market for cheap goods of dubious quality',[16] 'a cancer'[17]). For the traders, Arizona is a negotiation of customary, normative claims to subsistence against neo-

---

[15] *OHR Press Release*, 8 March 2001, available at <http://www.ohr.int/ohr-dept/presso/pressr/default.asp?content_id=4268>.
[16] *Oslobođenje*, 13 June 2002.
[17] *Time*, 13 November 2000.

liberal claims to profit. 'This here', trader Huso says, 'is mere existence, survival of a sort.' Beneath the simplistic descriptions of outside commentators and their straightforward prescriptions to legalize, sanitize, and rationalize Arizona, life at the market brims with tensions.

Situated along the regional Tuzla-Orašje highway (the lifeline of the market), the clutter of Arizona is well organized. First there is a dirt road that runs alongside the central market. Here very small scale vendors, the elderly, and Gypsies urge you to inspect their wares piled on the ground, into wheelbarrows, on their bodies, and to buy quickly, before 'the police chases them away' ('but they come back again' says Esad). They trade informally (*na crno*), paying no taxes or fees for the dirt on which they squat to trade. Here a Gypsy cries a tongue twisting line: '*Kikiriki, kokakola, kikiriki kokakola*' ('peanuts, Coca-cola'). The road coils and cuts through the markets, the whole way lined with very old looking peasant women sitting on stools selling *domaće* products: *kajmak*, milk, cheese, and eggs.

Then there is the *buvljak* (flea market), the part of the market furthest off the dirt road, where the hawking and sales are more sophisticated. A young Gypsy man uses a loudspeaker to advertise pyjamas and shorts. His words come across all garbled. The stands here are tiny, wide enough to hold one or two vendors, although customers squeeze in, hunching down behind the displays to try on clothing. Mostly clothing and shoes, goods at the flea market are out to be touched, felt, selected. Safet, working in the labyrinth, says of the flea market: 'I wouldn't work there even if someone gave me 2,000 Marks. It's all Gypsies [*ciganija*] there, they yell the whole time. Either I would kill someone there or someone would kill me.'

Finally, there is the *labirint* (labyrinth), the orderly looking core of the market. Here the passages are covered with plastic sheeting to shelter shoppers in bad weather. Wooden stands are fully built with walls and doors and many are large enough to receive customers. There are no Gypsies and, Gypsies being the main hawkers, no hawking either. Aside from clothing, there are household appliances, tools, office equipment, professional machinery and food. The goods, mostly from Turkey and the Chinese Market in Budapest, enter Bosnia through some 400 illegal border crossings or through official crossings by means of bribes or false reporting. Clothing, the single biggest item of trade at Arizona, sold both retail and wholesale, is displayed at the labyrinth in a variety of sizes and styles unmatched at the flea market.

Along the highway are larger shops that specialize in one product only: the signs advertise Nike, Levi's, a furniture store. At each end of the market are also Chinese run stores, the novelty of their owners living here and learning Bosnian having long worn off.

For the Office of the High Representative (OHR) and NATO's Stabilization Force (SFOR), the market is within the scope of the constitution which commits Bosnia(ns) to a multicultural state and a neo-liberal economy, both apparently having materialized at the Arizona market as a pragmatic antidote to all that is wrong with the region: ethnic strife and a centrally planned economy. In 1996, the market sprang up in the Zone of Separation monitored by NATO.[18] In 1999, a District with a special status placing it both within and outside of the Bosnian state was created out of the pre-war municipality of Brčko and the administration of the market passed to this District.[19] Western officials therefore claim that NATO was responsible for the market that ultimately 'enabled peace to break out'. In this account, NATO's invitation to trade was 'all that was necessary to bring people of all ethnic groups back together': in the words of an American NATO official, 'Say what you will about the evils of unregulated commerce today, Bosnia's traffic – personal, commercial and unfortunately criminal – flows across the former confrontation line as a result of the breathing space afforded by NATO troops'.[20]

At the market, Mico scoffs at the idea that Arizona is NATO's or OHR's project in ethnic reconciliation: 'They came to bring us together?!! Like they could do that if we hadn't been living like this before. Look at me [a Serb] and Suljo [a Muslim]. We've been here together since the first day. And worked together before that in *Polet* [a public company] for twenty years.' For the traders, Arizona is not the rational project of reconciliation between severed entities that the international observers imagine it to be but a continuation of interethnic relationships that were both accessible and socially validated even throughout the war.[21] Like exchanges across the frontlines during the war, the peacetime trade at Arizona happens without a foreign intermediary. Likewise, the trade is not replacing hostile nationalisms with an antiseptic form of multiculturalism but is displacing volatile issues to the periphery of popular discourse.[22] Mico will only talk about ethnicity and nationalism when I initiate the subject. Other traders, too, wait to be asked, and then tell me that ethnicity at Arizona is beside the point.[23]

As with nationalism, the economic rationality of free trade at Arizona is also trusted to displace the remnants of socialism. Thus the OHR, committed to the

---

[18]   See note 1.

[19]   See note 1.

[20]   Speech held on 18 November 2000 by Alexander Vershbow, US representative to the North Atlantic Council, available at <http://www.useu.be/ISSUES/vers1118.html>.

[21]   Many traders describe the interethnic relationships as a shared expectation, a legacy of the past but still a viable norm. So, Mustafa tells me: 'I grew up in that [socialist] system and there is no way you can change me now. I am not used to distinguishing whether someone is Serb, Croat, or Muslim. I didn't separate people out like that. I differentiate people according to their humanity. We can't say that all the Serbs are the same.'

[22]   It is an unstable periphery in the sense that disagreements threaten to re-centre the market around politicized identities, but a periphery nonetheless as the issues are evidently made obsolete through everyday work. At Zlata's stand, Huso (a Muslim) gives me a beautiful example of just how normalized – not neutralized – the issues of nationality and nationalism are at the market. He tells me that trader Rašo (a Serb) is the best neighbour they could have, and a very good man ('As good as bread'). 'But you start talking to him about politics and all is lost. That's how entrenched he is. So you let go.'

[23]   For other accounts on boundary economies and their (lack of) impact on interethnic relations, see Hann 1992; Konstantinov 1996; Wilson and Donnan 1998.

promotion of a 'single economic space, a central tenet of the Dayton Peace process',[24] cites the District, with the market boosting its revenues and its regional fame, as 'the future Bosnia-Herzegovina in microcosm'[25] and 'a paragon for the organization of de-centralized Bosnia-Herzegovina'.[26] Harnessing the spontaneous economic gathering and the transnational governance that Arizona stands for, the District plans are pulling Arizona away from the control of the Bosnian state while at the same time promoting a Bosnia with a 'free' market that is carefully planned and developed.

In the tales of its vendors, Arizona began with people who came 'of their own will' to trade along the road and across entity lines, in secrecy during the war ('while off duty from the front lines', remembers Haris), and openly after the peace, still in their respective uniforms. It all started with 'cigarettes, coffee and flour', says Sejo. The bare necessities, in Bosnian terms, thus brought the market to being. Throughout the war, warlords and common soldiers traded through the decades-old ties with the underground economy of Eastern Europe, but Arizona opened illegal trade opportunities to the wider public.[27] In the guise of retail and wholesale vendors, service providers and impoverished shoppers, ordinary people disseminate contraband, unrecorded and untaxed goods supplied by the organized crime networks. However, the various means for eluding state control (underreporting, employing unregistered workers, running firms under bogus names, to name just a few) are not unique to Arizona; most formal businesses in Bosnia resort to similar practices.[28] The subsequent 'developmental' initiatives of

---

[24]   *OHR Press Release*, 12 December 2001, available at <http://www.ohr.int/ohr-dept/presso/pressr/default.asp?content_id=6570>.

[25]   *OHR Press Release*, 8 March 2001, available at <http://www.ohr.int/ohr-dept/presso/pressr/default.asp?content_id=4268>.

[26]   *Oslobođenje*, 17 March 2001.

[27]   Far more exclusive is the trafficking of humans, mostly immigrants and women forced into the sex industry, although organized crime groups recruit wider local assistance for the logistics of this human flow. At the fringes of the market are night bars with signs now falsely advertising nudes since the sex trade was ended by a major police raid just a few months before my fieldwork. But the business, displaced further into the countryside or arranged by phone, still goes on. To distinguish among the extralegal activities at the market is an important but formidable task since conventionally 'the concept of an illegal or black market economy lumps illegal trading and small scale production together with violent criminal activities usually considered intrinsically immoral by state and society alike' (Clark 1988: 5).

[28]   This is precisely the weakness of theorizing the informal economy as radically separate and separable from the formal sector; in Bosnia such distinctions regularly do not hold. Furthermore, the terms 'informal', 'unofficial' and 'non-formal' are preferred over the 'black market economy', which presumably overemphasizes the issue of illegality and upholds a conventional notion of legitimacy that in many states, as in Bosnia, is no longer tenable. With this caution in mind, I use the term 'black market' here because it best fits the

the District to 'graduate' informal trade to the level of a conventional economy reflect a recent trend in global developmental policy that views the informal economy as 'a living expression of liberalism's ubiquitous economic men, a genuine force for modernization' (Duffield 2001: 148). Casting Arizona as a model of free market entrepreneurship, the state and the OHR burden the meagre earnings made there with high taxes and rent and thus infringe on the very possibility of subsistence. As Miralem observes: 'A year or two ago, every day used to be [busy] like Saturday and Sunday are now.' The revenues from Arizona comprise a 'significant source of budget incomes'[29] despite the accrued 30 million US dollars in unpaid taxes and ongoing unrecorded trade.[30] The most recent plan to relocate the market to a mall under construction further north is yet another step for economic development and a strike against the remainder of the regional 'Balkan' traditionalisms as embodied in the image of an open-air market.

The plan is a conspicuous departure from the very form of informal economy comprising a wide variety of income opportunities, simple facilities and minimal ties to the state bureaucracy (Clark 1988). But the plan also inconspicuously renounces the neo-liberal ideal of free competition that Arizona has stood for thus far and surrenders the traders to ultimately unaccountable, non-state interests – those of foreign investors. In December 2001, the District and the OHR allocated Arizona to *Italproject*, a coalition of anonymous Italian investors, and the local company *Santovac* that together committed themselves to an infrastructure development project worth over 300 million KM (150 million €). Allegedly using as a model an American legal clause on urban rehabilitation that entrusts the state with the development of private land defined as underdeveloped or criminal, the District entrusted to *Italproject*, for a period of twenty years, the public land of Arizona, as well as the private lands adjacent to it. *Italproject* had already taken over from the District the collection of rent for the existing market stands and, 'with our rent money', a vendor says, has begun construction of a shopping mall north of the central market. Perpetually preoccupied with the squalid appearance of the market, the OHR is now pleased to have turned 'an old probleme – the lack of infrastructure – into a real commercial opportunity'.[31] Miralem sums it up well: 'It will be nice to look at, like a real settlement. But it will no longer be this. It will be

---

popular image of Arizona and captures the local term for informal trade (*na crno*, literally 'in the black') as well as the historical model of *šverc*.

[29]   *Oslobođenje*, 17 March 2001.

[30]   Since the creation of the Brčko District in March 1999, Arizona has been policed by the District police department and the International Police Task Force (IPTF). Additionally, since June 2000, the State Border Service (*Državna granična služba*, DGS) has been monitoring the flow of goods across marked and unmarked borders. Nevertheless, informal goods continue to flow through ever more sophisticated channels carved out in the marriage of capital and officialdom.

[31]   *OHR Press Release*, 31 October 2001, available at <http://www.ohr.int/ohr-dept/presso/pressr/default.asp?content_id=6172>.

something else.' The restrooms and street lamps envisioned for the new mall are a small comfort to the traders who cannot afford the rent of 10,000 KM (5,000 €) in advance for the smallest unit of space and the additional 25,000 KM (12,500 €) in instalments during the first year. 'This is the biggest robbery there could be', Mico says. The amounts are incredible in Bosnia where the average (and regularly delayed) monthly salary amounts to 400 KM (200 €), or at the market where the average monthly turnover is about the same. Zlata speaks for many when she wonders: 'Who has the money for that? The small ones will not make it.' The head of the District's Department for Urbanization, Environmental Planning and Privatization agrees: 'Of the 3,500 traders who now work there, perhaps 1,000 will remain. The rest will find some other work'.[32] But Mico says: 'There is nothing else. This is the last resort.' The private owners of the land across the road from Arizona have initiated a legal suit to regain their rights to rent and to maintain a humbler market next to the *Italproject* one. However, when the landowners cancel a strike previously proposed to the traders, Mico's hopes wane: 'They must have been offered some good deal'.[33]

The *Italproject* scheme occupies the sphere that Karl Polanyi observes within the liberal economy and terms the 'non-market'. Removed from the sacred liberal creed of the self-regulating free market, in the non-market, capital and the state form a 'network of measures and policies … integrated into powerful institutions designed to check the action of the market' (Polanyi 2001 [1944]: 79). Eliminating the competition from private landowners at Arizona and transforming municipal land into a business concern, *Italproject* and the District are replacing the existing market, accessible to a range of interests from big to small, with a market for a select few. Moreover, the move expresses a more general ambivalence in the international policy towards Arizona that sees it both as an opportunity for an interethnic meeting ground and a showcase of planned development. The *Italproject* scheme indicates a swing towards the latter course, and the traders are quick to predict that the subsequent consolidation of capital and the exit of small traders will end the substantial level of interethnic interaction among the traders. As Mico puts it, 'They will break all this apart. Before, there was a project of bringing the people together, and now it's a project of dividing them.'

Far above the small traders, the market and non-market rules appear ominous, mighty, and unfair. There is the reach of ghostly, foreign capital and the legal

---

[32] *Oslobođenje*, 11 June 2002.

[33] One such deal is already known: after the war, the Croat veteran organization of the local 108th HVO brigade, based in the village of Bosanska Bijela, established a company called *Posavina 108* that seized a part of the Arizona land and built commercial facilities for rent on it. When *Italproject* signed the contract with the District, the director of *Posavina 108* at first threatened the mayor that his 'soldiers' (*borci*) would get involved 'if he allows foreigners to take our land' (*Oslobođenje*, 11 June 2002), but then quieted down after *Italproject* agreed to reimburse *Posavina 108* for the loss of land with monthly payments of 10,000 KM (5,000 €) for a period of two years (*Oslobođenje*, 6 November 2002).

arbitrariness of the national and transnational plans. When threatened in the past, the traders organized strikes and barricaded the highway. Now, watching and waiting, Miralem and Mico say: 'There will be social unrest.' The uncertain and incongruous takes on order in an uneventful everyday. Within the everyday experience of work, traders locate Arizona within a shared, normative body of needs and expectations, deemed customary and fair.

Tighter Pants, Bigger Stand

On my last day at the market, having had coffee with Miralem and Safet (Safet having shaved off his beard), I head for the flea market. At Zlata's stand, where six traders share a stand, used coffee dishes sit near by: the morning coffee is through. A customer asks Muho how much the long skirts are and he replies: 'Nine.' Zlata looks at him, puzzled – he has been selling them for eight the whole morning long. 'Too expensive', she says. 'I know', he replies, 'but let it be. I've sold enough since this morning. It's enough.'

The traders often invoke a limit to one's work and one's gain. In the metaphors of 'bread', 'survival' and 'life', the work at the market relates the idea of subsistence as the customary entitlement that it was during socialism and as an ideal of work within the market embodied in *domaće* goods. Muho's 'enough' exemplifies the logic of meaningful work as limited to subsistence. In contrast with the logic of profit generating schemes, this limit ensures the equal welfare of the workers and assumes personal relationships that permeate the working environment.

Mico, Haris and Miralem tell me that all traders, big and small, need to be able to work at the market since 'we all get our bread from this'. Haris concludes: 'We too ['the small ones'] need to survive.' The limit redraws the claims of traders, the state and non-state agents within normative and customary boundaries.

Some traders at Arizona, and by extension the District and the OHR planning the 'transition' to a rational capitalist economy, refuse such limits as alien to the very idea of profitable gain. 'We are eating off a stem', trader Mustafa says, describing the short-sighted ambition of his fellow traders. He goes on: 'Only those who have [something] will survive. Only the strong ones will win. It's the way it is. [It's] The West, capitalism.'

Later on the same day, Zlata points to a store being built straight across from them and says there will be trouble. A *Podrinjka*, a refugee from the Podrinje region (in eastern Bosnia), has apparently bought the spot and is building too close to the two stands on the left and right of her site. She is a bigmouth, they say, and quick to fight, and fist fight at that. Physical fights and arguments are common at the flea market, they add, but this *Podrinjka* is notorious for both. When the District officials (or those from *Italproject*? No one knows but the confusion is telling) and the *Podrinjka* march in, traders from the neighbouring stands neglect customers to follow the scene. Rašo, the indignant owner of the stand on the left, says: 'If only you'd left ten centimetres for the opening and closing of the stand.' She replies: 'I have a contract and what the contract says for me, that's how it will be, and I'm not giving up a centimetre of what's mine. What's mine is mine.' The neighbour to the right, Seka, also can't open her door because of the *Podrinjka*'s stand. At Zlata's stand, someone comments: 'They'll have to rub behinds getting into their stands.' Alma laughs: 'Yeah, but it'll be the end of anyone whom she [the *Podrinjka*] hits with her ass.' Alija adds, in a low voice: 'Make three meters like everyone else. Why did you spread out, why does she need seven?' According to the regulations, Muho explains, businesses at the flea market are spaced at half a meter on both sides, 'but she has to be greedy' ('*treba bit proklet*' – literally: damned, hogging something at another person's expense). Muho thinks it is all the fault of the District; some officials profit from selling the half meter assigned for spacing. The *Podrinjka* is shouting in the officials' faces, explaining how she already owns three spaces at the new (*Italproject*) market, for which she paid 140,000 KM (70,000 €), and that she will visit the District personally to straighten out this mess once and for all. Everyone at the stand laughs when Zlata comments: 'If only you built in the parking lot, there is plenty of space there. You could go ahead and spread out.'

Everyone sympathizes with Rašo. The *Podrinjka*'s conspicuous structure invokes disbelief ('why this big…'), disapproval ('she has to be greedy/damned'), distaste (revealed in the comments on the size of her behind 'squeezed into those tight pants in such heat!'). Everyone else is sharing the scarce space at the overcrowded market, but the *Podrinjka* shuns the others and thus should go to the parking lot, that is, truly exit the market since she has already symbolically left its 'people'. What everyone seems to be saying is that to be content with 'the same as everyone else' is to belong to the 'everyone else' whose vulnerable, indignant humanity is often invoked in the image of the producing peasant and stories about 'us': 'the people', 'the poor', 'the little ones'. The *Podrinjka*, with her open disdain, conspicuous wealth, legal contract and tight pants, remains outside.

As a rule, the state, the District and *Italproject* fall outside the customary economy; they overstep its limits. Miralem tells me: 'The state here arranges nothing, gives nothing, they are smothering the people [with revenue collections]. Already the smaller ones are not surviving. We are working here but for how much longer? They are asking for a lot and our earnings are small.' Haris puts it similarly: 'Here, to survive, to keep customers, see to your own interests, you have to buy as cheaply as possible and not record the sales. Otherwise, by the time you pay for the customs and everything to the state, you have nothing. I am not saying that you shouldn't give to the state, but there's a limit.' The state is both callous and greedy. It makes excessive claims on traders' earnings and gives nothing in return ('not even a single toilet'). It is up to the traders, then, to restore 'some limit' to the state's claims.[34]

---

[34] On the perception of the state as a predatory agent, see Grandits, Kolind, Helms, this volume.

Italproject, Haris says, knows no limits: 'If only he ['the Italian'] wanted to make less – say he can't make three million but he could make one million or so. We need to survive too. Don't suffocate us. I will not buy a space down there [at the mall]. I won't as a matter of principle.' Similarly, Mico says that *Italproject* is a scheme 'to suffocate this people, to prevent it from living or working. Just so they can get rich. The few of them will hold everything, and whatever happens to us is fine. And this supports some 150,000 people. The whole [region of] Tuzla lives from this'. He concludes: 'They will make poor people here. Even now it's the poor who are here, but they will be poorer. There will be social unrest.'

The traders' subsistence economy at the market is similar to the ideology of customary exchange theorized by Edward P. Thompson. His analysis is pertinent to the Bosnian context inasmuch as it posits a conflict between the capitalist process of legal and contractual rationalization and non-economic customary behaviour. The main feature of the customary claim, Thompson notes, is the 'priority afforded ... to the "non-economic" over direct monetary sanctions, exchanges and motivations' (Thompson 1991: 11).

The contractual and legal relationships that the *Podrinjka* and *Italproject* observe are unnatural and unfair when compared to the customary and personal relationships expected at the market. Although complicated by salaried contracts,[35] the work at Arizona is described as mobilized along axes of friendship and kinship rather than wages, and based on reciprocal assistance rather than on unilateral stipulation. Haris complains that '[*Italproject*] presented me with the contract that he has printed out. He did not ask me to write it, did not give me other options. He should tell us how he got this market, on what terms, and what are his and my rights and obligations'. Haris concludes: 'We are the sheep and he shears us.' *Italproject* is exploitative, its claims are unfair: by blatantly disregarding the concerns of the traders and forcing them into its own income generating scheme, it seeks to turn the people into a profitable, dumb mass: the sheep. *Italproject* denies subsistence, both as a possibility at Arizona and as an economic concept; it violates the normative order of customary claims.

The normative limit of 'enough' divides the market's economy in two: within the bounds of subsistence lies the sphere of belonging to 'the people', 'the little ones', 'the poor', those who, like the peasant-producer, have been displaced to the margins of the market but are dependent on it for 'survival'. This economy of subsistence redeems traditionally stigmatized work at the market in a legitimate

---

[35]   While wage work is not new to Bosnian peasants, its current form is unfamiliar to Bosnians. In the past most of them worked in public companies. Present day employment in private enterprises makes blatant the formal loss of social equality. However, outside of large scale projects mediated between companies by contracts, I argue that (a ghost of) the claims to social equality still inform relationships between owners and employees. Thus, for example, the skilled workers one hires for a personal project are treated no differently than friends and relatives recruited as traditional, reciprocal work parties. They are served a good meal, treated with coffee and sweets, and assisted by the 'contractor'.

commodity trade by relating it to the egalitarian idea of workers' welfare associated with the socialist and small scale agriculturalist 'past'. Transgressing the bounds of the customary and common is the other all-inclusive sphere comprising the state, non-state agents and investors, and other traders. By virtue of their presence beyond the limit and away from 'us', 'they' ('the big ones', 'the top'), like the other transgressional form of social imagination (*šverceri*, non-producing peasants), mark the insecurity of the everyday. The market is thus not traditional, but neither is it transitional in the sense that traders are realizing some type of neo-liberal potential bound to deliver Arizona to an anticipated state of development. Instead of the eternal, inevitable presence of peasant nationalisms, the freedom of the neo-liberal market, or the promise of planned development, in the routine of Arizona it is uncertainty that rules.

Everyday

At Zlata's stand on an ordinary day, we sit around and talk. Customers come and go. There is a shortage of small change, and the traders keep borrowing from one another. Velid gets some Euros (they are still very new in the region), two bills of 500, and he gets really nervous about whether they are 'real'. He repeats, 'I'm afraid of these Euros' and passes them around the stand for the rest to inspect. He gives it to each one of them in turn, saying, 'You would know', and each looks it over saying, 'I wouldn't know. They are fine'. Shortly afterwards, a tax collector shows up, looks at everyone's records one by one, and asks for paperwork that no one seems to have – some sort of tax declaration. With the tax collector gone, all gather to tell each other exactly what happened. And they are not sure. All seem to have received different instructions. Alma then says, 'Here you can't know whether to tell the truth or lie.' Amidst the mundane, the shortage of small change, long coffee sessions and tax collection, there is the unknowable. What exactly did the tax collector say? What should one say? Are the Euros real?

The aim of this study, as of any ethnography I think, is to move behind the apparent or extraordinary and into the ordinary as people experience it and explain it. So within a notorious regional black market I looked for the mundane values of work and found them very much connected, just as the market itself is, to the rest of Bosnian society.

While to me the notion of work as subsistence and the boundaries it implies are made explicit at Arizona (and in the wider society outside it), the continued validation of *domaće* products and the peasant-producer who sells goods at a market are far more convoluted and, some might suggest, entirely irrelevant to contemporary Bosnia. Absenting the peasantry from 'serious' transitional economics discourse as a quaint, obstinate category of culture, however, is a denial of the economic reality in which the quest for subsistence fuses and confuses the rural and the urban. I suggest that the peasant-producer and *domaće* products, even when they exit the core of the dominant economy (as in Arizona), are central to local notions of work and self produced within a society negotiating transgressional categories and claims. Recognition of transgressional forms of social imagination (*šverceri*, non-producing peasants) and violations of the normative ('the big ones', 'the top') is a pertinent exercise throughout the Bosnian market. Engaged in subsistence that no longer accords a 'natural' differentiation between productive and non-productive work, and powerless before the claims of capital and the law, traders displace themselves away from what is compromising and within the shared universe of right and wrong.

All appearances aside (the open sewage, the hawking, the squatting trade), Arizona is not peripheral. As a traditionally marginal form of trade that figures now as a prominent regional employment opportunity, Arizona speaks bluntly of the ongoing reshuffling of the Bosnian economy away from formal production to informal trade, of social fluidity outside the clear markers of urban and rural and away from ethnic or national distinctions. These are significant developments since the Bosnia of the 1960s, when Lockwood classified Bosnian peasant markets as 'peripheral' (Lockwood 1975: 208-11). Not only were the peasants self-sufficient within the village and only sporadically engaged in the market, but the peasant market was also marginal to the (cultural and normative) interethnic integration otherwise taking place in 'the more highly developed and rationalized economic and social institutions of the new nation state' (Lockwood 1975: 211). In contrast, Arizona is a site of regular employment for a host of full-time and part-time traders, and of daily economic and non-economic exchange, whereas the majority of formal economic and social institutions in the region have rested idle since the war. No longer a traditional peasant institution, the market recreates daily relationships across and around the lines of ethnicity, subsistence and residence that vary in intensity and form from friendship to partnership. Many relationships precede Arizona, having been forged through formal institutions before the war, and many extend outside the market.

Market relationships are subject to the shared, daily reinvented social norms ordered around the claim to subsistence and referenced in the ideal of market trade (*domaće* products) and market relationships (the independent peasant-producer). Thus, it is markets like Arizona rather than the institutions of a rational state or rituals of self-sufficient communities that are redrawing a larger social universe in post-war Bosnia. No longer occasioning merely the 'fleeting and materialistic contacts' that Lockwood observed as unsuitable for interethnic integration (Lockwood 1975: 210), neither are these new market forms the mechanisms of integration fuelled by amnesiac powers of trade that OHR and NATO envision. Instead, what is evident at Arizona is a more holistic exchange that reinvents both the socialist norms of worker welfare and peasants' independence from the state.

The experience of work for both socialist workers and peasant-producers (and the two often overlapped) is remembered in terms of subsistence, thus limited within the scope of 'enough' that is granted to everyone. In the personal experience of a socialist worker, 'enough' delineated an effort required at work to earn a salary on similar terms as every other worker. The peasant-producer defined 'enough' in similar terms; as the effort needed to support a family. On the other hand, the meaning of work for socialist peasants and workers hinged on the recognition of one's particularity within the community and an innate motivation to work without regard for the work's immediate, material utility.

Furthermore, the legacy of socialist and peasant notions of work informs an ideal of the state (see also Helms, Kolind, this volume). At Arizona, traders call for equality and welfare as well as the kind of independence that the Yugoslav socialist state bestowed on the landowners, whether producing peasants, peasant-workers or urbanite landowners making weekend pilgrimages to their land. But the state imagined at Arizona is also devoid of the socialist bureaucracy with its initiative-stunting pace and paperwork. The traders, who come to Brčko from all over the region to register their businesses, cite Brčko District as a model of an administration reformed to the needs of entrepreneurship.

Thus, the traders do not merely reinvent customary (socialist, peasant) expectations but instead invent novel customs and claims. What is claimed as customary transcends the distinctions of rural, urban, and ethnic without a formal ideology of 'Brotherhood and Unity', and without the assimilation required by multiculturalism. Navigating the uncertain and the unfair in the course of everyday work preoccupies the traders with ongoing differentiations, but the logic of subsistence limits the work and occupies the traders with everyday meanings.

Arizona is a metonym: its informal economy and the future enclosed in a mall, its claims to subsistence and the transnational investment plans, its uncertainties and the mundane all in a sense stand for the Bosnian whole. And in Bosnia, too, after the war, nothing extraordinary happens – just the orderly clutter of everyday life.

Bibliography

Adelkhah, F. (1998). *Being Modern in Iran*, London: Hurst.

Al-Ali, N. (2002). 'Gender Relations, Transnational Ties and Rituals among Bosnian Refugees', *Global Networks: A Journal of Transnational Affairs*, 2/3: 249-62.

Alispahić, F. (1996). *Krv boje benzina*, Tuzla: Radio Kameleon.

————— (2000). *Tuzland: knjiga o Tuzli*, Tuzla: Turistička zajednica općine Tuzle.

Allcock, J.B. (2000). *Explaining Yugoslavia*, London: Hurst.

————— (2002). 'Rural-Urban Differences and the Break-Up of Yugoslavia', *Balkanologie*, 6/1-2: 101-34.

Anderson, B. (1983). *Imagined Communities: Reflections on the Origins and Spread of Nationalism*, London: Verso.

Andjelic, N. (2003). *Bosnia-Herzegovina: The End of a Legacy*, London / Portland, OR: Frank Cass.

Andreas, P. (2004). 'The Clandestine Political Economy of War and Peace in Bosnia', *International Studies Quarterly*, 48: 29-51.

Antonić, Z. (1979, 1984 and 1987). *Tuzla u radničkom pokretu i revoluciji – knjiga I, II i III*, Tuzla: Univerzal.

Anzulović, B. (1999). *Heavenly Serbia: From Myth to Genocide*, London: Hurst.

Appadurai, A. (1998). 'Dead Certainty: Ethnic Violence in the Era of Globalization', *Public Culture*, 10/2: 225-47.

Arendt, H. (1994 [1963]). *Eichmann in Jerusalem: A Report on the Banality of Evil*, London: Penguin Books.

Aretxaga, B. (1997). *Shattering Silence: Women, Nationalism, and Political Subjectivity in Northern Ireland*, Princeton, NJ: Princeton University Press.

Armakolas, I. (2001a). 'A Field Trip to Bosnia: The Dilemmas of the First Time Researcher', in M. Smyth and G. Robinson (eds), *Researching Violently Divided Societies: Ethical and Methodological Issues*, Tokyo: United Nations University Press, pp. 165-83.

————— (2001b). 'Identity and Conflict in Globalizing Times: Experiencing the Global in Areas Ravaged by Conflict and the Case of the Bosnian Serbs', in P. Kennedy and C.J. Danks (eds), *Globalization and National Identities: Crisis or Opportunity?*, Basingstoke: Macmillan, pp. 46-63.

Asad, T. (ed.) (1995 [1973]). *Anthropology and the Colonial Encounter*, Amherst, NY: Prometheus Books.

Ashplant, T.G., Dawson, G. and Roper, M. (eds) (2000). *The Politics of War Memory and Commemoration*, London / New York: Routledge.

Babić, D. (1999). 'Sukobi i saradnja povratnika i useljenika u poslijeratnom razdoblju: brodsko-posavska županja', *Migracijske teme*, 15/4: 483-500.

————— (2000). 'Susjedstvo i prijateljstvo povratnika i useljenika u predratnom, ratnom i poslijeratnom ambijentu brodsko-posavske županije', *Migracijske i etničke teme*, 16/1-2: 7-27.

Bakić-Hayden, M. (1995). 'Nesting Orientalisms: The Case of Former Yugoslavia', *Slavic Review*, 54/4: 917-31.

————— (2004). 'National Memory as Narrative Memory: The Case of Kosovo', in M. Todorova (ed.), *Balkan Identities: Nation and Memory*, London: Hurst, pp. 25-40.

Bakić-Hayden, M. and Hayden, R.M. (1992). 'Orientalist Variations on the Theme "Balkans": Symbolic Geography in Recent Yugoslav Cultural Politics', *Slavic Review*, 51/1: 1-15.

Barsegian, I. (2000). 'When Text Becomes Field: Doing Fieldwork in Post-Communist Countries', in H.G. De Soto and N. Dudwick (eds), *Fieldwork Dilemmas: Anthropologists in Postsocialist States*, Madison, WI: University of Wisconsin Press, pp. 119-29.

Baskar, B. (1998). 'L'anthropologie sociale dans l'"autre Europe"', *Terrain*, 31: 113-28, available at <http://terrain.revues.org/document3143.html>.

Bass, G.J. (2000). *Stay the Hand of Vengeance: The Politics of War Crime Tribunals*, Princeton, NJ: Princeton University Press.

Bassiouni, C.M. (1994). *Final Report of the UN Commission of Experts Established Pursuant to Security Council Resolution 780 (1992) – document S/1994/674*, New York: United Nations, available at <http://www.ess.uwe.ac.uk/comexpert/REPORT_TOC.HTM>.

Bašić, N. (2004). *Krieg als Abenteuer: Feindbilder und Gewalt aus der Perspektive ehemaliger Kombattanten der postjugoslawischen Kriege 1991-1995*, Giessen: Psychosozial Verlag.

Bax, M. (1995). *Medjugorje: Religion, Politics and Violence in Rural Bosnia*, Amsterdam: VU Uitgeverij.

————— (1997). 'Mass Graves, Stagnating Identification, and Violence: A Case Study in the Local Sources of "The War" in Bosnia-Herzegovina', *Anthropological Quarterly*, 70 /1: 11-19.

————— (2000). 'Warlords, Priests and the Politics of Ethnic Cleansing: A Case Study from Rural Bosnia-Herzegovina', *Ethnic and Racial Studies*, 23/1: 16-36.

Beljkašić-Hadžidedić, Lj. (1988). 'Ethnological Work in Bosnia and Herzegovina from 1945 to the Present', *Etnološki pregled*, 23-24: 65-73.

Bellamy, A.J. and Williams, P.D. (eds) (2004). *Peace Operations and Global Order*, special issue of *International Peacekeeping*, 11/1.

Belloni, R. (2001). 'Civil Society and Peacebuilding in Bosnia-Herzegovina', *Journal of Peace Research*, 38/2: 163-79.

Bentley, G.C. (1987). 'Ethnicity and Practice', *Comparative Studies in Society and History*, 29/1: 24-55.

Bevrnja, A. and Strik, S. (2001). *Islamski propisi i običaji o smrti, dženazi i odnosu prema umrlim*, Sarajevo: Press Orient International.

Bieber, F. (2002). 'Nationalist Mobilization and Stories of Serb Suffering: The Kosovo Myth from 600th Anniversary to the Present', *Rethinking History*, 6/1: 95-101.

————— (2005). *Post-War Bosnia: Ethnicity, Inequality and Public Sector Governance* , Basingstoke: Macmillan.

Billig, M. (1995). *Banal Nationalism*, London: Sage.

Bjelaković, N. and Strazzari, F. (1999). 'The Sack of Mostar 1992-1994: The Politico-Military Connection', *European Security*, 8/2: 73-102.

Bliesemann de Guevara, B. (2005). 'External State-Building in Bosnia and Herzegovina: A Boost for the (Re)Institutionalisation of the State or the Establishment of Parallel Structures ?', paper presented at the 8th annual seminar *Democracy and Human Rights in Multiethnic Societies*, Konjic, Bosnia-Herzegovina, 10-15 July 2005, available at http://www.kakanien.ac.at/ beitr/theorie/BBliesemanndeGuevara2.pdf>.

Bloch, M.E. (1998). *How We Think They Think: Anthropolocial Approaches to Cognition, Memory and Literacy*, Boulder, CO: Westview.

Bogdanović, B. (1993). *Die Stadt und der Tod*, Klagenfurt: Wieser Verlag.

Bojičić, V. and Kaldor, M. (1999), 'The Abnormal Economy of Bosnia-Herzegovina', in C.-U. Schierup (ed.), *Scramble for the Balkans: Nationalism, Globalism and the Political Economy of Reconstruction*, Basingstoke: Macmillan, pp. 92-118.

Bokovoy, M.K. (1998). *Peasants and Communists: Politics and Ideology in the Yugoslav Countryside, 1941-1953*, Pittsburgh, PA: University of Pittsburgh Press.

Borneman, J. (1998). 'Toward a Theory of Ethnic Cleansing: Territorial Sovereignty, Heterosexuality, and Europe', in J. Borneman, *Subversions of International Order: Studies in the Political Anthropology of Culture*, Albany, NY: State University of New York Press, pp. 273-317.

————— (2002). 'Reconciliation after Ethnic Cleansing: Listening, Retribution, Affiliation', *Public Culture*, 14/2: 281-304.

Bose, S. (2002). *Bosnia after Dayton: Nationalist Partition and International Intervention*, London: Hurst.

Bougarel, X. (1995). 'Ramadan during a Civil War (as reflected in a series of sermons)', *Islam and Christian-Muslim Relations*, 6/1: 79-103.

————— (1996). *Bosnie: anatomie d'un conflit*, Paris: La Découverte.

————— (1999a). *Islam et politique en Bosnie-Herzégovine: le Parti de l'action démocratique*, unpublished Ph.D. Thesis, Institut d'études politiques, Paris.

————— (1999b). 'Yugoslav Wars: The "Revenge of the Countryside" between Sociological Reality and Nationalist Myth', *East European Quarterly*, 33/2: 157-75.

————— (2001a). 'Guerre et mémoire de la guerre dans l'espace yougoslave', in S. Yérasimos, *Le retour des Balkans (1991-2001)*, Paris: Autrement, pp. 44-59.

———— (2001b). 'L'islam bosniaque, entre idéologie politique et identité culturelle', in X. Bougarel and N. Clayer (eds), *Le nouvel Islam balkanique: les musulmans comme acteurs du post-communisme, 1990-2000*, Paris: Maisonneuve & Larose, pp. 79-132.

———— (2002). 'Travailler sur l'islam dans la Bosnie en guerre', *Cultures et conflits*, 47: 49-80.

Bowen, J.R. (1996). 'The Myth of Global Ethnic Conflict', *Journal of Democracy*, 7/4: 3-14.

Bowman, G. (1994). 'Xenophobia, Fantasy and the Nation: The Logic of Ethnic Violence in Former Yugoslavia', in V.A. Goddard, J.R. Llobera and C. Shore (eds), *Anthropology of Europe: Identity and Boundaries in Conflict*, Oxford / New York: Berg, pp. 143-71.

Bringa, T. (1993). *We Are All Neighbours*, documentary film, Manchester: Granada Television.

———— (1995). *Being Muslim the Bosnian Way: Identity and Community in a Central Bosnian Village*, Princeton, NJ: Princeton University Press.

———— (2002). 'Islam and the Quest for Identity in Post-Communist Bosnia-Herzegovina', in M. Shatzmiller (ed.), *Islam and Bosnia: Conflict Resolution and Foreign Policy in Multi-Ethnic States*, Montreal: McGill-Queen's University Press, pp. 24-34.

———— (2005). 'Reconciliation in Bosnia-Herzegovina', in A. Skaar, S. Gloppen and A. Suhrke (eds), *Roads to Reconciliation*, Lanham, MD: Lexington Books, pp. 187-99.

Bringa, T. and Loizos, P. (2001). *Returning Home: Revival of a Bosnian Village*, Sarajevo: Saga Film.

Brown, D.W. (2003). 'Martyrdom', in *Encyclopedia of Islam and the Muslim World*, Basingstoke: Macmillan, pp. 431-4.

Bulatović, Lj. (1996). *General Mladić*, Beograd: Evro.

Burawoy, M. (2000). 'Introduction: Reaching for the Global', in M. Burawoy (ed.), *Global Ethnography: Forces, Connections, and Imaginations in a Postmodern World*, Berkeley, CA: University of California Press, pp. 1-40.

Burawoy, M. and Verdery, K. (eds) (1999). *Uncertain Transition: Ethnographies of Change in the Postsocialist World*, Lanham, MD: Rowman & Littlefield.

Bureau of Government of RS for Relation with ICTY (2002). *Report about Case Srebrenica*, Banja Luka: Documentation Center of Republic of Srpska.

Burg, S.L. and Shoup, P.S. (1999). *The War in Bosnia-Herzegovina. Ethnic Conflict and International Intervention*, Armonk, NY: Sharpe.

Buturović, Đ. (2000). 'The National Museum of Bosnia and Herzegovina. Its Emergence and its Fall in the Overall Destruction of Bosnia and Herzegovina (from April 1992 to the End of 1995)', *Wissenschaftliche Mitteilungen des bosnisch-herzegowinischen Landesmuseums*, 7: 7-60.

Buturović, Đ. and Kajmaković, R. (1988). 'Naučna djelatnost u oblasti etnologije 1945-1988 godine', in A. Dautbegović and V. Palvestra (eds), *Spomenica stogodišnjice rada Zemaljskog muzeja Bosne i Hercegovine 1888-1988*, Sarajevo: Zemaljski muzej Bosne i Hercegovine, pp. 156-78.

Campbell, D. (1998). *National Deconstruction: Violence, Identity and Justice in Bosnia*, Minneapolis, MN: University of Minnesota Press.

Carlane, J. (2000). 'The "International" and the "Local": Globalisation, Capitalism and the Bureaucratisation of Post-Conflict Regeneration of War-Torn Societies', paper presented at the conference *Critical Citizenship: the Role of Non-Governmental Organizations in Civil Society*, San Diego, CA, 20 May 2000.

Carter, E., Donald, J. and Squires, J. (eds) (1993). *Space and Place: Theories of Identity and Location*, London: Lawrence & Wishart.

Caspersen, N. (2004). 'Good Fences Make Good Neighbours? A Comparison of Conflict-Regulation Strategies in Postwar Bosnia', *Journal of Peace Research*, 41/5: 569-88.

Cattaruzza, A. (2001). 'Sarajevo, capitale incertaine', *Balkanologie*, 5/1-2: 67-75

Cerić, M. (2002). 'Obraćanje Reisu-l-uleme u Begovoj džamiji', *Preporod*, 33/1 (1 January 2002): 7.

Chandler, D. (1998). 'Democratization in Bosnia: The Limits of Civil Society Building Strategies', *Democratization*, 5/4: 78-102.

————— (1999). *Faking Democracy after Dayton*, London: Pluto Press.

————— (2002). 'Anti-Corruption Strategies and Democratization in Bosnia-Herzegovina', *Democratization*, 9/2: 101-20.

————— (ed.) (2005). *Peace without Politics? Ten Years of International State-Building in Bosnia*, special issue of *International Peacekeeping*, 12/3.

Chaumont, J.-M. (1997). *La concurrence des victimes: génocide, identité, reconnaissance*, Paris: La Découverte.

Cibelli, K. and Guberek, T. (1999). *Justice Unknown, Justice Unsatisfied? Bosnian NGOs Speak About the International Criminal Tribunal for the Former Yugoslavia*, Tutfs: EPIIC, available at <http://www.epiic.com/class/ justicereport.pdf>.

Cigar, N.L. and Williams, P.R. (2002). *Indictments at The Hague: The Milošević Regime and Crimes of the Balkans Wars*, New York: New York University Press.

Clark, G. (1988). *Traders Versus the State: Anthropological Approaches to Unofficial Economies*, Boulder, CO: Westview.

Claverie, E. (2003). *Les guerres de la Vierge: une anthropologie des apparitions*, Paris: Gallimard.

Cockburn, C. (1998). *The Space between Us: Negotiating Gender and National Identities in Conflict*, London: Zed.

Cockburn, C. and Žarkov, D. (eds) (2002). *The Postwar Moment: Militaries, Masculinities and International Peacekeeeping in Bosnia and the Netherlands*, London: Lawrence & Wishart.

Coles, K.A. (2003). '"Nothing" Matters: The Practices of Passivity', paper presented at the conference *Democracy, Bosnia-Style?*, Providence, RI, 14

March 2003, available at <http://www.watsoninstitute.org/muabet/new_site/Kim_Coles_passivity.pdf>.

Cousens, E.M. and Cater, C.K. (eds) (2001). *Toward Peace in Bosnia: Implementing the Dayton Accords*, Boulder, CO: Lynne Rienner.

Cowan, J.K. (1991). 'Going Out for Coffee? Contesting the Grounds of Gendered Pleasures in Everyday Sociability', in P. Loizos and E. Papataxiarchis (eds), *Contested Identities: Gender and Kinship in Modern Greece*, Princeton, NJ: Princeton University Press, pp. 180-202.

Cox, M. (1998). 'The Right to Return Home: International Intervention and Ethnic Cleansing in Bosnia and Herzegovina', *International and Comparative Law Quarterly*, 47/3: 599-631.

————— (2001). *State-Building and Post-Conflict Reconstruction: Lessons from Bosnia*, Geneva: CASIN, available at <http://www.isn.ethz.ch/web/pdf/cox.pdf>.

Creed, G.W. (1998). *Domesticating Revolution: From Socialist Reform to Ambivalent Reform in a Socialist Village*, University Park, PA: Pennsylvania State University Press.

Čale-Feldman, L., Prica, I. and Senjković, R. (eds) (1993). *Fear, Death and Resistance. An Ethnography of War: Croatia 1991-1992*, Zagreb: Institute for Ethnology and Folklore Research.

Čolović, I. (1993). *Bordel ratnika*, Beograd: XX. vek.

————— (2002). *The Politics of Symbol in Serbia: Essays on Political Anthropology*, London: Hurst.

Ćimić, E. (1966). *Socijalističko društvo i religija*, Sarajevo: Svjetlost.

Dahlman, C.J. and O'Thuatail, G. (2005). 'The Legacy of Ethnic Cleansing: The International Community and the Return Process in Post-Dayton Bosnia-Herzegovina', *Political Geography*, 24/5: 569-99.

Das, V. and Kleinman A. (2000). 'Introduction', in V. Das, A. Kleinman et al. (eds), *Violence and Subjectivity*, Berkeley, CA: University of California Press, pp. 1-18).

————— (2001). 'Introduction', in V. Das, A. Kleinman et al. (eds), *Remaking a World: Violence, Social Suffering, and Recovery*, Berkeley, CA: University of California Press, pp. 1-30.

Dedijer, V. and Miletić, A. (1990). *Genocid nad Muslimanima 1941-1945: zbornik dokumenata i svjedočenja*, Sarajevo: Svjetlost.

Delpla, I. (2003). 'Une chute dans l'échelle de l'humanité: les topiques de l'humanitaire pour ses récipiendaires', *Mots*, 73: 97-116.

————— (2004a). 'Is There a Right to Return?', *Filozofski godišnjak*, 14: 121-44.

————— (2004b). 'La justice internationale dans l'après-guerre: la difficile évaluation des critères de justice', *Balkanologie*, 8/1: 211-28.

Denich, B. (1974). 'Why Do Peasants Urbanize? A Yugoslavian Case Study', in A.L. LaRuffa, R.S. Freed and L.W. Saunders (eds), *City and Peasant: A Study in Socio-Cultural Dynamics*, New York: New York Academy of Sciences, pp. 546-59.

————— (1977). 'Women, Work, and Power in Modern Yugoslavia', in A. Schlegel (ed.), *Sexual Stratification: A Cross-Cultural View*, New York: Columbia University Press, pp. 215-44.

————— (1994). 'Dismembering Yugoslavia: Nationalist Ideologies and the Symbolic Revival of Genocide', *American Ethnologist*, 21/2: 367-90.

Dizdar, E. (1998). *Dobro došli u Sarajevo: Novi turistički vodič 1998 / Welcome to Sarajevo: New Tourist Guide 1998*, Sarajevo: MB Publishers.

Doder, D. (1978). *The Yugoslavs*, New York: Random House.

Donais, T. (2005). *The Political Economy of Peacebuilding in Post-Dayton Bosnia*, London / New York: Routledge.

Donia, R.J. (1981). *Islam under the Double Eagle: The Muslims of Bosnia and Hercegovina, 1878-1914*, Boulder, CO: East European Monographs.

Donia, R.J. and Fine, John V.A. (1994). *Bosnia and Hercegovina: A Tradition Betrayed*, London: Hurst.

d'Onofrio, L. (2004). *Welcome Home? Minority Return in South-East Republika Srpska*, Brighton: Sussex Centre for Migration Research, available at <http://www.sussex.ac.uk/migration/1-3-3.html>.

Dragićević-Šešić, M. (1994). *Neofolk kultura: publika i njene zvezde*, Novi Sad: Knjižarnica Zorana Stojanovića.

Duffield, M. (2001). *Global Governance and the New War: The Merging of Development and Security*, London: Zed.

Duijzings, G. (1996). 'The Exodus of Letnica – Croatian Refugees from Kosovo in Western Slavonia: A Chronicle', in R. Jambrešić Kirin and M. Povrzanović (eds), *War, Exile, Everyday Life: Cultural Perspectives*, Zagreb: Institute for Ethnology and Folklore Research, pp. 147-70.

————— (2000). *Religion and the Politics of Identity in Kosovo*, London: Hurst.

————— (2002a). 'Part II, Chapter 7 – DutchBat in the Enclave: The Local Perspective', in NIOD [Nederlands Instituut voor Oorlogsdocumentatie], *Srebrenica – A 'Safe' Area: Reconstruction, Background, Consequences and Analyses of the Fall of a Safe Area*, Amsterdam: NIOD, available at <http://213.222.3.5/srebrenica>.

————— (2002b). *Geschiedenis en herinnering in Oost-Bosnië: De achtergronden van de val van Srebrenica*, Amsterdam: Boom, English version available at <http://213.222.3.5/srebrenica>.

————— (2002c). ' Part II, Chapter 4 – Srebrenica in the Time of CanBat: The Humanitarian Situation and the Arrival of the NGOs', in NIOD [Nederlands Instituut voor Oorlogsdocumentatie], *Srebrenica – A 'Safe' Area: Reconstruction, Background, Consequences and Analyses of the Fall of a Safe Area*, Amsterdam: NIOD, available at <http://213.222.3.5/srebrenica>.

Džanić, E. and Norman, E. (1998). 'Retraining the Federation Forces in Post-Dayton Bosnia', *Jane's Intelligence Review*, 10/1: 5-9.

Eriksen, T.H. (1995). *Small Places, Large Issues. An Introduction to Social and Cultural Anthropology*, London: Pluto Press.

Escobar, A. (1995). *Encountering Development: The Making and Unmaking of the Third World*, Princeton, NJ: Princeton University Press.

ESI [European Stability Initiative] (1999). *Reshaping International Priorities in Bosnia – Part One: Bosnian Power Structures*, Berlin / Sarajevo: ESI, available at <http://www.esiweb.org>.

———— (2000). *Reshaping International Priorities in Bosnia and Herzegovina – Part Two: International Power in Bosnia*, Berlin / Sarajevo: ESI.

———— (2001a). *In Search of Politics: The Evolving International Role in Bosnia and Herzegovina*, Berlin / Sarajevo: ESI.

———— (2001b). *Reshaping International Priorities in Bosnia and Herzegovina – Part Three: The End of the Nationalist Regimes and the Future of the Bosnian State*, Berlin / Sarajevo: ESI.

———— (2004). *Making Federalism Work: A Radical Proposal for Practical Reform*, Berlin / Sarajevo: ESI.

Faber, M. (2001). *Novi dani / Nieuwe dagen: oorlog en biografie in Banja Luka*, Amsterdam: Aksant.

Farmer, S. (1999). *Martyred Village: Commemorating the 1944 Massacre at Oradour-sur-Glane*, Berkeley, CA: University of California Press.

Fatma (2003). *Fatma, asocijacija za brigu o djeci šehida i palih boraca, 1993-2003. Odgoj, obrazovanje, dijalog*, brochure, Sarajevo: Udruženje građana Fatma.

Feldman, A. (1991). *Formations of Violence. The Narrative of the Body and Political Terror in Northern Ireland*, Chicago: University of Chicago Press.

Ferguson, J. (1994). *The Anti-Politics Machine: 'Development', Depoliticization, and Bureaucratic Power in Lesotho*, Minneapolis, MN: University of Minnesota Press.

———— (1995). 'From African Socialism to Scientific Capitalism: Reflections on the Legitimation Crisis in IMF-ruled Africa', in D.B. Moore and G.J. Schmitz (eds), *Debating Development Discourse: Institutional and Popular Perspectives*, Basingstoke: Macmillan, pp. 129-48.

Ferguson, J. and Gupta, A. (2002). 'Spatializing States: Toward an Ethnography of Neo-Liberal Governmentality', *American Ethnologist*, 29/4: 981-1002.

Fischel de Andrade, J.H. and Delaney, N.B. (2001). 'Field Report: Minority Return to South-Eastern Bosnia, a Review of the 2000 Return Season', *Journal of Refugee Studies*, 14/3: 315-30.

Fletcher, L., Stover, E. and Weinstein, H.M. (1999). 'Justice, Accountability, and Social Reconstruction: An Interview Study of Bosnian Judges and Prosecutors', *Berkeley Journal of International Law*, 18/1: 102-64.

Fletcher, L. and Weinstein, H.M. (2002). 'Violence and Social Repair', *Human Rights Quarterly*, 24: 573-639.

Fond Kantona Sarajeva za zaštitu i održavanje grobalja šehida i poginulih boraca (2001). *Šehidsko spomen-mezarje Kovači*, Sarajevo: Kanton Sarajevo.

Foucault M. (1991). 'Governmentality', in G. Burchell, C. Gordon and P.M. Miller (eds), *The Foucault Effect: Studies in Governmentality*, Hemel Hempstead: Harvester Wheatsheaf, pp. 87-104.

————— (1995 [1977]). *Discipline and Punish: The Birth of the Prison*, New York: Vintage Books.

Frankfort, T. (2002a). 'Part II, Chapter 8 – Peacekeeping and Humanitarian Action', in NIOD [Nederlands Instituut voor Oorlogsdocumentatie], *Srebrenica – A 'Safe' Area: Reconstruction, Background, Consequences and Analyses of the Fall of a Safe Area*, Amsterdam: NIOD, available at <http://213.222.3.5/srebrenica>.

————— (2002b). 'Part II, Chapter 9 – How DutchBat Functioned Internally until the VRS Attack', in NIOD [Nederlands Instituut voor Oorlogsdocumentatie], *Srebrenica – A 'Safe' Area: Reconstruction, Background, Consequences and Analyses of the Fall of a Safe Area*, Amsterdam: NIOD, available at <http://213.222.3.5/srebrenica>.

Frost, M. (1996). *Ethics in International Relations: A Constitutive Theory*, Cambridge: Cambridge University Press.

Gagnon, V.P. (2004). *The Myth of Ethnic War: Serbia and Croatia in the 1990s*, Ithaca, NY: Cornell University Press.

Gal, S. (1995). 'Language and the "Arts of Resistance"', *Cultural Anthropology*, 10/3: 407-24.

Gal, S. and Kligman, G. (2000). *The Politics of Gender after Socialism: A Comparative-Historical Essay*, Princeton, NJ: Princeton University Press.

Georgieva, C. (1999). 'Coexistence as a System in the Everyday Life of Christians and Muslims in Bulgaria', *Ethnologia Balkanica*, 3: 59-84.

Gilbert, A. (2003). 'Exploiting Humanitarian Spaces: Exploring the Politics of Antipolitics in the Refugee Return Process in Bosnia-Herzegovina', paper presented at the 102nd annual meeting of the American Anthropological Association, Chicago, 19-23 November 2003.

————— (2005). 'Humanitarianization and *Politika* in the Refugee Return Process in Bosnia-Herzegovina', paper presented at the conference *Politics and Society Ten Years after Dayton: Young Scholars Conference on the State of Social Science Research on Bosnia-Herzegovina*, Sarajevo, 10-13 November 2005.

Gledhill, J. (2000). *Power and its Disguises: Anthropological Perspectives on Politics*, London: Pluto Press.

Goffman, E. (1990 [1959]). *The Presentation of Self in Everyday Life*, London: Penguin Books.

Goldstein, J.S. (2001). *War and Gender: How Gender Shapes the War System and Vice Versa*, Cambridge: Cambridge University Press.

Gosztonyi, K. (1999). *Der Konfliktschlichtungsprozess in Mostar (Bosnien): Zwischen internationalem Druck und lokaler Obstruktion*, Berlin: Institut für Ethnologie.

————— (2003). 'Non-Existent States with Strange Institutions', in J. Koehler and C. Zürcher (eds), *Potentials of Disorder: Explaining Conflict and Stability in the Caucasus and in the Former Yugoslavia*, Manchester: Manchester University Press, pp. 46-61.

Gosztonyi, K. and Rossig, R. (1998). 'Bosnien-Herzegowina: Ohne "Raja" geht noch wenig', *Ost-West Gegeninformationen*, 10/4: 10-15.

Gow, J. (1997). *Triumph of the Lack of Will: International Diplomacy and the Yugoslav War*, New York: Columbia University Press.

———— (2003). *The Serbian Project and Its Adversaries: A Strategy of War Crimes*, Montreal: McGill-Queen's University Press.

Grandits, H. (1998). 'Über den Gebrauch der Toten der Vergangenheit als Mittel der Deutung der Gegenwart – Betrachtungen zum Krajina-Konflikt 1991-1995', in J. Köhler and S. Heyer (eds), *Anthropologie der Gewalt: Chancen und Grenzen der sozialwissenschaftlichen Forschung*, Berlin: Verlag für Wissenschaft und Forschung, pp. 179-86.

Grandits, H. and Gosztonyi, K. (2003). 'Nationalismus und diskrete Versöhnung: das neue interethnische Zusammenleben im Süden Bosnien-Herzegowinas', *Südosteuropa*, 52/4-6:198-228.

Grandits, H. and Leutloff, C. (2003). 'Discourses, Actors, Violence: the Organization of War-Escalation in the Krajina-Region in Croatia 1990/1991', in J. Köhler and C. Zürcher (eds), *Potentials of Disorder: Explaining Conflict and Stability in the Caucasus and in the Former Yugoslavia*, Manchester: Manchester University Press, pp. 23-45.

Green, L. (1999). *Fear as a Way of Life: Mayan Widows in Rural Guatemala*, New York: Columbia University Press.

Greenhouse, C.J. (2002). 'Introduction: Altered States, Altered Lives', in C.J. Greenhouse, E. Mertz and K.B. Warren (eds), *Ethnography in Unstable Places: Everyday Lives in Contexts of Dramatic Political Change*, Durham, NC: Duke University Press, pp. 1-34.

Gregson, K. (2000). *Veterans' Programs in Bosnia-Herzegovina*, Sarajevo: World Bank.

Grillo, R.D. and Stirrat R.L. (1997). *Discourses of Development: Anthropological Perspectives*, Oxford / New York: Berg.

Grodach, C. (2002). 'Reconstituting Identity and History in Post-War Mostar, Bosnia-Herzegovina', *City*, 6/1: 61-82.

Gullestad, M. (1992). *The Art of Social Relations: Essays on Culture, Social Action and Everyday Life in Modern Norway*, Oslo: Universitetsforlaget.

Gupta, A. (1995). 'Blurred Boundaries: The Discourse of Corruption, the Culture of Politics, and the Imagined State', *American Ethnologist*, 22/2: 375-402.

Gutman, R. (1993). *A Witness to Genocide*, Basingstoke: Macmillan.

Hadžibegović, I. and Kamberović, H. (1997). 'Građansko društvo u Bosni i Hervegovini: porijeklo i kontekst', *99 – Revija slobodne misli*, 9-10: 48-56.

Hagan, J. (2003). *Justice in the Balkans: Prosecuting War Crimes in the Hague Tribunal*, Chicago: University of Chicago Press.

Halilović, S. (1997). *Lukava strategija*, Sarajevo: Matica Sandžaka.

Halpern, J. and Weinstein, H.M. (2004). 'Empathy and Rehumanization after Mass Violence', in E. Stover and H.M. Weinstein, (eds), *My Neighbor, My Enemy? Justice and Community in the Aftermath of Mass Atrocity*, Cambridge: Cambridge University Press.

Halpern, J.M. and Kideckel, D. (eds) (1993). *War among the Yugoslavs*, special issue of *The Anthropology of East Europe Review*, 11/1-2.

————— (eds) (2000). *Neighbors at War: Anthropological Perspectives on Yugoslav Ethnicity, Culture and History*, University Park, PA: Pennsylvania State University Press.

Hammel, E.A. and Halpern, J.M. (1969). 'Observations on the Intellectual History of Ethnology and Other Social Sciences in Yugoslavia', *Comparative Studies in Society and History*, 11/1: 17-26

Hann, C.M. (1987). 'The Politics of Anthropology in Socialist Eastern Europe', in J. Anthony (ed.), *Anthropology at Home*, London / New York: Tavistock, pp. 139-53.

————— (1992). 'Market Principle, Market-Place and the Transition in Eastern Europe', in R. Dilley (ed.), *Contesting Markets: Analyses of Ideology, Discourse and Practice*, Edinburgh: Edinburgh University Press, pp. 244-59.

————— (1994). 'After Communism: Reflections on East European Anthropology and the Transition', *Social Anthropology*, 2/3: 229-47.

————— (1996). 'Introduction: Political Society and Civil Anthropology', in C.M. Hann and E.C. Dunn (eds), *Civil Society: Challenging Western Models*, London / New York: Routledge, pp. 1-26.

————— (ed.) (2002). *Postsocialism: Ideals, Ideologies and Practices in Eurasia*, London / New York: Routledge.

————— (2003). 'Is Balkan Civil Society an Oxymoron? From Königsberg to Sarajevo, via Przemyśl', *Ethnologia Balkanica*, 7: 63-78.

Hann, C.M., Sarkany, M. and Skalnik, P. (eds) (2005). *Studying Peoples in the People's Democracies: Socialist-Era Anthropology in East-Central Europe*, Münster: LIT Verlag.

Hayden, R.M. (1994). 'Recounting the Dead: The Rediscovery and Redefinition of Wartime Massacres in Late- and Post-Communist Yugoslavia', in R.S. Watson (ed.), *Memory, History and Opposition under State Socialism*, Santa Fe, NM: School of American Research Press, pp. 167-201.

————— (1996). 'Imagined Communities and Real Victims: Self-Determination and Ethnic Cleansing in Yugoslavia', *American Ethnologist*, 23/4: 783-801.

————— (1999). *Blueprints for a House Divided: The Constitutional Logic of the Yugoslav Conflicts*, Ann Arbor, MI: University of Michigan Press.

————— (2000). 'Rape and Rape Avoidance in Ethno-National Conflicts: Sexual Violence in Liminalized States', *American Anthropologist*, 102/1: 27-41.

————— (2002). 'Intolerant Sovereignties and Multi-Multi Protectorates: Competition over Religious Sites and (In)Tolerance in the Balkans', in C.M. Hann (ed.), *Postsocialism: Ideals, Ideologies and Practices in Eurasia*, London / New York: Routledge, pp. 159-79.

Hećimović, E. (1998). *Kako su prodali Srebrenicu i sačuvali vlast*, Sarajevo: Dani.

Helleiner, E. (1999). 'Historicizing Territorial Currencies: Monetary Space and the Nation-State in North America', *Political Geography*, 18/3: 309-39.

Helms, E. (2003a). *Gendered Visions of the Bosnian Future: Women's Activism and Representation in Post-War Bosnia-Herzegovina*, unpublished Ph.D. Thesis, University of Pittsburgh.

————— (2003b). 'Women as Agents of Ethnic Reconciliation? Women's NGOs and International Intervention in Post-War Bosnia-Herzegovina', *Women's Studies International Forum*, 26/1: 15-33.

————— (2004). '"East and West Kiss": Orientalism, Balkanism and Gender Bosniac Discourses', paper presented at the conference *Trouble with the Balkans*, Sarajevo, 1-3 November 2004.

Herzfeld, M. (1985). *The Poetics of Manhood: Contest and Identity in a Cretan Mountain Village*, Princeton, NJ: Princeton University Press.

Hoare, M.A. (2004). *How Bosnia Armed: The Birth and Rise of the Bosnian Army*, London: Saqi Books.

Hodžić, Š. (2003). *Dodir crnog kamena*, Sarajevo: DES.

Honig, J.W. and Both, N. (1996). *Srebrenica: Record of a War Crime*, London: Penguin Books.

Höpken, W. (1994). 'Von der Mythologisierung zur Stigmatisierung: "Krieg und Revolution" in Jugoslawien 1941-1948 im Spiegel von Geschichtswissenschaft und historischer Publizistik', in E. Schmidt-Hartmann (ed.), *Kommunismus und Osteuropa: Konzepte, Perspektiven und Interpretationen im Wandel*, München: Oldenbourg, pp. 165-201.

————— (1999). 'War, Memory and Education in a Fragmented Society: The Case of Yugoslavia', *East European Politics and Societies*, 13/1: 190-227.

————— (2001). 'Kriegserrinerung und Kriegsverarbeitung auf dem Balkan: Zum kulturellen Umgang mit Kriegserfahrungen in Südosteuropa im 19. und 20. Jahrhundert', *Südosteuropa-Mitteilungen*, 41/4: 371-89.

Hoppe, H.-J. (1998). *Das Dayton-Abkommen und die neue Führungselite in Bosnien-Herzegowina*, Köln: Bundesinstitut für ostwissenschaftliche und internationale Studien.

Howarth, D.R., Norval, A.J. and Stavrakakis, Y. (eds) (2000). *Discourse Theory and Political Analysis: Identities, Hegemonies and Social Change*, Manchester: Manchester University Press.

Humphrey, M. (2002). *The Politics of Atrocity and Reconciliation: From Terror to Trauma*, London / New York: Routledge.

Huntington, S.P. (1997). *The Clash of Civilizations and the Remaking of World Order*, New York: Simon & Schuster.

Hurem, R. (1972). *Kriza NOP-a u Bosni i Hercegovini krajem 1941. i početkom 1942. godine*, Sarajevo: Svjetlost.

Ibišević, B. (1999). *Srebrenica (1987-1992)*, Amsterdam: Besim Ibišević.

ICG [International Crisis Group] (1998). *Rebuilding a Multi-Ethnic Sarajevo: The Need for Minority Returns*, Brussels / Sarajevo: ICG, available at <http://www.crisisweb.org>.

———— (1999). *Rule of Public Administration: Confusion and Discrimination in a Post-Communist Bureaucracy*, Brussels / Sarajevo: ICG.

———— (2000). *War Criminals in Bosnia's Republika Srpska: Who Are the People in Your Neighbourhood*, Brussels / Sarajevo: ICG.

———— (2001). *The Wages of Sin: Confronting Bosnia's Republika Srpska*, Brussels / Sarajevo: ICG.

———— (2002a). *Bosnia's Alliance for (Smallish) Change*, Brussels / Sarajevo: ICG.

———— (2002b). *The Continuing Challenge of Refugee Return in Bosnia & Herzegovina*, Brussels / Sarajevo: ICG.

———— (2002c). *Implementing Equality: The 'Constituent Peoples' Decision in Bosnia and Herzegovina*, Brussels / Sarajevo: ICG.

———— (2003). *Bosnia's Nationalist Governments: Paddy Ashdown and the Paradoxes of State Building*, Brussels / Sarajevo: ICG.

ICTY [International Criminal Tribunal for the former Yugoslavia], *Prosecutor vs. Radislav Krstić – Judgment*, 2 August 2001, available at <http://www.un.org/icty/cases/indictindex-e.htm>.

Isaković, A. (1994). 'Riječ na otvaranju Bošnjačkog sabora', in A. Isaković, *Antologija zla*, Sarajevo: NIPP Ljiljan, pp. 378-84.

Ito, A. (2001). 'Politicisation of Minority Return in Bosnia and Herzegovina: The First Five Years Examined', *International Journal of Refugee Law*, 13/1-2: 98-122.

Ivanišević, M. (1994). *Hronika našeg groblja ili slovo o stradanju srpskog naroda Bratunca, Milića, Skelana i Srebrenice*, Beograd / Bratunac: Komitet za prikupljanje podataka o izvršenim zločinima protiv čovečnosti i međunarodnog prava.

Izetbegović, A. (1994). 'Ovo je posljedni genocid nad Muslimanima', *el-Liva*, 16 (November 1994): 4.

———— (1995a). 'Graditi jedinstvo i poštovati zakone (Sarajevo, 12. januara 1994. god.)', in A. Izetbegović, *Odabrani govori, pisma, izjave, intervjui*, Zagreb: Prvo muslimansko dioničko društvo, pp. 31-48.

———— (1995b). 'Povratak na čelo stranke (Sarajevo, 25. mart 1994. god.)', in A. Izetbegović, *Odabrani govori, pisma, izjave, intervjui*, Zagreb: Prvo muslimansko dioničko društvo, pp. 67-81.

———— (1999a). 'Govor na centralnom skupu Koalicije za cjelovitu i demokratsku Bosnu i Hercegovinu (Tuzla, 9. septembra 1998 god.)', in A. Izetbegović, *Govori, intervjui, izjave i pisma 1998*, Sarajevo: DES, pp. 95-103.

———— (1999b). 'Proslava 6. godišnjice Sedme viteške brigade (Sedme muslimanske) (Zenica, 17. novembar 1998. god.)', in A. Izetbegović, *Govori, intervjui, izjave i pisma 1998*, Sarajevo: DES, pp. 146-7.

Jalušič, V. (1994). 'Politics as a Whore: Women, Public Space and Anti-Politics in Post-Socialism', paper presented at the conference *The Politics of Antipolitics*, Vienna, 7-10 July 1994.

Jambrešić Kirin, R. and Povrzanović, M. (eds) (1996). *War, Exile, Everyday Life: Cultural Perspectives*, Zagreb: Institute for Ethnology and Folklore Research.

Jansen, S. (1998). 'Homeless at Home: Narrations of Post-Yugoslav Identities', in N. Rapport and A.H. Dawson (eds), *Migrants of Identity: Perceptions of Home in a World of Movement*, Oxford / New York: Berg, pp. 85-109.

————— (2002). 'The Violence of Memories: Local Narratives of the Past after Ethnic Cleansing in Croatia', *Rethinking History*, 6/1: 77-93.

————— (2005). 'National Numbers in Context: Maps and Stats in Representations of the Post-Yugoslav Wars', *Identities: Global Studies in Culture and Power*, 12/1: 45-68.

————— (forthcoming). 'The (Dis-)Comfort of Conformism: Post-War Nationalism and Coping with Powerlessness in Croatian Villages', in T. Otto, H. Thrane and H. Vandkilde (eds), *Archaeological and Social Anthropological Perspectives on Warfare*, Aarhus: Aarhus University Press.

Judah, T. (1997). *The Serbs: History, Myth and the Destruction of Yugoslavia*, New Haven, CT: Yale University Press.

Kalb, D. (2002). 'Afterword: Globalism and Postsocialist Prospects', in C.M. Hann (ed.), *Postsocialism: Ideals, Ideologies and Practices in Eurasia*, London / New York: Routledge, pp. 317-34.

Kaplan, R.D. (1993). *Balkan Ghosts: A Journey through History*, New York: St Martin's Press.

Karahasan, Dž. (1994). *Sarajevo, Exodus of a City*, New York: Kodansha Globe.

Karić, E. (1994). 'Agresija na Bosnu i Hercegovinu i pitanje džihada', in Press Centar ARBiH, *Duhovna snaga odbrane*, Sarajevo: Vojna biblioteka, pp. 73-7.

Katunarić, V. (1991). 'Uoči novih etnopolitičkih raskola: Hrvatska i Bosna i Hercegovina', *Sociologija*, 33/3: 373-85.

Keith, M. and Pile, S. (eds) (1993). *Place and the Politics of Identity*, London / New York: Routledge.

Kerney, M. (1995). 'The Local and the Global: The Anthropology of Transnationalism and Globalization', *Annual Review of Anthropology*, 24: 547-65.

Kolind, T. (2004). *Post-War Identifications: Counterdiscursive Practices in a Bosnian Town*, Ph.D. Thesis, University of Aarhus.

Kolstø, P. (ed.) (2005). *Myths and Boundaries in the Balkans*, London: Hurst.

Komisija za prikupljanje činjenica o ratnim zločinima (1996). *Ratni zločini na tuzlanskom okrugu 1992-1995 (drugo dopunjeno izdanje)*, Tuzla: Dom štampe.

Konstantinov, Y. (1996). 'Patterns of Reinterpretation: Trader-Tourism in the Balkans (Bulgaria) as a Picaresque Metaphorical Enactment of Postotalitarianism', *American Ethnologist*, 23/4: 762-82.

Korać, M. (1998). 'Ethnic-National Conflicts and the Patterns of Social, Political and Sexual Violence Against Women: The Case of Yugoslavia', *Identities: Global Studies in Culture and Power*, 5/2: 153-82.

Koschnick, H. (1995). *Brücke über die Neretva: Der Wiederaufbau von Mostar*, München: DTV.

Kožar, A. (1998). *Tuzla-podrinjski kanton / Tuzla-Podrinje Canton*, Tuzla: Tuzla-podrinjski kanton.

Kriger, N.J. (2003). *Guerilla Veterans in Post-War Zimbabwe: Symbolic and Violent Politics 1980-1987*, Cambridge: Cambridge University Press.

Kurtanović, S. (1993). 'Vrijeme mudžahida i šehida', *el-Liva*, 4 (May 1993): 13.

Laclau, E. and Mouffe, C. (1985). *Hegemony and Socialist Strategy: Towards a Radical Socialist Strategy*, London: Verso.

Lafontaine, A. (2002). 'Réfugié ou "Local Staff"? Changement de statut et enjeux de pouvoir au Kosovo d'après-guerre', *Anthropologie et sociétés*, 26/1: 89-105.

Latić, Dž. (1996). 'Vatropoklonstvo u Tuzli', *Ljiljan*, 4/177a (5 June 1996): 40.

Laušević, M. (1996). 'The *Ilahiya* as a Symbol of Bosnian Muslim Identity', in M. Slobin (ed.), *Retuning Culture: Musical Changes in Central and Eastern Europe*, Durham, NC: Duke University Press, pp. 117-35.

Ler-Sofronić, N. (1998). 'Women', in UNDP [United Nations Development Programme], *Human Development Report: Bosnia and Herzegovina*, Sarajevo: UNDP.

Leutloff-Grandits, C. (2005). *Claiming Ownership in Post-War Croatia: The Dynamics of Property Relations and Ethnic Conflict in the Knin Region*, Münster: LIT Verlag.

Liggett, H. and Perry, D.C. (eds) (1995). *Spatial Practices: Critical Explorations in Social/Spatial Theory*, London: Sage.

Lilly, C.S. (2001). *Power and Persuasion: Ideology and Rhetoric in Communist Yugoslavia 1944-1953*, Boulder, CO: Westview.

Lilly, C.S. and Irvine, J. (2002). 'Negotiating Interests: Women and Nationalism in Serbia and Croatia 1990-1997', *East European Politics and Societies*, 16/1: 109-44.

Lockwood, W.G. (1973). 'The Peasant-Worker in Yugoslavia', *Studies in European Societies*, 1: 91-110.

————— (1975). *European Moslems: Economy and Ethnicity in Western Bosnia*, London / New York: Academic Press.

Loncle, F. (président) (2001). *Srebrenica: rapport sur un massacre – Tome I: rapport et annexes*, Paris: Assemblée nationale.

Maček, I. (1997). 'Negotiating Normality in Sarajevo during the 1992-1995 War', *Narodna umjetnost*, 34/1: 25-58.

————— (2000). *War Within: Everyday Life in Sarajevo under Siege*, Uppsala: Acta Universitatis Upsaliensis.

————— (2001). 'Predicament of War: Sarajevo Experiences and Ethics of War', in B.E. Schmidt and I.W. Schröder (eds), *Anthropology of Violence and Conflict*, London / New York: Routledge, pp. 197-224.

———— (2005). 'Sarajevan Soldier Story', in P. Richards and B. Helander (eds), *No Peace, No War: An Anthropology of Contemporary Armed Conflicts*, Athens, OH: Ohio University Press, pp. 57-76.

Magaš, B. and Žanić, I. (eds) (2001). *The War in Croatia and Bosnia-Herzegovina*, London / Portland, OR: Frank Cass.

Malcolm, N. (1994a). 'Balkan Ghosts: Response to Article by Robert Kaplan in this Issue', *National Interest*, 33: 110-11.

———— (1994b). *Bosnia: A Short History*, Basingstoke: Macmillan.

Malkki, L.H. (1994). 'Citizens of Humanity: Internationalism and the Imagined Community of Nations', *Diaspora*, 3/1: 41-68.

———— (1995). *Purity and Exile: Violence, Memory, and National Cosmology among Hutu Refugees in Tanzania*, Chicago: University of Chicago Press.

———— (1998). 'Things to Come: Internationalism and Global Solidarities in the Late 1990s', *Public Culture*, 10/2: 431-42.

Mandel, R. and Humphrey, C. (eds) (2002). *Markets and Moralities: Ethnographies of Postsocialism*, Oxford / New York: Berg.

Maners, L. (2000). 'Clapping for Serbs: Nationalism and Performance in Bosnia and Herzegovina', in J.M. Halpern and D.A. Kideckel (eds), *Neighbors at War: Anthropological Perspectives on Yugoslav Ethnicity, Culture, and History*, University Park, PA: Pennsylvania State University Press, pp. 302-15.

Marcus, G.E. (1998). *Ethnography through Thick and Thin*, Princeton, NJ: Princeton University Press.

Massey, D. (1993). 'Politics and Space/Time', in M. Keith and S. Pile (eds), *Place and the Politics of Identity*, London / New York: Routledge, pp. 141-61.

Mašić, N. (1996). *Istina o Bratuncu: agresija, genocid i oslobodilačka borba 1992-1995*, Tuzla: Općina Bratunac sa privremenim sjedištem u Tuzli.

———— (1999). *Srebrenica: agresija, otpor, izdaja, genocid*, Srebrenica: Općina Srebrenica.

Mayeur-Jahouen, C. (ed.) (2002). *Saints et héros du Moyen-Orient contemporain*, Paris: Maisonneuve & Larose.

Mead, G.H. (1967 [1934]). *Mind, Self, and Society: From the Standpoint of a Social Behaviorist*, Chicago: University of Chicago Press.

Mertus, J. (1994). '"Woman" in the Service of National Identity', *Hastings Women's Law Journal*, 5/1: 5-23.

Mihrović, A., Salihović, Z. and Kržalić, A. (eds) (2002). *Žrtve srebreničke apokalipse*, Tuzla: Organizacija demobilisanih boraca općine Srebrenica – sjedište u Tuzli.

Miljanović, B. (1996). *Krvavi Božić sela Kravice*, Bad Vilbel: NIDDA Verlag.

Minow, M. (1998). *Between Vengeance and Forgiveness: Facing History after Genocide and Mass Crime*, Boston, MA: Beacon Press.

Mitchell, T. (1989). 'The World as Exhibition', *Comparative Studies in Society and History*, 31/2: 217-36.

————— (1999), 'Society, Economy and the State Effect', in G. Steinmetz (ed.), *State/Culture: State-Formation after the Cultural Turn*, Ithaca, NY: Cornell University Press.

Moser, C.O.N. and Clark, F. (eds) (2001). *Victims, Perpetrators or Actors? Gender, Armed Conflict and Political Violence*, London: Zed.

Mostov, J. (1995). '"Our Women"/"Their Women": Symbolic Boundaries, Territorial Markers, and Violence in the Balkans', *Peace and Change*, 20/4: 515-29.

Mujačić, M. (1972). 'Međunacionalni odnosi u jednom gradu: primer Dervente', *Gledišta*, 12/8: 1081-92.

Muminović, R. (1994). 'Uloga Islamske zajednice u ostvarivanju vjerskih upotreba pripadnika ARBiH', in Press Centar ARBiH, *Duhovna snaga odbrane*, Sarajevo: Vojna biblioteka, pp. 79-86.

Muslimović, F. (1993). 'Aktuelni problemi i zadaci na izgradnji morala, informativnog, propagandnog, političkog i vjerskog djelovanja u jedinicama ARBiH', in Press Centar ARBiH, *Borac Armije Republike Bosne i Hercegovine*, Sarajevo: Vojna biblioteka, pp. 39-45.

————— (1994). 'Uloga komandovanja i rukovođenja u ostvarivanju vjerskih potreba pripadnika Armije RBiH', in Press Centar ARBiH, *Duhovna snaga odbrane*, Sarajevo: Vojna biblioteka, pp. 87-94.

Mustafić, I. (2001). *Spasite nas od Dejtona*, Sarajevo: Udruženje građana Majke Srebrenice i Podrinja.

Naumović, S. (1999). 'Identity Creators in Identity Crisis: Reflections on the Politics of Serbian Ethnology', *Anthropological Journal of European Cultures*, 8/2: 39-128.

Neuffer, E. (2001). *The Key to My Neighbour's House: Seeking Justice in Bosnia and Rwanda*, London: Bloomsbury.

NIOD [Nederlands Instituut voor Oorlogsdocumentatie] (2002). *Srebrenica, een 'veilig' gebied: reconstructie, achtergronden, en analyses van de val van een Safe Area*, Amsterdam: NIOD, English version available at <http://213.222.3.5/srebrenica/>.

Nordstrom, C. (1992). 'The Backyard Front', in C. Nordstrom and J. Martin (eds), *The Paths to Domination, Resistance, and Terror*, Berkeley: University of California Press, pp. 260-74.

————— (1995). *Fieldwork under Fire: Contemporary Studies of Violence and Survival*, Berkeley: University of California Press.

————— (1997). *A Different Kind of War Story*, Philadelphia, PA: University of Pennsylvania Press.

Novick, P. (1999). *The Holocaust in American Life*, Boston, MA: Houghton Mifflin.

Occhipinti, L. (1996). 'Two Steps Back? Anti-Feminism in Eastern Europe', *Anthropology Today*, 12/6: 13-8.

Omeragić, S. (2001). 'Državotvorna tijela', *Ljiljan*, 9/461 (19 November 2001): 5.

Omerdić, M. (1997). *Šehidi, svjedoci vjere*, Sarajevo: Vijeće kongresa bošnjačkih intelektualaca.

Orić, N. (1995). *Srebrenica svjedoči i optužuje: genocid nad Bošnjacima u istočnoj Bosni (srednje Podrinje), april 1992. – septembar 1994. god.*, Srebrenica / Malmö / Ljubljana: Općina Srebrenica.

OSCE [Organization for Security and Cooperation in Europe] (1998). *Women's Representation in Elections in Bosnia and Herzegovina: A Statistical Overview 1986, 1990, 1996, 1997*, Sarajevo: OSCE.

Osiel, M. (2000). *Mass Atrocity, Collective Memory and the Law*, New Brunswick, NJ: Transaction.

Općina Centar (2003). *Osnovni podaci 2003*, brochure, Sarajevo : Općina Centar Sarajevo.

O'Thuatail, G. and Dahlman, C.J. (2004). 'The Efforts to Reverse Ethnic Cleansing in Bosnia-Herzegovina: The Limits of Return', *Eurasian Geography and Economics*, 45/6: 439-64.

Palavestra, V. (2004). *Historijska usmena predanja iz Bosne i Hercegovine*, Sarajevo: Buybook / Zemun: MostArt.

Pandolfi, M. (2002). '*Moral Entrepreneurs*, souverainetés mouvantes et barbelé: le biopolitique dans les Balkans post-communistes', *Anthropologie et sociétés*, 26/1: 29-50.

————— (2003). 'Contract of Mutual (In)Difference: Governance and Humanitarian Apparatus in Albania and Kosovo', *Indiana Journal of Global Legal Studies*, 10/1: 369-81.

Paris, R. (1997). 'Peacebuilding and the Limits of Liberal Internationalism', *International Security*, 22/2: 54-89.

————— (2005). *At War's End: Building Peace after Civil Conflict*, Cambridge: Cambridge University Press.

Pašalić, E. (1995). *Genocid našeg doba*, Ljubljana: Esperia.

Perry, V. (2003). *Reading, Writing and Reconciliation: Educational Reform in Bosnia and Herzegovina*, Flensburg: ECMI, available at <http://www.ecmi.de/download/ working_paper_18.pdf>.

Philpott, C. (2005). 'Though the Dog is Dead, the Pig Must Be Killed: Finishing the Property Restitution to Bosnia-Herzegovina's IDPs and Returnees', *Journal of Refugee Studies*, 18/1: 1-24.

Pickering, P.M. (2003). 'The Choice that Minorities Make: Strategies of Negociation with the Majority in Postwar Bosnia-Herzegovina', in D. Keridis, E. Elias-Bursac and N. Yatromalonakis (eds), *New Approaches to Balkan Studies*, Dulles, VA: Brassey's, pp. 255-309.

————— (2006). 'Generating Social Capital for Bridging Ethnic Divisions in the Balkans: Case Studies of Two Bosniak Cities', *Ethnic and Racial Studies*, 29/1: 79-103.

Polanyi, K. (2001 [1944]). *The Great Transformation: The Political and Economic Origins of Our Time*, Boston, MA: Beacon Press.

Pollack, G.E. (2003a). 'Burial at Srebrenica: Linking Place and Trauma', *Social Science and Medicine*, 56: 793-801.

———— (2003b). 'Intentions of Burial: Mourning, Politics, and Memorials following the Massacre at Srebrenica', *Death Studies*, 27: 125-42.

———— (2003c). 'Returning to a Safe Area? The Importance of Burial for Return to Srebrenica', *Journal of Refugee Studies*, 16/2: 186-201.

Popovic, A. (1996). 'Morts de saints et tombeaux miraculeux chez les derviches des Balkans', in G. Veinstein (ed.), *Les Ottomans et la mort: permanences et mutations*, Leiden: Brill, pp. 97-115.

Pouligny, B. (2005). *Peace Operations Seen from Below: UN Missions and Local People*, London: Hurst.

Povrzanović, M. (1998). 'Practice and Discourse about Practice: Returning Home to the Croatian Danube Basin', *Anthropology of Eastern Europe Review*, 16/1: 69-75, available at <http://condor.depaul.edu/~rrotenbe/aeer/aeer16_1.html>.

———— (2000). 'The Imposed and the Imagined as Encountered by Croatian Ethnographers', *Current Anthropology*, 41/2: 151-62.

Povrzanović-Frykman, M. (1997). 'Identities in War: Embodiment of Violence and Places of Belonging', *Ethnologia Europaea*, 27: 153-62.

———— (2001). 'Construction of Identities in Diaspora and Exile: Croats in Sweden in the 1990s', in M. Povrzanović-Frykman (ed.), *Beyond Integration: Challenges of Belonging in Diaspora and Exile*, Lund: Nordic Academic Press, pp. 166-94.

———— (2003). 'The War and After: On War-Related Anthropological Research in Croatia and Bosnia-Herzegovina', *Etnološka tribina*, 33/26: 55-74.

Press Centar ARBiH (1994). *Duhovna snaga odbrane*, Sarajevo: Vojna biblioteka.

Pugh, M. (2000). *The Regeneration of War-Torn Societies*, Basingstoke: Macmillan.

———— (2002). 'Postwar Political Economy in Bosnia and Herzegovina: The Spoils of Peace', *Global Governance*, 8/4: 467-82.

Pugh, M. and Cobble, M. (2001). 'Non-Nationalist Voting in Bosnian Municipal Elections: Implications for Democracy and Peacebuilding', *Journal of Peace Research*, 38/1: 27-47.

Purišević, F. (2000). *Boračka zaštita u Federaciji Bosne i Hercegovine*, Sarajevo: Institut za istraživanje zločina protiv čovječnosti i međunarodnog prava.

Repatriation Information Centre (2000). *Municipality Information Fact Sheet – Pale (RS)*, brochure, Sarajevo: Repatriation Information Centre.

Revival of Stolac (2001). *Written Memory against Apartheid in the Municipality of Stolac*, Sarajevo: Edin Mulać, available at <http://www.haverford.edu/relg/sells/stolac/MemoryofApartheid.html>.

Ribičič, C. (2000). *Geneza jedne zablude: ustavnopravna analiza nastanka i djelovanja Hrvatske zajednice Herceg-Bosne*, Zagreb: Jesenski i Turk / Sarajevo: Sejtarija.

Rihtman-Augustin, D. (1993). '"We Were Proud to Live with You, and Now Immensely Sad to Have Lost You": A Chronicle of the War through Newspaper Death Notice', *Narodna umjetnost*, 30/1: 279-302.

———— (2004). 'The Ethno-Anthropologist in his Native Field: To Observe or to Witness?', in D. Rihtman-Auguštin and J. Čapo Žmegač (eds), *Ethnology, Myth and Politics: Anthropologizing Croatian Ethnology*, Aldershot: Ashgate, pp. 93-104.

Rihtman-Auguštin, D. and Čapo Žmegač, J. (eds) (2004). *Ethnology, Myth and Politics: Anthropologizing Croatian Ethnology*, Aldershot: Ashgate.

Robinson, G.M., Engelstoft, S. and Pobric, A. (2001). 'Remaking Sarajevo: Bosnian Nationalism after the Dayton Accord', *Political Geography*, 20/8: 957-80.

Roćenović, L. (1993). 'Rituals Commemoring Deceased Croatian Soldiers (the Example of the Town of Samobor)', in L. Čale-Feldman, I. Prica and R. Senjković (eds), *Fear, Death and Resistance. An Ethnography of War: Croatia 1991-1992*, Zagreb: Institute for Ethnology and Folklore Research, pp. 151-62.

Rohde, D. (1997). *A Safe Area: Srebrenica, Europe's Worst Massacre since the Second World War*, London: Pocket Books.

Roksandić, D. (1995). 'Shifting References: Celebrations of Uprisings 1945-1991', *East European Politics and Societies*, 9/2: 256-71.

Rolland, S. (2004). 'Autochtones étrangers: les déplacés à Mostar après la guerre de Bosnie-Herzégovine', *Balkanologie*, 8/1: 189-209.

Rotim, K. (1997). *Obrana Herceg-Bosne*, Široki Brijeg: Karlo Rotim.

Rousso, H. (2002). *The Haunting Past: History, Memory, and Justice in Contemporary France*, Philadelphia, PA: University of Pennsylvania Press.

RS Commission for the Investigation of the Events in and around Srebrenica (2004). *The Events in and around Srebrenica between 10th and 19th July 1995*, Banja Luka: RS Government.

Ruga, G. (2001). 'Sixth Anniversary Commemoration of the Srebrenica Massacre', *Friends of Bosnia Newsletter*, 8/1 (December 2001): 3.

Sack, R.D. (1981). 'Territorial Bases of Power', in A.D. Burnett and P.J. Taylor (eds), *Political Studies from Spatial Perspectives*, Chichester / New York: J. Wiley, pp. 53-71.

Said, E. (1978). *Orientalism*, New York: Pantheon.

Salimović, S. and Sekulić, M. (2003). *Srebrenica-Potočari spomen obilježje i mezarje*, Srebrenica: Opština Srebrenica.

Sampson, S. (2002a). 'Beyond Transition: Rethinking Elite Configurations in the Balkans', in C.M. Hann (ed.), *Postsocialism: Ideals, Ideologies and Practices in Eurasia*, London / New York: Routledge, pp. 297-316.

———— (2002b). 'Weak States, Uncivil Societies and Thousands of NGOs: Benevolent Colonialism in the Balkans', in S. Resic and B. Törnquist-Plewa (eds), *The Balkans in Focus: Cultural Boundaries in Europe*, Lund: Nordic Academic Press, pp. 27-44.

Scarry, E. (1985). *The Body in Pain: The Making and Unmaking of the World*, Oxford: Oxford University Press.

Scharf, M.P. (1997). *Balkan Justice: The Story behind the First International War Crimes Trial since Nuremberg*, Durham, NC: Carolina Academic Press.

Scott, J.C. (1990). *Domination and the Arts of Resistance: Hidden Transcripts*, New Haven, CT: Yale University Press.

Segev, T. (1994). *The Seventh Million: The Israelis and the Holocaust*, New York: Owl Books.

Sekelj, L. (1993). *Yugoslavia: The Process of Disintegration*, Boulder, CO: Social Sciences Monograph.

Sell, L. (2000). 'The Serb Flight from Sarajevo: Dayton's First Failure', *East European Politics and Societies*, 14/1: 179-202.

Sells, M.A. (1996). *The Bridge Betrayed: Religion and Genocide in Bosnia*, Berkeley, CA: University of California Press.

Senjković, R. (2002). *Lica društva, likovi države*, Zagreb: Biblioteka nova etnografija.

Shields, R. (1991). *Places on the Margin: Alternate Geographies of Modernity*, London / New York: Routledge.

Shore, C. (2000). *Building Europe: The Cultural Politics of European Integration*, London / New York: Routledge.

Sijarić, R. (1996). 'Zemajski muzej u ratu 1992/93. godine', *Glasnik zemaljskog muzeja*, 47: 7-39.

Simic, A. (1973). *The Peasant Urbanites: A Study of Rural-Urban Mobility in Serbia*, New York: Seminar Press.

———— (1983a). 'Machismo and Cryptomatriarchy: Power, Affect, and Authority in the Contemporary Yugoslav Family', *Ethos*, 11/1-2: 66-86.

———— (1983b). 'Urbanization and Modernization in Yugoslavia: Adaptive and Maladaptive Aspects of Traditional Culture', in M. Kenny and D.I. Kertzer (eds), *Urban Life in Mediterranean Europe: Anthropological Perspectives*, Urbana, IL: University of Illinois Press:, pp. 203-24.

Sivac, N. (2004). 'La lettre de Nusreta Sivac', *Astérion*, 2, available at <http://asterion.revues.org/document89.html>.

Smillie, I. (1996). *Service Delivery or Civil Society? Non-Governmental Organizations in Bosnia and Herzegovina*, Zagreb: CARE Canada.

Solioz, C. (2005). *Turning-Points in Post-War Bosnia: Ownership Process and European Integration*, Baden-Baden: Nomos.

Sorabji, C. (1989). *Muslim Identity and Islamic Faith in Sarajevo*, unpublished Ph.D. Thesis, University of Cambridge.

———— (1992). *Bosnia's Muslims: Challenging Past and Present Misconceptions*, London: Action for Bosnia.

———— (1993). 'Ethnic War in Bosnia?', *Radical Philosophy*, 63: 33-5.

———— (1994). 'Mixed Motives: Islam, Nationalism and Mevluds in an Unstable Yugoslavia', in C.F. el-Solh and J. Mabro (eds), *Muslim Women's*

Choices: Religious Belief and Social Reality, Oxford / New York: Berg, pp. 108-27.

———— (1995). 'A Very Modern War: Terror and Territory in Bosnia-Hercegovina', in R.A. Hinde and H.E. Watson (eds), *War: A Cruel Necessity? The Bases of Institutionalized Violence*, London: Tauris, pp. 80-95.

———— (2006). 'Managing Memories in Postwar Sarajevo: Individuals, Bad Memories and New Wars', *Journal of the Royal Anthropological Institute*, 12/1: 1-18.

———— (forthcoming). 'Bosnian Neighbourhoods Revisited: Tolerance, Commitment and *Komšiluk* in Sarajevo', in J. de Pina Cabral and F. Pine (eds), *On the Margins of Religion*, New York / Oxford: Berghahn.

Spangler, M. (1983). 'Urban Research in Yugoslavia: Regional Variation in Urbanization', in M. Kenny and D.I. Kertzer (eds), *Urban Life in Mediterranean Europe: Anthropological Perspectives*, Urbana, IL: University of Illinois Press, pp. 76-108.

Spasić, I. (2000). 'Woman-Victim and Woman-Citizen: Some Notes on the "Feminist" Discourse on War', in S. Slapšak (ed.), *War Discourse, Women's Discourse: Essays and Case-Studies from Yugoslavia and Russia*, Ljubljana: Institutum Studiorum Humanitatis, pp. 343-57.

Stančić, Lj. (1994). 'Merhaba, gospodine!' *Stećak*, 1/3: 25.

Stefansson, A. (2003). *Under My Own Sky? The Cultural Dynamics of Refugee Return and (Re)integration in Post-War Sarajevo*, unpublished Ph. D. Thesis, University of Copenhagen.

———— (2004a). 'Refugee Returns to Sarajevo and Their Challenge to Contemporary Narratives of Mobility', in L.D. Long and E. Oxfeld (eds), *Coming Home? Refugees, Migrants, and Those Who Stayed Behind*, Philadelphia, PA: University of Pennsylvania Press, pp. 170-86.

———— (2004b). 'Sarajevo Suffering: Homecoming and the Hierarchy of Homeland Hardship', in F. Markowitz and A. Stefansson (eds), *Homecomings: Unsettling Paths of Return*, Lanham, MD: Lexington Books, pp. 54-75.

Stojaković, V. (1982). 'Etno-socijalni okviri života stanovništva Drežnice', *Glasnik zemaljskog muzeja (etnologija)*, N.S. 37: 189-218.

———— (1986-87), 'Društveni odnosi i društvene institucije stanovništva tešanjskog kraja', *Glasnik zemaljskog muzeja (etnologija)*, N.S. 41-42: 223-47.

Stojanov, D. (2001). 'Bosnia-Herzegovina since 1995: Transition and Reconstruction of the Economy' in Ž. Papić (ed.), *Policies of International Support to South-East European Countries: Lessons (not) Learnt in Bosnia and Herzegovina*, Sarajevo: Open Society Fund, pp. 44-70.

Stolac Municipality (2001). *Crimes in Stolac Municipality (1992-1996)*, Sarajevo: Edin Mulać, available at <http://www.haverford.edu/relg/sells/stolac/CrimesSt.pdf>

Stover, E. and Shigekane, R. (2002). 'The Missing in the Aftermath of War: When Do the Needs of Victims' Families and International War Crimes Tribunals Clash?', *International Review of the Red Cross*, 84/848: 845-66.

Stover, E. and Weinstein, H.M. (eds) (2004). *My Neighbor, My Enemy? Justice and Community in the Aftermath of Mass Atrocity*, Cambridge: Cambridge University Press.

Stubbs, P. (1997). 'NGO Work with Forced Migrants in Croatia: Lineages of a Global Middle Class?', *International Peacekeeping*, 4/4: 50-60.

————— (1999). *Displaced Promises: Forced Migration, Refuge and Return in Croatia and Bosnia-Herzegovina*. Sweden: LPI.

————— (2000a). 'Partnership or Colonisation? The Relationship between International Agencies and Local NGOs in Bosnia-Herzegovina', in B. Deacon (ed.), *Civil Society, NGOs and Global Governance*, Sheffield: GASPP, pp. 23-31, available at <http://www.stakes.fi/gaspp/publications/occasional%20papers/GASPP7-2000.pdf>.

————— (2000b). 'Peacebuilding, Hegemony and Integrated Development: The UNDP in Travnik', in M. Pugh, *The Regeneration of War-Torn Societies*, Basingstoke: Macmillan, pp. 157-76.

————— (2001). '"Social Sector" or The Diminution of Social Policy? Regulating Welfare System in Contemporary Bosnia-Herzegovina', in Ž. Papić (ed.), *International Support to South-East European Countries: Lessons (not) Learnt in Bosnia-Herzegovina*, Sarajevo: Open Society Fund, pp. 95-107.

————— (2005). 'Stretching Concepts Too Far? Multi-Level Governance, Policy Transfer and the Politics of Scale in South East Europe', *Southeast European Politics*, 6/2: 66-87, available at <http://www.ceu.hu/archives/issue62/stubbs.pdf>.

Stubbs, P. and Deacon, B. (1998). 'International Actors and Social Policy Development in Bosnia-Herzegovina: Globalism and the "New Feudalism"', *Journal of European Social Policy*, 8/2: 99-115.

Suárez-Orozco, M. (1992). 'A Grammar of Terror: Psychocultural Responses to State Terrorism in Dirty War and Post-Dirty War Argentina', in C. Nordstrom and J. Martin (eds), *The Paths to Domination, Resistance, and Terror*, Berkeley, CA: University of California Press, pp. 219-59.

Subašić, S. and Gardel, F. (2001). *Viol, une arme de guerre*, documentary film, Paris: Doc en stock / Arte.

Sugar, P.F. (1963). *Industrialization of Bosnia-Herzegovina, 1878-1918*, Seattle, WA: University of Wasington Press.

Sundhaussen, H. (1994). 'Ethnonationalismus in Aktion: Bemerkungen zum Ende Jugoslawiens', *Geschichte und Gesellschaft*, 20: 402-23.

Sunić, T. (1998). 'From Communal and Communist Bonds to Fragile Statehood: The Drama of Ex-Post-Yugoslavia', *The Journal of Social, Political, and Economical Studies*, 23/4: 465-75.

Šabani, A. (not dated). 'Titova Street and Its Sociological Significance', *The Best of 'Lica' (Issues 1-10: May 1996 to June 1998)*, Sarajevo: Lica, pp. 3-6, 44-6 and 86-8.

Šaćirbegović, N., Malešević, M. and Ajanović, I. (eds) (2000). *I Begged Them to Kill Me: The Crime against the Women in Bosnia-Herzegovina*, Sarajevo: Savez logoraša Bosne i Hercegovine.

Šivrić, I. (1982). *The Peasant Culture of Bosnia and Herzegovina*, Chicago, IL: Franciscan Herald Press.

Taussig, M. (1992). *The Nervous System*, London / New York: Routledge.

Teitel, R. (1999). 'Bringing the Messiah through the Law', in C. Hesse and R. Post (eds), *Human Rights in Political Transitions: Gettysburg to Bosnia*, New York: Zone Books, pp. 177-93.

Thiéblemont, André (2001). *Expériences opérationnelles dans l'armée de terre: unités de combat en Bosnie (1992-95) – Tomes I, II et III*, Paris : Centre d'études en sciences sociales de la défense.

Thompson, E.P. (1991). *Customs in Common*, New York: New Press.

Tica, O. (1996). 'Otvoreno pismo gospodinu Aliji Izetbegoviću', *Ljiljan*, 4/158 (24 January 1996): 311.

Todorova, M. (1997). *Imagining the Balkans*, Oxford: Oxford University Press.

Tomić, S. (1988). *Lokalni nivo nacionalnih odnosa*, Sarajevo: Institut za proučavanje nacionalnih odnosa.

Torsti, P. (2003). *Divergent Stories, Convergent Attitudes: Study on the Presence of History, History Textbooks and the Thinking of Youth in Post-War Bosnia and Herzegovina*, Ph.D. Thesis, Helsinki: University of Helsinki, available at <http://www.valt.helsinki.fi/staff/ptorsti>.

————— (2004). 'History Culture and Banal Nationalism in Post-War Bosnia', *Southeast European Politics*, 5/2-3: 142-57, available at <http://www.ceu.hu/archives/issue52/torsti.pdf>.

Trifković, D. (1981, 1983, 1988 and 1990). *Tuzlanski vremeplov – knjiga I, II, III i IV*, Tuzla: Grafičar.

Trouillot, M.-R. (2001). 'The Anthropology of the State in the Age of Globalization: Close Encounters of a Deceptive Kind', *Current Anthropology*, 42/1: 125-38.

Turner, V.W. (1970 [1967]). *The Forest of Symbols: Aspects of Ndembu Ritual*, Ithaca, NY: Cornell University Press.

United Nations (1999). *The Fall of Srebrenica: Report of the Secretary-General Pursuant to General Assembly Resolution 53/35,* UN Document A/54/549, New York: United Nations, available at <http://www.un.org/peace/srebrenica.pdf>.

UNHCR [United Nations High Commissioner for Refugees] (1994). *Information Notes on Former Yugoslavia,* 8/94: 7.

————— (1999). *Population Structure in BiH (September 1999)*, Sarajevo: UNHCR.

————— (2003). *Survey on Displaced Persons in Tuzla Canton for the Podrinje Area, Eastern Republika Srpska*, Tuzla: UNHCR.

van de Port, M. (1998). *Gypsies, Wars and Other Instances of the Wild: Civilisation and Its Discontents in a Serbian Town*, Amsterdam: Amsterdam University Press.

Väyrynen, T. (2003). 'The Search for Meaning in Global Conjunctions: From Ethnographic Truth to Ethnopolitical Agency', in P.G. Mandaville and A.J. Williams (eds), *Meaning and International Relations*, London / New York: Routledge, pp. 106-16.

Vego, M. (1993). 'The Croatian Forces in Bosnia and Herzegovina', *Jane's Intelligence Review*, 5/3: 99-103.

Verdery, K. (1994). 'From Parent State to Family Patriarchs: Gender and Nation in Contemporary Eastern Europe', *East European Politics and Societies*, 8/2: 225-55.

————— (ed.) (1996). *What Was Socialism, and What Comes Next?*, Princeton, NJ: Princeton University Press.

————— (1999). *The Political Lives of Dead Bodies: Reburial and Postsocialist Change*, New York: Columbia University Press.

Vlaisavljević, U. (1997). 'Der Krieg als grösstes Kulturereignis', *Dijalog*, 3-4: 23-34.

von Carlowitz, L. (2005). 'Resolution of Property Disputes in Bosnia and Kosovo: The Contribution to Peacebuilding', *International Peacekeeping*, 12/4: 547-61.

Vrcan, S. (2001). *Vjera u vrtlozima tranzicije*, Split: Dalmatinska akcija.

Vujović, S. (2000). 'An Uneasy View of the City', in Nebojša P. (ed.), *The Road to War in Serbia: Trauma and Catharsis*, Budapest: Central European University Press, pp. 123-45.

Vuković, Ž. (1993). *Ubijanje Sarajeva*, Podgorica: Kron.

Walzer, M. (1994). *Thick and Thin: Moral Arguments at Home and Abroad*, Notre Dame, IN: University of Notre Dame Press. '

Warren, K.B. (ed.) (1993). *The Violence Within: Cultural and Political Opposition in Divided Nations*, Boulder, CO: Westview.

Wedel, J.R. (1998). *Collision and Collusion: The Strange Case of Western Aid to Eastern Europe 1989-1998*, New York: St Martin's Press.

————— (2004). 'Studying Through a Globalizing World: Building Method through Aidnographies', in J. Gould and H.S. Marcussen (eds), *Ethnographies of Aid: Exploring Development Texts and Encounters*, Roskilde: IDS, pp. 149-73.

Wesselingh, I. and Vaulerin, A. (2005). *Raw Memory: Prijedor, Laboratory of Ethnic Cleansing*, London: Saqi Books.

Wieviorka, A. (1998). *L'ère du témoin*, Paris: Plon.

Willekens, L. (2003). '*Porodične slike* / Family Photos. The Changing Role of Family Photography in Sarajevo', *Etnofoor*, 16/1: 62-74.

Wilson, T.M. and Donnan, H. (eds) (1998). *Border Identities: Nation and State at International Frontiers*, Cambridge: Cambridge University Press.

Winter, J. (1995). *Sites of Memory, Sites of Mourning: The Great War in European Cultural History*, Cambridge: Cambridge University Press.

Woodhead, L. (1999). *A Cry from the Grave*, documentary film, London: Antelope.

Woodward, S.L. (1985). 'The Rights of Women: Ideology, Policy, and Social Change in Yugoslavia', in S.L. Wolchik and A.G. Meyer (eds), *Women, State and Party in Eastern Europe*, Durham, NC: Duke University Press, pp. 234-56.

————— (1995a). *Balkan Tragedy: Chaos and Dissolution after the Cold War*, Washington DC: Brookings Institution Press.

————— (1995b). *Socialist Unemployment: The Political Economy of Yugoslavia, 1945-1990*, Princeton, NJ: Princeton University Press.

World Bank (2002). *Bosnia and Herzegovina: Local Level Institutions and Social Capital*, Washington DC: World Bank.

Wubs, D.C. (1998). *The Way Back? A Study of the Obstacles for Minority Return in the Municipalities of Tuzla and Bijeljina*, Tuzla: Forum građana Tuzle.

Yuval-Davis, N. (1997). *Gender and Nation*, London: Sage.

Zakošek, Nenad (1998). 'Elitenwandel in Kroatien 1989-1995', in W. Höpken and H. Sundhaussen (eds), *Eliten in Südosteuropa: Rollen, Kontinuitäten, Brüche in Geschichte und Gegenwart*, München: Oldenbourg, pp. 279-88.

Zaum, D. (2003). 'The Paradox of Sovereignty: International Involvement in Civil Service Reform in Bosnia and Herzegovina', *International Peacekeeping*, 10/3: 102-20.

Zur, J. (1998). *Violent Memories: Mayan War Widows in Guatemala*, Boulder, CO: Westview.

Žanić, I. (1998). *Prevarena povijest: Guslarska estrada, kult hajduka i rat u Hrvatskoj i Bosni i Hercegovini*, Zagreb: Durieux.

Žarkov, D. (1995). 'Gender, Orientalism and the History of Ethnic Hatred in the Former Yugoslavia', in H. Lutz, A. Phoenix and N. Yuval-Davis (eds), *Crossfires: Nationalism, Racism and Gender in Europe*, London: Pluto Press, pp. 105-20.

————— (1999). *From Media War to Ethnic War: The Female Body and Nationalist Processes in the Former Yugoslavia, 1986-1994*, unpublished Ph.D. Thesis, University of Nijmegen.

————— (2001). 'The Body of the Other Man: Sexual Violence and the Construction of Masculinity, Sexuality and Ethnicity in the Croatian Media', in C.O.N. Moser and F. Clark (eds), *Victims, Perpetrators or Actors? Gender, Armed Conflict and Political Violence*, London: Zed, pp. 69-82.

Živković, M. (2000). 'The Wish to Be a Jew: The Power of the Jewish Trope in the Yugoslav Conflict', *Cahiers de l'URMIS*, 6: 69-84, available at <http://www.unice.fr/urmis-soliis/ Docs/Cahiers_6/cahiers_n6_zivkovic.pdf>.

————— (2001). *Serbian Stories of Identity and Destiny in the 1980s and 1990s*, unpublished Ph.D. Thesis, University of Chicago.

Index